Dostoevsky
and the
Affirmation
of Life

Dostoevsky and the Affirmation of Life

Predrag Cicovacki

Transaction Publishers
New Brunswick (U.S.A.) and London (U.K.)

First paperback edition 2014
Copyright © 2012 by Transaction Publishers, New Brunswick, New Jersey.

This book is printed on acid-free paper that meets the American National Standard for Permanence of Paper for Printed Library Materials.

Library of Congress Catalog Number: 2011040541
ISBN: 978-1-4128-4606-6 (cloth); 978-1-4128-5383-5 (paper)
Printed in the United States of America

Library of Congress Cataloging-in-Publication Data

Cicovacki, Predrag.
   Dostoevsky and the affirmation of life / Predrag Cicovacki.
        p. cm.
   ISBN 978-1-4128-4606-6
      1. Dostoyevsky, Fyodor, 1821-1881--Criticism and interpretation.
   2. Life in literature. I. Title.

PG3328.Z7L543 2012
891.73'3--dc23

                                                          2011040541

To Jadranka

"I think that everyone should love life before everything else in the world."

"Love life more than its meaning?"

"Certainly, love it before logic, as you say, certainly before logic, and only then will I also understand its meaning."

– Dostoevsky, *The Brothers Karamazov*

Contents

Prologue

Marcel Proust once stated that "Crime and Punishment" could be the title of all of Dostoevsky's novels.[1] Since Proust was a great admirer of the Russian novelist and many of his concerns were similar to Dostoevsky's own, we need to take his statement seriously. What, then, do Proust's words teach us about Dostoevsky? Does his formulation succeed in expressing what is most characteristic for Dostoevsky's novelistic and philosophical approach?

In Dostoevsky's Russian, the word for "crime" is *prestuplenie*, which literally means "transgression." To commit a crime refers, then, to the transgression of a certain limit or boundary defined by law. There are boundaries, and when they are crossed, a crime is committed and an appropriate punishment should follow.

Although the "transgression of boundaries" indeed plays a central role in Dostoevsky's novels, this phrase is significantly broader than what Proust intends to convey by the word "crime."[2] There

---

1   Marcel Proust, "Dostoievski," *On Art and Literature*, 381.
2   The relevance of transgression of boundaries in Dostoevsky has been emphasized by various critics: Stefan Zweig, *Three Masters: Balzac, Dickens, Dostoeffsky*, 172 and 202–5; Helen Muchnic, *Russian Writers: Notes and Essays*, 143–50; Edward Wasiolek, *Dostoevsky: The Major Fiction*, 83; and Joseph Frank, *Dostoevsky: The Mantle of the Prophet, 1871–1881*, 727. See also Vyacheslav Ivanov, *Freedom and the Tragic Life: A Study in Dostoevsky*, 14, where the expression used is not "transgression" but "infringement." Malcolm V. Jones similarly approaches Dostoevsky's work in terms of the contrast between sliding into discord and subsequent attempts to restore order; see his *Dostoyevsky: The Novel of Discord*, 9–54.

are quite different kinds of boundaries – legal and non-legal, individual and social, spatial and temporal, artificial and natural – and many of them do not relate to crimes at all. Thus, the word "transgression" need not have the negative connotation always associated with the word "crime." We are all familiar with both impermissible and permissible transgressions of boundaries, just as we all understand that along with the undesirable there are desirable crossings of existing borders. Even if our first inclination may be to associate transgressions of boundaries with crime or evil, no good would ever occur without inappropriate boundaries being violated or removed. Boundaries can be unjust and oppressive, and for the sake of progress they must be rejected and replaced. Without transgressions of boundaries there might not be any victims, but nor would there be any heroes. Without transgressions of boundaries there may be no evil, but also no good.

Proust may have implicitly understood all of this, and by saying that all of Dostoevsky's novels could be entitled "Crime and Punishment," he may have wanted to call our attention to something peculiar for the Russian writer. The so-called *Bildungsroman*, popular in Europe since Goethe's time, emphasizes the developmental story and the process of maturation of the main hero. The story is told in linear time, and it often covers the entire biological cycle of the protagonist's birth, development, and death. This approach was also widespread in Russia. We can read even a complex work like Tolstoy's *War and Peace* as the development over a long period of time of the novel's main character, Pierre Bezukhov.

Dostoevsky, however, mostly ignores this pedagogically required developmental account of the main characters. He portrays them in a relatively short time-span, in which they are not able to undergo a time-consuming process of maturation. Dostoevsky is not as interested in their gradual evolution as he is in their sudden reversal of fortune. Crime, or more generally transgression of some significant boundary, is his point of departure, and then he places the characters under a magnifying glass. Dostoevsky's main concern is to examine the inner life of his characters, an approach that may seem more appropriate for philosophical or psychological analysis than for works of fiction. This interior probing of the soul attracted an immediate attention of philosophers and psychologists, such as

Nietzsche and Freud, and then gradually became a major focus of the twentieth-century novel.

The reversal of the common narrative approach creates an impression that Dostoevsky's novels begin in the middle of the story. Indeed they do, if we consider them through the perspective of linear time and linear plot developments. Eventually we recognize – at first more intuitively than fully consciously – that Dostoevsky's novels deal with a transformation typical of a cyclical conception of time. In this conception the cycle of symbolic death and rebirth replaces a linear development in terms of birth, growth, and death. The usual storytelling begins with a state of innocence, with some primordially desirable state of affairs, and then proceeds to tell us how a fall from grace occurs. Crime can be compared to a fall from innocence; it is pollution of something pure or clean, a stain of some kind. What is distinctive of Dostoevsky's novelistic approach, and what Proust may be helping us realize, is that Dostoevsky is less interested in how and why the fall occurs, than in what happens afterwards. *Crime and Punishment*, for example, describes the hero's murder of two women in the first part, which then sets the stage for the central theme of this work: Raskolnikov's confrontation with his conscience, his torturous acceptance of responsibility for the crime, along with his self-inflicted punishment and resulting spiritual transformation.

Although typical for Dostoevsky, this reversal of the customary narrative approach is by no means arbitrary. As we will see later in greater detail, it is the result of some of his deepest insights concerning human nature. Let us consider just one example. When crimes occur, we lock those who commit them in jail, deprive them of their freedom, often of their dignity, sometimes of their lives. Our justification is that the criminals themselves compromise their humanity by violating the boundaries of law and morality of their own free will. For Dostoevsky, by contrast, crime does not constitute a denial of the criminal's humanity, or a justification to eliminate it. Goethe once said that he could not think of any crime which he himself could not have committed; Dostoevsky subscribes to the same view. The four years he spends in Siberia with the worst criminals of Russia convinces him that, though crimes often appear monstrous, they are performed by human beings, not by monsters. It is remarkable that Dostoevsky sees the potential saintliness in a sinner, and what Blake famously called "the marriage of Heaven and Hell" is for Dostoevsky a very real possibility. No wonder, then, that his first-hand witness report from Siberia, *The House of the Dead*, gives the impression that crime is one of the very expressions of our humanity. Not that Dostoevsky thinks that crime is good, but that, because of his peculiar understanding of crime in terms of transgression of boundaries, he sees transgression as an act that every human being commits. Each of us transgresses existing boundaries every day – because of our desires for what is not and our disagreements with what is; because each of us sees the rift between how the world is, how it could be, and how it ought to be. The crux of the matter does not consist in transgressing boundaries, for transgress them we certainly will. A far thornier obstacle consists in not always knowing which of these transgressions are appropriate. In many situations we are forced to choose not between good or evil, but between two goods, or between two evils. Dostoevsky realizes that to know what to do once the boundaries are crossed and order needs to be restored is even more difficult. The crucial issue for him is what happens after the transgression. This may be the reason why Proust insists on crime *and punishment*.

We might have the following concern with Proust's characterization of Dostoevsky's entire opus. Despite the fact that it happens to be the title of one of Dostoevsky's novels, "crime and punishment" is a general expression we take for granted; the two seem always to go together, like day and night, male and female, good and evil. Significantly, we take it for granted because we are confident that there is a boundary that separates crime and punishment. The idea that the former should be followed by the latter lies at the very foundation of our trust in the world order. We hope to live in a world in which vice leads to punishment and virtue to reward.

A point against Proust's statement is that in Dostoevsky's novels the connection between crime and punishment does not always exist. Like all of us, Dostoevsky learns in his own life that many innocent suffer unjustly and that those who are virtuous are not always rewarded. His rebellious characters – Ivan Karamazov standing at the last point of the line which begins with the underground man – never tire of reminding us that life is far less ordered and more arbitrary than we would like it to be. Justice should prevail, but often it does not. The unpredictable flow of contingencies, rather than a benevolent, omniscient, and just God, appears to dictate what happens in the world.

We can cite a long list of Dostoevsky's characters to show that he is attentive to the voice of victims who are aware that their personal boundaries are often transgressed, though these injustices are not punished. They all know that meaningless suffering is one of our worst fears. The suffering of the innocent appears pointless and life itself seems to lack meaning for us. If we believe that the cause of the pain is justified or that the pain will lead to good consequences, it is almost always possible to bear. In our often naïve reasoning, it appears that life is a learning process, that there is a teacher who is trying to teach us a lesson. But what if there is no teacher and no lesson to learn?

Ivan Karamazov addresses this issue in the most disturbing way. He presents a challenge perhaps unmatched in the entire history of Western philosophy, literature, or theology. We will consider this challenge in detail in the course of the book, but here will gloss on only its simplified version. Ivan's challenge – and many of his confusions and disappointments – hinges on the following dilemma:

What comes first – the meaning of life or the affirmation of life?

After citing the most horrifying stories of the torture and death of innocent children, Ivan brings his brother Alyosha to agree with him that the ends do not justify the means. Ivan thereby undermines the traditional theodicy: Even if God has some plan in mind, His actions in creating this unjust world cannot be justified because of the endless suffering that has resulted. The price is too high. The challenge for God is this: Would it not be better if God had never created the world, than to have made it as it is? The challenge for human beings is no less formidable: Why live in the world of suffering, if suffering can have no meaning?

In this book, we are interested in the part of Ivan's challenge that deals with *our* position in the world. There is no denial that human beings have a strong, animal-like desire to live. Ivan himself claims to have "indecent thirst for life."[3] What if, despite this "indecent thirst," life has no meaning? If there is so much undeserved and pointless suffering, if life is indeed as meaningless as it often appears, how can we affirm life? Why not commit suicide? Why not trespass all boundaries?

A thinker like Ivan cannot but be disturbed by such questions. In the face of unjust suffering, what can demonstrate that death is not a better option? Ivan demands proof of that and, predictably, cannot find any. Life does not offer enough guarantees to make such proof possible. All Ivan knows with certainty is that by affirming life, he condones a scheme of things in which there is evil and that makes him an accomplice in the suffering of the innocent. Thus, for his part, Ivan turns against his "indecent thirst for life" and declares that he is going to "return [his] ticket" (Bk. V, Ch. 4, 245).

An obviously puzzling aspect of Proust's characterization of Dostoevsky's work in terms of "crime and punishment" is that it does not relate to this crucial issue. Proust does not say anything about Ivan's rebellion, which, according to his contemporary Albert Camus and many other admirers and critics of the Russian novelist, is the culminating point of Dostoevsky's entire opus. No one can deny that there is a horrible crime at the focal point of *The Brothers Karamazov*, or that there is punishment as well. Proust's characterization does not, however, capture the essential problem of the novel. This is why, although useful, Proust's insight must be corrected in more than one way. Dostoevsky is not focused on the issue of crime *per se*, but on the more general problems of the affirmation and meaning of life, even in the presence of evil. He is not interested in punishment in its legal sense, but focuses on the individual's inner voice, which so often reveals to him the crossing

---

3   *The Brothers Karamazov*, trans. Richard Pevear and Larissa Volokhonsky, Bk. V, Ch. 3, page 230. All subsequent references to substantial quotations from Dostoevsky's works will be given in the text, immediately after the quotation. For the full references of the translations used, see Part I of the Bibliography.

of boundaries that separate good from evil and which demands an appropriate reaction.

Understanding exactly what kind of reaction is needed is the key to comprehending Dostoevsky's entire outlook. It is far easier to understand the transgressions of boundaries. They are an expression of freedom, of curiosity, of our desire to change the world according to our visions and needs. Not all the transgressions are crimes, and not all reactions to them are punishments. Yet there is an intimate connection between the transgressions and our reactions to them – a desire to restore order, to curb freedom, to accept responsibility for what we have done. Dostoevsky does not connect the voice of conscience directly to punishment because he believes that God has something to do with that voice. His God is not the God of punishment, not the terrifying and judging Yahweh from the Old Testament, but the compassionate God of the New Testament who bestows His grace upon the world. Dostoevsky's God is loving but not overprotecting, He is like the father from the biblical tale of the prodigal son who would always welcome his stray child home.

Proust also seems to forget that, notwithstanding its title and its preoccupation with the murderer (Raskolnikov), *Crime and Punishment* is as much about the oppressed as it is about the oppressor. This is especially true of the young prostitute, Sonia, who, in the face of her personal and family tragedies, finds enough faith and strength to help Raskolnikov accept the responsibility for his transgression and to be reborn. Dostoevsky is deeply attuned to the voice of victims, but Proust's formula does not indicate that this is the case.

A less obvious but no less consequential omission of Proust's insistence on crime and punishment deals with his inability to account for the possibility of there being heroes in Dostoevsky. The picture of reality which Dostoevsky paints is often so bleak that the reader may become convinced there is no room for genuine goodness and authentic heroes. Pessimists like Lev Shestov and Jean-Paul Sartre, who mistakenly identify Dostoevsky's voice with the voice of the underground man, argue that all the talk about heroism is only one of our many life-supporting illusions; if such illusions were entirely expelled, there would be nothing to trust.

Ivan similarly considers any heroic ideal as a dangerous and irresponsible seduction of an already disoriented mankind. In his view,
the crucified "Son of God" is certainly not a hero. If this "title" were
appropriate for anyone, it would be his Grand Inquisitor.

Deep inside his soul, Dostoevsky must have been terrified of the
world in which the likes of the Grand Inquisitor would be considered the only heroes. But whom else would he regard as worthy
of the title "hero"? This question will preoccupy us, especially in
Part II, when we consider Dostoevsky's most "constructive" novels,
The Idiot and *The Brothers Karamazov*. Here only a few remarks
are in order. Although there are no noble warriors in Dostoevsky's
novels, numerous characters strive toward greatness and purity.
We may not immediately think of them as heroes, but Dostoevsky
admires those who stand up after falling down, those who do not
lose their faith even after witnessing unspeakable evils of dehumanization. If they can learn to die for the old self and be purified and
reborn through their suffering, they may be the only ones deserving
to carry the torch of heroism. Purification and redemption through
pain and suffering are among Dostoevsky's central preoccupations.

The notion that Dostoevsky's consistently gloomy worldview preserves enough room for heroes and heroism is connected with the
most remarkable feature of his approach – his optimism. This is
the point at which Proust's formula deserts us. The optimism of
Dostoevsky deserves further attention and a detailed account. His
favorite part of the Bible was the Book of Job, and it is not too difficult to understand why. Dostoevsky's life resembled that of Job in
many ways: It was a life of enormous suffering, incurable disease,
and loss of those he loved most. And yet, as much as Dostoevsky
may have anticipated Kafka, Camus, or Faulkner, in his work, there
is no ominous sense of helplessness or resignation. A small but
steady light of hope is always present and recognizable. This hope
is not self-deluding – a naïve, childish, unfounded hope that blindly
justifies all misfortune and stubbornly repeats that our Creator
must have a good reason for permitting tragedy. Dostoevsky never
deceives himself that in this world "everything happens for a reason." He is aware that the world is, has always been, and will always
be full of examples of purposeless evil.

Dostoevsky does not see evil as a kind of a curable disease which can be eradicated once and forever when we finally restructure society in the right way. Evil for him is like a malaise inherent in the human condition because it is part of the same drive that leads us toward greatness and heroism, the drive to transgress existing boundaries and open new frontiers. Although there must be limits to such strivings, we should not try to overprotect the innocent by eliminating freedom (which includes the freedom to choose evil).

Ivan recommends precisely such a denial of freedom and the overprotection of a weak and disoriented humanity in his "Legend of the Grand Inquisitor." But this is not Dostoevsky's last word on the subject. As Job had to learn long ago, and as Father Zosima realizes as well, it is not sufficient merely to live so as not to do evil. For Dostoevsky, despite its continuous failings, the essence of humanity is to hope and strive for better. Although a firm believer, he kindles this hope without any religious fanaticism, and without dogmatically asserting the coming of a "Golden Age." If we are realistic, we have to question and – together with Ivan – reject every theodicy and all grandiose eschatological expectations. We must learn to live with evil, without losing hope and without ceasing to strive toward a more humane world.

In Dostoevsky's novels there are two deadly dangers for humanity: having hopes and ideals that are not congruent with reality, and having no hopes and ideals at all. The former warns us never to close our eyes to what the real world is, the latter never to abandon a healthy hope. This unique combination of clear-headed realism and undeniable optimism is the most striking – and perhaps the least understood – feature of Dostoevsky's worldview. That Dostoevsky himself never fully succeeds in articulating where this vitalizing optimism comes from, or how it could coexist with his uncompromising realism, makes his optimism so under-appreciated. We feel unmistakably this optimism in his novels and appreciate it like a sudden ray of sunshine on a gloomy winter day. (As the narrator of *The Insulted and the Injured* says on the opening page, "It is amazing what one ray of sunshine can do for a man!") When in voluminous journalistic writings Dostoevsky tries to articulate his deepest religious and philosophical convictions, his vision often comes out as dogmatic, narrow-minded, and national-istic. All the vitality and purity intuited while reading *The Idiot* or *The Brothers Karamazov* seems either perverted or irretrievably lost in his non-fiction.

A sounder and more adequate articulation of this unique combi-nation of realism and optimism in his great novels requires showing (i) on what ground he bases his affirmation of life, and (ii) how his affirmation can be reconciled with the overwhelming presence of evil in the world. The perimeters within which this task must be accomplished have been indicated in a sporadic manner, and now must be outlined more precisely. Because life appears arbitrary, unjust, and often pointless, Ivan first argues that the meaning of life must come before the affirmation of life and then maintains that the suffering of the innocent invalidates any attempt to prove that life has meaning. Dostoevsky, and we with him, would like to counter Ivan's prioritization and posit a different view. Although we can agree with Ivan that there cannot be a systematic justi-fication of suffering, it is equally unacceptable not to see that in many cases suffering leads to purification and positive transforma-tion. Contrary to Ivan's insistence, if the affirmation of life comes first, life will have genuine meaning. The affirmation of life, and its subsequent meaning, can only come within certain constrains. The affirmation and meaning of life must be grounded:

(1) without denying the reality of evil,
(2) without accepting any self-deluding ideal about every suffering having meaning,
(3) without giving in to resignation or despair, and
(4) without basing this affirmation on a sheer animal instinct for preservation.

According to Dostoevsky, we must learn how to accept the reality of evil and live with it, and yet affirm and love life. We need to find a way to feel at home in the world without grounding that feeling either on false denials of past and present reality or on unfounded utopian promises of a glorious future and a "new world." Dostoevsky believes that qualified optimism is not only possible, but actually indispensable for our mental balance and health. Our primary task in the analysis of Dostoevsky's central novels – the five works we will closely analyze in the book: *Notes from the Underground*, *Crime and Punishment*, *The Idiot*, *The Possessed*, and *The Brothers Karamazov* – will be to examine whether and how this optimism may be attained.

The obstacles in fulfilling this goal will be formidable. One of them is that Dostoevsky is a most unusual thinker. He could give brilliant expression to Ivan's challenge, but could not find a convincing and equally persuasive expression for the opposite line of thought, the viewpoint he defends as his own in his correspondence and journalistic writings. More importantly, the view he claims to be defending – that unique blend of realism and optimism – appears to contain something paradoxical. In attempting to articulate and defend this combination of realism and optimism, we will strive against strongly ingrained psychological mechanisms which seem to prevent the reconciliation of these views. If we accept a pervasive presence of evil in the world, how can this acceptance not lead to skepticism, relativism, resignation, depression, or profound pessimism? On what grounds can any reasonable hope be sustained in the face of evil? And is not optimism a sign that our eyes are turned away in denial from the actual world? To many readers it seems that any form of optimism must be based on illusion or self-deception. It may be no wonder, then, that moralists dealing with the problem of evil tend to take one of the two following stances: Either we have to deny that there is a problem of evil, or we have to deny that there may be an adequate solution to it.

Dostoevsky has a flair for paradoxes and the very fact that a viewpoint contains a paradox would not be sufficient for him to reject it. On the contrary, he is convinced that "there is nothing more fantastic than reality itself."[4] Dostoevsky not only firmly follows this powerful insight throughout his literary career; he even ascribes to it his very birth as a writer. Moreover, his works display a conscious and systematic transgression of all three fundamental laws of logic: of non-contradiction, of sufficient reason, and of the excluded middle. For Dostoevsky reason and rationality are far less important aspects of our nature than they are for philosophers. In fact,

---

4   Quoted from Konstantin Mochulsky, *Dostoevsky: His Life and Work*, 27.

for him our stubborn overestimation of rationality is part of the contemporary problem. Dostoevsky realizes that one of the most recurring motives of Western civilization is "the dream of Faust": The educated man yearns for a systematic interpretation of all the phenomena of experience, informed by one central idea. Put differently, in the history of Western culture there has always been a struggle between two elements: the intuitive and aesthetical on the one hand, and the abstract and theoretical on the other. What characterizes a Western approach to life is not so much the mere existence of the tension between these two kinds of elements – their struggle is universally present in every culture – but rather the fact that in the West the intuitive and aesthetic component is virtually always subordinate to, and in the service of, its theoretical and abstract counterpart.[5]

Dostoevsky weaves the tension of intuitive elements (which are immediately apprehended) and of abstract thoughts (which need an indirect confirmation by an intuitive apprehension of the real world) into his novels. Ivan, for example, demands a (theoretical) proof that life is worth living, but all Alyosha (or Father Zosima) can offer him is its aesthetic counterpart – if you could only open yourself to the aesthetic dimension of human existence, if you could appreciate the beauty of life, you would see not only that such a proof is impossible but also that it is unnecessary. The appreciation of the aesthetic component opens the door for the affirmation of life and our love of it, and this door leads us further toward the restoration of our trust into the meaning of existence – toward faith and hope.

Dostoevsky's criticism of rationalism is closely connected with his view of our divided nature and, more generally, with his conviction that life itself is paradoxical. Life does not develop along the rationally discernable linear ascent of progress, as the advocates of the Enlightenment envision it. Dostoevsky does not believe in the modern conception of an ever-unfolding progress, just as he does not believe in the eschatological expectations of the end of

---

5   For further discussion of this tension and its implications, see F.S.C. Northrop, *The Meeting of East and West: An Inquiry concerning World Understanding*, especially pages 300–11 and 440–96.

history and the establishment of the Kingdom of God on earth. Human destiny unfolds, not in customary linear time, but in cycles of symbolic and literal death and rebirth. Thus, the central motivation of Dostoevsky's entire outlook is more adequately expressed in terms of cycles of "transgression and restoration," rather than as "crime and punishment."

The main task of this book is to reconstruct and examine Dostoevsky's "aesthetically" motivated affirmation of life, based on these cycles of transgression and restoration. Ivan claims that, if life has no meaning, it is absurd to affirm life and it is pointless to live. Since Ivan's doubts concerning the meaning of life resonate so deeply throughout our age of pessimism and relativism, the central question of this book is: Can the author overcome the skepticism of his most brilliant creation?

Part I
Life without Meaning

Introduction to Part I

What are we looking for when we search for the meaning of life?

A novelist may say that we are looking for something like glue. We need a kind of glue that would hold together an enormous swirl of individuals and events, all of which partake in the drama we call reality. We need something that would make sense of the world's past, present, and future.

A philosopher, who aspires to be more precise than a novelist, would argue that we are searching for something akin to the purpose of life. Life has meaning if it has purpose, which gives every person a sense of direction and helps her figure out her role and place in reality. Being a lover of distinctions, our philosopher would point out two distinct senses of the word "purpose." According to its ancient meaning, to have a purpose is to be made or used as a means toward the achievement of some objective. In the modern and quite contrary sense, to have a purpose is to choose a goal toward which a person's efforts and activities – perhaps her entire life – are directed.

The difference between these two meanings of purpose is based on where the glue of life comes from: Is it supplied from the outside, by some transcendent source, or does it emerge from within, from an individual or his social group? Who or what is the source of purpose which gives meaning to our lives?

This difference is reflective of two alternative conceptions of life and its meaning. We will call one of them metaphysical and religious, since it assumes that the purpose and glue of life is supplied by a divine Creator, or at least by something bigger than and independent from the human world. According to the second, humanistic and typically secular approach, human beings create meaning for themselves and the world around them.

We must also take into account a third viewpoint to the issue of meaning of life. Although this approach has never been dominant – except perhaps in our own time – it has always lingered in the undercurrents of the Western culture and has occasionally erupted to its surface as a violent, destructive force. We are talking about a skeptical and pessimistic approach to life, which sometimes takes on the form of radical nihilism.

How are these three approaches related and how are they important for our understanding of Dostoevsky? The metaphysical and religious approach has reigned the longest, and it is by no means without significant influence even today. This is not accidental, for this approach may be the one that most reassures our deepest existential anxieties. It leaves us believing that we are in the hands of a benevolent Creator, a caring, protective, and wise parent who will always be there for us.

The problem with this viewpoint is that, in the face of the harsh reality we experience, it requires a significant leap of faith into something intangible and mysterious. The glue of life is supposed to come from a transcendent Creator, but the experience of life often leaves us dumbfounded as to what the Creator's plan may be. This viewpoint tells us that something is meant by being human which involves more than sheer existence. Life is a task of a certain kind, yet what exactly is at stake in being human remains impenetrable. Man is an obscure text to himself, often left in doubt as to his purpose in life.

The Enlightenment breaks away from such wonderings. As Dostoevsky's contemporary Alexander Herzen puts it in his book, *From the Other Shore*, "Human history has no libretto: The actors must improvise their parts."[1] Not transcendence but

---

1   Herzen's words are quoted from Isaiah Berlin, *The Crooked Timber of Humanity*, 201. For a valuable discussion of immanence as the source of values and norms, see Yermiyahu Yovel, *Spinoza and Other Heretics*, vol. 2: *The Adventures of Immanence*.

immanence is the source of values and normativity. The self-aware individual must confront the world with his own indomitable will and critical reason, the only two capacities which humanity can trust.

As it develops throughout several centuries, the twin project emerges from the European Enlightenment: the death of God and the deification of reason. The death of God does not leave man as an orphan but as a master, a potential mini-god. As Dostoevsky's character Kirillov expresses it, we have advanced from God-man to Man-god (*The Possessed*, Pt. II, Ch. i, 241).

The excitement of the Enlightenment epoch has passed, and it has turned out that man is not such a great master, after all. The purposes we set for ourselves time and again result in consequences we do not expect or welcome. The improvisations of the actors of our history without libretto turn too frequently into a nightmare of incompetence and inhumanity. The Enlightenment is motivated by the idea that as human beings we cannot and should not trust anything but what we make ourselves. Our repeated individual and collective failures undermine that trust as well. No small wonder that, not only in our times but already in Dostoevsky's nineteenth century, the voices of some of the smartest and most concerned human beings had begun assuming skeptical, pessimistic, even nihilist tones. Their criticism of the entire Western tradition is based on what Isaiah Berlin calls the three-fold dreadful and eye-opening humiliation. The first of them is the recognition that man is not the purpose of creation, preceded by the realization that the earth is not the center of the universe. The second humiliation is that rather than being created in the divine image, man is a creature of nature, just as any other animal. The third humiliation, directed more against the humanistic approach than its religious counterpart, is that human reason is not as autonomous and objective as previously believed: Reason is subject to passions and subconscious urges.

The picture of humanity that emerges from such humiliations is, indeed, a humbling one. The human being appears to be a confused, superfluous creature that cannot control even its own thoughts and decisions, much less the destiny of the entire world.

Dostoevsky struggled throughout his adult life with these competing viewpoints regarding the meaning of life. For him, however, they are not abstract or theoretical points of view, which we may or may not rationally adopt, but voices coming from within our souls. They represent the existential choices that haunt every human being. These voices are by no means as sharply separated in the depths of our souls as they look when presented as theoretical viewpoints. Perhaps they are not even fully separable. We waver between them, and at different crossroads of life either one of them may present itself to us as the voice of the ultimate truth.

But is there an ultimate, or at least objective truth?

Dostoevsky certainly wants us to believe that these choices are not equally valuable. There is no doubt that he has often struggled with the voice of the skeptic. "God has tormented me my whole life," confesses Kirillov (Pt. I, Ch. iii, 115), and later, in a manner anticipating Ivan, points his finger toward the source of his agony: "All evil comes from the desire for immortality that Christ foolishly sparked in us." Nonetheless, replies another of Dostoevsky's alter-egos – Makar Ivanovich Dolgoruky from *The Adolescent* – "life without God is nothing but torture . . . a man cannot live without worshiping something; without worshiping he cannot bear the burden of himself" (Pt. III, Ch. 2, sec. iii, 373). Both of these voices represent Dostoevsky's own trials, as he admits to his friend Strakhov: "It is not as a child that I believe in Christ and profess His teaching; my hosanna has burst through a purging flame of doubts."[2] How else but by purging his thoughts through the furnace of doubts would Dostoevsky be able to make Ivan sound so persuasive? Yet it may also be fair to say that Dostoevsky abhors nothing more than the resonances of that skeptical voice within his soul.

---

2   This quotation comes originally from Strakhov's biography of Dostoevsky; reprinted here from V.V. Zenkovsky, "Dostoevsky's Religious and Philosophical Views," in *Dostoevsky: A Collection of Critical Essays*, ed. R. Wellek, 130. See also Dostoevsky's letter to A.N. Maikov of March 25, 1870.

Dostoevsky also knows well the other two viewpoints. In his youth, at the beginning of his writing career and before the sentence that sent him to Siberia, the humanistic view appeals to him very much. This is not to say that in that period, or any other, he fully abandons the religious view which he firmly appropriated in his childhood, but only that it plays a secondary role. The years in Siberia, spent far away from the progressive intellectual circles of Petersburg, turned the tables. For the rest of his life Dostoevsky's faith emerges as his dominant outlook. What is perhaps more surprising is that in some of his best novels after Siberia – *Notes from the Underground, Crime and Punishment*, and partially *The Possessed* – he is strongly, sometimes unjustly, opposed to the humanistic outlook. Dostoevsky fights against it as a dangerous viewpoint that seduces us to identify with our rational capacities and moral autonomy. If it is correct to say that the religious and metaphysical view misleads us to ascribe reality to the creatures of our imagination, then it should also be admitted that the humanistic view denies reality to some aspects of human existence without which human life is impoverished beyond repair.

We will leave for the second part of the book a discussion of what Dostoevsky's religious and metaphysical attitude is and how it differs from what usually falls under that name. After considering how he challenges the commonly accepted assumption that the meaning of life is related to purpose, plan, or anything similar, we will argue there that his outlook is not only far more original and viable but also less orthodox and dogmatic than usually assumed by numerous Dostoevsky scholars.

In the first part of this book, however, we need to prepare the ground for this central discussion. In Chapter 1 our intent will be to reconstruct Dostoevsky's conception of realism and his general assessment of the direction which the modern world has taken. This assessment will be developed, challenged, and reevaluated in Chapters 2–4, where we will analyze his criticism of the humanistic and the nihilistic approaches. For Ivan, these two approaches are not fully separated. The humanistic approach creates high expectations which, when they fail to be obtained, lead to a sense of despair and meaninglessness. For Dostoevsky, the glue on which humanism relies is neither strong enough nor of the right kind.

Our central questions in the first part of the book will be the following: Why is Dostoevsky so utterly discontent with the humanistic and pessimistic viewpoints? What is the cause and what is the effect of the problem? Is the objective state of affairs in the world really the cause of the feeling of homelessness? Or is it rather that our inappropriate subjective attitudes toward life negatively affect the objective position of humanity in the world?

1
Sorrow and Injustice

A World Delivered to Evil?

Dostoevsky's Realism

In the Swiss city of Geneva, there is a small cemetery – *Cimetière de Plainpalais*. Located between the majestic old part of the town with its imposing cathedral above it, and the broad, calm Rhone river underneath it, the well-maintained cemetery welcomes random passersby. When you step in and walk along the first row toward the left, at its very end you will find a small, barely visible grave. A child – born on February 22, 1868, died on May 12 of the same year – is buried there.

As much as the birth of this first-born brought joy to then-forty-seven-year-old Dostoevsky and his noticeably younger second wife, the child's sudden death had a devastating effect on them. A few days after a modest, unceremonial funeral, Dostoevsky pours out his sorrow in a letter to his friend Maikov:

> My Sonia has died, three days ago we buried her. . . . Oh, Apollon Nikolayevich, say, say my love for my first baby was comical, say I expressed myself ridiculously about her in many letters to many people who congratulated me. For them I was only comical; to you, *to you* I am not afraid to write. This little three-month-old creature, so poor, so

tiny, was already a person and a character for me. She was beginning to know me, to love, and smile when I came near. When with my comical voice I used to sing songs to her, she liked to listen to them. She didn't cry and didn't frown when I kissed her; she used to stop crying when I came near. And now they say to me in consolation that I'll have other children. But where is Sonia? Where is this little personality for whom, I say boldly, I would accept the cross's agony if only she might be alive.[1]

We can trust what Dostoevsky tells his friend in the last sentence, for he knew what "the cross's agony" was. His whole life looked like one nightmarish agony after another. From the premature deaths of his parents, of his first wife, of his beloved brother Michael, of his two children (first Sophia and later his three-year-old son Alexei), to his own trembling in front of the firing squad, years of penal servitude in Siberia, a gambling passion and devastating poverty, and often recurring epileptic fits, Dostoevsky experienced an enormous share of misery and suffering.

The agonizing litany of sorrow is all too familiar to Dostoevsky. He knows what irreplaceable losses, suffering, and evil are – not as abstract ideas or theoretical concepts, but as living experiences. The problem of evil is for him a matter of the most real confrontation with everyday life. Strakhov – his collaborator of many years – testifies that Dostoevsky wrote his works "with the blood of his heart." Out of this "blood" emerged some of the most memorable characters in literary history: the underground man and Raskolnikov, Kirillov and Stavrogin, Dmitri and Ivan. Each one of them is echoing Dostoevsky's agony: Where is justice in the death of an innocent child? Where is justice in this world?

Under the influence of Gogol, Dostoevsky's early literary preoccupations are with the injustices committed against the weakest and most defenseless, as well as with their horrifying living conditions. "We have all come from under Gogol's *Overcoat*," admits Dostoevsky. Like Akaky Akakievich, a poor clerk from

---

1   Letter to A.N. Maikov of May 18, 1868. (Sonia is Russian nickname for Sophia.)

The Overcoat, Dostoevsky's first hero, Makar Devushkin (*Poor Folk*), lives a life of humble resignation. Makar's only bright spot, his only love, Varenka, agrees to marry a proprietor who is young and rich, but also coarse and tyrannical. Makar does not complain. Trying to be of use, he even participates in the preparations for the nuptials. Makar would recoil from any humiliating expedient if he could only preserve his modest place in the shadow of his adored Varenka. Cruel fate will not grant him even that.

Makar represents one type of Dostoevsky's characters who can be called – to borrow Turgenev's vivid phrase – "superfluous human beings."[2] They feel that nobody wants them or needs them, that their existence is dispensable and disposable, that they are individuals who do not make a difference, that it might be better if they were not alive, that they present a greater burden to others while alive than dead. Their suffering is the pain of poverty, of need, of being powerless. Can we comprehend what evil means to those who are oppressed? What do they think of the meaning of life?

Although the superfluous, "the insulted and the injured" human beings continue to crowd Dostoevsky's writings to the end, after his penal servitude in Siberia, another preoccupation becomes more discernible in his novels: The powerlessness of those unfortunate creatures may provoke them to transgress the boundaries of the permissible. Gruesome crimes and violated taboos, such as atrocious murders and rapes of children, find their way into Dostoevsky's pages and become the nightmares of his leading characters. The problem of evil gains thereby a different dimension. The emphasis shifts from the repressive social conditions to the transgression of boundaries, from the perspective of a victim to the perspective of a victimizer: What does evil mean for a tormenter? How can an individual who commits a horrible crime come to terms with his own evil? Through Raskolnikov and Svidrigailov, Stavrogin and Peter, Ivan and Smerdyakov, Dostoevsky expresses what he must have always intuitively felt – that the greatest moral struggles go on within people, not between them.

---

2   They are so named after Turgenev's *Dnevnik lishnega cheloveka* (Diary of a superfluous man), first published in 1850.

Dostoevsky's fascination with appalling crimes, together with his incomparable ability to describe the dark side of the human soul, has always puzzled his readers and critics. Many have accused him of being sick, or insane, or a sadist, or a masochist, or a child molester, or of committing a terrible crime which haunted him and which he could not bring himself openly to confess. Thomas Mann claims he esteems Dostoevsky because he risks his sanity to make art – a devotion foreign to insulated, self-protective geniuses like Goethe or Tolstoy.[3] Nevertheless, Mann considers Goethe and Tolstoy as the prototypes of "healthy" writers and individuals, and tellingly names one of his essays as: "*Dostoevsky – mit Massen*" (Dostoevsky – but in Moderate Doses). Even Proust, who owes Dostoevsky so much, does not hesitate to assert how "there was certainly a crime in his life."[4] Whether there is something to such accusations, we will never know. To dwell on them needlessly is, however, to miss the mark, to forget that he alone among all other writers was capable of creating as powerful a character as Ivan Karamazov. Dostoevsky clearly realizes that evil is not just a social phenomenon. It has much deeper psychological, metaphysical, and religious roots. Unlike Arthur Schopenhauer, who comes to similar insights, Dostoevsky does not simply focus upon the spectacle of human wickedness, greed, or vanity in order to support his preconceived notion of the meaninglessness and unworthiness of this world. Nor is Dostoevsky yet another Marquis de Sade, perversely trying to put in front of our eyes the dirtiest and the ugliest of what human beings are capable. Nor does Dostoevsky think about those criminals he met in Siberia as perverse, or as necessarily evil people. In *The House of the Dead* he often calls criminals "the

---

3   Thomas Mann, "Goethe and Tolstoy," *Essays of Three Decades*, 108. See also Mann, "Tolstoy," *Past Masters and Other Papers*, 156–60. For a significantly different comparison of the two greatest Russian novelists, see George Steiner, *Tolstoy or Dostoevsky*, especially pages 231–348.

4   "*Crime and Punishment* could be the title of all Dostoievski's novels. . . . But probably he makes two persons by dividing what really appertained to one. There was certainly a crime in his life, and a punishment (which perhaps had no connection with the crime), but he has preferred to allot them severally, to attribute in case of need the impressions of punishment to himself (*The House of the Dead*), and the crime to others"; Marcel Proust, "Dostoievski," *On Art and Literature*, 381.

unfortunate ones." Nor does he take poverty, oppression, or crime as the only realities of the world. But they are certainly indicative of a serious crisis that Dostoevsky could sense was shaking the Russia and Europe of his epoch.

For a long time Dostoevsky was unable to put his finger on the exact source of this crisis. He achieves a clearer insight of it only in the last fifteen years of his life. Then he begins exploring a particular type of transgression which René Girard describes as a crime that attacks the very foundation of societal and cultural order, a crime against the symbols of supreme authority.[5] This new orientation is latently present in *Crime and Punishment*, more pronounced in *The Idiot*, *The Possessed*, and *The Adolescent*, and reaches its climax in *The Brothers Karamazov*. Raskolnikov is a fatherless character, a fact brought to our attention at several crucial points of the novel. Prince Myshkin from *The Idiot* also has no father, nor does he have any recollection of one. Several leading young characters in *The Possessed* are the biological or spiritual children of Stepan Verkhovensky, but he turns out to be a failure as a parent, disoriented and in need of spiritual guidance. The old Fyodor Karamazov symbolizes a nominal power-figure whose authority is compromised. Fyodor is an indifferent and unconcerned father. He is selfish, greedy, lustful, and despicable. If he indeed symbolizes a deity, our Father in Heaven – and there are many indications that this is what Dostoevsky intends – it is a fallen one. The whole novel is a tale of how his children, that is, humanity, plot to get rid of their Father and how the orphans react to a chaotic new reality without a supreme authority. If there is nothing sacred, Ivan wonders, how can any norm be valid? If God is dead, everything is permissible.

What Dostoevsky believes must happen to such orphans he nicely expresses in *The Adolescent*. Makar Dolgoruki, a prototype of Zosima, an old and wise man without children of his own, concludes there that:

> a man cannot live without worshiping something; without worshiping he cannot bear the burden of himself. And that goes for every man. So that if a man rejects God, he will

have to worship an idol that may be made of wood, gold, or ideas. So those who think they don't need God are really just idol worshipers (Pt. II, Ch. 2, sec. iii, 373).

Life without worship is the transgression of boundaries which captivates Dostoevsky the most and of which he is utterly horror-struck – the reality in which man attempts to play the role of God.[6] Realizing this dreadful direction of modernity, he completes a full circle and connects his early sympathies for the insulted and the injured with his insight about man's obsession with idols and his identification with God. Dostoevsky believes that he can now unveil, if not the whole account, then at least the foremost reason for the pervasive victimization of the world that he so masterfully portrays in his novels. This key is in the shift from theocentrism to anthropocentrism: We begin our asecent with God-man and then tumble to Man-god.

Whether or not we always agree with his ideas, any reader of Dostoevsky's novels would hardly be able to avoid the impression that human life is indeed bound up with injustice and evil. He does not offer any definition of evil, nor does he intend to develop an innovative conception of evil. All he claims to do is portray reality as he experiences it. Yet even Dostoevsky is aware that this form of realism – which he persistently defends in numerous letters – is of an uncommon sort:

> I have my own particular opinions about the real. What most call fantastic and impossible is often for me real in its actual and deepest meaning – the true reality. A record of everyday events is for me far from realism, rather it is the opposite. In every single newspaper, you can find stories about absolutely real yet absolutely strange facts that our writers would reject and call fantastic – these things

6 According to Joseph Frank, *Dostoevsky: The Seeds of Revolt, 1821–1849*, 31, "[Dostoevsky] was always to remain both fascinated and horrified by the temptation of sacrilege, and all of his great novels deal with the theme in one form or another." Later in the same book (103) Frank claims that already in 1838, at the age of seventeen, "Dostoevsky exhibits a horrified fascination with the theme of man's sacrilegious aspiration to dethrone God and substitute himself in God's place."

hold no interest for them. And yet these stories are the deep and living reality, because they are facts. They happen every day, every moment; they are in no way exceptional.[7]

There is no other word in literary criticism as used, and abused, as the word "realism." It is often prescribed that art should give a truthful representation of the real world and almost every writer wants to be faithful to reality and life. But where are the boundaries between real and unreal? By what criteria can we distinguish what should represent a norm (and thus is normal) from what should not be a norm (and thus is abnormal)? What does it mean to be faithful to reality and life in the first place?

Dostoevsky gives us a clear idea of what it does not mean to him. Realism in literature should not be understood as imitation of reality; it has nothing to do with photographic naturalism, concerned with recording the surface of everyday life and the average. Realism is not the description of commonplace events, characters, or settings. We must aim at a truthful representation of reality without presuming that it can be done completely dispassionately or impersonally.

Every experience of reality involves a subjective element, a selection of one kind or another. For Dostoevsky such a selection must be centered on facts that are not ordinary but extraordinary, bordering on what he calls fantastic. It is not commonplace events but limiting situations and the confrontation with principal boundaries that reveal to us what reality is like. As Stefan Zweig points out,

> [Dostoevsky's] characters do not come to life until they are excited, are filled with passion, have to face a tense moment. Whereas those other authors endeavor to convey an impression of the spiritual by describing the bodily attributes, [Dostoevsky] builds up the body by way of the soul . . . only around the soul does the body take shape; only around a passion, the picture.[8]

7   Letter to Strakhov of February 26, 1869. See also a letter to Maikov of December 11, 1868. For further discussion of Dostoevsky's realism, see Joseph Frank, *Dostoevsky: The Miraculous Years, 1865–1871*, 308–15.

8   Stefan Zweig, *Three Masters: Balzac, Dickens, Dostoeffsky*, 170.

What thus emerges as most relevant for our portrayal of reality is not people's appearance or behavior, but the interior motives of their actions. The writer's task is not to judge his or her characters – neither to love nor to hate them – but to make their souls appear before us. They emerge in front of us as if they are part of their author's psyche, as if they are revelations of his or her inner being.

In this regard Dostoevsky is much closer to existentialism of the twentieth century than to historicism which, under the influence of Hegel and German romantics, dominates his own time.[9] Historicism may be understood as a way of depicting reality insofar as that reality is conditioned by the dynamic concreteness of the stream of historic events. In a work of art, this stream can be captured by a chain of deeds which, like glue, represents the novel's plot. Plot is centered on the development of the main character; its culminating point is the character's ultimate success or failure.

Dostoevsky believes that with historically oriented novelists plot is an effort to make reality seem more cohesive than it is. This is why we like a well-defined plot in a novel: It creates an illusion of structure, order, and certainty in life. Dostoevsky needs no such illusion, nor does he create any. If anything, he wants to liberate himself and his readers from such deceptive assurances. This is why Dostoevsky is not concentrated on plot. (His *Notes from the Underground*, which so impressed the existentialist philosophers, has no discernable plot.) Dostoevsky is interested in life itself, its fluidity, unpredictability, and apparent disconnectedness. The glue keeping his novels and the lives of his characters together is not plot but the revelations of the main characters' souls when they find themselves in the limiting situations, facing the extreme.

In his biography of Dostoevsky, Strakhov repeats the novelist's annoyance at being continually misunderstood: "They call me a psychologist – this is not true; I am a realist in the highest meaning of this word, that is, I depict the deepest regions of a man's soul."[10] Dostoevsky's realism seems fantastic and psychological to his critics because he does not want to stay on the surface of

---

9   See Walter Kaufmann, *Existentialism from Dostoevsky to Sartre*, 12–14.
10   Quoted from Peter Sekirin, *The Dostoevsky Archive*, 169.

things but to reach toward the depths of the soul. If we understand metaphysics as "a drive to find a real order behind the apparent one,"[11] then Dostoevsky's orientation can be most adequately called "metaphysical realism." He trusts that this is the only realism worthy of its name, because the ordinary commonplace reality must be based on the hidden grounds; they can be found in the depths of the human soul and are revealed in the unusual and extreme.

Realism does not have to appear realistic. In fact, Dostoevsky comes to understand that nothing is more fantastic than reality itself. To this insight he ascribes his very birth as a writer, and this same realization can help us understand why he treats Cervantes's *Don Quixote* as the prime example of a realistic novel. As Rabelais's *Gargantua and Pantagruel* unearths the human body with all its coarse delights, *Don Quixote* reveals the soul of that body. Before Cervantes (and Shakespeare), authors wrote what happens to their heroes, not about what happened inside them. Like his contemporary Shakespeare (who Dostoevsky also greatly admires), Cervantes makes us see what is happening within his hero's soul.

We may be puzzled by Dostoevsky's considering Cervantes's novel as realistic, for there are many exaggerations in it. "All art," replies Dostoevsky, "consists in a certain portion of exaggeration, provided . . . one does not exceed certain bounds."[12] We find a further support of this view in the "Author's Preface" to *The Brothers Karamazov*: "For an eccentric is not necessarily an exception or an isolated phenomenon; indeed, it often happens that it is he who embodies the very essence of his time while his contemporaries seem to have been cut loose from it by gusts of an alien wind." *Don Quixote*, Dostoevsky maintains, strikes just the right balance between the eccentric and the essential, between the fantastic and the real, and he is thus not afraid to ascribe such an exemplary value to this novel: "In all the world there is nothing more profound and more powerful than *Don Quixote*. Further than this, it is

11 This is how Susan Neiman aptly characterizes metaphysics in her book, *Evil in Modern Thought: An Alternative History of Philosophy*, 203.
12 Quoted from Donald Fanger, *Dostoevsky and Romantic Realism*, 216.

the last and greatest word of human thought, the most bitter irony that man can express."[13]

What is so profound in Cervantes and in what does Dostoevsky find that "most bitter irony"? As is also the case with Dostoevsky's own works, one of the deepest problems of Cervantes's novel is to distinguish appearance and reality. Although Don Quixote on the surface seems to be the least capable one of drawing that line, his real task does not consist in attacking windmills, but in offering a tireless resistance to what is habitual and customary. He feels constantly challenged to invent new gestures and new evaluations of things, in order to awaken the world from its misperceptions. This is a task doomed to failure, a battle no human being can win. After many glorious but unsuccessful adventures, the noble knight of La Mancha is compelled to realize that man cannot shape his own destiny, much less reality as a whole, in the image of his chosen ideal.

Thinking in the same vein, Joseph Conrad argues that the language of art seeks to present its object with maximum clarity and a minimum of emotional or stylistic deformation. The task of that language is "to make you hear, to make you feel – it is, before all, to make you *see*. That – and no more – is everything."[14] Dostoevsky would gladly emphasize this last point, since he believes that the important thing "is not in the object but in the eye: If you have an eye, the object will be found; if you don't have an eye, if you are blind – you won't find anything in any object."[15] The defining feature of Dostoevsky's realism is that it is directed toward making the secret life of the human soul *visible*. His characters educate the eye rather than inform the intellect. Dostoevsky does not merely want us to believe or be able to explain something, but rather to see that which is hidden in plain view.

Although we usually associate eyes and vision with space and spatial representations, Dostoevsky is more focused on time and

---

13   Quoted from Ernest J. Simmons, *Introduction to Russian Realism*, 6. For further thoughts on Don Quixote, see Dostoevsky's essay, "A Lie Is Saved by Lie," *A Writer's Diary*, September 1877, 1127–31.

14   Quoted from Simmons, *op. cit.*, 6. See also Iris Murdoch, *The Sovereignty of Good*, 61–65.

15   Quoted from Fanger, *op. cit.*, 217.

what we grasp in a short span of intensely experienced moments. Not counting its epilogue, *Crime and Punishment* deals with the events of only two weeks; *The Adolescent* covers seven days; the main action of *The Brothers Karamazov* only six. In *The Idiot*, Dostoevsky tells us about the moments of radiant clarity before the epileptic seizure, when the whole cosmos, with its past, present, and future, seems to appear almost simultaneously in front of our eyes. In the same novel he talks about a few precious moments before the guillotine falls down and the whole film of one's life unfolds with a fantastic speed in front of the convicted. In *Netochka Nezvanova* Dostoevsky sums it all up: "There are minutes in which one experiences, mentally, more than in whole years" (Ch. 3, 57; translation modified.)

Dostoevsky's novels are written about precisely such moments. They are not organized around plot, nor do they intend to express any doctrinal view. They are a series of visual experiences or pictures. Recall, for instance, the bath scene of the chained convicts from *The House of the Dead* (Pt. I, Ch. 9), which appears as if coming straight from Dante's "Purgatory." Or remember Prince Myshkin and Rogozhin laying down next to the murdered corpse of Nastassya Filippovna, with a fly buzzing over them (Pt. IV, Ch. 11). These pictures captivate us because they make the outer and the inner life of their characters appear in front of us with utmost clarity and intensity. Once immersed into the fantastic metaphysical reality of his novels we are forced to keep reading and returning back to them.

It is not accidental that Dostoevsky speaks about paintings (and icons) with a considerable regularity. He was a frequent and passionate visitor of the major galleries in cities like Dresden and Florence; a copy of Raphael's "Sistine Madonna" decorated the wall of his study until his death. We will later discuss his use of several paintings in his novels, but here we will only illustrate his own realism by means of the drawing by Albrecht Dürer. Dostoevsky knew several of Dürer's paintings and drawings from Dresden's *Gemäldegalerie*. This particular drawing belongs to Dürer's early works; it is undated and without title. (In the University Library in Erlangen, where it is located, it is catalogued as B 155v.)

If you were to give this drawing a title, what would you call it?

Dostoevsky would call it "A witness," and would argue that it illustrates two main features of his own brand of realism. First, it focuses on certain aspects of reality and disregards others. Second, the drawing manifests his central interest in psychological expressiveness.

The face and the right hand are worked out in fine details, but the person's hair and clothes are given in barest outlines. Some features are, as it were, put under a magnifying glass, while others are left uncharted. As Dostoevsky himself notoriously ignores any description of nature, in this drawing all the features of the background are similarly neglected. Not everything we perceive is impressive enough to cross the threshold of consciousness, nor is everything we see important. By selecting a certain aspect of the given situation, both Dürer and Dostoevsky focus on what they believe is truly significant in the picture. Both artists call our attention to the pain and suffering of the real world, which a mechanical reproduction of the same reality would obscure.

The genders of Dostoevsky's characters are mostly irrelevant; what matters is their common humanity. Similarly, in Dürer's drawing, it may be difficult to identify the gender of the person: The lips and the long hair may suggest a female, but a closer look at the right hand leaves little doubt that it is a male. (Art critics believe that this is Dürer's self-portrait.) The facial expression, and especially the despondent mood which the eyes reveal, can belong to either sex. These are the eyes of a witness. This man has witnessed something which has left him searching for an explanation. This is the face of someone who does not judge. But nor does he know how to respond to what he has witnessed.

How can we know that these are the eyes of a witness and not of a victim? Prince Myshkin, whose extraordinary skill in "reading faces" we will discuss in Chapter 5, would reply that the eyes of a victim would be facing down, in agony, perhaps also in shame, over what had happened. The eyes of a witness, by contrast, are looking straight into the world, trying to establish a contact with a reality which does not seem to make sense.

One of the distinguishing marks of Western civilization is its focus on the visual aspect of reality. Since its first days of glory among the ancient Greeks, visual elements are considered crucially significant in all attempts to establish the meaning of the life. Our sense of life's meaning can be told in terms of pictures and visual images which hold us captive – whether it be Plato's cave, or the Christian image of Jesus on the cross, or the grave of a three-month-old baby. The picture that is most vivid in front of our eyes is the one that determines how we look at the world as a whole; it settles on how we comprehend our own role and place in that reality; it establishes how we conceive life's meaning.

Eyes have a double role in our comprehension of reality: They act both as subjects and as objects. Our own eyes are like the windows through which a picture may enter our mind's chambers, so that we can make sense of what we see. The eyes of other persons are the openings through which we penetrate their inner lives. Eyes are the boundaries that both separate and connect. They are like the thresholds of a cathedral which establish the distance between the outer and the inner, between the profane and the sacred. Eyes are also the thresholds which allow the passage from one space to another, or from one person to another.

Eyes are not, however, sufficient for our full grasp of reality, either literally or figuratively. The pictures that hold us captive influence what we see as real, but eyes cannot tell us why these (and not some other) pictures make such an impact on us. This limitation of sight is the reason for the distinction between a body's eye and a mind's eye on which the ancient Greeks insisted. Taken in isolation, Dostoevsky's realism is similarly insufficient: It does not reveal his entire vision of the world. Yes, it is difficult to live like a human being in this vale of sorrow. But this sorrow does not exhaust our experience of the world. Similarly, realism – with its admission of the everlasting presence of evil – is the ground which must not be neglected or denied, but on which further building must be based. Realism is like the eyes on Dürer's drawing: They show us the openings of the soul, but we have to figure out what hides behind the threshold.

The Epoch of Homelessness

Ivan builds his case for nihilism on the suffering of little children, those who "have not eaten [the apple] and are not yet guilty of anything" (Bk. V, Ch. 4, 238). Facing the flawed creation, Ivan requires justice. If this justice demands that the Creator be forever detached from the creation, so that man can correct the injustices of this world, so be it. *Fiat iustitia, ruat caelum.* (Let justice prevail, even if the heavens collapse.)

Unlike Ivan, some of Dostoevsky's characters do not demand justice; they hope for grace. Yet grace is in short supply as well. When we think of the death of an innocent child, we wonder: Grace for whom? The parents of little Ilyusha, who dies at the end of *The Brothers Karamazov*, do not receive any grace but go mad in their sorrow. They hit the bottom of the emotional abyss. This must also be how Dostoevsky and his wife felt when they first lost Sonia and, a decade later, a three-year old Alyosha.

Many of Dostoevsky's characters lament that life is not fair: They feel betrayed, alone. "Do you understand, sir," the drunkard Marmeladov addresses Raskolnikov during their first meeting, "do you understand what it means when you have absolutely nowhere to turn? No, that you don't understand yet" (Pt. I, Ch. 2, 13).

Marmeladov suggests that being alive feels like being a victim of an unknown crime. Without any sin that can be ascribed to us, we feel fallen, we are treated like orphans. The expression of this troublesome homelessness, of the profound loneliness and disorientation of modern man is by no means unique to Dostoevsky's works. He may have been one of the first to feel it so acutely, but the tragic proportion of this crisis is even more obvious in the twentieth century. How have we arrived at such a deep point of despair?

Martin Buber, who experiences this crisis no less deeply than Dostoevsky, offers an explanation. He divides the history of spirit into "epochs of habitation" and "epochs of homelessness."[16] In the former, human beings live in the world as in their home. In the

16   Martin Buber, "What is Man?" in *Between Man and Man*, 150.

latter, we feel as if we are living on an open field, without even being able to find four pegs with which to set up a tent. In the former epochs, the anthropological thought is contained within a wider-reaching cosmological thought. In the epochs of homelessness, our sense of identity and our general conception of the world do not complement each other.

Buber identifies three epochs of habitations, and argues that they receive their most convincing advocates in Aristotle, Aquinas, and Hegel. The ancient Greeks marvel at the order of the universe, which they appropriately call *kosmos*. Plato and Aristotle consider the wonder which this ordered universe evokes as the origin of all critical thinking. The central motive of all Greek thought is to offer a systematic account of the order of the cosmic edifice, with special attention to man's place in it. For the Greeks, all words whose meaning is associated with "boundless," "unlimited," and "indefinite" have a bad connotation. In their view, order is opposed not only to chaos but also to anything that is not confined, limited, and fully determinable.[17]

The spatial image of a confined, limited, and determined *kosmos* is further related to another word with spatial references: *kentron* (center). Symbolically speaking, the center is that around which everything revolves. It is the focal point, the most important place. In opposition to what is "center" and "central" stand the "periphery" and the "peripheral" – that which is of little importance, even superfluous.

The hegemony of the visual over the other senses leads the Greeks to base both their ordinary and philosophical thinking on the formation of images. Plato's world of ideas is a visual world of forms that can be seen by the mind's eye. It is with Aristotle, however, that the visual image of the universe is realized in unsurpassable clarity as a universe of *things*. According to Buber, with Aristotle,

> man ceases to be problematic, with him man speaks of himself always as it were in the third person, is only a

---

17   The Greek view is masterfully illustrated in Albert Camus's essay "Helen's Exile," in *The Myth of Sisyphus*, 134–38.

'case' for himself, he attains to consciousness of self only as 'he', not as 'I'. The special dimension, in which man knows himself as he can know himself alone, remains unentered, and for that reason man's special place in the cosmos remains undiscovered. Man is comprehended only in the world, the world is not comprehended in him. The tendency of the Greeks to understand the world as a self-contained space, in which man too has his fixed place, was perfected in Aristotle's geocentric spherical system.[18]

As a rational being, man is, with Aristotle, given his own dwelling-space and his home in the *kosmos*: not in one of the lower storeys, as in Plato's cave, nor in the highest, where the Olympian gods dwell, but in the respectable middle.

Without mentioning Socrates, Buber argues that the first to pose the genuine anthropological question, and in the first person – not "What is man?" but "Who am I?" – was Augustine. Several centuries after Aristotle, the round and integrated world of the ancient thinker collapsed. Instead of a unified heavenly sphere, Augustine contrasts two autonomous and hostile kingdoms, the kingdom of light and the kingdom of darkness: The city of God and the city of man. Human beings consist of soul and body which pull them in opposite directions, toward opposite kingdoms. Cain ends up suffering in the city of man, while his victim, Abel, is mercifully admitted into the city of God.

In Augustine, light and darkness are irreconcilable, and so are the different aspects of the same human being. Man becomes an internally divided, homeless creature. Yet the further development of Christianity, culminating in Aquinas's magisterial *Summa* and Dante's *Divine Comedy*, marks a new epoch of man's domestication. In Buber's words:

> Once again, there is a self-enclosed universe, once again a house in which man is allowed to dwell. This universe is still more finite than that of Aristotle, for here finite time too is taken into the image in all seriousness – the finite time of the Bible, which here appears, however, transformed into

18 Buber, *op. cit.*, 150–51.

a Christian form. The pattern of this image of the universe is a cross, whose vertical beam is finite space from heaven to hell, leading right across the heart of the human being, and whose cross-beam is finite time from the creation of the world to the end of days; which makes time's centre, the death of Christ, fall coveringly and redemptively on the centre of space, the heart of the poor sinner. The medi- aeval image of the universe is built around this pattern. In it Dante painted life, the life of men and spirits, but the conceptual framework was set up for him by Thomas Aquinas.[19]

Aquinas and Dante visibly soften Augustine's conflict between soul and body. The human soul is the lowest of the spirits, while the body is the highest of physical things. Man appears as the dividing line of spiritual and physical nature. He is an organic part of the objective order of the world, the *divine* cosmos: Heaven is above him, Hell below him. The central role in the universe belongs to God, perfect and separated from His imperfect creation. Man is cre- ated in the image of God, and his planet is the central point of the physical universe. As soon as the six days of creation are over, man takes the central stage and God assumes the passive role of react- ing to human deeds and pronouncing judgment on them. While in the beginning of history God Himself appears to man, He gradually recedes from sight and His voice is heard only through His inter- preters, first through the prophets and then, exclusively, through the Church.

Modernity's drive toward orientation and the center of the cos- mic order is no less powerful than it was in ancient and medieval times, yet it undergoes a radical transformation. Although still hailed as omnipotent, omniscient, and most benevolent, the hid- den God and His order appear increasingly less comprehensible to man. If He exists, God is invisibly located somewhere outside of space and time, outside of all human frames of meaning.

---

19 *Ibid.*, 153–54. On Dante's (and Aquinas's) conception of man and its contrast with Dostoevsky's view, see Nicholas Berdyaev's *Dostoevsky*, 46–48.

Modernity chooses to battle the problem of orientation on two fronts. Using Kant's terminology, they can be called the "metaphysics of nature" and the "metaphysics of morals" (instead of the Christian distinction of body and soul). The first appears less central, since it pretends not to have any direct impact on human affairs. To the modern mind, nature does not function as a living *kosmos*, nor does it participate in any universal hierarchy with Heaven and Hell. Nature is now understood as a giant, center-less mechanism, a soul-less and spirit-less universe without purpose or meaning, operating according to its own laws.

Although the starry heavens above are a source of constant fascination, the moral law within is far more intriguing. Humanity no longer feels bound by any objective world order from above. Modern man feels free, yet he is puzzled by his freedom. He neither fully understands how he can be free in the midst of the mechanically determined world, nor does he quite know what to do with his freedom. According to Kant, our humanity is not something that is given to us (as a gift from God), but an endless task to which the realization of all other tasks, and even the entire physical world, must be subordinated. No house is inherited by us, but, as the builders of the new world order, we must figure out how to put together a home for ourselves. The question "Who is man?" is for Kant as open as it is for Augustine. While Kant cannot offer a definitive response to it, Hegel can. According to Buber:

> Hegel's system is the third great attempt at security within Western thought . . . The universal reason goes its undeflectable way through history, and knowing man knows this way, rather, his knowledge is the real goal and end of the way in which truth as it realizes itself knows itself in its realization. The stages of the way follow one another in an absolute order: The law of dialectic, in which the thesis is relieved by the antithesis and the antithesis by the synthesis, is sovereign over them. As one goes with sure step from storey to storey and from room to room of a well-built house with its solid foundations and walls and roof, so

> Hegel's all-knowing man goes through the new world-house,
> history, whose whole meaning he knows.[20]

What man knows, according to Hegel, is not that he is at home in the world, as Aristotle and Aquinas think, but that he *can* and *will* become at home. Human beings and the world are made for each other, because of the iron laws of an underlying rationality which permeate every aspect of being: Everything that exists must have a sufficient reason for its occurrence. According to Hegel, Kant's metaphysics of nature and metaphysics of morals must be reunited because behind the demand to understand the world and to act in it lies the same mandate that the world be intelligible. The modern rift between nature and morality, between "is" and "ought," is just as unnecessary as the distance between the human and the divine. Such distinctions do not lie in the nature of things but are created. They are only the byproducts of history, the temporary stages of the civilization's development: Reality will become what it should be with the passage of time. Instead of Aristotle's image of the sphere and Aquinas's image of the cross (both of which separate the center from its periphery), Hegel offers the conception of an inevitable ascent and progress. He reassures us that we should not feel helpless in the face of the world's contingency. The proper philosophical understanding of the real and the rational will eliminate the contingent and unveil the unstoppable march of the historical necessity.

Once the creative work of God is rejected as an explanatory ground, the most natural way to justify the creation is in terms of the unfolding stages of development. Hegel does not offer any new image of the world, with its center and its periphery. Instead, he comes to realize that although the infinite and open-ended universe cannot be visualized any more, it can still be conceptualized. The conceptualization relies not on space but on the dimension of time, in the form of history whose meaning can be clearly conceived. The completion of man's new house, the meaning of human existence, and Hegel's optimism with regard to them, are projected

---

20   Buber, *op. cit.*, 165–66.

into an eschatologically conceived future, which will in retrospect justify as indispensable all of the preceding stages of the historical development.

Despite Hegel's assurance, the magic formula which equates the real and the rational cannot close the gap between what "is" and what "ought to be." Their rift can neither be overlooked nor easily overcome. In establishing a new epoch of habitation, Hegel fails to solve the manifest lack of the most basic trust in the world – the problem that stands behind the pervasive presence of evil and our sense of homelessness. Human existence is as problematic as it has ever been. In fact, claims Buber, the contemporary crisis of man's identity, his confusion with regard to his meaning of life and the place and role in reality, has never been deeper.

Dostoevsky is in full agreement with such an assessment. In his works, the uprootedness of modern man has two distinguishable yet related symbolic manifestations. One of them deals with the perception of chaos, the other with the preoccupation with pollution.

Chaos is a spatial phenomenon, literally a place that is a non-place, symbolically a waste land. The manifestations of chaos are understood by all who attempt to establish a dwelling place for man in the world: Chaos strikes us as the lack of order, or as the lack of center. Dostoevsky's primary concerns are not with the world's chaos but with its pollution. If, as Dudley Young points out in his book, *The Origins of the Sacred*, chaos is spatial and static, pollution is dynamic; it is an event in time.[21] As chaos appears as lack of order and absence of center, pollution also has two major manifestations: dirt and blood. In *Crime and Punishment*, for instance, Dostoevsky never tires of reminding us of the stinky streets and dirty staircases of Petersburg. In *The Possessed*, he masterfully describes the muddy streets of back alleys. Nor does Dostoevsky forget to describe in detail the filthy outfits of many of his heroes (e.g., Raskolnikov or Marmeladov), or the

---

21 See Young, *The Origins of the Sacred: The Ecstasies of Love and War*, xix, 212, 233–35, 263–65, and 446n19. See also Mary Douglas, *Purity and Danger: An Analysis of the Concepts of Pollution and Taboo*.

dirty underwear and socks which Dmitri is ashamed of during his interrogation.

Blood plays an even more important role in Dostoevsky's portrayals of the evil world in which modern man unsuccessfully tries to establish his home. Raskolnikov makes his hands dirty with human blood, as does Dmitri. Rogozhin kills the person he loves most. Dostoevsky indicates the depth of Rogozhin's derangement by making him marvel at how just a few drops of blood came out of Nastassya Filippovna's corpse. The madness of the world contaminates the beautiful soul of Prince Myshkin. Subdued by it, he spends the night with Rogozhin, lying down next to Nastassya's lifeless body. Myshkin, this prince of compassion, cannot find home in this world and must head back to the asylum for the lunatics. Chaos and pollution are victorious, once again.

The shedding of blood plays a symbolic role in all mythologies and religions of the world, and it points toward one of the deepest wounds of any epoch: How to stop this endless spilling of human blood? Dirt may be cleansed by water – there is an omnipresence of rivers and rainstorms in Dostoevsky's novels. But what do we do about blood-shedding? Are – as Christianity teaches us – the tears of lamentation enough?

Ivan certainly does not think so. Tears or no tears, he takes the torture and murder of innocent children (= pollution) as a proof of the systematic distortion of justice (= chaos), and indirectly as a proof that life has no meaning (= homelessness).

This, then, is the problem that his own realism poses for Dostoevsky. Since the world appears to be full of sorrow and injustice, since it appears to be delivered to evil, how can we possibly continue to long for a home in this world? This problem of homelessness appears virtually unsolvable when we (a) realize that the world is not made to our advantage, (b) lose trust that it is part of a secret design by God, and (c) do not have enough faith in humanity's capacities – theoretical or practical, rational or otherwise – to cope with its problems. In the face of such obstacles, should we keep searching for the way to make ourselves at home in this world, or should we perhaps give up on this ancient quest?

C.S. Lewis recognizes that some concessions must be made and, in order to defend the old religious and metaphysical approach, suggests that "the government of the universe is temporarily in enemy hands."[22]

Humanistically oriented intellectuals do not think much of such a proposal. Erich Fromm, for example, argues that the apparent absence of justice in divine institutions is no excuse for tolerating it in human ones. If anything, it makes the request for establishing justice more pressing.

Sigmund Freud decisively opposes both proposals. First, the whole idea of "the government of the universe," with its underlying expectation that good is rewarded and evil punished, simply does not square with reality. Second, human institutions seem no less fallible than their alleged divine counterparts. Neither divine nor human justice can correct the evils of the world.

Freud believes that many of the debates which have preoccupied intellectuals for centuries are based on ill-grounded conceptual and linguistic constructions. They endlessly argue whether nature and morality can be reconciled in any fruitful manner, without realizing not only that the gap between them is unbridgeable, but even that the words "nature" and "morality" are ambiguous and misleading. Instead of "nature" Freud leads his discussion in terms of the instinctual forces of the "*id*" and, in the later stages of his career, of the pursuit of the pleasure principle. Instead of morality, focusing on the issue of justice and injustice, Freud sees the controversy as dealing centrally with fear – fear of death, fear of chaos, fear of losing the security of parental protection. Even religion, with its so-called "oceanic feeling" ("a feeling as of something limitless, unbounded, something oceanic"), really begins with the longing of a frightened child for security, love, and pleasure.[23]

Freud's analytical knife keeps cutting even deeper. In his *Civilization and Its Discontents* he takes the metaphor of homelessness seriously, yet argues that our desire for home, as well as our expectation of justice, reveals not our depth but our infancy.

---

22   Quoted from Armand M. Nicholi, Jr., *The Question of God: C.S. Lewis and Sigmund Freud Debate God, Love, Sex and the Meaning of Life*, 206.
23   Sigmund Freud, *Civilization and Its Discontents*, 1.

This desire is not something we should nourish but outgrow. The intensity of our longing for home derives from the intensity of the terror and helplessness we feel as children. This feeling is not simply prolonged from childhood days, but is permanently sustained by fear of the superior power of fate. The perplexity and helplessness of the human life cannot be remedied. Our choices are either to face reality and give up our unfounded hope, or to keep deceiving ourselves. We continually choose the latter and imagine that a solicitous "Providence" watches over us. This attitude, claims Freud, is "so patently infantile, so incongruous with reality, that to one whose attitude to humanity is friendly it is painful to think that the great majority of mortals will never be able to rise above this view in life."[24] The obsessive desire to make ourselves feel at home in the world does not represent a worthwhile endeavor. If anything, it is embarrassing.

Instead of deluding ourselves with a naively optimistic search for home and the meaning of life, all we should hope for are bare survival and normal functioning. Even "the meaning of culture" – in Freud's eyes the greatest accomplishment of the human race – is nothing but "the struggle between Eros and death, between the instincts of life and the instincts of destruction, as it works itself out in the human species. This struggle is what life essentially consists of and so the evolution of civilization may be simply described as the struggle of the human species for survival."[25]

In his late works, Freud offers a dark vision of human nature and bleak prospects for the future. Neither does he find much to be appreciated about the past. Freud writes about the human condition as if any epoch of domestication had never existed, and as if all the magnificent accomplishments of humankind had been at best the acts of sublimation and at worst hopeless attempts to escape recurring fears and the libidinous drives of man's insatiable *id*.

Many have likened Dostoevsky and Freud's penetration into the dark secrets of the human soul. Such comparisons are neither arbitrary nor unjustified. Dostoevsky and Freud had little reason to

---

24 *Ibid.*, 9.
25 *Ibid.*, 49. For discussion of Freud's opinion of Dostoevsky, see Frank, *Dostoevsky: The Seeds of Revolt, 1821–1849*, 379–91.

disagree about the facts regarding either the external or the internal aspects of reality. Their realism with regard to the overwhelming presence of evil in the world was reinforced by the sorrow and pain that left unhealable wounds in their own lives. There is, nevertheless, one principal difference in their attitudes. For Dostoevsky, life does not reduce to a struggle for survival, nor does pessimism ever fully overtake his soul. No amount of suffering and injustice can lead him to deny the worthiness, even sanctity, of life. When his beloved Sonia passes away and his pain is unbearable, Dostoevsky does not think that life is pointless, or that Sonia may be better off dying so early, rather than suffering through the torture of this life. Fully aware of the implications of his words, he writes to his close friend Maikov: "I would accept the cross's agony if only she might be alive."

2
Notes from the Underground

Evil out of Spite?

The Anatomy Lesson

In 1844 Dostoevsky published his first work, *Poor Folk*, and it was an instant success. Russian literary critic Belinsky went as far as to designate the previously unknown author as the successor of the great Nikolai Gogol. Twenty years later, Dostoevsky published *Notes from the Underground*, and his Russian critics did not know what to make of it. In retrospect, it is clear that with this work Dostoevsky comes out of the shadow of Gogol and every other writer. Even now, almost a hundred and fifty years after its publication, after we have experienced Kafka, Camus, and Faulkner in literature, Nietzsche, Heidegger, and Wittgenstein in philosophy, Kandinsky, Klee, and Picasso in painting, and Schönberg, Bartok, and Stravinsky in music, Dostoevsky's work is barely comprehensible on first reading. It is so profoundly original and revolutionary that, had Dostoevsky never published again, his fame as a writer would have been assured. Yet, as Konstantin Mochulsky remarks, this work is just "the philosophical preface to the cycle of his great novels."[1]

---

1 Konstantin Mochulsky, *Dostoevsky: His Life and Work*, 254. See also Leonid Grossman, *Dostoevsky: A Biography*, 315.

Notes from the Underground is unconventional with respect both to its form and its content. It is hard to say to what genre it belongs. It is not a novel; it is not a story. *Poor Folk* is written in the epistolary form, and the *Notes* appears to be a confession of an "underground man." A few direct and several subtle references to Rousseau's *Confessions* confirm this, except that Dostoevsky's work mocks not only Rousseau, but also the institution of confessing itself. Confession is a voluntary admission that something has gone wrong, and there is much that has gone amiss with the nameless hero of Dostoevsky's work. He is an isolated man, yet despite his self-disclosure it is not clear either what exactly has gone wrong, or who is responsible for it. There is some kind of curse on the underground man, and indirectly on humanity as a whole, but it is hard to identify what the curse is and what to do about it. To confess means not to accuse others for what we are responsible, and not to cover up the truth about ourselves. Dostoevsky's twisted confessional work consists of two parts: The first represents the accusation of others, the second the underground man's contempt for himself.

The content of the *Notes* is even more experimental than its form. There is no visible plot, and it is far from clear how the two parts are related; if the first represents a transgression of some unnamed boundary, the second fails to bring a desired reconciliation. Although the underground man does not explicitly identify his opponents, he fires a whole battery of charges: against the rationalistic orientation of the Enlightenment; against the utopian visions of the happy future of humanity; against Chernyshevsky's obsession with rationally calculated interest; against Rousseau's celebration of the independence of an autonomous individual; and against the Romantic fascination with "the beautiful and sublime." The underground man rebels against entire modernity.

Dostoevsky prefaces his work by emphasizing that, "Both the author of the *Notes* and the *Notes* themselves are, of course, fictitious. Nevertheless, such persons as the author of such memoirs not only may, but must, exist in our society. . . . He is one of the representatives of a generation that is still with us."[2]

2 *Notes from the Underground,* in *Great Short Works of Fyodor Dostoevsky,* trans. David Magarshack, Pt. I, sec. i, page 263. Since there

Who is this underground creature who "must exist"? How does he represent an entire generation? Dostoevsky never gives him a name. A person without a name is no person, no human being. Spiders and mice do not have names, and this underground man compares himself more than once with such creatures. He has no parents, no background, no religion, no friend, no lover. Although Dostoevsky insists that the underground man must exist, he has virtually no identity. He is an isolated atom, one among the infinite number of atoms. And that is exactly what Dostoevsky wants us to wonder about: the identity, not just of this man but of all modern humanity.

How can man not be homeless if he does not know who he is and with whom or what to identify? His own boundaries – between death and life, between body and soul – are obscure to him. In the *Notes* the underground creature does not contrast himself against a beast or a mass-man without identity. He is a citizen of a cultivated society, and he perceives our humanity in such terms. Man is not stupid, he claims, but "monstrously ungrateful": "The best definition of man is – a creature who walks on two legs and is ungrateful. But that is not all, that is not his principal failing; his greatest failing is his constant lack of moral sense" (Pt. I, sec. vii, 287).

The Latin word *definitio* means a boundary. To define means to bound and determine, to limit and fix the essence of something.[3] The underground man's definition indicates that something is wrong with humanity: Not only that we grow accustomed to that to which we should not have grown accustomed (lack of moral sense), but also that we are ungrateful. The underground man does not clarify what to make of this ungratefulness: Toward whom is man ungrateful? For what should he be grateful? Nor can we gather

---

are many various translations and editions of the *Notes*, in the following, after quoting this work, I will give reference first to the part, than section, and finally the page number of the used translation: e.g. (Pt. I, sec. i, 263).

3 According to the Aristotelian tradition, definition is a statement of the inherent essence or nature of a thing. The underground man makes fun of this tradition by showing that definitions do not add to our factual knowledge about the essence or nature of things. This rejection of essentialism is one of the reasons why existentialist philosophers admire Dostoevsky's *Notes*: they also argue that there is no essential human nature which precedes and determines our actual existence.

in what way man lacks moral sense. What the underground man clearly states is that he is educated and conscious; in fact, he is too conscious. It is precisely to this "super-consciousness" that he ascribes the source of his problems. In contrast to him, we associate consciousness with surface, not underground; with light, not darkness; with health, not disease; with knowledge, not ignorance. Why does the underground man make such paradoxical claims? In order to cope with this problem, we need to place *Notes from the Underground* in a historical context.

Since Dostoevsky names the underground man's servant Apollon, we can assume that the underground man knows of the most famous Greek temple in Delphi, the temple of Apollo. Above the entrance of this temple there were two inscriptions which served as the intellectual and moral foundation of the Athenian civilization: "Know thyself," and "Nothing in excess." The first inscription is immortalized in Plato's account of Socrates' speech during his trial, in the *Apology*. The second finds its philosophical articulation in Aristotle's ethics of virtue. Moral virtue consists in finding the right measure in everything we do, in the mean between too much and too little. The first inscription is the more important of the two, for even Aristotle believes that above moral virtues tower the virtues of the intellect, where the ultimate demand is to know oneself – one's mortality in contrast to the immortality of gods.

Christianity respects the first prescription but turns away from the second: Love of God and dedication to living a life that would bring us closer to God knows no limits and should not be bound by moderation. While moderation helps the Greeks feel at home in this world, Christians are asked to overcome that same world. Human beings can find their home not in this valley of tears, but only in following the will of the transcendent God. The Gospel of John and the Epistles of Paul give the strongest expression to this otherworldly orientation.

Modernity is equally hostile to moderation. Unlike the Greek and Christian traditions which presuppose that the past has a powerful grip on us, modernity rejects any such influence of the past as a prejudice from which we must liberate ourselves. Modernity is directed toward the future, not the past, and it is obsessively focused on what is new, on what makes news. Moderation does not make newspaper headlines, nor does it attract the attention which modern man craves. In this regard the underground man is a prototype of modern man.

The problem with modernity is that it has no world to which to turn. It makes a decisive break from the otherworldly orientation of Christianity, while also retaining the Christian contempt for this world. But in what world, then, are we supposed to find a dwelling place? Like an ungrateful prodigal son, modern man turns away from his own roots and tradition. Unlike the prodigal son, if he fails to establish a new home, he will have nowhere to return.

With almost all of his bridges burned behind him, modern man turns to his inner world. With modernity everything transposes from the outside toward the inside. The boundaries of the world are redefined one more time. If Heaven and Hell exist, they must be within our psyche, not in the seventh circle of Dante's *Divine Comedy*. As this shift toward the interior world becomes more pronounced with Shakespeare and undeniable with Dostoevsky, it becomes apparent that if life is a comedy, it must be a human comedy.[4] Yet is life really a comedy? Does it have a happy ending? After the centuries of wandering, can modern man finally find himself a home?

The founders of modernity certainly expect so. For them, self-knowledge becomes an imperative of renewed significance. Following Descartes and Rousseau, Kant answers the question: "What is Enlightenment?" with *Sapere aude!* "Dare to know," encourages Kant. Dare to use your own reason! It is in our vital interest to find enough courage to use reason against any traditional authority, against any source of prejudice. The use of reason will lead not only to an advancement of freedom but also to the increase of knowledge. Reason is the source of light that dispels the darkness of this world and serves as the ultimate authority of truth. *Scientia est potentia*: Knowledge is the power which will help us transform the world in the image conceived by reason.

---

4   For an insightful comparison of the conception of man in Dante, Shakespeare, and Dostoevsky, see Nicholas Berdyaev, *Dostoevsky*, 46–49. One of the most provocative accounts of the modern shift toward inwardness can be found in Carl Gustav Jung's *Answer to Job*.

Rousseau's *Confessions* is an attempt at self-knowledge of man, which will empower him to control the circumstances life deals him. Descartes's *Meditations* is also a search for self-knowledge, in a different form of "confession." It is an admission of the mistakes that the best representatives of human kind have made in their effort to understand and master the world. Descartes has no doubt that Plato and Aristotle are men of superior, perhaps unmatched intelligence. What puzzles him is that they develop so many mistaken beliefs. Descartes reasons that these giants did not use their intellectual capacities correctly, that they did not discover the right method. He describes his new method in two complementary ways. The first of them is known as "the method of doubt," the second as "the method of analysis."

The method of doubt begins with the assumption that *all* of our beliefs can be mistaken. Thus, they should be mistrusted and treated as guilty until proven innocent. Proving them innocent requires exposing them to most rigorous examination. Only those beliefs which can be thoroughly demonstrated will be readmitted within the body of our beliefs. The first belief which, according to Descartes, passes even the most scrupulous test of doubt is the famous *cogito ergo sum*: "I think, therefore I am." I am conscious, and the act of consciousness establishes my identity as a thinking being. After that, Descartes moves on to present a proof of the existence of a benevolent, omniscient, and omnipotent God. At the end of his *Meditations*, he also offers a reassurance of the existence of a body. The material body is less valuable than the immaterial soul, but remains an indispensable component of every human being.

The method of analysis is based on the insight that many of our mistakes arise from premature judgments about things or problems which are too complex. The proper procedure is to reduce every complex body or problem to its irreducible parts. We should analyze each elementary part separately, form simple but indubitable truths about them, and then proceed toward judging complex problems and compound things.

Armed with these methodological tools, Descartes and his followers hope they can establish a body of certain and indubitable beliefs. They also suppose that the proper application of these methods will lead not only to our liberation from the shackles of the past but also to a resolution of virtually all human problems, including the mastery of the external world. Descartes's epistemological optimism is the foundation for the moral, political, and economic optimism of modernity.

In *Notes from the Underground* Descartes's twin methods are at work. Yet although using Descartes's methodology, Dostoevsky's intention is not to imitate the great philosopher. There are three deviations in his approach. The first is that the underground man's style combines a serious examination and strange playfulness. His gestures and words are ironic, and there is also much jest. He is a strange mishmash of a confidant who saps those illusions we are so prone to believe in and a buffoon who speaks the truth most of us would not dare pronounce. While reading the *Notes*, we may wonder if the underground man is more similar to Don Quixote or to Sancho Panza? To Ivan Karamazov or to his father Fyodor?

The second difference is that the underground man develops his doubt more consistently than Descartes. If we are to doubt everything, why exempt the rules of rational thinking by means of which we are to scrutinize all of our beliefs? If nothing remains sacred, why would consciousness and reason be treated as such?[5] If we do not believe in religious miracles, why believe in those performed by science?

The third deviation is in the end product. Descartes argues that radical doubt and the method of analysis will ultimately lead to an unshakeable foundation not only for our rational knowledge but for our faith as well. None of this is the case. For the underground man, doubt leads only to greater doubt. Consciousness remains caught in its own vicious circle and, detached from the real world, leads to no action. What we doubt and analyze, what we dissect

---

5   The underground man intentionally challenges the main principles of classical Aristotelian logic. Against the principle of non-contradiction, he asserts that sometimes 2 + 2 = 5. Against the principle of sufficient reason, he insists that he does things out of spite, for no (other) reason whatsoever. Against the principle of the excluded middle, the underground man argues that man is neither good nor evil, neither rational nor irrational, but both.

and decompose, we cannot again recompose and bring back to life. The anatomy lesson that Descartes initiates leads not to a grand synthesis but ends up in a general deconstruction. The unhappy conclusion of the *Notes* underscores the paradox of the modern approach to life as a whole: Man thinks of himself in comparison with God. Yet man is a creator of a strange kind, for he ends up being more successful at analysis than synthesis, in destruction than construction, in killing than promoting life.

I find it hard to think about Dostoevsky's *Notes* without remembering one other disturbing work of art, Rembrandt's "Anatomy Lesson of Dr. Jan Deyman." Rembrandt painted it in 1656, less than two decades after the appearance of Descartes's *Meditations*.[6] Although only the central fragment of this painting is preserved from a fire (in 1723), what survived, together with preparatory drawings, indicates that this may have been one of Rembrandt's most powerful works. At the center of the preserved fragment, we see a dissected corpse and an anatomist standing above it while performing an autopsy. Rembrandt portrays here both a unique event and also something that has established itself as a tradition in Amsterdam and a few other Dutch cities.

Amsterdam was then a booming corporation city, a beehive of the rapidly developing capitalism. Events like public autopsies were performed in arenas especially built for this purpose; they were eagerly anticipated and well-attended. Besides all the eminencies of the city, those in regular attendance included not only professors and students of anatomy, but also the ticket-paying public which filled out many back rows. During and after the show, the audience thoroughly enjoyed itself. There were intestines and heart and

6   It is quite possible that Rembrandt was acquainted not only with Descartes's most influential works, but with their author himself. According to John Cottingham, Descartes took up residence in Holland in 1629 and decided to make that country his permanent home: "He lived first in Franaker, but within a year he had moved to Amsterdam, and then, after two years, to Leiden. . . . While living in Amsterdam, in Kalverstraat (quarter were many of the city's butchers were to be found), he was able to pursue his anatomical studies by purchasing numerous carcasses for dissection"; *Descartes*, 11.

brain to see. After the event, there was food and drink, music and gossip.[7]

Rembrandt was commissioned to do this painting on the occasion of Dr. Deyman's dissection of the corpse of Joris Fonteyn. (Fonteyn was arrested a few days earlier after attempting to rob a draper's store and then attacking with a knife those who tried to stop him.) Our strongest impression after looking at Rembrandt's painting may be an unsettling sense of cohabitation that lingers over it – of the sacred with the profane, of the living with the dead. The first thing we notice is not the honorable Dr. Deyman but the corpse. Resembling the portrayal of the dead Christ (e.g., "*Cristo sorto*," by Andrea Montegna), the corpse is represented very realistically, with the stomach cavity open and emptied of the alimentary and excretory organs. Then we notice Dr. Deyman's hands, exposing for examination the lobes of the brain. Unlike Rembrandt's "The Anatomy Lesson of Dr. Tulp," painted twenty-four years earlier, where the illustrious anatomist is examining the muscles on the corpse's arm, the procedure here has progressed to the corpse's brain. This novelty symbolizes a more advanced examination of the center of thinking and consciousness, the sapient marks of humanity. Initially, there must have been some discomfort over such a desacralization of the body by inappropriate penetration into it – a boundary of something previously considered sacred has been violated – but the illustrious anatomist and his audience have clearly overcome it. The quest for self-knowledge should not be slowed by any sense of discomfort, or anything deemed sacred. Although we cannot know where it will lead us, the anatomy lesson of modernity should not be stopped.

Had Dostoevsky been aware of Rembrandt's painting, he could have renamed his *Notes* "The Anatomy Lesson of an Underground Man." Anatomy is the opposite from confession. Confession is a voluntary revealing of our mistakes; anatomy is a forced extraction

---

7 My presentation relies here on Simon Schama, *Rembrandt's Eyes*, 342–53; Ludwig Münz, *Rembrandt*, 26–28; and Dudley Young, *Origins of the Sacred: The Ecstasies of Love and War*, 18–20. Schama indicates (353) that one of the placards hanging in such anatomy theaters was commending *Nosce te impsum* – Know thyself!

of the truth. In both Rembrandt and Dostoevsky, man dissects not animals but human beings in order to find out who he is. In Dostoevsky's work, the inappropriate penetration is made into the body of a prostitute: For little money, we can desacralize a body of another human being. Unlike the criminal on Rembrandt's painting, Lisa is still alive. Yet because she is polluted, penetration into her body is socially accepted. Both Rembrandt and Dostoevsky suggest that by desacralizing others we also desacralize ourselves. The anatomy of others may ultimately be the anatomy of ourselves.

Descartes and Rousseau assume that the self is given at birth, and thus that our identity is then established as well. Even if that is so, and Dostoevsky's underground man rejects the idea, we need to identify what exactly that identity is. Just like Rembrandt's painting, the *Notes* includes the dissection of both the body and the brain. Yet Dostoevsky reverses the sequence. Perhaps mindful of the order of presentation in Descartes's *Meditations*, he first proceeds to analyze human consciousness and reasoning, then focuses on the body, with its passions and drives. This is the procedure we will follow in our attempt to penetrate the darkness of the underground.

An Anatomy of Reason

In the first part of the *Notes* Dostoevsky displays his dialectical skill – and his irony. From the very first sentence he confronts us with a strange fellow who, by going against his self-interest, tries everything in his power to convince us how extreme and irrational he is. This man appears to come from a world of different values. Naturally, we approach him from the position of common sense and its norms. Gradually, however, this eccentric creature convinces us that his voice may not stand for that of the isolated lunatic he appears to be at first. It may rather be he who represents our interests more faithfully, and not those which we initially took as the norm. And just as we start warming up to this character and recognize ourselves in him, Dostoevsky reverses direction in Part II of the *Notes*. The underground man's inability to overcome his dreadful isolation and establish a genuine human relationship turns us away from him. At the end of the *Notes*, he remains alone in his underground cellar.

Following the model of Rousseau's *Confessions*,[8] the *Notes* begins with a "confession" none of us would make: "I am a sick man. . . . I am a spiteful man. No, I am not a pleasant man at all." Just as we start to form the first impression of our interlocutor, the rollercoaster begins: "I believe there is something wrong with my liver. However, I don't know a damn thing about my liver; neither do I know whether there is anything really wrong with me" (Pt. I, sec. i, 263).

This "confession" brings us to the borderline of the absurd, and the underground man continues to exploit our confusion:

> I am not under medical treatment, and never have been, though I do respect medicine and doctors. In addition, I am extremely superstitious, at least sufficiently so to respect medicine. (I am . . . educated enough not to be superstitious, but I am superstitious for all of that.) The truth is, I refuse medical treatment out of spite. I don't suppose you will understand that (Pt. I, sec. i, 263).

Of course not. Who could? There comes an instant response: "Well, I do. I don't expect I shall be able to explain to you who it is I am actually trying to annoy in this case by my spite" (Pt. I, sec. i, 263).

---

8   Rousseau begins his *Confessions* with the following two passages: "I have resolved on an enterprise which has no precedent, and which, once complete, will have no imitator. My purpose is to display to my kind a portrait in every way true to nature, and the man I shall portray will be myself. Simply myself. I know my own heart and understand my fellow man. But I am made unlike any one I have ever met; I will even venture to say that I am like no one in the whole world. I may be no better, but at least I am different. Whether Nature did well or ill in breaking the mould in which she formed me, is a question which can only be resolved after the reading of my book." For a valuable discussion of the relationship of the *Notes* to Rousseau's *Confessions*, and the earlier Augustine's *Confessions*, see René Efortin, "Responsive Form: Dostoevsky's *Notes from Underground* and the Confessional Tradition," 291–14, and Liza Knapp, *The Annihilation of Inertia: Dostoevsky and Metaphysics*, 15–43.

Even after reading Kafka's *Trial* or Camus's *Stranger*, the reader must be shocked. But why? What is so astonishing about these statements?

They undercut our expectations. They violate the rules of our reasoning.

This chap appears irrational and we are trying to adjust him to our world: You do not do things out of spite, especially if you are educated, respect medicine, etc. There must be a more convincing reason than spite for our choices and behavior. We try to be rational and expect him to express himself rationally – especially since he is the one who initiated this ridiculous exchange – yet he tells us that we cannot understand this whole charade and he can.

The underground man continues his assault on how we understand the world and what we esteem, without giving us any pause. Among other things, he asserts that "any sort of consciousness is a disease" (Pt. I, sec. ii, 267), and that "man is stupid, phenomenally stupid" (Pt. I, sec. vii, 282).

This barrage astonishes enough to confuse us completely, so that we have temporarily to put the book down and wonder how an educated person can make claims like this. Consciousness (or, more precisely, self-consciousness) and reason are the capacities that separate us from animals and make us human. Descartes and Rousseau take our self-consciousness as the foundation of our identity. The adherents of the Enlightenment believe in the universality and objectivity of reason and its capacity to provide permanent solutions to all genuine problems of life and thought. Their dream is to demonstrate that everything in the universe occurs according to the laws of nature, that all evils can be cured by appropriate technological advancements, and that we can master not only the engineering of human bodies but also that of human souls.

In Russia, under the strong influence of such modern sentiments, Nicolai Chernyshevsky published his provocative book, *What Is to Be Done?* (1862). In this seminal novel, which had a profound effect on the Russian political scene for decades to come, Chernyshevsky expounds his theory of "rational egoism."[9] Free will is impossible,

---

9   Orlando Figes argues in *Natasha's Dance: A Cultural History of Russia*, 221, that Chernyshevsky's book "became a bible for the revolutionaries,

for science has proven that the world is completely determined by mechanical causation. Freedom of the will is not the only apparition in which people blindly believe. Chernyshevsky's outlook relies on the most precious dogma of the Enlightenment – the harmony of nature and reason. Human beings do only what they understand to be in their best interest. Rational egoism is at the bottom of all ethical strivings, of all virtue and sacrifice. Once accepted as scientifically sound, rational egoism would so enlighten people that the very possibility of behaving irrationally or contrary to self-interest would disappear.

Chernyshevsky points at the Crystal Palace in London as the crowning accomplishment of materialistic determinism and rational egoism. This monument of modern architecture was originally constructed for the first London World's Fair in 1851 by Sir Joseph Paxton. In this huge cast-iron and glass building, covering nineteen acres and located on high grounds just outside the city, Chernyshevsky sees the most glorious triumph of science and technology which promises that modern man can build an appropriate home and preside over the material world by means of reason and technology.

Dostoevsky, who came to see the famous Palace during the second London World's Fair in 1862, shares his very strong impression in *Winter Notes*:

> Can this really be the accomplished ideal? – you think; – is not this the end? is not this really the "one herd"? Will we not have to accept this really as the whole truth and remain silent once and for all? All this is so majestic, victorious, and proud that it takes your breath away. You observe these hundreds of thousands, these millions of people, obediently flowing here from all over the world – people coming with one thought, peacefully, unceasingly, and silently crowding into this colossal palace; and you feel that something

---

including the young Lenin, who said that his whole life had been transformed by it." On Dostoevsky's negative reactions to Chernyshevsky's book, see Joseph Frank, *Dostoevsky: The Stir of Liberation, 1860–1865*, 286–95; and also Frank, *Dostoevsky: The Mantle of the Prophet, 1871–1881*, 72–74.

has been finally completed and terminated. This is some sort of Biblical illustration, some prophecy of the Apocalypse fulfilled before your eyes. You feel that one must have perpetual spiritual resistance and negation so as not to surrender, not to submit to the impression, not to bow before the fact and deify Baal, that is, not to accept the existing as one's ideal.[10]

"Baal" refers to the god of the flesh execrated in the Old Testament, a false idol which Dostoevsky takes as a symbol of modern materialism and rational egoism. Once we come to comprehend that this is what the underground man is opposed to, we recognize why he claims that we cannot understand him.

For the underground man the Crystal Palace stands for everything contrary to his world and his values. A symbol of light and transparency, the Palace belongs to the Euclidean surface world, as precise as $2+2=4$. The Crystal Palace is the summit of the accomplishments of human rationality and civilization, a symbol of the perfectly ordered world in which there is no room for human freedom and suffering.

In contrast to the splendor of the Crystal Palace, the main character of the *Notes* lives in the underground. We can understand this spatial metaphor in more than one way. The first is that the underground man lives far away from the center of Petersburg, in his peripheral "mouse hole." Second, the underground also refers to something dark, secret, or hidden, most likely to the darkness within man. We realize that there is more darkness in man than Chernyshevsky and the followers of the Enlightenment want to admit. Third, the word "underground" suggests a world of crime, and this involves women who earn their money by prostitution. In the second part of the *Notes*, Lisa reminds us of the connection between the underworld and moral pollution. Fourth, the underground is also traditionally associated with world of the dead, and the underground man underscores this symbolism at the end of the second part of the *Notes*.

10 Quoted from Joseph Frank, *Dostoevsky: The Stir of Liberation, 1860–1865*, 239.

The underground man does not present in any systematic way his contempt for the Crystal Palace and what it symbolizes, but what he has to say sufficiently convinces us to accept his opinion: Chernyshevsky's program will not lead to the realization of heaven on earth, but it may lead to the elimination of humanity.

The underground man admits that we do not want to suffer for suffering's sake, nor do we like to see others, especially innocent people, experience pain. But even Descartes asks in the *Meditations*: "Is there anything more intimate or internal than pain?" The underground man gives a negative answer; pain and suffering are the sole origin of consciousness. They are what moves us. The ability to experience pain and suffering are the signs that we are alive. Suffering and pain occur when, with or without our intentions, borders are crossed which separate the exterior and the interior, the public and the private. No matter how we arrange the external world, conflicts of interests and the transgressions of personal boundaries will never cease. Even if we manage to eliminate all external enemies, we will still experience pain and suffering. The underground creature can declare his first victory: I suffer, therefore I am.

The underground man is aware of how highly we esteem civilization and its progress. The philosophers of the Enlightenment hope to insure this progress by means of a twin project: a simultaneous advancement of reason and freedom. This project is revolutionary with regard to the traditional treatment of reason and free will. For instance, while the Greeks insist on reason, they rarely use the concept of the will; Aristotle does not even have a term for it. For Augustine and later Christian theologians, will is a free power of choice, but also a negative principle: Free will is the source of moral weakness, sin, and evil. Will is the irrational element which Augustine associates with the body, and even Descartes remains within this Augustinian tradition. Rousseau, by contrast, promotes will into something positive: Our will is rational, at least potentially, and it can serve as the source of individual autonomy. The *Notes* refers to Rousseau's conception by citing his *l'homme de la nature et de la vérité*. Rousseau's "man of nature and truth" is the man whose nature – his will and his reason – is essentially unified and good. The underground man's ironic rebuttal of this view is worth citing at length:

> You see, gentlemen, reason is an excellent thing. There is no doubt about it. But reason is only reason, and it can only satisfy the reasoning ability of man, whereas volition is a manifestation of the whole of life, I mean, of the whole of human life, including reason with all its concomitant head-scratchings. And although our life, thus manifested, very often turns out to be a sorry business, it is life none the less and not merely extraction of square roots. For my part, I quite naturally want to live in order to satisfy all my faculties and not my reasoning faculty alone, that is to say, only some twentieth part of my capacity for living. What does reason know? Reason only knows what it has succeeded in getting to know (certain things, I suppose, it will never know; this may be poor comfort, but why not admit it frankly?), whereas human nature acts as a whole, with everything that is in it, consciously and unconsciously, and though it may commit all sorts of absurdities, it persists (Pt. I, sec. viii, 285–86).

Despite the expectations of the Enlightenment philosophers, man's reason and his will power can stand in an irreconcilable opposition to each other. Our reason can construct the Crystal Palace, but our will prefers freedom in the darkness of an underground cellar. The underground man is acutely aware of his own inner division. Moreover, he believes that this is not only his problem, but a truthful portrayal of the entire modern humanity. As he sees it, the problem of human schism can have two possible solutions, neither of which is fully satisfactory, but one of which is preferable.

The first option is to deny the existence of the inner division. Most people are not even fully aware of this schism, because they have drowned themselves in a group identity. Baal, the false idol before whom the mass-man of advanced civilization bows, eliminates any consciousness of the problem. If, however, there is an awareness of the inner schism, its denial and a life of a lie is still on option. When he complains that Rousseau's *Confessions* is no real confession but a sham and a cover up, the underground man accuses the leading figures of modernity of duplicity.[11]

The second option, more difficult but more honest, is favored in the *Notes*. Yes, the underground man admits that he often desires to be transformed into a stupid insect which does not understand anything. But like it or not, he is a human being, fully aware of how internally divided he is. Man's nature is not united: not one at a time, but always double – two at a time.[12] That is why we cannot offer a definition of man, for man has no rigid unified essence which can be captured through such a definition. All definitions being determinations or interpretations of *what* man is are possible only if we ignore his forever unpredictable, rebellious nature – only if we ignore *who* man is. For Descartes and Rousseau, the self is not a mystery; there is no riddle of human identity, if only we approach this issue with the right method. With the underground man, our humanity becomes an enigma again.

Augustine thinks that man is a riddle unto himself because of the division between body and soul. The underground man points out that the riddle is even more disturbing because the rift separates us not only into a body and a soul, but further divides the soul itself into two: reason and will. Philosophers and religious leaders have always preached how the increase of knowledge and consciousness can liberate us and make us worthy of happiness. The underground man asserts that just the opposite is the case. The increased consciousness, the refined awareness of the human condition, leads to misery and unhappiness.

Why would this be so? It is so because the acute consciousness of the underground man's inner schism paralyzes his actions. Its effects on him are like those of a disease or a toothache – one part

---

11 See, for example, *Notes from the Underground*, Pt. I, sec. v, 275, and Pt. I, sec. xi, 295–96.

12 Dostoevsky starts exploring the idea of the human personality divided into doubles already in his second publication, *The Double*. This psychological study of a split personality was not received well by Dostoevsky's contemporaries and he himself was critical of the way in which he originally presented the idea. Nonetheless, he considered the idea itself brilliant, and continued to develop it throughout his later works, all the way through *The Brothers Karamazov*.

of the body hurts, and yet his keen awareness of this pain prevents the normal functioning of the entire organism. Heightened awareness does not lead to happiness but to increased suffering; it leads to sickness. His liver hurts. "Let it damn well hurt," replies the underground man (Pt. I, sec. i, 263). Even if he cures his liver, this would provide no cure for his divided nature. And if consciousness, rational egoism, the laws of nature, and the Crystal Palace cannot do that, concludes the underground man, the only principal attitude is that of *amor fati*. Embrace your fate, whatever it is: "And so three cheers for the dark cellar!" (Pt. I, sec. xi, 294).

An Anatomy of Passion

The first part of the *Notes* demonstrates the limitations of human reason. Reason can establish and clarify the facts, but the existence of a unified human nature cannot be derived from them. Nor can we infer what human beings value and what choices they will make. The proponents of the Enlightenment assume that all human beings want roughly the same things. There is, however, a plurality of values and ends which we pursue and not all of them are compatible. If we can conclude anything about human nature, it is the existence of conflicting values and choices. Such conflicts can never be entirely eliminated from human life, at either the individual or the social level.[13] The presence of such conflicts leads to suffering and to consciousness – of ourselves and of our unsettled position in the world.

Reason determines and clarifies facts, but our choices are the acts of will, of our passions and drives. The underground man establishes the primacy of will over reason, yet this primacy leaves many questions open: If we should not be reduced to organ pedals and piano keys, if we need to suffer, for what should we suffer? Is there anything about which the underground man is passionate? Does he know what he wants? What do we learn in the second part of the *Notes*?

13 The best discussion of the conflict and incompatibility of certain fundamental values can be found in Nicolai Hartmann's *Ethics*, vol. II, and in various writings of Isaiah Berlin; e.g., "Two Concepts of Liberty," in *The Proper Study of Mankind*, 191–242.

Alfred North Whitehead argues in *Science and the Modern World* that what characterizes each century and each culture is which of these two values they prefer: order or freedom.[14] Whitehead is right in emphasizing how these values, both of which we hold in high regard, often go against each other. Freedom does not only mean freedom to choose good, but also freedom to choose evil – freedom to prefer chaos to order.

Dostoevsky would add that Whitehead's observation holds for every human being as well. We also are characterized by our preference for order or freedom. The conflict between these basic values is all the more dramatic at the individual level where the decision in favor of freedom or order shifts far more frequently than in the case of large social groups. In fact, Dostoevsky insists that such changes not only may but even must happen numerous times in the course of the life of every individual. The two parts of the *Notes* illustrate this conversion in the underground man.

In Part I, this isolated individual stakes everything on freedom, because he fears that materialistic determinism and rational egoism will deprive him of his humanity. In Part II, the focus is not on the intellect but on the passions; not on the detachment but on his craving for companionship; not on freedom but on his desire for an escape from freedom. The contrast between the two parts of the *Notes* illustrates the divided nature of humanity. We are pulled in different directions; we change our values unsure of the course we should follow. In Part I, the underground man tells us how he prefers chaos and freedom to order and determination. In Part II, he complains that we need more discipline. In the beginning, the underground man abhors the utilitarian and hedonistic calculus, yet later he comes to prefer "cheap happiness" to "exalted suffering." The following passage gives a magnificent exposition of this changed viewpoint: "Is the world to go to rack and ruin or am I to have my cup of tea? Well, as far as I'm concerned, blow the world so long as I can have my cup of tea" (Pt. II, sec. ix, 370). The criticism of romantic egoism of Part II supplants the criticism of rational egoism of Part I.

14 Alfred North Whitehead, *Science and the Modern World*, 249.

While Part I of the *Notes* mocks the modern, oversimplified reduction of the psychic life to rational and conscious thinking, Part II parallels this mockery with respect to the modern distortion of the human body. At one point the underground man tells the story of a dead woman whose body is nearly dropped from the coffin while it is carried out of the cellar where she died. If body is nothing but what our superstition-free science teaches us it is, what difference would it make whether the dead body is dropped out? The body – any body, dead or alive – is reduced to the role of *subiectum anatomicum*: It is just a thing, an object, no better and no worse than a piece of rock. As the soul and the spirit are reduced to a mechanism, so the body is understood as a machine which can be dissected and inspected by means of scientific experiment and demonstration. As the meaning of the Greek word *autopsia* suggests, the inner springs of the body can be "seen with one's own eyes."

Both Rembrandt and Dostoevsky are uncomfortable with this treatment of bodies as inanimate objects. They are opposed to this reduction of the human body to what can be called a "positive" body, an object of anatomical knowledge and, in the economy of the rapidly developing capitalism, an object prepared for disciplined labor and consumerism. Both artists manifest their firm belief in the existence of a "negative" – hidden and absent – body, whose boundaries are usually denied and whose passions are repressed.[15] If our bodies are to be what materialistic determinism tells us they are, there can be nothing sacrilegious with regard to their treatment, nor any reason for a sense of guilt or shame related to them.

Yet as Heraclites already knew, that what is seen is always related to something unseen, to some "unseen measure (*logos*)" which "holds the limit of things." When we look at Rembrandt's "Anatomy Lesson," we cannot but feel uncomfortable about what is being done to the body of someone who only a while ago was a living human being. The painting appears to pose the question: What happened to the boundary between permissible and impermissible,

---

15 I borrow the distinction between a negative and a positive body from F. Barker, *The Tremulous Private Body*.

legitimate and illegitimate entry into the body? To make sure such a question would occur to us, Rembrandt does something highly unusual for that genre: He paints the parts of the cadaver, especially the face, with the same attention as he has done with the esteemed doctors. The artist makes it look as if the corpse is very much a part of the company of the living beings.

The *Notes's* portrayal of Lisa's character and behavior does something analogous to Rembrandt's portrayal of the body. We hardly find any description of the appearance of the underground man, or of his "friends," yet Lisa is described in detail: "Now her eyes were soft and beseeching, and at the same time trustful, tender, and shy. So do children look at people they are very fond of and from whom they expect some favor. She had light-brown eyes, beautiful and full of life, eyes which could express love as well as sullen hatred" (Pt. II, sec. vii, 354–55). Why does he need to describe Lisa in such detail? As a prostitute, she is a polluted creature and a criminal. Should she not be treated as an object?

Dostoevsky wants to convince us that Lisa is far more than a body. The crucial moment in the *Notes* occurs during their second meeting, when she refuses to take the underground man's money although she depends on it for her existence. And not only does Dostoevsky paint her with warmer colors than those used for the underground man, he also makes the underground man fully aware of Lisa's moral superiority.

Through the few encounters between the underground man and the other characters in the *Notes*, Dostoevsky makes apparent the two archetypal patterns in which human beings relate to each other. The more prominent pattern is concerned with power relationships – those of rank, status, discipline, order, and possession. The other pattern deals with passions and emotional attachments; it manifests itself through care-giving and care-receiving, compassion and love. As Chernyshevsky asserts, the first pattern is analogous to the work of the forces in nature: The more powerful dominate over those who are weaker or powerless. This is the pattern through which the underground man relates to everyone he meets, including his initial dealings with Lisa. He is in the position to pay; she must obey. Few feelings are involved; no attachment is desired.

Toward the end of their first meeting the underground man commits a terrible blunder. After he receives her service and pays for it, he delivers a long and sentimental lecture about love. The underground man reveals a bit of his humanity: He makes a promise and takes a risk; he makes himself vulnerable. A day or so later, with full horror the underground man becomes conscious of what he had done. Irritated that his servant Apollon does not obey the pattern of their power relationship, the underground man trembles with fear that Lisa might take seriously his bookish talk about love. Sure enough, she appears at the doorsteps. Because of his blunder, Lisa is allowed to peek over the protective wall of his wretched hole, carefully guarded from intruders for years. Not finding himself up to the task, the underground man wavers between one pattern of behavior and the other, thereby revealing his crippled humanity: Despite his vehement protests to the contrary, he himself may be nothing but a piano key, a superfluous screw in the giant machine of the world.

And then the most unexpected occurs – the worst possible scenario for the underground man. Lisa, who would not understand much of what we are discussing here in such a learned manner, intuitively comprehends his wretchedness. Instead of being offended by his offensive behavior, she takes pity on him. Lisa feels sorry for the underground man!

This reversal of roles in the power-game irritates the underground man. In the days before Lisa appears in his apartment, he is imagining himself as her romantic hero, as her savior. During their fateful second meeting, he grasps that Lisa is the heroine and he a miserable anti-hero. On her part, Lisa has stopped playing the power-game. She recognizes his misery and is willing to help him. His wounded pride does not allow that. In Part I of the *Notes*, the underground man welcomes suffering. In Part II he reveals he does not understand suffering. Suffering is not just a mix of pain and vanity, the combination we find in the underground man. Although he rejects Chernyshevsky's rational egoism, voluntary sacrifice of one human being for another is beyond his comprehension. The underground man can talk about love, but he does not know what it means to feel love. In one of the most beautiful sentences of the *Notes*, this super-conscious mouse realizes that there

is a difference: "But how much love, good Lord, how much love
I used to experience in those dreams of mine, during those hours
of 'salvation through the sublime and beautiful'" (Pt. II, sec. ii,
311–12).[16] In Part I the underground man mocks Schiller's romantic notions of the "sublime and beautiful." In Part II he recognizes
just how much he craves them.

The second part of the *Notes* begins with a quotation from
Nekrasov's poem entitled "When from the Darkness of Delusion,"
which deals with a regeneration of a fallen woman through the aid
of the man who loves her. Ignored by the mighty Zverkov and his
company, the underground man turns himself toward the powerless
Lisa. He initiates their sentimental exchange about little children
and domestic happiness: "Are you fond of little children, Lisa? I am
very fond of them. Just imagine a rosy little baby boy sucking at
your breast – what husband's heart is not touched at the sight of
his wife nursing his child?" (Pt. II, sec. iv, 347).

Strange words from a creature not capable of love! Even the
uneducated Lisa suspects that this may be nothing but bookish
chatter: "Why, you – you're speaking as though you were reading
from a book" (Pt. II, sec. iv, 348). Yes, he is. Only in romantic
fairy tales can a fallen woman be converted from the error of her
ways by the pity of another human being, so that Nekrasov can
proudly declare at the end of his poem: "And my house, fearlessly
and freely/As mistress you can enter now!" (Pt. II, sec. ix, 366).
When Lisa visits the underground man's mouse-hole, she neither
enters nor exits as his mistress. While she enters with some hope,
she exits with all of her romantic illusion shattered.

Yet Lisa is not ungrateful to the underground man. She is able
to ignore the humiliation he inflicts and extends her hands toward
him in a gesture of compassion and forgiveness. He abuses her one
more time, placing money in her hands to make sure she understands who she is in his eyes. Lisa leaves the money behind and
departs, bearing her cross on her own.

16 Dostoevsky explores similar distinctions between pseudo-love and real
love, and the tragic consequences of their confusions, in the stories "White
Nights" and "A Gentle Creature."

Lisa is gone. She manages to gather enough strength to break away from being an object of pleasure for a sinful stranger. A happy end for Lisa? Hardly. How is a lone woman to survive in a rotten society built on power-games? Dostoevsky leaves little doubt about what kind of ending should be expected.

What will happen to the underground man? Most likely, he will remain forever in his underground hole, lonely and wretched. As with Lisa, Dostoevsky leaves it to our imagination to fill the gap. Where he has to give us some help is in the interpretation of the opening remarks that such a man "must exist" and that he is "one of the representatives of a generation that is still with us." Are we in a better position to understand such puzzling remarks at the end of the *Notes* than we are at the beginning?

What this anti-hero shares with others is often unjustly termed a tragedy of human nature – the internal split between will and reason. Dostoevsky himself does not consider this rift tragic; it is simply part of our human condition. The tragedy occurs at a different level. What makes the underground man different is not the primacy of will over reason, but his inability to decide what he really wants. Chernyshevsky's rational man believes in his self-interest and focuses on the rational choice of the means suitable for the realization of his goals. Schiller's romantic hero follows his noble impulses, in "the pursuit of the beautiful and the sublime." Dostoevsky's underground man complains about his super-consciousness – he knows too much; he cannot be so easily deluded. The underground man can believe neither in crystal palaces nor in romantic fairy tales. He can trust neither other people's reason, nor his own – especially not his own.

The underground man is free, but he does not know what to do with his freedom. He is passionate, but does not know where to direct his passion. The underground man has no goal, no object of devotion, no trust in anything or anyone. That is why he is a tragic figure – he suffers greatly and he would like to suffer for something great, but his suffering is aimless and pointless. Since passion has to be channeled somehow, the underground man lets it go against his rational intentions. He ends up acting not because of his conscience but out of spite.

There is a long tradition of thought, stretching from Socrates and Augustine to Nicolai Hartmann and Hannah Arendt, which denies any "substantiality" to evil. As Hartmann sums it up, "No one does wrong for the sake of the wrong. . . . This view has not been seriously challenged since Socrates. He who plots injury to another does not desire the other's harm, but his own advantage."[17] Augustine similarly denies that good and evil are on the same ontological footing, for evil is nothing but a deprivation of the good (*privatio boni*). Following Augustine, Arendt asserts that evil has no roots and can be compared to fungus. Even a mass-murderer, like Eichmann, is not a monster, not an exponent of radical evil, but simply a thoughtless bureaucrat.

There is plenty of material in the first part of the *Notes* to undermine this tradition. Evil is not shallow; evil is not due to ignorance, or to the lack of understanding of what is in our best interest. Dostoevsky does not speak of evil explicitly, but of freedom, for it is the precondition of both good and evil. He denies that freedom can be "naturalized," in the way which Chernyshevsky proposes. The elimination of freedom would mean the eradication of the distinction between good and evil. Free will must be different from the stone wall of nature – it belongs to the layers beneath the wall, the mysterious underground beneath the world of nature. Freedom is not a physical category, just as it is not primarily a moral or a psychological one. For Dostoevsky, freedom is a metaphysical category.[18]

If the drive toward freedom is metaphysical and primordial, so must be the drive toward its counterpart, order. The tragedy of the underground man consists precisely in his inability to comprehend what order is and how it could be reconciled with the drive toward freedom. In Part I of the *Notes*, he desperately clings to freedom,

17   Hartmann, *op. cit.*, 177.
18   Of Dostoevsky's numerous commentators, the metaphysical aspect of freedom is most clearly recognized by Berdyaev. In his book, *Dostoevsky*, Berdyaev has an entire chapter on the problem of freedom where he, for instance, makes the following important statements: "freedom is the centre of his conception of the world" (67), and "freedom that is arbitrary destroys itself" (76). See also Vyacheslav Ivanov, *Freedom and the Tragic Life: A Study in Dostoevsky*, 3–45.

but in Part II he reveals that this same cherished freedom is a terrible burden as well: What is he to do with his freedom?

This is the problem the underground man is unable to solve, and he only formulates it in different ways. The most memorable of them is the following: "Which is better: cheap happiness or exalted suffering? Well, which is better?" (Pt. II, sec. x, 376). The underground man would like to say that exalted suffering is better, but he cannot understand what to suffer for and thus cannot in clear conscience give such an answer.

If *Notes from the Underground* is a confession of any kind, it is a confession that the underground man does not know whether there is anything worth suffering for. He confesses not to know how to use his freedom in a positive and constructive way, not to know how to reconcile the drive toward freedom and the drive toward order. For all the underground man can see, freedom implies chaos and destruction (ultimately: self-destruction), while order means for him determinism and slavery (ultimately: loss of human dignity).

This is the dilemma that paralyzes the underground man. Dostoevsky believes that the same dilemma paralyzes all those who are fully conscious of themselves and their position in a hostile world. The pursuit of self-knowledge, followed with the conviction of a religious creed from ancient Greece to modern Europe, does not lead to liberation but to desperation. The mob flows with the current; it does not know itself, nor does it desire to know itself. Perhaps it is better that way, the underground man could say. Or, if not better, it certainly makes life easier. Self-knowledge can only bring to the surface the dark secrets of man, his lies and pretensions. Self-knowledge can only make us aware of our vanity.

Vanity is nothing but false self-satisfaction, a cover up for our emptiness and worthlessness. The underground man associates vanity with death – the death of spirit. The spirit is dead when, caught in unsolvable paradoxes, it ends up choosing cheap happiness over exalted suffering. The underground man is aware of his choice: "I have merely carried to extremes in my life what you have not dared to carry even half-way" (Pt. II, sec. x, 377).

Unable or unwilling to confront the paradoxes which real life so tirelessly poses to us, we hide behind the bookish knowledge and "noble lies" called confessions and virtues. And this, the underground man asserts, is not just his problem, but the problem of his generation, the problem of every modern man:

> Why, we do not even know where we are to find real life, or what it is, or what it is called. Leave us alone without any books, and we shall at once get confused, lose ourselves in a maze, we shall not know what to cling to, what to hold on to, what to love and what to hate, what to respect and what to despise. We even find it hard to be men, men of *real* flesh and blood, *our own* flesh and blood. We are ashamed of it. We think it a disgrace. And we do our best to be some theoretical "average" man. We are stillborn, and for a long time we have been begotten not by living fathers, and that's just what we seem to like more and more. We are getting a taste for it. Soon we shall invent some way of being somehow or other begotten by an idea. But enough – I don't want to write any more "from a Dark Cellar" (Pt. II, sec. x, 377).

And so ends this strange book, *Notes from the Underground*. In Rembrandt's painting, you can be dead and look very much alive. Dostoevsky realizes, by contrast, that life can be like death, not just in a Siberian camp, but also in a metropolis like Petersburg. Paradoxically, then, at any place and any time you can be alive and dead at the same time. What, then, does it mean to be fully alive? What does it mean to be free?

If *Notes from the Underground* is really the philosophical preface to Dostoevsky's great novels, for what does this work prepare us? Will Dostoevsky's later characters find their way out of the underground, so that they can establish their dwelling place on the lighted surface of the earth? Or will they, on the contrary, lead us even deeper into the underground, only to show us that there is light even in the heart of darkness?

The underground man warns us not to expect too much. If he is the messenger of what is forthcoming, his words foretell more turmoil, more soul searching, more wondering as to what our human identity is:

> The excellent ants began with the ant-hill and with the ant-hill they will most certainly end, which does great

credit to their steadfastness and perseverance. But man is a frivolous and unaccountable creature, and perhaps, like a chess-player, he is only fond of the process of achieving his aim, but not of the aim itself. And who knows (it is impossible to be absolutely sure about it), perhaps the whole aim mankind is striving to achieve on earth lies in this incessant process of achievement, or (to put it differently) in life itself, and not really in the achievement of any goal, which, needless to say, can be nothing else but twice-two-makes-four, that is to say, a formula; but twice-two-makes-four is not life, gentlemen. It is the beginning of death (Pt. I, sec. ix, 290).

3

Crime and Punishment

Victimizer or Victim?

Monologue and Dialogue

Notes from the Underground is a provocative work. *Crime and Punishment* is more so. The *Notes* is intended as an openly polemical and disturbing piece. The polemical nature of *Crime and Punishment* is subtle and unfolds in several layers. As Dostoevsky explained to M.N. Katkov, the editor of the magazine *Russian Messenger* in which *Crime and Punishment* was later printed,

> It is a psychological account of a crime. The action is contemporary, this year. A young man from a bourgeois background has been expelled from the university and is living in dire poverty. Because of his rashness and instability he has become prey to certain strange, "unfinished" ideas which are in the air and has decided to free himself from his miserable position in a single stroke. He has resolved to murder an old woman who lends money on interest. This old woman is stupid, deaf, sick, and greedy, takes horrific interest rates, is cruel, and torments her younger sister who works for her. "She's fit for nothing. What is she

living for? Is she of any use to anybody?" Such questions drive the young man out of his mind. He decides to murder and rob her in order to find happiness for his mother, who lives in the provinces, to rescue his sister, who lives with a family of a landowner as a paid companion, from the lascivious advances of the head of the family (advances which threaten to ruin her) to finish his university course, to go abroad and then for the rest of his life to be honest, resolute, and steadfast in the performance of his "humane duty to mankind," by means of which he will, of course, "expiate his crime," if in fact such an act (against a deaf, stupid, malicious and sick old woman, who herself does not know why she lives on this earth and who would possibly die a natural death in a month's course) can be called a crime.

In spite of the fact that crimes of this kind are extremely difficult to execute – it almost always happens that evidence is left around and loose ends stick out all over the place, and an enormous amount is left to chance, which almost always gives the criminal away – he succeeds, completely by accident, and manages to carry out his plan quickly and successfully.

Nearly a month passes between the crime and the final catastrophe. There is no suspicion of him nor cause for any. In this month the entire psychological process of the crime unfolds. The murderer is faced with insoluble problems; undreamed, unexpected feelings torment him. God's truth and earthly law triumph, and in the end, he understands that he must turn himself in. He is compelled to do this, for even if he is to perish in prison, he will be reunited with people again. The feeling of being isolated and separated from mankind, which he began to experience immediately after he had committed the crime, torments him beyond endurance. The law of truth and human nature have won out. The criminal himself resolves to accept suffering and thereby atone for his deed.[1]

1   Dostoevsky's letter to M.N. Katkov, September 1865.

An intriguing aspect of this description is how adequate it is in one sense, and how insufficient in another. To someone who has not read the novel, this outline gives a good account of what it is about. To the reader familiar with Dostoevsky's work, too much is left out. From this description we cannot sense the depth of the struggle that rages in the young man's soul. Nor does this description tell us anything about another central personality, Sonia Marmeladova. Raskolnikov is the leading character, but Sonia, who some critics consider to be the real axis of the novel, provides the needed counterbalance for his immense pride and misguided ambition. While Raskolnikov is a victimizer, Sonia stands for the novel's many victims. Raskolnikov's and Sonia's fates become intertwined, their torments measured against each other. In this confrontation of power and powerlessness, sacrifice and suffering, life and death, the novel forces us to ask ourselves with whom we identify: a victimizer or a victim? The dilemma is an ancient one, taking us back to the Book of Genesis: If we were put in the situation to choose, who would we rather (not) be – Cain or Abel?

Unlike *Notes from the Underground,* which poses its questions directly, the symbolic complexity of *Crime and Punishment* offers no semblance of that straightforwardness. We can look at the book many times; we are not going to find the names of Cain and Abel. They reside in our psyche, and the fictional story of a murder in nineteenth-century Petersburg brings to life the archetypal dilemma one more time.

The artistic beauty of *Crime and Punishment* conceals its polemical side. Dostoevsky's artistry can be compared to Raphael's "Sistine Madonna," the painting mentioned several times throughout the novel. According to the *Reminiscences* of Dostoevsky's second wife, Anna Grigorievna, he considered Raphael to be an artist of the greatest class and this painting the most beautiful he had ever seen.[2] A decade or so after the publication of *Crime and Punishment*, Dostoevsky received as a gift a reproduction of a portion of the painting (only the Madonna with the child) from his wife. Like his private icon, it sanctified Dostoevsky's study for the rest of his life.

2   Anna Dostoevsky, *Reminiscences*, 119.

There is nothing polemical about Raphael's painting, not a shade of doubt that life has meaning and that with the help of the divine power man can find home in the world. Raphael's superbly harmonious painting is an expression of faith – pure, profound, and unshakable. Dostoevsky hoped for that kind of faith all his life. Although he never manages permanently to silence his internal voice of doubt, in *Crime and Punishment* he is also a champion of faith. Far more so than in the times of Raphael, Christianity needed defenders against mounting denials. The divine radiance that illuminates man's position in the world has dissipated, clouded by the uncertainties regarding man's identity and purpose.

In Russia of the 1860s, Chernyshevsky's novel *What Is to Be Done?* was the "bible" of young atheists and revolutionaries. The previous chapter briefly considered some of Chernyshevsky's scientific and philosophical views concerning rational egoism and materialistic determinism. Dostoevsky will continue his polemics with these and related viewpoints throughout *Crime and Punishment.* For the moment we are more interested in another issue: Why does Chernyshevsky choose the medium of a novel, rather than that of a treatise, to expose his views? Even more importantly, why does Dostoevsky change the form of his counterattack against Chernyshevsky? Why does he switch from the monological form of the *Notes* to the dialogical form of *Crime and Punishment?*

Ever since the time of Aristotle, the treatise has been an indisputable and virtually unanimous choice for any scientific or philosophical work. Using this form presumes that there is a voice of authority presenting the problem and proposing its solution. This voice has to be as clear and persuasive as possible. A treatise is comparable to a straight line of Euclidean geometry: For any problem (A) there must be an adequate solution (B), and the treatise is our guide to the shortest path from A to B.

The danger of the treatise arises in its presumption that there is more structure and clarity in the world than is really present. If something is left obscure or unsolved, our assumption is that such lapses are due to the author's lack of knowledge or depth of insight. Dostoevsky's insistence on the divided nature of humanity forces us to reconsider this conclusion. If, for example, cruelty and compassion can coexist in the same person, our failure to provide a complete and rational theory of human nature need not be due to our subjective intellectual shortcomings. Rather, it may be based on the non-transparency and antinomian character of our nature. The uncritically accepted assumptions that (i) a definitive theory of human nature must be possible and that (ii) such a theory is needed to explain how we can find a dwelling place in this world, may only be further obstacles toward a fuller understanding of ourselves and our role and place in reality.

To avoid the trap of these two assumptions, we should recall that the treatise is not the only option. Before Aristotle, there was Plato and his incomparable mastery of the dialogical form. Only artificial dialogues can provide the shortest path from A to B, but we are not going to find those in Plato. His early (the so-called "Socratic") dialogues offer no solution at all. Socrates engages his interlocutors in an animated exchange, only to help them realize their ignorance. Once they are cleansed of their misconceptions, the ground is prepared for a genuine insight. For himself, Socrates denies the possession of any positive knowledge. He considers himself a philosopher in the authentic sense of that word (*philosophia*) – a lover of wisdom and a seeker of truth – not a wise man. Socrates may not have solved a single philosophical enigma, but he showed that the journey, not the destination, carries greatest significance.[3]

---

3   Compare this approach with the claim in the *Notes* (Pt. I, sec. ix, 290) that "man is a frivolous and unaccountable creature, and perhaps like a chess-player, he is only fond of the process of achieving his aim, but not of the aim itself. And who knows (it is impossible to be absolutely sure about it), perhaps the whole aim mankind is striving to achieve on earth lies in this incessant process of achievement, or (to put it differently) in life itself, and not really in the achievement of any goal." According to Helen Muchnic, *Russian Writers: Notes and Essays* (229), "It is probably the ambiguities of Tolstoy and Dostoevsky that, as much as anything else, are the marks of their greatness. The questions they pose can be answered only by further questions. The realms of thought in which they move are unfathomable and their fictional creations are correspondingly complex."

Chernyshevsky attempts to combine the best features of both approaches (the monologue form of a treatise and the dialogue form of a novel). He wants to deliver the truth, an objective and scientifically established truth. Chernyshevsky believes that the questions of morality have been resolved once and for all, principally by John Stuart Mill, whom he translated into Russian. According to Chernyshevsky, Mill correctly argues that every individual pursues what is in his or her rational and enlightened self-interest and, as Henry Thomas Buckle adds, only ignorance with respect to self-interest leads to misconduct.

While writing his novel, Chernyshevsky is in jail, in the Peter-and-Paul fortress, expecting hard labor in Siberia for his underground activities. Not only does he attempt to present a theoretical explanation concerning rational egoism and materialistic determinism, but also he outlines a manifesto for the radical transformation of the world. The treatise is not very suitable as a call for action which would lead to universal happiness and harmony. Its monological form does not affect at the emotional (conscious and subconscious) level, which is what Chernyshevsky hopes to accomplish. The dialogical form is much better suited to provoke and involve the readers.

From Dostoevsky's quoted description of *Crime and Punishment* we can sense the uncertainties in the monological preoccupation of his main hero. After the crime, he feels alienated from other human beings, including his mother and sister. A significant degree of estrangement exists, however, even before the transgression. We first encounter Raskolnikov as a gifted but lonely man, expelled from the university, and living in extreme poverty in his little garret. He spends his days in monologue with himself, arrested in his own stream of thoughts which gradually lose contact with the external reality. At this stage of the novel, Raskolnikov reminds us of the underground man, who claims his disease is due to his super-consciousness. The difference in Raskolnikov's case is that super-consciousness leads to action, and the action is based on the lunatic idea of murdering an old money lender.

Raskolnikov does have occasional exchanges with other human beings, but these conversations do not seem to touch him. He has to relearn that other people are not extensions of his self, not mere projections of his psyche, but human beings with lives and concerns of their own. The underground man never manages to relate to another human being except through power relationships, and Raskolnikov has to relearn how to establish authentic interactions with other persons. Raskolnikov's maturation unfolds only after the crime.

Dostoevsky is convinced that Raskolnikov's alienation is not the primordial state of affairs, but rather a result of the modern way of life. The transgression of murder does not belong to Hobbes's "natural state of affairs" but, as Raskolnikov recognizes in an article he publishes as a student, is a result of some distortion or illness. We are not born strangers but become alienated in the course of our artificially lived lives. Raskolnikov is an example of such an individual who is not only separated from other people, but whose psyche is internally divided. The first part of his last name, *raskol*, means "schism" in Russian.[4] His intellect detaches itself from his feelings, and Raskolnikov operates on two levels: one full of contempt for life, the other quite capable of generosity and compassion. Very early in the novel we intuitively recognize that Raskolnikov is not a bad human being, even though he plans and executes a horrible murder for which there can be no excuse. We recognize an intrinsic incongruity between the "theoretical" Raskolnikov and the "spontaneous" Raskolnikov, between the transgression and the person who commits it.

Following the philosophers of the Enlightenment, Chernyshevsky assumes that human values can be rationally derived from facts about human nature, that all human beings value and desire the same things, and that these objects of desire are not in conflict. Dostoevsky again attacks this conception of man as a unified rational animal through the struggles of Raskolnikov as

4   According to Vyacheslav Ivanov's *Freedom and the Tragic Life: A Study in Dostoevsky*, 72n, Raskolnikov's last name comes from the word raskol, which means "split," "schism," "heresy"; *raskolnik* is an "apostate" and "heretic." Philip Rahv points out in his essay, "Dostoevsky in *Crime and Punishment*," 611, that Raskolnikov "is a dissenter and rebel (*raskol*, the word from which his name derives, means *schism* or *dissent*), in essence the type of revolutionary terrorist of that period, whose act of terror is somehow displaced unto a private object."

he explains to himself why exactly he commits the crime. In the course of the novel he proposes and defends several explanations, most of which mitigate rather than illuminate why he carries out this impermissible transgression. How rational and autonomous are we, Dostoevsky seems to be asking, if we cannot understand the motives for our own actions? How unified is our nature when we are constantly pulled in opposite directions?

The novel unfolds in such a way as to lead to these questions. For those who have not previously read *Crime and Punishment*, the title may suggest a detective novel. Nothing could be further from the truth.[5] A story of crime is normally shaped around the discovery of the murderer. In Dostoevsky's scenario, it is not the readers who have to discover the criminal, but the criminal who must discover himself. In a typical detective novel, the culmination is reached by the accumulation of all the relevant facts. Raskolnikov knows all the relevant facts, yet what he needs is a special kind of insight. Dostoevsky's novel demands a different attitude to what we already know. At this point Raskolnikov's conscience and dreams play a significant role, in combination with his dialogical encounters with Svidrigailov, Porfiry, and especially Sonia. A polyphony of voices, not a monological treatise, is needed to find the truth about what it means to be a human being.

Why assume, however, that if the truth cannot be discovered in a completely analytical and rational way through the monological form of a treatise, it is made available by means of a dialogue? Why would not one approach be as insufficient as the other?

Isaiah Berlin voices such skeptical concerns. In *The Crooked Timber of Humanity* he exposes an unstable "three-legged stool" which supports the central tradition of Western thought.[6] The first leg assumes that to all genuine questions there can be only one

---

5   My presentation of the view that *Crime and Punishment* is not a detective novel follows Anthony J. Cascardi, *The Bounds of Reason: Cervantes, Dostoevsky, Flaubert*, 111–16; and Philip Rahv, *op. cit.*, 596–601.

6   Isaiah Berlin, *The Crooked Timber of Humanity*, 24–25. Berlin claims that the three-legged stool is presupposed by the central tradition of Western political thought, but it clearly applies to Western thought in general.

correct answer, all other answers being incorrect. If there is no correct answer, then the question cannot be genuine. The second leg is that there must exist a method by which correct answers can be found, a procedure for establishing what is right. The third and the most important premise of this approach is that, at the very least, all correct answers must be compatible with one another. At best, these answers will logically interact to build a single, systematic, and interconnected whole. Building such a whole is the foundation of the age-old dream that there is a final solution to all human ills.

Berlin rejects all three legs because they seduce us into one or another version of an ideological "-ism," the harmful consequences of which have been clearly demonstrated by the twentieth century course of events. Instead, Berlin defends a radical version of pluralism of values as the only healthy attitude toward life. He finds the motivation for this approach in Tolstoy. In the piece that made him famous, "The Hedgehog and the Fox: An Essay on Tolstoy's View of History," Berlin takes seriously a fragment from the ancient Greek author Archilochus: "The fox knows many things, but the hedgehog knows one big thing."[7] Following this dictum, Berlin divides all writers and thinkers, even human beings in general, into two kinds. The hedgehogs relate everything to a single central vision, more or less coherent and articulate, in terms of which all that they do and say has significance. Then there are the foxes, who pursue many ends, often unrelated and sometimes contradictory, traceable to no single moral principle. In Berlin's view, Dante belongs to the first category, Shakespeare to the second. Plato, Lucretius, Pascal, Hegel, Nietzsche, Ibsen, and Proust are, in various degrees, hedgehogs. Herodotus, Aristotle, Montaigne, Erasmus, Molière, Goethe, Pushkin, Balzac, and Joyce are foxes.[8]

One of the central claims Berlin defends in his essay concerns Tolstoy: the Russian novelist tries to convince himself that he is a hedgehog, even though by nature he is a fox. How about Dostoevsky?

7   Isaiah Berlin, "The Hedgehog and the Fox: An Essay on Tolstoy's View of History," in Berlin, *The Proper Study of Mankind*, 436.
8   *Ibid.*, 437.

Berlin places Dostoevsky squarely among hedgehogs. This means that Dostoevsky should more or less approve of the three legs that Berlin criticizes and should support one ultimate voice, a monologue rather than a dialogue.

I believe that Berlin is mistaken in his assessment of Dostoevsky, and a close reading of *Crime and Punishment* shows this to be the case. Unlike the other novels we discuss in this book, which cannot be molded to support Berlin's judgment because of their more or less open-ended conclusions, the Epilogue of *Crime and Punishment* may seem to suggest that Berlin is right: Dostoevsky appears to display a firm support of the Christian doctrine, as unwavering as Raphael's in his famous painting.

Dostoevsky may have wanted to possess this kind of faith, he may have dreamt of being a hedgehog, but is that who he really was? Would not a hedgehog let Sonia and her Christian message have the final word in *Crime and Punishment*? Instead, the novel closes without unequivocally negating Raskolnikov's transgression.

Does that make Dostoevsky a fox? The reader familiar with Mikhail Bakhtin's *Problems of Dostoevsky's Poetics* may be inclined to conclude so. He demonstrates the polyphony of voices in Dostoevsky's novels and undermines any complete identification between, for instance, the voice of the underground man (or of Ivan) with Dostoevsky's own voice. More than one voice in any of Dostoevsky's works expresses his thoughts and concerns. The dialogues between his characters do not serve a mere pedagogical role but create genuine encounters in which the outcomes are not obvious or pre-established.[9]

Bakhtin's theory does not turn Dostoevsky into a fox or a radical pluralist like Berlin. Not all of the voices in Dostoevsky's novels are equally important, just as not all of the values equally valuable. Moreover, discovering the truth is not his only motivation for the dialogues. The tension Dostoevsky maintains prevents any view to prevail and cautions us against any dogmatism. It also serves an important "therapeutic" function: Sincere dialogue with others, not rational analysis, leads to trust in others and life. We must

9   See, for instance, Chapter 1, 5–46, of Mikhail Bakhtin's *Problems of Dostoevsky's Poetics*.

understand the concept of interest in its literal Latin meaning as *inter-est* – that which goes on in our co-existence with other human beings. Only genuine dialogues can lead us to realize our indebtedness to others and gratitude to them. Such encounters provide the sought-after glue for a meaning to life.

Dostoevsky focuses on the tensions between human beings and the world in which they live, on the dynamism between transgressing and restoring, freedom and order, life and death. He plays neither the role of a typical hedgehog, nor of a typical fox. What remains to be seen is whether he lies somewhere in between the two, or whether we need an altogether different categorization to capture his approach.

Murder

Murder is a frequent theme in Dostoevsky's works. In *The House of the Dead* he catalogues a number of astonishing murders, which he heard from the convicts. In several of his later novels murder also plays a prominent role, but the blueprint of the crime is always different. In *Crime and Punishment*, the victims are barely related to the murderer. In *The Possessed*, the connection between the victimizers and their victim is tighter: A group of revolutionaries slay a colleague whom they think betrays them. In *The Idiot*, Ragozhin kills Nastassya Filippovna, the person he loves the most. In *The Brothers Karamazov*, the theme is parricide; as Ivan (and Freud) would explain it, it is the murder of the one you hate the most. In all these works murder is antithetical to the very idea of dialogue – it is the result of an inability to engage in or sustain a dialogue.

In *Crime and Punishment* this inability is not a result of an animal-like urge for blood, but of a rationally conceived idea. Raskolnikov struggles with numerous explanations for his murder, which seem to reduce to three. The first is sociological: The murderer is himself a victim of the circumstances, someone deprived of normal life. The second explanation is utilitarian: The wrongness of murder is offset by the good which can be performed with the stolen money. The third explanation is the most important for the novel as a whole. It is centered on the issue of an exceptional individual, on the challenge of becoming more than his limited existence indicates he is. Raskolnikov is determined to find out how worthy as a human being he is: Is he an ordinary or an extraordinary individual? Does he not have the right to overstep the boundaries established by society?

According to the first account, Raskolnikov's murder – and crime in general – is the result of an unhealthy environment. Terrible external circumstances of life are the cause, and crime is their effect. In many of his writings Dostoevsky associates such depriving circumstances with life in a metropolis. When Raskolnikov's mother and sister arrive in Petersburg for the first time, they cannot overcome their shock: "This is a town of crazy people!"[10] On the dirty and stinking streets of Petersburg they can see all kinds of nastiness and indecency. Even Raskolnikov, who is used to living in Petersburg, tells Sonia that this is not the place for the orphaned Polenka and her siblings to grow up: "Children can't remain children there! At seven the child is vicious and a thief" (Pt. IV, Ch. 4, 261). What future is there for little Polenka? As Sonia's father Marmeladov remarked earlier, "Do you suppose that a respectable poor girl can earn much by honest work?" (Pt. I, Ch. 2, 13).

The insides of the houses offer no more hope than the streets. Only in a big city can you find a room like Raskolnikov's garret in which you can barely turn around or stand up. Such places do not feel like homes, but like coffins in which you are buried alive. The big city creates this sickly atmosphere in which one is constantly surrounded by people, and yet lonely, with no one to turn to.

Dostoevsky rejects the influence of an unhealthy environment as the determining cause of crime. He refuses to look at evil from a merely sociological point of view. Raskolnikov occasionally entertains the idea that extreme poverty leads toward crime, yet he becomes aware that the attitude of his only friend, Razumihin, is a refutation of this view. Razumihin, who lives in similarly impoverished social conditions as Raskolnikov, earns enough by giving private lessons and by translating, and is never tempted to find a

---

10   *Crime and Punishment*, trans. Constance Garnett, Pt. VI, Ch. 3, page 366. All subsequent references to this work will be given in the text, immediately after the quotation.

solution to his problems in crime. His example teaches that even in the most depraved circumstances we have a choice with respect to our attitudes, decisions, and actions. If we do not, the underground man rightly considers us as piano keys. Dostoevsky knows that human choices are demanded even under the worst possible circumstances, even in the prisons of Siberia. Whether human beings behave as dignified creatures or not depends not on their external circumstances but on their attitudes toward life.

Let us now turn to the second account for Raskolnikov's transgression, which plays a prominent role in the first two parts of *Crime and Punishment*. This account is based on the utilitarian approach to life: If utility is the ultimate criterion, "What value has the life of that sickly, stupid, ill-natured old woman in the balance of existence?" Before Raskolnikov commits the murder, he overhears a conversation in a bar between a student and an officer about the old lady Raskolnikov intends to kill. By a remarkable coincidence – so characteristic of Dostoevsky's works – the student considers the same utilitarian calculus as Raskolnikov. The equation seems just a bit more complex than the underground man's "$2 + 2 = 4$." On the one side, there is that old woman, who is greedily hoarding money and is going to die soon anyway.

> On the other side, fresh young lives [are] thrown away for want of help and by thousands, on every side! A hundred thousand good deeds could be done and helped, on that old woman's money which will be buried in a monastery! Hundreds, thousands perhaps, might be set on the right path; dozens of families saved from destitution, from ruin, from vice, from the Lock hospitals – and all with her money! Kill her, take her money and with the help of it devote oneself to the service of humanity and the good of all. What do you think, would not one tiny crime be wiped out by thousands of good deeds? (Pt. I, Ch. 6, 54).

The officer offers limited resistance: "Of course she does not deserve to live, but there it is, it's nature" (Pt. I, Ch. 6, 54).

The excited student has a powerful answer, which brings us to the heart of the matter: "Oh well, brother, but we have to correct and direct nature" (Pt. I, Ch. 6, 54).

We cannot but recognize that the student makes a point about which we have thought many times: Nature has to be corrected and directed. Is it not what civilization is about? Is it not what striving toward justice and the pursuit of happiness are about? As Berlin's criticism of the "three-legged stool" already indicated, the problem is to find answers to the following questions: Who has the authority to change nature, and in what direction? Should not there be some limits to our redirection of nature? Is murder an acceptable means toward that goal?

Experience suggests that the most thriving utilitarian is the one who successfully hides his or her utilitarian motives.[11] What should we do, however, when we are dealing with extreme cases where our ultimate principles must be brought out and tested? The murder of the old money lender is one such case. Let us then return to the conversation Raskolnikov overhears between the student and the officer.

"Tell me," asks the student, "would you kill the old woman *yourself*?"

(An officer is the perfect person to be asked this question because he is often asked to perform dutifully all kinds of evil deeds, "for the common good," or "the greater glory of his country.")

"Of course not! I was only arguing the justice of it. . . . It's nothing to do with me."

"But I think, if you would not do it yourself, there's no justice about it" (Pt. I, Ch. 6, 54).

As they are about to start another game of billiards, the student and the officer change their conversation. They drop out of the picture, but Raskolnikov remains there, perplexed and overexcited. And he recognizes the key point: Can you, or can you not, live out

---

11 It is a common criticism of utilitarianism that the long-range consequences of our actions cannot be predicted (adequately or at all), but Joseph Frank adds one objection that may well sum up Dostoevsky's own sentiment: despite all the talk of greatest happiness for the greatest number of people, utilitarianism seems to involve contempt, even hatred, for the common humanity; see Frank, *Dostoevsky: The Years of Ordeal, 1850–1859*, 107. For a general criticism of utilitarianism and egoism, see Nicolai Hartmann, *Ethics*, vol. 1, 119–39.

in practice what you think is right in theory? If murdering the old woman is just and beneficial, why not go ahead and kill her?

Why not, indeed? Yet many of us are reluctant and would not dare overstep the boundaries of conventional morality and law. And Raskolnikov, can he do this?

From the very first sentence of the novel, Raskolnikov's indecisiveness is the dominant theme. When the narrator first reports Raskolnikov's thoughts, we gain an insight into the dilemma that makes him so tentative: ". . . all is in a man's hands and he lets it all slip from cowardice, that's an axiom. It would be interesting to know what it is men are most afraid of. Taking a new step, uttering a new word is what they fear most" (Pt. I, Ch. 1, 2).

The underground man daydreams and complains, but he does not act. Raskolnikov sees the daring to act as the very criterion of whom he is. The underground man offers a devastating criticism of rational egoism in Part I of the *Notes*, but he does not equally tear to pieces his romantic egoism of Part II. Raskolnikov's third explanation of his crime focuses precisely on this romantic picture of man. "Everything is in man's hands," thinks Raskolnikov, which means that who we are is not determined by our past, or by some supernatural power. It is up to us to change the world, "to correct and direct nature," but we do not do it because we are afraid. "That's an axiom."

If that is indeed an axiom, Raskolnikov asks a very disturbing question: What are human beings afraid of? Even stronger: What are they most afraid of? Raskolnikov then offers an answer that not only determines the course of the novel but reveals a new way of understanding the human condition: "Taking a new step, uttering a new word is what they fear most." As the underground man ties the issue of the preservation of our human dignity to the preservation of freedom, Raskolnikov ties it to the transgression of boundaries: Do I dare? Or do I not? As he puts it: "A louse or a Napoleon?"

Raskolnikov's "either – or" reasoning is crude and unsophisticated; he does not see the difference between various kinds of transgressions and various kinds of boundaries. The same dualistic reasoning initially pervades all of his thinking. A few months before the murder, Raskolnikov wrote an article on crime. In it he divides people into ordinary and extraordinary. A vast majority of human beings are submissive creatures with no choice, born to obey someone like the Grand Inquisitor or a Nietzschean Superman. Weak and lost when left on their own, they need external authority to control them and tell them what is permissible and what is not, what is good and what evil.

Raskolnikov is far more concerned with the other kind of people, those rare human beings who dare – and have every right to – overstep the boundaries. Yes, they have the right to commit crime. They allow humanity as a whole to move toward the final solution, toward greatest happiness for the greatest number of people. By an inner light which only the chosen can see, they are called to cross all boundaries, even if it means leaving piles of dead bodies behind them. Indeed, there may be no other way to guide the countless mass of people who, blind and insecure, are looking at and worshipping every move their leader makes.

Napoleon is Raskolnikov's representative of these extraordinary creatures who blur the distinction between heroes and victimizers. He symbolizes the power of those who dare, the masters who would step on every trembling creature and on the whole ant-hill. In order "to correct and direct nature," he would break "what must be broken."

In Russia immediately after 1812, Napoleon was far more hated than admired. Tolstoy's majestic epic *War and Peace*, which appeared in the same magazine and at the same time as *Crime and Punishment*, exposes the vanity of the so-called great people like Napoleon. Thomas Carlyle prefaces his series of lectures published as *Heroes and Hero Worship* by assuming that "universal history is at bottom the history of the great men who worked here."[12] In contrast to Carlyle, Tolstoy argues that it is a dangerous illusion to believe extraordinary individuals can, by their intellect and will, understand and control the course of events. In his novel Tolstoy

---

12 *The Best Known Works of Thomas Carlyle*, 159. Carlyle's view relies on Hegel's conception of the historic hero as the agent of "the World-Spirit." According to Hegel's *Philosophy of History*, the history of the world moves on a higher level than that of morality. Philip Rahv emphasizes that Hegel's theory, very well known and widely endorsed in Russia in the middle of the nineteenth century, may have been "a direct and obvious source of Raskolnikov's notion of inferior and superior men"; *op. cit.*, 612.

uses a vivid, although exaggerated simile in which people like Napoleon are compared to the ram that the shepherd is fattening for slaughter. Because he is treated preferentially and grows fatter than others, the ram may imagine that he is the leader of the flock which will follow him wherever he goes. The ram is seduced by events whose aims neither he nor the rest of the flock can fathom.

Other Russian writers also refer to Napoleon with negative feelings. Before Dostoevsky and Tolstoy, Pushkin portrays him in *Eugene Onegin* and also in his celebrated story "Queen of Spades." In his thirst for power, Hermann, the leading character of "Queen of Spades," imagines that he is a Napoleon and ends up murdering an old woman.

In his controversial essay "Dostoevsky and Parricide," Freud diagnoses that "two traits are essential in a criminal: boundless egoism and a strong destructive impulse. Common to both of these, and a necessary condition for their expression, is absence of love, lack of an emotional appreciation of (human) objects."[13] Against his intentions, Freud's points apply more accurately to Raskolnikov than to Dostoevsky's attitude toward the murder of his father. Raskolnikov is the one who strikes us as a boundless egoist with an apparently strong destructive impulse. During several encounters with Porfiry and Svidrigailov, the thought crosses Raskolnikov's mind that he should kill them as well. The absence of love and appreciation of other human "objects" is closely associated with Raskolnikov's immense pride and egoism.

Had he been familiar with Freud's characterization of a criminal, Dostoevsky would probably have pointed out how close it lies to the legitimate description of a hero and to Raskolnikov's idea of an extraordinary man. An extraordinary man is someone whose passion is of great intensity and whose drive is directed toward a goal of great value. No one can deny the intensity or the depth of Raskolnikov's drive, even though his passion is misdirected. Like the underground man, Raskolnikov associates the greatest human

---

13 Sigmund Freud, "Dostoevsky and Parricide," 42. For detailed discussion of Freud's article on Dostoevsky, see Fritz Schmidl's essay "Freud and Dostoevsky," as well the Appendix to Joseph Frank's *Dostoevsky: The Seeds of Revolt, 1821–1849*, 379–91.

values with freedom. In both cases, this is freedom in a negative sense, or "freedom from" external obstacles and influences. Just like the underground man, Raskolnikov is confused about freedom in a positive sense: Provided that I am free to make my own decisions, what am I "free for"?

The underground man does not advance much in this direction, but this issue preoccupies Raskolnikov. Is everything really in man's hands, or are there some forces higher than man that (also) shape his destiny? If there are such forces, why is there so much suffering on earth? Is there not a moral imperative to make the world better than it is? If there is, should not every transgression be permissible in order to accomplish the highest good?

In the confusion that results from being overwhelmed with these questions, Raskolnikov's "rebellion" becomes an inverted heroism and leads to crime. In heroism, I am free to sacrifice myself for a noble goal, for something higher than my life. Raskolnikov, the underground man, and modern humanity in general have plenty of difficulties with self-sacrifice: How can I sacrifice myself for something higher if I do not believe in anything higher? The old heresy that "man, not God, is the measure of all things" is radicalized even further: The chosen few are the measure of all things. In the inverted heroism, if I am one of the chosen few, I am free to sacrifice the insignificant others for my own goals. Following Dostoevsky, Camus characterizes this point of view as belonging to a "romantic rebel" – he sides neither with God, nor with mankind, but with himself.[14]

In his obsession with himself, Raskolnikov does not understand the underlying dialectic of the two different senses of freedom. Nor does he draw a sharp line between sacrificing others and sacrificing oneself. Raskolnikov is not sure whether his task should consist in trying to correct injustices or in conquering the world. His question is exclusively monological, an example of the perverted heroism that is not a means for any end but becomes its own goal. In this confusion, everything turns on the misguided dilemma: Am I a man, or a louse? If I am a man, I have the right to overstep the boundaries and kill the old money lender.

14 See Albert Camus, *The Rebel: An Essay on Man in Revolt*, 55–61.

Pollution and Suffering

Raskolnikov kills – not once, but twice. First the old woman, as he had planned. Then he murders her sister, "the gentle Lizaveta," who returns home before he had expected.

Raskolnikov realizes right away that by means of his transgression he does not prove himself "a man." Instead, he becomes a "riddle unto himself." The murder turns out to be a bloody affair, far more complicated than a simple calculus of one death in exchange for a hundred lives. The spilling of "sticky, warm blood" irrevocably triggers his confrontation with reality. Raskolnikov is shocked to learn how many people are affected by his deed. The lonely monologue is first replaced by a dialogue with the previously hidden layers of his psyche, and then gradually with the real people surrounding him. In the Epilogue Dostoevsky writes how, finally, "Life had stepped into the place of theory and something quite different would work itself out of his mind" (Epilogue, 430). Raskolnikov has to travel a long road to come to this point and endure much suffering along the way.

Even in his bookish, internally trapped mind, Raskolnikov should have anticipated that the shedding of human blood would turn everything upside down. The shedding of blood is more exciting than the confrontation with reality a day after. Or, as the veterans of all wars know, not only the day after, but the year after. And the rest of life after, as well.

Dostoevsky's *Crime and Punishment* is in that sense comparable to Homer's *Iliad* and *Odyssey*. It is easier to wage war than to come back home again. It took ten years to conquer Troy, but twenty altogether for Odysseus to find his way home. This may be the reason, as Dudley Young points out, for the greater coherence of the *Iliad*, with its bursting nobility of spirit and body and its "judicious silence on the mutilating ecstasy to which that nobility is tied."[15] Homer already knew that once human blood is shed and violence unleashed, there immediately arises the bewildering problem of how to contain its deadly cycle and cleanse its dangerous pollution. Young connects the Latin word *polluere* (= to defile),

15 Dudley Young, *The Origins for the Sacred: The Ecstasies of Love and War*, 369.

with the closely related *pollere* (= to be powerful); pollution then comes to mean "letting loose of strength." But, according to Young, there is more to it: "The word 'pollution' . . . points to something essentially bad, even horrible; and yet, because its root meaning is 'a coming into presence of the usually absent divinity,' it also caries an ambiguous shadow, the possibility of a spasm that may kill or cure, or kill as it cures."[16]

This "spasm that may kill or cure, or kill as it cures," is present in Raskolnikov's struggles to come to terms with his own deeds. Yet Dostoevsky does not have the Homeric tradition in mind but the biblical one. Some commentators rightly point out that the first word of the title of Dostoevsky's novel – *prestuplenie* – contains "Biblical connotation" which is lost when this word is translated as "crime."[17] What exactly is this "Biblical connotation" and why does it not relate to Homer?

In Homer's epics, the representation of daily life remains within the realm of the peaceful and idyllic. In the Bible the problematic and the tragic take shape precisely in the domestic sphere: The domestic quarrels between Cain and Abel, Noah and his sons, or Abraham, Sarah, and Hagar are inconceivable in the context of Homer's *Iliad* and *Odyssey*. The Homeric heroes must have palpable reasons for their conflicts, and these work themselves out in their heroic battles. In the biblical stories, by contrast, daily life is permeated with perpetually smoldering jealousy and enmities. In the Bible the realms of the sublime and the everyday are inseparable, as they are in Dostoevsky's novels.[18]

16   *Ibid.*, 232; see also 446n19.
17   Edward Wasiolek, *Dostoevsky: The Major Fiction*, 83. According to Robert L. Jackson's editorial note, "The Russian word *prestuplenie* conveys the Biblical sense of moral violation or 'overstepping' the Law, while at the same time, like 'crime,' it serves to define actions contrary to the laws of the state"; Jackson, ed. *Twentieth Century Interpretations of Crime and Punishment*, 21n5.
18   See Erich Auerbach, "Representations of Reality in Homer and the Old Testament," 45–58, especially page 58.

Both Judaism and Christianity are "blood" religions.[19] In the Hebrew of the Old Testament there is an intimate connection between *dam* (= blood), and *'adam* (= human being), and the word "bliss" has its origin in the word for blood as well. In Exodus we read how Moses sanctifies the altar that God has commanded him to build with the blood of oxen, and in the tenth chapter of John that, "He that eateth my flesh and drinketh my blood, dwelleth in me, and I in him." The first human act in Genesis is that of disobedience, the second an act of murder. Cain kills his brother Abel, and "the blood cries out from the ground." (The servant woman Nastassya – the abbreviated version of Anastasia, which means Resurrection – repeats this phrase to Raskolnikov after the murder.) God marks Cain, and Raskolnikov feels equally marked. Cain shouts: "*Gadol avoni miniso*," which is usually (mis)translated from Hebrew as "My punishment is too great to bear." What the Hebrew text really says is something significantly different: "My sin, my iniquity, is too great to bear."[20]

Despite its title, Dostoevsky's novel is not about the difficulty of bearing the punishment, but about the difficulty of bearing the sin. Dostoevsky learns in Siberia that punishment, legal punishment, need not touch the soul of the one who commits a terrible crime. He is more interested in the inner change provoked by the transgression of the boundary and the blood crying out from the ground. With his transgression, Raskolnikov discovers yet another plane of existence, for which Dostoevsky does not assign a specific name: We can call it the sacred versus the ordinary plane of existence, or perhaps the tragic as opposed to the trivial. More important than the name itself is the recognition that, despite the spatial associations of words like "transgression" and "overstepping boundaries," Dostoevsky is more concerned with the temporal dimension of Raskolnikov's deed.

---

19 Girard argues that all religions are "blood" religions: "violence is the heart of the sacred"; *Violence and the Sacred*, 31.

20 This statement by Burton Visotzky is quoted from Bill Moyers (ed.), *Genesis: A Living Conversation*, 87.

The artistic device which Dostoevsky uses to call our attention to this temporal dimension, later skillfully explored by Joseph
Conrad, Henry James, Virginia Woolf, and James Joyce, is the
manipulation of the temporal sequence.[21] This device is by no
means arbitrary. Unlike chaos, which is a derangement in space,
pollution is an event that takes place in time. Dostoevsky manifests
this manipulation of the temporal sequence through the contrast
between the exact account of events in Part I and Raskolnikov's
confusion with regard to time in Part II. Before the murder,
Raskolnikov follows the linear progression of events without difficulty. As soon as he murders, Raskolnikov is thrown into a
whirlwind in which he loses track of time. He feels sick and lies
in coma. He has dreams and nightmares, which make it difficult
for him to figure out what is real and what is not. Raskolnikov
is transposed into an archetypal order of his psyche, where his
consciousness and conscience, rationality and irrationality mingle
together and produce unpredictable outcomes.

What is going to happen to Raskolnikov? What are the options of
a victimizer?

There are five of them, and Dostoevsky gives us the whole spectrum. One: escape where nobody knows you and will never hear
about your crime. On a few occasions, Raskolnikov thinks about
escaping to America, but quickly rejects this idea. Two: continue
with victimizations. Once one starts the chain of violence, it is not
easy to escape from its dehumanizing cycle. This is in a sense what
happens, because Raskolnikov does not plan to kill Lizaveta but
only the old money lender. As he will find out later, this continuous victimization is also what Svidrigailov does. Raskolnikov is
not inclined to go in this direction any further. Three: if accused,
deny any allegations connected with the crime. Raskolnikov delib-
erates about turning himself in, but encounters a powerful inner
resistance to any such inclination. Fourth: if the burden of bearing your sin becomes intolerable, commit suicide. This possibility

21 This point is made by Joseph Frank; see *Dostoevsky: The Miraculous
    Years, 1865–1871*, 93. On the role of temporal distinctions and the aban-
    donment of the liner time sequence in *Crime and Punishment*, see also
    Konstantin Mochulsky, *Dostoevsky: His Life and Work*, 297–98.

is never too far from Raskolnikov's mind.[22] Unlike Svidrigailov, who ends up killing himself, Raskolnikov's desire to live and his hope for a second chance help him in resisting this temptation. Five: come to terms with the deed by accepting responsibility for its consequences. Sonia is instrumental in helping Raskolnikov confess his crime, although Porfiry and Svidrigailov play a role as well.

After the murder, Raskolnikov's first confronts his own psyche. Instead of the Promethean ascent of which he was dreaming, he begins a descent into the belly of the whale. Dostoevsky believes that a genuine dialogue between the divided parts of Raskolnikov's psyche can take place only after the transgression.[23] Notice, however, that his subconsciousness triggers and then interferes with his conscious processes even before he crosses the threshold of crime. A day before the murder Raskolnikov receives a letter from his mother containing a compelling analogy to what he is planning to do. Just as he is going to use the old pawnbroker as a means for his own purposes, Luzhin coldly calculates that he can use Raskolnikov's sister, Dounia, to advance his selfish interests.

The letter also triggers the memories of a different time, when his father was still alive, the time of innocence and family happiness. Later than night, Raskolnikov dreams about the old mare, one of the most poignant moments of the novel. In the dream, a drunken peasant Mikolka beats the useless old horse to death. As a child, Raskolnikov passes by with his father. The child is so touched by

22 It is clear from Dostoevsky's notes that for a long time he intended to finish the novel with Raskolnikov's suicide. See, for instance, *The Notebooks for Crime and Punishment*, 243.

23 This is the point of Hermann Hesse's short book, *Blick ins Chaos* (translated as "In Sight of Chaos"), a series of essays on Dostoevsky, whom Hesse considered his closest fellow-traveler into the abyss of the human soul. As Oscar Seidlin argues, *Blick ins Chaos* could have been the proper title of almost all of Hesse's works; "Hermann Hesse: The Exorcism of the Demon," in *Hesse: A Collection of Critical Essays*, ed. Theodor Ziolkowski, 62. Malcolm Jones takes this "glance into chaos" to be one of the main motives of Dostoevsky's opus as well; see Jones, *Dostoyevsky: The Novel of Discord*, 9.

the madness of the adults' behavior and the fate of the old mare that he breaks away from his father and embraces the head of the helpless, dying horse. Mikolka's drunken rage is analogous to Raskolnikov's blind intoxication with ideas. Raskolnikov himself is not a child any more, but an adult who has no power to break away from his own madness.

Besides such confrontations with his own subconsciousness, the dialogues with Svidrigailov and Porfiry also play an indispensable role in Raskolnikov's struggles. Svidrigailov is Raskolnikov's double; he is to Raskolnikov what Mephistopheles is to Faust. In the terminology of Jungian psychoanalysis, Svidrigailov is Raskolnikov's "Shadow." This psychological archetype refers primarily to the dark, feared, and unwanted side of our personality. The shadow personality, our double, is also the unlived part of our life. Svidrigailov is the parody of the extraordinary man Raskolnikov hopes to become. He is someone who can murder without remorse. For Svidrigailov, good and evil are relative notions, and that is why his actions can range from committing premeditated murder to giving a huge amount of money to charity. One minute he tries to take advantage of Raskolnikov's sister Dounia, and the next he lets her go.

While Svidrigailov represents the rejection of all authority and anticipates Ivan's slogan that "everything is permissible," Porfiry stands on the other side of transgressions. As a police inspector, he symbolizes the external authority concerned with protecting the public law and morality, and thereby preserves a sense of order and stability. Porfiry invites Raskolnikov to confess and accept responsibility for the murder. According to Porfiry, the cause of the crime is Raskolnikov's pride: "That proud suppressed enthusiasm in young people is dangerous!" Pride hardens people's hearts; they become insensitive toward each other. Life in this wretched city has bad effects and will not make anything easier, but there is only one solution to prideful egoism – suffering: "For suffering, Rodion Romanovitch, is a great thing. . . . Don't laugh at it, there's an idea in suffering" (Pt. VI, Ch. 2, 362).

Porfiry's words about suffering mean much to Raskolnikov, yet his main teacher in suffering is not a police inspector but a harlot. Everything about Sonia – the Russian nickname for Sophia –

betrays suffering. Dostoevsky introduces Sonia as "a small thin girl of eighteen with fair hair, rather pretty, with wonderful blue eyes" (Pt. II, Ch. 7, 147). Raskolnikov hears about her early in the novel from her father (who also tells him about the indispensability of suffering, but claims that man is made "in the image of the Beast"). Raskolnikov meets Sonia when he brings the dying Marmeladov home. Dressed as a prostitute, she arrives in time for her ill-fated father to die in her arms. Death brings Raskolnikov and Sonia together, the death of Marmeladov but also – as they realize later – of Sonia's friend Lizaveta. These two unhappy women used to read the New Testament together. Sonia and Lizaveta held their faith in common.

The contrast between Sonia and Porfiry is symbolic of the various layers implied in the title of Dostoevsky's novel. For Porfiry, law and morality provide a sense of stability and order in the world. For Sonia, that stability and order come from God. Porfiry stands for authority and justice, Sonia for compassion and redemption. Porfiry has to engage in a cat-and-mouse power game with Raskolnikov for him to confess. Sonia plays no such game, but she recognizes a tormented soul. She does not treat Raskolnikov's deed primarily as a crime but as a sin. Unlike crime, which is a breech of the conventional law or morality, Sonia grasps intuitively that sin hides within itself the assumption that "I am God." She senses that Raskolnikov rebels not so much against human law as against that of the divine. If he is ever to atone for what he did, he must address the metaphysical and religious dimension of his deed.

Obsessed with his "unfinished" theoretical ideas, Raskolnikov struggles to understand Sonia's point of view. Versed only in power games, he cannot at first comprehend who Sonia is and how she can bear her cross. Her suffering initially strikes Raskolnikov as pointless. Sonia's non-judgmental embrace of who he is helps him to recognize in her someone with whom he can fully open his soul and unite in genuine dialogue. But this transformation does not happen immediately and without resistance. Indeed, Raskolnikov's behavior toward Sonia mirrors his tormented soul. He refuses to commit suicide after a double murder, but he is not embarrassed to ask her: "Tell me how this shame and degradation can exist in you side by side with other, opposite, holy feelings? It would be better, a thousand times better and wiser to leap into the water and end it all!" (Pt. IV, Ch. 4, 255).

Following Sonia's silence, Raskolnikov asks her to read him the biblical story of Lazarus, but all he can say to her afterwards is: "You, too, have transgressed . . . have had the strength to transgress. You have laid hands on yourself, you have destroyed a life . . . *your own* (it's all the same!)" (Pt. IV, Ch. 4, 261).

It is not the same. It cannot be the same if you sacrifice your own life or that of someone else. It cannot be the same if you assume the role of a judge about who lives and who does not, or if you refuse any such "privilege." Raskolnikov does not see that yet; he does not see how good can come out of suffering.

When Raskolnikov is finally ready, he confesses to Sonia. This time, he finally opens his polluted soul in front of her: "I murdered myself!" (Pt. V, Ch. 4, 330).

Moved by his suffering, which Sonia begins to realize may be greater than hers, she tells him what to do: "Go at once, this very minute, stand at the cross-roads, bow down, first kiss the earth which you have defiled and then bow down to all the world and say to all men aloud, 'I am a murderer!' Then God will send you life again." (Pt. V, Ch. 4, 330).

After some reluctance, yet without public admission that he is the murderer, Raskolnikov kisses the earth at the cross-road, and confesses his crime at the police station.

Rebirth

In *Notes from the Underground* the inner contraction of the underground man paralyze his action. In *Crime and Punishment* Raskolnikov's schism does not assume the character of contradictions but more of contrasts. Indeed, the whole novel displays archetypal contrasts: between monologue and dialogue, pollution and purity, thinking and feeling, power and powerlessness, life and death, death and rebirth.

To illustrate how deeply such contrasts permeate in the structure of the novel, let us consider why Dostoevsky's characters mention Raphael's "Sistine Madonna." This painting portrays such serenity and harmony which stands in complete contrast to the turmoil of *Crime and Punishment*. The most touching disparity is between the Madonna walking through the clouds of the spiritual heaven with Christ in her hands, and Katerina Ivanovna begging with her children on the streets of Petersburg. Born in the upper class family and raised with a prospect of comfortable life, Katerina Ivanovna has seen all of her dreams shattered. She never marries the prince she fantasizes about, her first husband dies and leaves her with three little children, she buries her drunken second husband, and is left on the street with Polenka, Kolya, and Lida. Without any source of income and dying of tuberculosis, feeling betrayed by humanity and by God, the desperate woman loses her mind. She dresses her poor children in whatever remains of their festive clothes and takes them to the streets to sing and dance, hoping to shame people, perhaps even God, into righteousness. Soon she recognizes that "the ball is over," but, in a last act of defiance, she refuses to see a priest.

Minutes before Katerina Ivanovna dies, she is taken to Sonia's room, where she faces for the first time the reality of Sonia's shameful life. On Raphael's painting, the gesture of St. Sixtus and St. Barbara seem to be directed toward the faithful, whom we can imagine beyond the balustrade at the bottom of the painting. As the curtains open, the saints are indicating to the faithful that their prayers are answered, that the miracle has occurred. Katerina Ivanovna has not lived to see any such miracle. Her death, like her life, was one of mounting agony.

Katerina Ivanovna dies in Sonia's arms, just as her father Marmeladov did a few days earlier. Sonia is left to shed the tears of lamentation, and even Raskolnikov cannot but recognize in her a representative of the suffering of all humanity. Seconds after he ridicules Sonia's faith in God, Raskolnikov kneels down and, in a completely irrational yet sincere gesture, kisses her feet. Her full name alone – Sofia, or Sofya – suggests "the Divine Wisdom," attained through suffering and humility. In his book on Dostoevsky, L.A. Zander connects her name with another Russian word – *tselomudrie*. This word literally means the wisdom of wholeness, and is the translation of the Greek word *sophrosyne*, which indicates wholeness, soundness, integrity, and unity. The proper English translation for *tselomudrie* is chastity. "Isn't Sonia a harlot?" asks Zander, and admits: "Yes, she is." Nevertheless, continues Zander, Dostoevsky himself says that "all that infamy had only touched her mechanically, not one drop of real depravity had penetrated to her heart." Sonia being a harlot is Dostoevsky's "literary device used to emphasize the magnitude of her sacrifice: there is not a single word in the novel referring to any facts, feelings or experiences testifying to her being 'a harlot'."[24]

This may be an exaggeration, but there is no question that Sonia symbolizes purity, similar to the Madonna on Raphael's painting. Sonia's heart is unstained by evil, and this purity of heart is a fundamental Christian virtue, so potent that the guilty are powerless in its presence. Dostoevsky clearly wants Raskolnikov to feel his own powerlessness, but also to feel his trust in the presence of such a pure being as Sonia. The deeper the consciousness of guilt, the higher the admiration for the person of the pure heart. Although they have warm feelings for each other, Raskolnikov does not perceive Sonia as a lover. She is more like a spiritual sister, and he is not the only one to treat her in such a way: because of her unusually small size and childlike appearance, the convicts in Siberia end up calling her their "little mother, Sofya Semyonovna."

Unlike Raskolnikov, who is portrayed as a victimizer, Sonia is a victim. She is certainly the victim of worse circumstances than his. To earn some money, he can do some translations, or give private lessons. Sonia does not have such choices. The only thing she has to offer – and Dostoevsky makes even her father say this – is her body. To ensure that we perceive Sonia as a victim, Dostoevsky later introduces an episode in which, during her father's funeral dinner, Luzhin accuses her of stealing his hundred rubles.

In this episode we find a typical pattern of victimization. Luzhin has nothing personal against Sonia, but uses her for his schemes against Raskolnikov. Sonia is treated as a peripheral and superfluous creature. Unlike English, in Russian (as well as French, German, and most other Indo-European languages), one word (zhertva) means both victim and sacrifice. A victim is someone who is sacrificed against her or his will, who is denied either the common core of humanity, or her or his specific individuality.

24   L.A. Zander, *Dostoevsky*, 78.

A victim is someone transgressed against and polluted. Cain goes on to live, but Abel is dead. Raskolnikov lives, but Alyona Ivanovna and her sister Lizaveta are dead.

Sonia is not dead, but what are her choices? What are the choices of a victim?

There are four of them and Dostoevsky explores them all. The first option is resignation. Somebody else, a victimizer, has already made a choice. What difference does it make what a victim wants? Should not a victim simply accept her or his shame, together with a life of degradation?

The second option is suicide. Why should a victim continue to live the life of humiliation? Can a victim expect anything but a meaningless subsistence? If so, why not commit suicide? Is not this the last dignified choice a victim can make?

The third possibility is that a victim turns into a victimizer: Someone has sacrificed me, so I can victimize others. The merry-go-round of revenge and scapegoating goes on and on, whether it is pushed on by personal vengeance or institutional justice.

There is one more option, and this is the one in which Dostoevsky is most interested. Instead of continuing the cycle of violence, the victim may try to stop it. Instead of punishment, the victim may choose forgiveness; instead of justice, compassion. This is what Dostoevsky has in mind when he creates Sonia. In *Notes from the Underground*, Lisa takes pity on the underground man, but then turns around and walks away. Sonia, by contrast, follows Raskolnikov to Siberia, determined to wait eight long years to start their new life together.

Sonia, the weak and defenseless victim, opts for the path of suffering and self-sacrifice. She affirms life, instead of choosing resignation, suicide, or victimization of others. Sonia chooses to willingly participate in existence, whose preconditions she cannot alter. All around her Sonia sees the process of life consuming life; life ends on the one side and begins on the other. Like the mother of God, Sonia must have a premonition that she is only a vehicle of life, not the life itself. She cannot understand or explain these mysteries of death and life, nor does she try to control them. Sonia simply affirms life, with faith and hope. This is that chastity, of which Zander speaks, which is not merely a spiritual condition, but a spiritual energy and force. Sonia is thereby the well-spring of love, faith, and hope, and for that she is called by the convicts "our little mother."

Sonia's choice and her self-sacrifice is by no means something ordinary, nor can it be demanded as a moral norm. Raskolnikov intuitively recognizes that she too has transgressed the boundary of the ordinary, but he cannot grasp exactly what makes her so unique. Although searching for how to be a hero and an extra-ordinary man, he is so blindly obsessed with the question of whether he is such a man that he cannot see that Sonia is a truly remarkable person, a heroine.

Raskolnikov's blindness does not mean that Sonia is perfect. Dostoevsky is always suspicious of perfection. He makes Sonia human, with utilitarian impulses. In one memorable episode, Sonia refuses to give Katerina Ivanovna some cuffs that Sonia brought to adorn herself. Already losing her mind, Katerina Ivanovna repeat-edly begs her to give her those cuffs, but Sonia refuses with a bitter reproach: "What use are they to you, Katerina Ivanovna?" (Pt. IV, Ch. 4, 253).

Of no use, indeed, just as Lebeziatnikov remarks that for a hungry worker Raphael and Pushkin are of no use. Unlike Lebezi-atnikov, Sonia trusts that there are values that cannot be measured with utilitarian yardsticks, and, moreover, that the greatest values are of a non-utilitarian kind. Love is such a value, as is self-sacrifice. Although Sonia never blames herself for being a prostitute, she bitterly regrets not giving Katerina Ivanovna these cheap cuffs. Even her prostitution belongs to a different "economy" of life than the one defended by Lebeziatnikov (and Luzhin) – the "economy of gifts." "The gift symbolizes a central triumph for culture over Nature," points out Dudley Young. Dostoevsky would agree. He might prefer, however, to substitute the word "spirituality" for the world "culture."[25]

In ethics – utilitarian or not – once innocence and purity are lost, they cannot be restored. Yet ethics never has the last word for Dostoevsky. In Raphael's painting religion tries to do what is ethically impossible. Despite the horrifying reality that surrounds

25 Dudley Young, op. cit., 260.

her, Sonia believes the impossible, the "good news" of the Gospel. Guided by her faith, she responds to her victimization with a gift, the highest gift of which she is capable. She gives her love to Raskolnikov and her gift transgresses ordinary boundaries. But is Raskolnikov worthy of such a gift? Can his old self fully die in order for him to be reborn again?

If Sonia is a more saintly version of Lisa, Raskolnikov is a far more sophisticated adaptation of the underground man. The analogy is not straightforward, however, for their similarities and differences develop in various directions. The underground man's primal element is, so to say, earth; he lives as a mouse in the darkness under its surface. Raskolnikov is also a nocturnal creature, yet his element is not earth but air. He lives in the upper floor of a building, among the clouds. Like Don Quixote, he lives in the clouds of illusory ideas. The underground man is an anti-hero with no ideals, while Raskolnikov aspires to be a genuine hero. The underground man is arrested within the confines of his ego in a way in which Raskolnikov is not. Like Don Quixote, Raskolnikov strives toward the highest values, and he is willing to sacrifice his life for the attainment of his ideals. Indeed, to a hero of the sort of Don Quixote and Raskolnikov, death may be more valuable than life, provided that the sacrifice advances the chosen goal. What both need to learn is that life, too, can be a sacrifice. This sacrifice need not be a flamboyant one, but it requires patient energy, time, and service to others. From those like Sonia, Don Quixote and Raskolnikov must learn that to live can be more heroic than to die.

Far more than Don Quixote, Raskolnikov has strayed from striving to be a hero to becoming its opposite. Through Raskolnikov's struggle, Dostoevsky displays the negative aspects of heroism: that it can turn into victimization of the innocent, that striving toward heroism can become its own goal (rather than a means toward the realization of a noble goal), and that a hero can become tempted to regard himself as a god.

As Raskolnikov himself recognizes, along with the two women, he has killed something in himself. Yet through suffering and his love for Sonia he has also created a possibility of a new beginning. The whole novel, with its multiple layers and complex symbolism, centers on this transformation: from death to rebirth. It is incorrect to believe, however, that *Crime and Punishment* fits into the happy ending of a melodrama. It is true that for Raskolnikov "Life had stepped into the place of theory" (Epilogue, 430), and Sonia and Raskolnikov "were renewed by love; the heart of each held infinite sources of life for the heart of the other" (Epilogue, 429). By the end of *Crime and Punishment*, Dostoevsky warns us that Raskolnikov does "not know that the new life would not be given for nothing, that he would have to pay dearly for it, that it would cost him great striving, great suffering." That, however, "is the beginning of a new story – the story of the gradual renewal of a man, the story of his gradual regeneration, of his passing from one world into another, of his initiation into a new unknown life. That may be the subject of a new story, but our present story is ended" (Epilogue, 430).

Does Dostoevsky ever write that "new story"? What would it look like? We will return to this subject in Part II. What is important for now is Dostoevsky's warning: Raskolnikov may have been reborn, but more suffering is still ahead of him. What will his "initiation into a new unknown life bring," we simply do not know.

The question that must be addressed here is: What part of Raskolnikov dies and what survives? Raskolnikov has certainly learned to distinguish between crime and sin. For his crime, he willingly accepts punishment both at his trial and during the penal servitude. His sin, and his attitude toward it, is a more complicated affair.

Speaking of *Crime and Punishment*, Jaroslav Pelikan claims that for Dostoevsky sin is not a moral but a religious fact: Sin is not primarily something I *do*, but something I *am*. "A sense of sin was more than a feeling of guilt, it was the feeling of profanes and unworthiness."[26] Raskolnikov is led to this sense of profanes and unworthiness by his egotistical drive (so typical of our civilization) to become more than his limited existence allows him to be. In his dialogues with Raskolnikov, Porfiry uses the language of fire and thunderbolts several times. Driven by his yearning to be the highest and the most powerful, Raskolnikov turns not only against the prevailing moral norms, but also against God. He imagines that

---

26   Jaroslav Pelikan, *Fools for Christ*, 72.

man can steal the thunderbolt from Zeus and be God. The demonic element is thereby unleashed and Raskolnikov sheds human blood.

For a long time, Raskolnikov does not understand why things went wrong. He is tempted to think that it was a flaw in the execution, not in the plan itself. Human life to him does not have the same value which it holds for everyone around him. But there are moments of awakening. One occurs after he manages to protect an abused girl from the repulsive advances of a stranger on the streets of Petersburg:

> Where is it I've read that someone condemned to death says or thinks, an hour before his death, that if he had to live on some high rock, on such a narrow ledge that he'd only have room to stand, and the ocean, everlasting darkness, everlasting solitude, everlasting tempest around him, if he had to remain standing on a square yard of space all his life, a thousand years, eternity, it were better to live so than to die at once! Only to live, to live and live! Life, whatever it may be! . . . How true it is! Good God, how true! Man is a vile creature! . . . And vile is he who calls him vile for that (Pt. II, Ch. 6, 127).

The capacity for having such an excitement for life distinguishes Raskolnikov from Svidrigailov. And this is only one example when Raskolnikov escapes from his dark, Svidrigailov-like mood. Another reversal of his usual devaluation of life occurs after Marmeladov's accident. His death and the misery of the rest of the family prompt Raskolnikov to leave on their window the money that he just received from his mother. On the way out, after overcoming the desire to go back and take at least a portion of the money for himself, he feels "a new overwhelming sensation of life." The narrator tells us that this sensation might be compared to that of a man condemned to death who has suddenly been pardoned. Raskolnikov himself exclaims: "Life is real! Haven't I lived just now? My life has not yet died with that old woman!" (Pt. II, Ch. 7, 151).

This sensation that rises in Raskolnikov after he does good, establishes a genuine contact with another human being; he recognizes himself as a participant in the larger whole of humanity. Where does this affirmation of life come from? It is not a mere animal drive to live. This positive sensation is rather a remnant of his deeply buried spirituality. Dostoevsky has his typical way of revealing this to the reader. Whenever we find Raskolnikov obsessed with his "unfinished" theoretical ideas, the air is hot and stiff; he is barely capable of breathing. But before his confession, there is a tremendous thunderstorm: The heavens open up and Zeus reminds us that he is still the one in charge of the thunderbolt. The rain cleanses the pollution and the air is fresh. In Russian, more than in English, the meaning of the word air (*vozdukh*) is connected to spirit (*dukh*), which in the original Greek (*pneuma*) meant the breath of life.[27]

In his mastery of using various contrasts, Dostoevsky makes Svidrigailov (of all the characters in the novel) talk about Raphael's "Sistine Madonna." He mentions it not once but twice. With his perverted mind, Svidrigailov shows that he can distort the meaning of anything valuable when he compares the face of his sixteen-year-old fiancée with the face of the mother of God on Raphael's painting. Since Svidrigailov is Raskolnikov's double and his shadow, the painting must also be of significance for our understanding of Raskolnikov.

The main connection between Raskolnikov and Svidrigailov is directly related to air and, indirectly, to spirit. The Madonna walks through the air; she is in the clouds above the earth, above the ordinary. This is what Raskolnikov aspires toward, but he walks through the wrong kind of clouds and breaths the wrong kind of air. (Recall how Svidrigailov remarks enigmatically: "All men need air, air, air.") On a painting that is consciously structured in terms of hierarchies, the mother of God is very high in the air. Nonetheless, there is no illusion that she is on the summit, that there could not be anyone above her. Her function is quite different. As Goethe famously expresses it in the conclusion of his *Faust*: "*Das Ewig-Weibliche/Zieth uns hinan*" (The Eternal Feminine/Draws us onward). Sonia plays the same role in *Crime and Punishment*.

---

27 The Russian word *dukh* can be translated as spirit, breath, smell, scent, odor, ghost, apparition, courage, heat, and in several other ways. The related Greek word *pneuma* has also a variety of meanings, the most relevant of which are breath, wind, and spirit.

In his striving onward, Raskolnikov divides human beings into extraordinary and ordinary – everyone belongs to one group or to the other. Raphael's painting offers a different story from our usual either-or reasoning. Virgin and Christ, who are on the top of the painting, are the symbols of the unity of what appears to be contradictory: virginity and motherhood, divinity and humanity, heaven and earth. Raphael's painting suggests the possibility of a synthesis between these apparent contradictions. Sonia comes much closer to this synthesis than Raskolnikov. She reconciles the death that strikes her parents and her friend Lizaveta on the one hand with her affirmation of life on the other. Sonia represents the unity between evil reality and undeniable faith, between the ordinary and the extraordinary. Raphael's painting displays an eternal, yet, to someone like Raskolnikov, abstract archetype. Through Sonia, Dostoevsky brings this ideal closer to earth. Through her, Dostoevsky shows how a Christian ideal, walking through the air/spirit, is a concrete and living thing. Sonia is the first great heroine of Dostoevsky's affirmation of life – even in the face of evil.[28]

In his abstract preoccupation with self-knowledge and self-realization, Raskolnikov tends to forget that he cannot sacrifice the lives of others for his "noble" ideals. When it comes to real life, he has difficulty connecting abstractions and ideas with experiences and emotions. Even at the news of his mother's death, silence is his only response. Raskolnikov needs to learn from Sonia about life, especially that suffering is not a punishment from God but can be an affirmation of life.

Sonia's suffering is neither ordinary nor easy. Nor is her faith something that brings any guarantees; it does not save Lizaveta, or her father and stepmother. If anything, Sonia's faith may appear as useless and irrational. Her faith requires sacrifice but does not promise anything in return. Sonia's faith, however, does not pretend to be useful or rational. It is not based on calculation but on trust. It is like walking on the clouds of spirit, without any firm ground underneath.

---

28 As Eduard Thurneysen expresses it, "So in Dostoevsky there comes a full acceptance of life, of nature, and of man, a paradoxical affirmation of that which is, as it is, for the sake of that which it is *not*"; *Dostoevsky*, 70.

Raskolnikov is a divided creature because he comprehends Sonia's faith on one level, but not on another. Every time he actually helps someone, every time he sacrifices himself and suffers for others, he is overwhelmed by a new appreciation of life. Dostoevsky's dialogical message is that "I" need "we" to be truly "I." Yet Raskolnikov has difficulty understanding this, even in Siberia.

Is he a slow learner, or only a reluctant one? How is it that Sonia grasps it and he does not? Or is Raskolnikov perhaps right in refusing to learn this lesson? We often think that it is easier to be a victimizer than a victim. Abel is dead; Cain lives. The old money lender and her sister are gone, Raskolnikov gets another chance. Even a living victim seems worse off than a victimizer.

Dostoevsky wants us to reconsider this view. Sonia's character is more beautiful than Raskolnikov's, and her cross may be easier to bear than his. Why? Because Sonia has a different attitude toward carrying her cross: She has faith and Raskolnikov does not. Sonia's faith gives her life a sense of meaning. Where Sonia has faith that leads her on, no matter how thorny the path may be, Raskolnikov stumbles. And as Dostoevsky makes it clear in the Epilogue, he will continue to stumble.

Cain asks God: "Am I my brother's keeper?" Because we are so poor at being our brothers' keepers, the question is still with us, burning like an open wound. Countless tragedies of life force us to pose this question again and again. The problem is that, even when we raise it, the question is so often just a rhetorical one, as it is for Cain.

Dostoevsky may well have thought that our destiny depends on our willingness and determination to give an affirmative, non-rhetorical answer to Cain's question: Yes, we are supposed to be our brothers' keepers. Sonia does it. Raskolnikov is not so sure. They both understand what a positive answer means: humbling our narcissistic egos, restricting our almost boundless desire to possess and dominate. Moreover, the affirmative answer also means that when the choice is between being wronged and doing wrong, between being killed and killing others, we have to consciously and willingly choose to find ourselves on the receiving end.

Sonia would do that. Raskolnikov would hesitate. It takes so long before he can distinguish between an apology he tries to find for his transgression and a genuine confession. It takes so long before his quest for self-knowledge begins transforming itself into a search for forgiveness. Even those prisoners in Siberia who adore Sonia as their "little mother" are suspicious of him: "You're an infidel! You don't believe in God," they shout. "You ought to be killed" (Epilogue, 427).

To be readmitted into a human society, Raskolnikov needs to wake up from his monological obsession and relive the history of mankind, the never-ending cycle of transformations: "Through the age of Abraham and his flock," to the resurrection of Jesus, to the realization of how much he misses Sonia when she is ill and does not visit for several days. When she finally appears, he gains a painful but happy awareness of what Sonia means to him:

> He thought of her. He remembered how continually he had tormented her and wounded her heart. He remembered her pale and thin little face. But these recollections scarcely troubled him now; he knew with what infinite love he would now repay all her sufferings. And what were all, *all* the agonies of the past! Everything, even his crime, his sentence and imprisonment, seemed to him now in the first rush of feeling an external, strange fact with which he had no concern. But he could not think for long together of anything that evening, and he could not have analyzed anything consciously; he was simply feeling. Life had stepped into the place of theory and something quite different would work itself out in his mind (Epilogue, 430).

A romantic happy-ending? A moral lesson worthy of a hedgehog?

Not quite. The categories here contrasted – feeling versus theory, purity versus pollution, life versus death, death versus rebirth – are not themselves of the moral kind. We may be seduced by Dostoevsky's language in the quoted passage, but he is not primarily interested in morality. Just as Sonia's purity should not be identified with the good, nor should the category of the holy – so manifest in Dostoevsky's favorite painting – be identified with the good. Purity and holiness point toward a metaphysical and religious dimension of reality which Dostoevsky is not yet ready to confront. We have, nonetheless, traveled a significant distance from the mouse-hole of the underground man. When we first meet Raskolnikov, who thinks "all is in a man's hands and he lets it all slip from cowardice" (Pt. I, Ch. 1, 2), he reminds us of his underground cousin. Yet with his last words, "Can her convictions not be mine now? Her feelings, her aspirations at least . . ." (Epilogue, 430), Raskolnikov has broken from the confines of his lonely "unfinished" ideas. He is now a participant in the dialogue – manifested not only through the polyphony of different voices mingling together, but in a co-existence and co-dependence of a higher order. Based on his trust in Sonia, Raskolnikov has established a vital contact with another human being. His logic of either-or is softened, and his self-obsession weakened. Raskolnikov now realizes that we do not individually control the situations in which we find ourselves, that they always involve a multitude of forces which render the outcomes unpredictable. Following Sonia, he is developing a sense of trust in life, perhaps also in a higher will.

While Raskolnikov is discovering what life in a dialogue means, we should not assume that such a life and a trust in a higher will must exclude differences in opinions and dissimilar attitudes toward reality. Nor should we be seduced by the quoted passage to forget that the intensity and direction of Raskolnikov's feeling do not represent a whole picture of his dynamic nature. They show only one side of the see-saw that represents his life. Even after Raskolnikov's rebirth, even in his new life – the story we will never read – Dostoevsky would preserve a little bit of Ivan Karamazov in him. And Ivan would hardly resist asking what Sonia – or any other hedgehog – would never dare: If we are contemptuous of Cain for not being his brother's keeper, why are we not contemptuous of God for not being the keeper of His children?

4
The Possessed

Is Nothing Sacred?

"From the Real to the More Real"

The Possessed is Dostoevsky's most complex novel; its final structure emerges only in the long process of writing and rewriting. Dostoevsky admits that *The Possessed* cost him more labor than any other work: He feared "not to be equal" to the theme he has chosen.[1] In fact, it would be more precise to say that Dostoevsky weaves together three main themes in this work; he does it in a way that sometimes makes the unity of this novel far from obvious. One theme deals with generational conflict – a motif prominent in

---

1   Letters to N.N. Strakhov of October 9, 1870, and of April 23, 1871. See also Dostoevsky's letters to A.N. Maikov of December 5, 1870, and of March 2, 1871, as well as Edward Wasiolek's Introduction for *The Notebooks for The Possessed*, 5. Wasiolek argues that despite such doubts and struggles, Dostoevsky created "one of the world's greatest novels." Konstantin Mochulsky similarly concurs that this (in the West under-appreciated) novel is "one of the greatest artistic works in world literature"; *Dostoevsky: His Life and Work*, 433. Orhan Pamuk maintains that *The Possessed* is "the greatest political novel of all time"; *Other Colors: Essays and a Story*, 143. See also Joseph Frank's appraisal of *The Possessed* in *Dostoevsky: The Miraculous Years, 1865–1871*, 497.

Russian literature since the appearance of Ivan Turgenev's novel *Fathers and Sons* (1862). In *The Possessed* this conflict is displayed through the dissonance between the highest hopes and the deepest fears of the two generations – the romantic idealists of the 1840s and the nihilistic revolutionaries of the 1860s. In Dostoevsky's novel (published in 1871–72), the father – in one case biological, in the other intellectual – is Stepan Trofimovich Verkhovenski. We will look at his fall from grace and his resurrection in the next section.

The famous Nechaev affair inspired the second theme: revolutionary conspiracy. In 1869, the body of a student named Ivanov was found in a pond in Moscow. He was a former member of the secret revolutionary society, "The People's Justice." Sergei Nechaev, the leader of this society and a disciple and friend of the anarchist Bakunin, killed Ivanov because he had threatened to expose them to the authorities. Nechaev fled abroad, but was arrested and tried upon his return. The whole affair shocked Russia, and Dostoevsky followed it with great interest.

After the Nechaev affair, the term "nihilist" became widely used to describe the views of persons like Bazarov – the protagonist of Turgenev's novel. This character idolized Diderot and La Mattrie and emulated their tendency to regard nature as a machine or factory. Turgenev himself appeared to endorse similar views: "Is there God? I don't know. But I do know the law of causality. Twice two is four."[2]

Chernyshevsky argued in *What Is to Be Done?* that Turgenev's Bazarov is an untenable caricature of the new generation of revolutionaries. He viewed Turgenev's work as typifying the reaction of the last generation of the Romantics who, hiding behind the tradition of Western liberalism, failed to evolve a concrete political program, whether of reform or of revolution, for their country. Led by Chernyshevsky, the radicals of the 1860s rejected sentimental romanticism for hard-headed realism, spurned philosophical idealism for materialism, and replaced metaphysics with science; they renounced empty chatter and demanded action.

2   Quoted from Mochulsky, *op. cit.*, 329.

While Dostoevsky addressed some of the emerging problems and the ideological views behind the new revolutionary movement in *Notes from the Underground*, he soon realized that his treatment of this looming specter of nihilism had been too superficial. *Crime and Punishment* emphasized the timeless truth that isolated, desperate, and ideologically confused young men were capable even of mindless murder in order "to correct and direct nature" (Pt. I, Ch. 6, 54). The Nechaev affair helped Dostoevsky realize that the situation in Russia was far more alarming than had been generally assumed; what was prepared in the name of the revolution was terror of apocalyptic proportions. Unlike Turgenev's Bazarov, who was merely swept up by the modernist vision of the man-machine, Dostoevsky saw that Nechaev and the other young revolutionaries were spiritually diseased; their souls were literally possessed. Peter Stepanovich Verkhovenski, the only biological son of a typical intellectual liberal of the previous generation, plays the role of Nechaev. While his father's follies were unintentional, the arrogant and shameless Peter is fully aware of the evil animating his own actions.

The third theme, the Prince of Darkness himself, was the last to be conceived but the first in order of importance. Nikolai Vsevolodovich Stavrogin, a pupil of Stepan and a friend of Peter, is a mysterious man of seemingly supernatural qualities. To Peter he is what Napoleon is to Raskolnikov. A man of extraordinary power and fearlessness, Stavrogin attracts everyone but remains detached from all. Yet inside this superman is really a human cripple, a man possessed by demonic evil, incapable of conscience, self-sacrifice, or love. Unable to deal with his interior emptiness, the mysterious Stavrogin, one of the greatest villains of literature, commits suicide. We will take a closer look at Stavrogin and his demonic evil in the fourth section.

There are two main reasons to consider *The Possessed* and its counter-Trinity (Stepan, Stavrogin, Peter) in the context of our inquiry. The first deals with the deepening of Dostoevsky's understanding of evil, the second with the sharpening of his metaphysical comprehension of reality. Dostoevsky examines why there is so much evil in the world and why it is so difficult for human beings to feel that they belong here, that this is their home. He looks at the facts – the Nechaev affair being one of them – as the symptoms of the hidden ills of society and tries to decode them. In its increasing turning away from religion, modernity gradually narrows the problem of evil to the problem of *moral* evil; its religious and metaphysical aspects have either disappeared or have been relegated to an irrelevant background. According to Dostoevsky's decoding of the facts, the problem of evil (and of good, as well) cannot be restricted to purely anthropological and moral realms. As L.A. Zander explains,

> The significant fact is that although human standards are of central and fundamental importance for Dostoevsky, he consciously and consistently relinquishes them as soon as good or evil reach the highest degree of intensity in the human heart. When this happens, the limits of personality cease, for him, to be clear and definite: Man, as it were, is no longer merely himself, but is merged into something else, attaining a different kind of being. He describes this process of de-humanization in a particularly vivid and many-sided way with regard to evil. In a whole series of characters Dostoevsky shows how the evil principle, increasing in strength, expresses itself first by automatism, then by becoming a man's "double," and finally by completely splitting his personality so that the unity of the human self is finally lost. Thus evil proves to be *human* when it is only of medium degree of intensity, when it still struggles with the good and has not yet finally conquered. As soon as it becomes the dominant force it immediately dissolves the human personality, destroys its uniqueness and appears to man as something formless and featureless [as, in Stavrogin's words], "rational and ironical, present in different persons and different characters but always one and the same."[3]

We have already noticed this "increase in strength" of evil by comparing *Notes from the Underground* and *Crime and Punishment*. The underground man is afraid of losing his freedom and being turned into a sub-human automaton. With Raskolnikov, the evil principle has intensified: He behaves like a man of

3   L.A. Zander, *Dostoevsky*, 13.

double standards, and the schism dominates his being. Fortunately, he does not step over the edge that separates the human from the diabolical. After a series of dialogical confrontations, *Crime and Punishment* ends with a promise of the reintegration of Raskolnikov's emotional and intellectual components into one personality. What would happen had he failed? *The Possessed* gives the answer. The dehumanization continues to such a degree that human beings are transformed into something else. Into what? Into demons, answers Dostoevsky. In fact, "Demons" is the precise meaning of *Besy*, the Russian title of this novel.

Who are these demons with whom Dostoevsky is concerned?

We both can and cannot understand who they are, and this is typical of his style of writing and of his conception of realism. Let us clarify this by briefly comparing Dostoevsky with Turgenev. In *Fathers and Sons*, the main character Bazarov is the representative of the younger generation: He personifies the chief characteristics of that group. Stavrogin is also a representative of that generation, but that means something else for Dostoevsky. Stavrogin symbolizes certain phenomena, types, and forces expressed in his character. Yet in Dostoevsky, unlike Turgenev, their essence remains half-concealed and mysterious. Dostoevsky insists that this is not a game he plays with language. In his view, words – and thoughts – are approximations of the truth and allusions to it, but they cannot capture the truth itself. It is in the very nature of human language (and thought) that, although being a way toward revealing the truth, it is at the same time inadequate to it. As Yuri Lotman puts it, "The truth glimmers dimly" through our words, but the words are incapable of naming the truth precisely.[4]

---

4   Yuri Lotman, *Universe of the Mind: A Semiotic Theory of Culture*, 108. Lotman contrasts Dostoevsky's view with that of Tolstoy, for whom the words are always true or false, and for whom truth and falsehood are manifest: "Truth is the natural order of Nature. Life purged of words (and social symbolics), life in its essential nature is truth." For Dostoevsky, however, "the words do not name things and ideas but as it were allude to them, at the same time letting it be understood that things cannot be precisely named" (107). For further discussion of this contrast, see George Steiner, *Tolstoy or Dostoevsky: An Essay in the Old Criticism*, especially pages 258, 261, and 345.

Dostoevsky does not have in mind factual and trivial truths, but the ultimate nature of reality, what philosophers call metaphysical truths. In most cases there is nothing problematic about facts, and we can establish what they are. The important thing is that the facts we observe are the symptoms of different layers of reality. Stavrogin's face, we are told several times in the course of the novel, is "like a mask."[5] Decoding what is behind that surface mask, penetrating to the bottom layers of reality is Dostoevsky's central preoccupation. In Vyacheslav Ivanov's apt phrase, the art of Dostoevsky leads "from the real to the more real."[6]

How can we progress "from the real to the more real"? We can understand what determines the surface behavior of people, which can be easily observed. To bring us under the surface and toward "the more real," Dostoevsky uses a particular technique of writing and a specific content. With regard to his technique of writing, Lotman points out how Dostoevsky relies on the law of "least probability."[7] When acquainted with real or fictional characters, we create expectations as to what is most likely to happen in the next step in the plot based on our previous experience. Dostoevsky intentionally violates our expectations: In *The Possessed*, the episodes follow each other in the order of least probability.

To clarify this further, let us make a comparison with a detective novel. The sequence of events in a detective novel and the connections between its protagonists are at first intentionally portrayed as obscured, even mysterious, though a later revelation of secret crimes will show how non-accidental they are. Once we learn certain hidden facts, everything appears logical and meaningful. In *The Possessed*, no discovery of facts connects the disconnected; the identity of the previously hidden criminal is not revealed. The causal laws and the cliché "twice two is four" are not taken for granted. The world is not a well-structured place. Dostoevsky intentionally disrupts our expectations at the level of everyday

---

5   *The Possessed*, trans. Constance Garnett. All subsequent references to this work will be given in the text, immediately after the quotation. For the full references of the translation used, see Part I of the Bibliography.

6   Vyacheslav Ivanov, *Freedom and Tragic Life: A Study in Dostoevsky*, 49.

7   Lotman, *op. cit.,* 166.

events so that we can focus on the connections that are not factual, that are hidden under the surface. He lets us know everything there is to know on the factual level. What we do not know, and what Dostoevsky wants us to wonder about, are the eschatological questions, those "accursed questions" about the ultimate meaning of life and death. At this level, Dostoevsky does not follow the law of least probability, but on the contrary tries to reveal the most probable though hidden connections between human aspirations and actions.

This brings us to the second consideration: How does Dostoevsky lead the reader to progress "from the real to the more real" with regard to the content of his novel? He focuses on our deepest fears and highest hopes, for these ultimately mold our choices and guide our behavior. Perhaps the most fundamental question of the entire novel is whether such fears and hopes are justified by reality, or whether they are merely the projections of the inner self. This question points to one of the reasons why this extraordinary novel is not sufficiently appreciated – it is not only highly complex but also excessively demanding. We are not even clear about what our deepest fears and highest hopes are, yet Dostoevsky wants us to address the troubling question of their foundation in reality.

What are our deepest fears? It is difficult to give a precise list, or an exact hierarchy of them, but human beings have always been troubled by the following fears: of pain, of darkness, of eternal nothingness, and of death. In children, the most pronounced fear may be that of abandonment, in mature adults the fear of sterility, in the old age the fear of decay. Our whole lives seem to consist in trying to building something – ourselves and the world around us – yet all of this so easily collapses and evaporates. Life presupposes some order, but what if that order is an illusion? What if there is no sequence to life? What if everything ends in an eternal nothingness?

As if that is not enough, Dostoevsky wants to confront our fears from a different perspective as well – it is not just *what* but *whom* we fear the most? Some kind of superhuman – possibly demonic – power? Other human beings? Ourselves?

Whom, then, can we trust?

Our highest hopes are correspondingly difficult to pin down. As it is impossible to be a human being without having fears, we cannot live without nourishing hopes. There are collective utopias, dreams of a Paradise, a Golden Age, a New Jerusalem, the Kingdom of God on earth, of the eschatological end of time. Claude Lorrain's painting "Landscape with Acis and Galatea," which Dostoevsky saw several times in Dresden and which Stavrogin mentions in his confession, portrays one such vision of a Golden Age. The painting shows a magnificent coastal landscape with the gently towering mountains and the tranquil immensity of the sea. The whole painting is suffused with the calm golden light of the sun, and – in the sharpest possible contrast with Dostoevsky's novel – everything gives the impression of order, measured restraint, beauty, and serenity. It is a dream landscape for the blissful mythical pair, but one that could be imagined only as long as human beings – or demons – do not disturb the solemn magnificence of Mother Nature.

Claude Lorrain's painting, with its depiction of Acis and Galatea, is inspired by Ovid's *Metamorphoses*. As its name indicates, *Metamorphoses* deals with transformations of situations and reversals of fortune. Triumph may easily turn into despair, bliss into misery, life into death. Our highest hopes concern not only attaining happiness, but also sustaining it. Transcending death has been a perpetual human preoccupation: How can that be accomplished?

There are two radical options, and both play a significant role in Dostoevsky's *Possessed*. One is positive, the other negative. According to the first, immortality can be attained by some kind of perfection, or by self-deification. Stepan, Peter, and Stavrogin are all tempted by this dream of making themselves "larger than life." Dostoevsky wants to expose the danger of this attitude. Just as an individual lamp cannot be identified with light itself but is only a temporary vehicle of light, no individual life can be identified with life. Not only can I never become a god, but the stronger my desire for self-deification, the greater is my self-deception and, at the end, my despair. "Ever" then comes close to "never," "everything" to "nothing." If I cannot attain perfection and eternal life, I may reverse my attitude and strive toward eternal nothingness. If I cannot live "for ever," let everything collapse with me into "never." The search for a future eternal light transforms into a descent to the eternal darkness of the past, a return to the primordial womb-tomb. This is the metamorphosis of Stepan Verkhovenski into Peter and Stavrogin.

By a strange dialectic, the highest hopes need not be far removed from the greatest fears. As Dostoevsky knew, one moment you can be standing in front of the firing squad, and in the next your life is given back to you. What appears as the most opposed may turn out to be intimately connected. This is the point of Dostoevsky's frequent references to the Apocalypse, the most prophetic book of the New Testament. The literal meaning of the Greek word *apokalypsis* is that of development, uncovering, disclosure, discovery, and revelation (the last book of the New Testament is also called the Book of Revelation). Apocalypse is the disclosure of the hidden future, the end of time. (Stavrogin reminds Kirillov: "In the Apocalypse, the angel promises that there'll be no more time," to which Kirillov adds: "Time is not a thing, it's an idea. It will vanish from the mind" [Pt. II, Ch. 1, sec. v, 224].) The negative meaning usually associated with the word apocalypse – a catastrophic conclusion – comes from the strange dialectic of which Dostoevsky is deeply aware: The apocalypse is the unfolding and revelation that ends in the destruction of what it has unfolded and revealed.

The message of *The Possessed* is that when our hopes are unrealistic and ill-founded, they lead to their own opposite, to despair. The ambiguous hopes of the generation of 1840s were radicalized by their sons and transposed to a disaster of apocalyptic proportions. While Dostoevsky was planning *The Possessed*, he did not envision even a trace of optimism in its outcome. The final version of the novel, however, shows that the fate of Stepan Verkhovensky keeps a small window of hope open. May there, after all, be light at the heart of darkness?

Stepan Trofimovich Verkhovenski

Imagine Don Quixote, but with children and pupils; that is a good initial characterization of Stepan Trofimovich Verkhovenski. This good-natured man is a homeless wonderer, living in the clouds of his own visions and ideals. Although in his fifties, he leaves the impression of a child, incapable or unwilling to adjust to the harsh reality of the world. Stepan is a professor, but he does not teach anywhere. He views himself as an important author, yet he has written only a few obscure pieces. Stepan preaches happiness for all mankind, yet gambles away his serf Fedka at cards. He claims to be a true Russian, but expresses himself in French. Stepan is seemingly one of the most respected people in town, yet everyone mocks him. He is a free man, yet completely dependent on Mrs. Stavrogin. In his tormented and long-lasting attraction for her (over two decades), he writes her a letter or two a day, although they live in the same household. The letters are carefully read, enumerated and catalogued by Mrs. Stavrogin, but they are never discussed. Stepan's life is like a soap bubble, some kind of unreal dream from which someone will violently wake him. His children will take that task on themselves.

When we meet him at the beginning of *The Possessed*, Stepan does not suspect a reversal of his fate. His worst fear is that of prosecution. As a representative of the 1840s generation, as a liberal idealist and humanist who imagines himself an "old fighter for social justice" (Pt. I, Ch. 1, sec. v, 21), he believes he is carefully observed by the government. This fear, so typical of many provincial intellectuals, amounts to nothing but a vain hope that he is more important than he actually is. Stepan's deeper fear is his recurring dream of being devoured by the beast he himself has taken a hand in creating. This is the point we need to explain in more detail.

Dostoevsky clearly grasps that we cannot, so to say, create a map of reality without having an object of devotion. We need someone or something on our map of reality that we can consider sacred. We need someone or something higher than our own egos, an idol toward whom we can direct our hopes and toward whom we can turn in the moment of crisis. Stepan (whose last name derives from the Russian word *verkhovenstvo*, meaning "pre-eminence," "supremacy," "sovereignty") expresses a related idea: "The whole life of human existence is that man should worship something immeasurably great. . . . The immeasurable and infinite are just as necessary to man as is the tiny planet on which he lives" (Pt. III, Ch. 7, sec. iii, 679–80).[8]

8   Nicolai Hartmann (*Ästhetik*, Ch. 31, sec. b) formulates a similar principle: "The fundamental law . . . is this: Man has always been attracted to great

Stepan's life is centered on defending the principle of worshiping "something immeasurably great." As a private tutor of the young and fatherless Stavrogin, Stepan tries to instill the highest ideals into his mind and heart. Sometimes he wakes up the child in the night, "pours out his wounded sensibilities," and the two of them sob together. Stepan manages to "touch the deepest-seated chords in the boy's heart, causing the first, still undefined, sensation of the undying, sacred longing that a superior soul, having once tested, will never exchange for vulgar satisfaction" (Pt. I, Ch. 2, sec. i, 41–42).

What exactly does Stepan mean by "something immeasurably great"? This is the point where he becomes elusive and vague, where his limitations become clearer to us. He lives by a "higher thought," which he often understands as the ideal of eternal beauty, and considers himself a poet with the presentiment of world harmony. During the literary matinee Stepan defends his idea of beauty:

> [T]o me, Shakespeare and Raphael are of greater value than the emancipation of the serfs, than nationalism, than socialism, than the younger generation, than chemistry – and perhaps even than mankind itself! And it is this way because they represent the very highest human achievement, an achievement of beauty without which I wouldn't be willing to go on living (Pt. III, Ch. 1, sec. iv, 504).

When Stepan attempts to give a lesson to the nihilists that mankind "could subsist without science and even without bread," but not "without beauty," the audience loses all restraints and scandal erupts. His listeners believe that he had pushed the argument too far, and in the wrong direction. Yes, the older generation has "different aesthetics" than its children – they appreciate boots more than Shakespeare, petroleum more than Raphael – but these "different aesthetics" are the effect rather than the cause of their disagreements.

Dostoevsky traces the general ideal of Stepan's generation (which includes Belinsky and Granovsky, Herzen and Turgenev) back to

---

and superior. All his life he can live with a quiet longing for the great and superior and where and when he finds it, his heart will fly toward it."

"the same old Rousseau and the dream of changing the world on the basis of reason and experience (positivism)."[9] Dostoevsky identifies the problem with this orientation: "A moral basis for society that is derived from positivism not only fails to yield results, but it cannot even define itself, and its gets lost in aspirations and ideals."[10] He ascribes this fault to Stepan: He cannot really say what the highest ideal is, and the problem can indeed be traced all the way back to Rousseau.[11]

Following Rousseau, Stepan's answer may be that the highest ideals concern human freedom and happiness for all. Until Rousseau, the idea of freedom was always understood negatively, as the absence of obstacles to our chosen course of thought and action. With Rousseau, and later with the Romantics, comes the idea of freedom in the positive sense, the idea of realizing our innermost nature. Freedom in the positive sense then becomes synonymous with self-expression and self-creation. In the first half of the twentieth century, existentialists develop a similar theme in terms of the search for authenticity.

Dostoevsky does not think that either Rousseau or Stepan could tell us what our innermost nature is, nor how we should re-create humanity. As he remarks in the already quoted letter to Strakhov, "They desire the happiness of mankind, but they get no further than Rousseau's efforts to define the word *happiness*; that is, they get no further than an abstract idea not even justified by experience."

Re-creation of humanity means for Dostoevsky turning against God: The Romantics try to "correct and direct nature" not according to the image of God but according to the image of Man. Is it

9   Letter to Strakhov of May 18, 1871.
10   *Ibid.*
11   Since Rousseau was born in Geneva, in *The Adolescent* Dostoevsky criticizes the same view under the name of "Geneva ideas." As his character Versilov expresses it, "By Geneva ideas, I mean virtue without Christ, which is the contemporary concept or, we may even say, the idea underlying today's civilization" (Pt. II, Ch. 4, 212). In a different context, Dostoevsky argues that Rousseau's philosophy also stands behind Tolstoy's world-view; for further discussion, see George Steiner, *op. cit*, 326.

possible to transform the world into a realization of the Christian ideal without believing in Christ? Can there be a brotherhood of human beings without a common father?

Even more than in the novel itself, in his correspondence Dostoevsky turns against the generation of the 1840s. Their detachment from their own soil, culture, and people sometimes appears to Dostoevsky as even more problematic than open nihilism of their sons: "Our secret villains may at least possess a certain repulsive odor, but among the fathers one finds only agnosticism and indifference, and that is even worse."[12]

Whether or not Dostoevsky is right – and we will return to this issue in the following sections – he has Stepan realize his share of responsibility and open his way back to the ordinary people and their native religion. After a series of disappointments, culminating with the scandal at the literary matinee, Stepan runs away from his adopted home. Instead of Don Quixote's old mare Rocinante, Stepan rides on a peasant cart. Instead of Sancho Panza, Stepan journeys with a peasant and his wife. He does not know where he is going or why, but – like the knight of La Mancha – at the end he is granted a gift of clear insight and peaceful death.[13]

Before his "last wandering," Stepan's attitude toward religion is well known among his friends. He does not shy from admitting that, in the spirit of his generation, he is "not a Christian" but rather a pagan, "like the great Goethe or the ancient Greeks" (Pt. I, Ch. 1, sec. ix, 39). Since the journey represents Stepan's turn toward the native soil and the religion of its people, Dostoevsky relies on multiple Christian symbols in his presentation of Stepan's last days. His pilgrimage is a journey of salvation, which takes him to the village of Ustevo (*uste* means "mouth" in Russian), the place where his final judgment will be pronounced. Stepan begins his pilgrimage in rain and comes to a lake, and both rain and lake – water in general – are symbols of purification and regeneration. He is on his way to the town of Spasov (*spas* means "the Savior" in Russian), and he

---

12   Quoted from Geir Kjetsaa, *Fyodor Dostoyevsky: A Writer's Life*, 258.

13   For further comparison of Stepan with Don Quixote, see Steiner, *op. cit.*, 307; René Girard, *Deceit, Desire and the Novel*, 291; and Leonid Grossman, *Dostoevsky: A Biography*, 476.

wants to reach it by crossing the lake. In Ustevo, Stepan meets an ex-nurse who now lives by selling copies of the New Testament. Her name is Sophia (Ulitin), a symbol of the Divine Wisdom. In her presence Stepan "forgives all his enemies" and, like the Elder Zosima in *The Brothers Karamazov*, accepts that "we're all guilty toward one another, all of us" (Pt. III, Ch. 7, sec. ii, 661). He is ready to spend the rest of his life selling the holy book with Mrs. Ulitin, but a merciful death arrives.

A reading of the Sermon on the Mount stirs Stepan to acknowledge that all his life has been a lie: "I never spoke for the sake of truth, only for my own sake, and although I always knew it, I only really see it now. . . . The main trouble is that I believe myself even while I'm lying. The most difficult thing in life is to live without lying and – and not to believe in one's own lies" (Pt. III, Ch. 7, sec. ii, 668).

On his deathbed Stepan asks that the passage in Luke about the Gadarene swine be read to him, the passage which Dostoevsky uses as the epigraph to the novel. In this tale Stepan recognizes for the first time that all forms of civil life are riddled with demonic forces and also that his own "civil role" is implicated in the demonic possession that has overtaken Russia:

> It's *us*, us and the others – my son Peter and those around him; and we'll hurl ourselves from the cliff into the sea and I'll be the first perhaps, and all of us, mad and raving, will drown and it will serve us right because that's all we're fit for. But the sick man will recover and will sit at the feet of Jesus and they will look at him in surprise (Pt. III, Ch. 7, sec. ii, 671).

Stepan's last wondering has cleared his mind and heart of many of the previous self-delusions. Instead of his fear of prosecution, there is now hope; instead of an abstract idea of eternal beauty, a new understanding of the central significance of love:

> My immortality is necessary if only because God would not wish to do anything unjust and put out the flame of love once it was kindled in my heart. And what is more precious than love? Love is higher than existence – love is the crown

of existence, so how can existence not be subordinate to love? (Pt. III, Ch. 7, sec. iii, 678–79).

Stepan's last hope is that the younger generation will learn what he now clearly sees: "Every man, whoever he may be, needs to bow before the fact that the Great Idea exists. Even the most stupid man needs something great. Peter – oh, how much I want to see them all again! They don't know that the eternal Great Idea dwells in them too!" (Pt. III, Ch. 7, sec. iii, 680).

Does "the eternal Great Idea" really dwell in Peter and his friends? If it does, it must be so distorted that we are forced to reiterate Dostoevsky's main concern with the generation of the 1840s: What exactly is their "eternal Great Idea"?

Peter Stepanovich Verkhovenski

Had he been familiar with it, Stepan would have shown much admiration for Claude Lorrain's "Landscape with Acis and Galatea." It would have fit perfectly into his vision of the "eternal Great Idea." The landscape is sublime, with every element of the painting beautifully balanced. The first impression of the painting is that of the harmonious sequence of forms, which creates a sense of unity within variety. The eye travels effortlessly from one portion of the canvas to another. The handling of space is masterful. As in Raphael's majestic "Sistine Madonna" (Stepan's favorite painting), air serves as the unifying element. The painter appears to have captured the moment of eternity. Time has stopped; we have come to the end of time. By imperceptible modulations the eye is guided toward the radiant void of the painting: the horizon, the threshold of the sky, and the invisible source of light. The horizon recedes even beyond the limit of the canvas, beyond the given reality, toward the transcendent. In the pursuit of the source of light, the artist leads us to the borderland of dream and reality; he takes us over the edge of the tangible and into the field of the imaginary. The landscape is realistic enough to be believable, yet imaginary enough to invite us to break away toward its unexplored realm. The visual experience brings us to pure contemplation.[14]

14 My presentation of Claude Lorrain's painting relies on Sabina Colté, *Toward Perfect Harmony*, 57–58.

The young nihilists, Turgenev's Bazarov and Stepan's son Peter, would not appreciate this painting. It is too archaic for Bazarov. The painting does not reveal even a trace of the modern, scientifically minded curiosity. Such curiosity leads painters from Leonardo to Rembrandt to penetrate into the anatomical mysteries of their objects of examination.

Peter would object to the quiet adoration of nature. The painting reveals no attempt to "correct and direct nature." On the contrary, the artist creates the impression that we can trust nature and let her guide us in our pursuit of the perfect world. And yet, in 1657, when Lorrain painted the work, Rome (where he then lived) was hit hard with the plague that forced most of its citizens to flee. Neither can we trust nature, nor those who glorify it, Peter would conclude.

Peter is annoyed by a similar kind of "hypocrisy" in his father: To Stepan, life is a playground for various kinds of games and theatrical performances. We are told on the first pages of the novel that Stepan has a "civic role" to play, that Mrs. Stavrogin has dressed him in a special kind of "costume" in which he would spend the rest of his life, and that he likes playing cards, usually for "small" stakes. He always loses on cards, and that is how he lost his former serf Fedka and the land his son Peter inherited from his deceased mother.

Stepan is by no means the only idle character who spends his life playing. Mrs. von Lembke, the wife of the new governor of the province, tries to "establish herself" and organizes a major gala with literary festivities and dance. Her husband's hobby is to make miniature models of a railroad station, a theatre, and a church. Captain Lebiadkin's pastime is writing poems which reveal scant literary value. His crippled sister, secretly married to Stavrogin, spends her lonely days putting a powder on her face and foreseeing the future by looking at cards. Perhaps the most impressive of them all, Lyamshin, a post-office clerk, is often invited to parties to "give imitations of a pig, a thunder storm, a confinement, the first cry of the baby, etc., etc." (Pt. I, Ch. 1, sec. ix, 36; translation modified).

Some of the games are less than appropriate. The ex-convict Fedka steals an icon from the church and puts a mouse in its place. Some other rascals secretly place pornographic pictures in the copies of the New Testament that Sophia Ulitin goes around selling. Most of the protagonists are bored and they need to come up with ways of entertaining themselves. The younger generation is so desperate for amusement that some of them go to see the body of the nineteen-year old who hanged himself. A few of them even try the wine that is left in the room next to the body of the unfortunate boy. Peter is among them.

Peter is an idle character, who admits that, like his father, he has "adopted a certain role." Stavrogin introduces Peter to his mother as "a universal peacemaker" who "cannot lie" (Pt. I, Ch. 5, sec. vii, 186), but nothing could be further from the truth. Peter seems to be everywhere, not as a peacemaker but to stir unrest and trouble. He seems to know everything, and uses this knowledge to mock or deceive people. Besides playing a buffoon and a gossip, Peter involves himself with a revolutionary gang. He plays with fire and his games are power games of violence and destruction. The stakes are much higher than those in the pretentious games of his father.

Peter was born in an unhappy marriage that did not last very long, and then there was also the premature death of his mother. When she dies, the parents have already been separated for three years, and the five-year-old Peter is then packed off to some distant relative in a far-away province. During the next twenty years, the father and the son see each other only once. At the time of the events chronicled in the novel, they are unhappily united again.

Peter has never loved anyone. He even appears incapable of loving, and from his actions we conclude that he firmly subscribes to the biblical phrase, "The world lieth in evil" (I John V, 19). Peter is a homeless wonderer, an exile with no roots in the province or in the capital, in Russia or in the West, where he also spends a considerable amount of time. We are told that he attended the famous 1867 congress of the revolutionaries in Geneva. Since Dostoevsky happened to live in Geneva at that time, out of curiosity he visited this "Congress of Peace," as it was officially called. Among the leaders of socialism and world revolution, Bakunin was the ring master and his anarchist pledges left an unforgettable – although quite diverse – impression on everyone present. This master-manipulator got into the heads of the young revolutionaries by encouraging violent nihilism: "Let us put our trust in the eternal spirit which destroys and annihilates only because it is the unsearchable and eternally creative source of all life. The passion for destruction is also a creative passion."[15]

Besides Bukunin, Peter idolizes Machiavelli and Robespierre. He revolts against the idle talks and empty ideals of his father's privileged generation. With all of its past idols, that world needs to be burned and destroyed, so that a new world order can emerge with a new man in it.

Does Dostoevsky have any right to criticize the members of the old idealistic and romantic generations for the destructive fire of the new revolutionaries and nihilists? He does insofar as there is continuity between the socialist aspirations of the older generation and the revolutionary zeal of the younger. Recall again Isaiah Berlin's "three-legged stool" which supports the central tradition of Western political thought. The first leg is the assumption that to all genuine questions there can be only one correct answer. The second is that it must be possible to establish a method by which correct answers can be found. The third and the most important leg of this approach is that these answers will build a single, interconnected whole. The optimistic expectation related to this third leg is that which, according to Dostoevsky, betrays a bridge between the two generations, which share the hope of discovering the foundation of an age-old dream in the final solution to all human ills. The fathers instilled in their children the expectation that rational methods and the rejection of the prejudices of the past (religion included) will lead to the final solution. In the words of Berlin,

> It can be achieved; by revolution or peaceful means it will surely come; and then all, or the vast majority, of men will be virtuous and happy, wise and good and free; if such a position can be attained, and once attained will last forever, what sane man could wish to return to the miseries of man's wandering in the desert? If this is possible, then surely no price is too heavy to pay for it; no amount of

15 Quoted from J.W. Burrow, *The Crisis of Reason: European Thought, 1848–1914*, 3.

cruelty, repression, coercion will be too high, if this, and
this alone, is the price for the ultimate salvation of all men.[16]

Stepan and his generation of idealists are not sure whether the
final solution should be attempted by peaceful or revolutionary means. The true representative of this generation, Alexander
Herzen, famously stated that, "Human history has no libretto: the
actors must improvise their parts."[17] While the secular humanism remains paralyzed by its own indecisiveness, Peter, Chernyshevsky, and the revolutionaries of the 1860s resolve the issue
decisively: Revolution is the way! One of the main themes in *The
Possessed* is to show how the pretentious and inactive posturing
of the old generation is replaced by the intolerant, narrow-minded
fanaticism ready to overstep all established boundaries and destroy
all the fruits of civilization. "Only the indispensable is indispensable," claims Peter, "that will be the motto of our globe from now
on" (Pt. II, Ch. 8, sec. ii, 399). Down with culture! Down with the
lies of morality and religion! The boundaries imposed by society
are man-made, conventional, and arbitrary. There is no such thing
as conscience and honor. Karmazinov helps Peter understand that
the essence of the revolutionary zeal lies in the negation of honor,
and Peter enthusiastically embraces this idea.

Stepan believes that human beings have always been attracted to
what is great and superior. While his ideal is the heavenly Madonna,
Peter shows us that Stepan has forgotten the other, no less important side of humanity: the adoration of Sodom. If asked to postulate
the law of human existence, the idea with which his father is preoccupied, Peter would say that the law is quite different from the
one Stepan advocates: Human beings have always been attracted to
what is low and inferior. Stepan dreams of personal immortality and
postulates that, "if God exists, then I, too, am immortal!" (Pt. III,
Ch. 7, sec. iii, 679). Peter has no such pretension: Forget the illusions that Russians are a God-fearing people – "the Russian God
has already capitulated to cheap liquor" (Pt. II, Ch. 8, 401). There
is nothing immortal or sacred, nothing but the nothingness itself.

16 Isaiah Berlin, *The Crooked Timber of Humanity*, 47.
17 Herzen's words are quoted by Berlin, *op. cit.*, 201.

Peter and the revolutionaries overlook how easy it is to slip from using violence and destruction as a means to violence and destruction becoming a goal. Nechaev has famously written: "Our business is terrible, complete, universal, and merciless destruction."[18] Peter echoes these words in *The Possessed*: "We can cause such a mess that anything will go flying to hell" (Pt. II, Ch. 8, 398).

The burning fire, the killing fields, the gospel of destruction – it is not just that we got used to them, but rather that we are addicted to them. Yearning for immortality, searching for paradise, striving toward the absolute, the world falls in love with bloodshed, violence, and destruction. As if we were possessed by the forces of malice, hatred, and annihilation, Dostoevsky would say. The demons have entered us, and like the biblical herd of swine, we are rushing toward the cliff, toward our annihilation.

Where have these demons come from? How have we become the prisoners of false idols? Is there enough wisdom left in us to avoid the cliff?

Nikolai Vsevolodovich Stavrogin

Is Peter a monster? Is he one of the demons in the title of the book?

Dostoevsky's answer seems to be both affirmative and negative. Compared to the underground man and Raskolnikov, Peter and his gang are the real demons. Contrasted with the true Prince of Darkness, Stavrogin, they do not look so evil.

Although he remains passive, the underground man defends freedom as the ultimate criterion of humanity. Raskolnikov takes that freedom further and understands it as freedom of action, as freedom to step over the boundaries imposed by society. Even more than *Crime and Punishment*, *The Possessed* is a novel of action and violation of all possible boundaries. In his revolutionary zeal, Peter turns against God and humanity and anticipates some of the ideas later developed by Ivan Karamazov and expressed by his Grand Inquisitor. Revolution is the ultimate defiance of the world as it is; it is the destruction of the old so that the new can arise on the ashes of the unjust past. The ultimate end of destruction, however,

18   *Ibid.*, 421.

is not the destruction of others but the destruction of oneself. Peter and his revolutionaries are not willing to go that far. Stavrogin is.

Had he been able to witness all the revolutionary violence of the twentieth century, Dostoevsky would perhaps reconsider his judgment and admit that Peter and similar revolutionaries stand at the edge of the monstrous and demonic. In one of his letters Dostoevsky seems to identify himself more with the generation of the 1860s than with the generation of their fathers; under different circumstances he himself might have become a Nechaev. Dostoevsky is referring to the progressive Petrashevsky circle to which he belonged in the second half of the 1840s; as one of the members of this circle, he is arrested and sentenced to the maximum security prison in Omsk, Siberia. Even there, living with cold-blooded murderers, Dostoevsky does not imagine them demons.

Even Dostoevsky's later experience of Bakunin and other hot-headed anarchists does not lead him to accuse them of being diabolical. His judgment somewhat anticipates Hannah Arendt's perception of Adolf Eichmann. Arendt uses the famous phrase "banality of evil"; Dostoevsky may have preferred "the poverty of evil." In a letter to his niece, written after the "Congress for Peace," he reports his astonishment by the inner poverty of the anarchists and nihilists he met there. They openly preach atheism and the abolishment of large governments and private property. "But mainly – fire and the sword, and after that, as everything will be destroyed, then, in their opinion, there will also be peace."[19]

The anarchists and nihilists like Peter are not monsters and demons, but confused youngsters seduced by false idols. Of course, the degree of seduction can be very high, and Peter represents a good illustration of it. Stepan sentimentally recalls how, afraid as a little boy that he may die during the night, Peter used to cross his pillow before going to sleep. Peter has changed much since that time. While Stepan has a clear line dividing the worst fear and the highest hope, in Peter the two merge together. It is hard to resist the impression that, for Peter, life itself is the enemy, that the world's

19 Letter to Sofya Alexandrovna, September 29, 1867.

existence is the cause of his greatest anxiety. How else could he perceive chaos as peace and destruction as his goal?

While the Nechaev affair motivates Dostoevsky to start working on *The Possessed*, his correspondence reveals that he relegates Peter to a secondary position because Stavrogin imposes himself as the central character. Why Stavrogin rather than Peter?

Unlike Peter, Stavrogin is endowed with superhuman qualities. He is "one of those people who do not know what fear is," who "even in the moments of unbounded hatred retains complete control over himself" (Pt. I, Ch. 5, sec. viii, 194). Stavrogin kills a man in a duel and shoots another, crippling him. He defies social norms and conventions without fear or remorse. Stavrogin is an exemplar of an "ungovernable wildness" who behaves any way he pleases. In a spur of the moment Stavrogin grabs hold of Gaganov's nose, kisses Liputin's wife at her party in the presence of her husband, and "sinks his teeth" into the governor's ear. He displays an absolute autonomy of ungovernable self-will. Stavrogin is the superman of whom Raskolnikov dreams.

Stavrogin's last name derives from the Greek word *stavros*, meaning "cross," but also involves the Russian word *rog*, meaning "horn." His patronymic, Vsevolodovich, suggests someone who "leads all others." Peter ignores the mixed symbols, which suggests a perversion of the cross and the falsification of the Savior, and sees Stavrogin as the bearer of the cross, as the mythological savior, Ivan the Tzarevich: "I love idols, and you're my idol. . . . You think nothing of sacrificing your own or someone else's life. You're just what I need. I don't know anyone like that except you. You are the leader, you are the sun, and I'm your worm" (Pt. II, Ch. 8, 400).

Is Stavrogin the true pretender to the throne? Is he the Savior everyone seems to be expecting?

When Peter kisses his hand, Stavrogin pushes him away in disgust. Unlike Peter, he is not caught in any revolutionary frenzy and is suspicious of any grand eschatological design – "Nothing ever ends in this world" (Pt. II, Ch. 3, sec. iv, 276).

Peter has invested too much into the idea of Stavrogin as the Savior to give up so easily. He thinks Stavrogin is reluctant only because he does not understand that Peter has destined him for the throne. Stavrogin refuses the crown; his horn would stick out.

If he is a Man-god, he would be the Antichrist. Stavrogin knows that he is not the Savior, that he has to bear a different kind of cross, which will ultimately lead to his suicide.

There is no short supply of suicides in Dostoevsky's works. N.N. Shneidman has counted fourteen suicides in his five major novels, and has compiled a detailed table of successful and unsuccessful attempts of suicide in his works.[20] In *The Possessed*, three suicides are mentioned: one in passing, of an unknown nineteen-year-old boy; Kirillov's suicide, which is of central significance for the novel; and the suicide of Stavrogin. Described with great artistic and philosophical mastery, Kirillov's thoughts on suicide are inspired by Stavrogin and will be discussed first.

From the occasional encounters with this mysterious man, we can conclude how passionately Kirillov loves life and pities people. The night of his suicide, Kirillov tells Peter about the leaf of a tree as a symbol of cosmic beauty and innocence, but Peter cannot understand him. All Peter wants from Kirillov is his signature on the suicide note in which Kirillov accuses himself of Shatov's death, so that nobody suspects that the real murderers are Peter and his revolutionary comrades.

Why would a person so much in love with life commit suicide?

We always find Kirillov in his room, spending nights drinking tea and in contemplation of the meaning of life and death. He is totally absorbed in the idea of the existence of God, and we are led to believe that Stavrogin installed this idea in his mind. "God has tormented me all my life" (Pt. I, Ch. 3, sec. viii, 112), says Kirillov. It is hard to believe that this is not Dostoevsky's autobiographical confession.[21]

"God is indispensable and therefore must exist," intuitively reasons Kirillov, "but I rationally know there can be no God" (Pt. III, Ch. 6, sec. ii, 634). Kirillov's schism consists in this separation of the emotional from the rational. The truth of the heart and the truth of the mind clash violently in his conscience. The key point in Kirillov's decision to commit suicide is that these two sides

---

20   See N.N. Shneidman, *Dostoevsky and Suicide*, 103.

21   Dostoevsky confessed that the question of God's existence has tormented him all his life in the letter to Maikov, March 25, 1870.

do not weigh equally on his scale: There is not enough support for the emotional side, while its rational counterpart has many arguments in its favor. Since the rational side wins, Kirillov finds enough strength of will to live up to what he believes is the most rational thing to do. He takes his freedom to its extreme: The ultimate act of freedom is to transgress the boundary of one's own existence.

Why could Kirillov not support the emotional side of his existential antinomy? Is he not so emotionally attached to life and God that he cannot live without God? He is, but that is the source of the problem. His own emotional commitment is driving him to look for a rational proof of God's existence and, when he finds none, he disregards his own emotions. This point is of crucial significance for the understanding of the entire novel. The possessed are those who are emotionally crippled: They are uprooted and have lost touch with their own native soil, people, and religion. Virtually all of the characters in the novel are homeless in this sense: Kirillov, Stepan, Peter, and Stavrogin even more than others. They have never learned of their own spiritual heritage, or have rejected it to accept Western ideas. Without their native roots, they are left at the mercy of whatever fashionable foreign ideas they happen to accept.

The ancient Book of Job teaches that fear of the Lord is the greatest wisdom, but the modern world turns against such prejudices of the past. In the fashion of the moment, which shapes Kirillov's rational reasoning, we recognize the influence of Bakunin and Feuerbach. Bukunin reasons that, "As long as God exists, man is a slave." Since "man is rational, just, and free," this must imply that man is not a slave and "consequently there is no God."[22] Although Feuerbach's reasoning is more subtle, his conclusions are similar. In Kirillov's interpretation, Feuerbach's doctrine requires a real sacrifice and not just a verbal dismissal of God. Human beings have invented the idea of God, because of their fear of death. The worst fear of man is the fear of death and of the mystery beyond

---

22 Quoted in Geir Kjetsaa, *op. cit.,* 252. My presentation here relies on Kjetsaa's book, especially 250–52, and on J.W. Burrow, *op. cit.,* 6–9, and 28–30.

the grave. To this fear, man has given the name of "God."[23] This fear must be conquered and the idea of God extinguished. For that to be possible, thinks Kirillov, only one path is open: Man must find enough courage to kill himself, so that he does not have to fear death and invent God any longer. Feuerbach expects that once man overcomes God, he will be physically transformed into a different kind of a creature. Kirillov also concludes that, by killing himself, man rids himself of God and transforms himself into a Man-god.

Stavrogin treats Kirillov with more respect than anyone else (with the possible exception of Dasha). He is impressed by Kirillov's reasoning, but is experienced enough to recognize the delusions in Kirillov's intoxicating optimism. Kirillov convinces himself that if human beings are free from pain and fear, they would – like God at the end of creation – perceive and understand that "all is good." Stavrogin lives out what Kirillov only rationalizes about – he is free from pain and fear, but not all is good. His world is the world of numbness and indifference. Stavrogin also knows that no amount of knowledge would make him happy. If anything, it is precisely what he knows that makes him so sick.

Through Stavrogin's character, Dostoevsky masterfully delivers an important message: The shortcoming of rational belief and knowledge does not consist only in ignorance. What we do and do not believe in is also a matter of coincidence, of a given set of circumstances. There is nothing in the nature of rational belief to prevent it from going in one direction or another, in supporting the existence of God, or in denying it. Many would reason that the existence of evil in the world is, if not a proof, then a solid indication that God does not exist. Berdyaev, however, thinks he can support the opposite conclusion: "The existence of evil is a proof of the existence of God. If the world consisted wholly and uniquely of goodness and righteousness there would be no need for God, for the world itself would be god. God is, because evil is."[24] Kant famously tries to show in his *Critique of Pure Reason* that we are not capable

---

23 Clear echoes of this doctrine are still preserved by Freud throughout *Civilization and Its Discontent*.
24 Berdyaev, *Dostoevsky*, 87.

of rationally resolving such antinomies: Does God exist? Or does He not? The resolution is reached through the decisive role of interest (speculative, moral, or practical), not by means of reasoning.

Kirillov is a sensitive and honest man, burning with a self-tormenting love for truth. He wants to determine his will by the sheer power of his reasoning. Unlike Raskolnikov, he does not take other lives to prove his point. Kirillov is willing to lead the way for the rest of humanity by his own example and through his own sacrifice. In the madness of the surrounding world, Kirillov's deluded but honest act is overlooked. His suicide ends up being one more of the numerous parodies in *The Possessed*.[25]

While talking to Kirillov, Stavrogin comes closer to his final self-confrontation, yet this encounter is of a limited value. Like Stepan, Kirillov lives in the clouds of ideas, and Stavrogin needs to be in touch with the real world. Peter dwells in chaos of the real world, which he hopes to intensify to the point of complete negation, but Stavrogin is different from Peter. They represent two different dangers for humanity: possessing no ideals at all, and harboring ideals incongruent with reality. Stavrogin's element is pollution, not chaos. Can Stavrogin find a way to cleanse himself?

Stavrogin's confession to Tikhon reveals the sickness of his soul. The underground man wonders what is better: cheap happiness or exalted suffering? Raskolnikov may have come to recognize that exalted suffering is a better alternative, but Svidrigailov, his Shadow, does not. Stavrogin is an even more potent character than Svidrigailov – more central, more demonic. Svidrigailov has a nightmare in which a five-year girl turns into a tempting prostitute; Stavrogin actually violates a child. The only impressions strong enough to stir his dead soul is the recurring memory of his abuse of the twelve-year-old-girl and the repeated visits of the cousin with the horns and a tail.

Stavrogin represents the worst degradation of the human soul in Dostoevsky's novels. He lacks the capacity to distinguish between good and evil, true and false, beauty and ugliness. This modern

---

25 Albert Camus has a different take on it; see *The Myth of Sisyphus and Other Essays*, 80.

superman, the colossal force that soils everything it touches, collapses under the burden of his own tainted soul. Stavrogin seeks his cross, he wants to be crucified, yet he does so without really believing either in his sin or in Christ. Even Tikhon, the old priest who has seen countless sinners, is shocked by the pollution of Stavrogin's soul.

To pollute means to defile, soil, taint, debase, deprive, or violate – to mismanage sex and violence. It is a violation of innocence and of individual integrity. Dostoevsky ascribes to Stavrogin what he believes to be the worst crime a human being can commit. Bored with his life, desperately searching for any kind of amusement, Stavrogin is drawn to the child Matryosha. After he seduces her, the short-lived excitement he has felt passes; like everything else, she bores him. With complete indifference, he allows the girl to hang herself and returns to his customary card-playing and drinking. Stavrogin admits in his last letter to Dasha, "Today as before, I'm still capable of wishing to do something decent and I derive some pleasure from this; but the next moment I want to do evil things and that also gives me pleasure" (Pt. III, Ch. 8, 690).

In search of another pleasure, or just sheer distraction, Stavrogin decides impulsively to marry a lame and insane girl, Marya Timofeevna Lebyadkina. This represents yet another violation, another inexcusable overstepping of sacred boundaries. Stavrogin does not care about the fulfillment of the apocalyptic prophecy: "It wasn't simply that I had lost the feeling of good and evil, but that I felt there was no such thing as good and evil (I liked that); that it was all a convention; that I could be free of all convention; but that if I ever attained that freedom, I'd be lost" (Pt. II, Ch. 9, sec. ii, 426).

Marya is one of Dostoevsky's most enigmatic characters, a figure out of myth. She is a mirror-image of Stavrogin's crippled soul, and at the same time an image of the violated soul of Russia. Many commentators also see in this lame figure a symbol of the desecrated Mother Earth and the Mother of God. The demons are all masculine in Dostoevsky's novel, and their principal orientation toward the world is through consciousness, manifested as reason and will without emotion. Marya's insights are not rational but intuitive. Before anyone else, she recognizes in Stavrogin a broken, cynical Christ, a Savior no longer capable of redeeming anyone. Marya longs for a Prince, but she recognizes him as the Antichrist. Annoyed by Marya's recognition of who he is and her refusal to play the role he intends for her, Stavrogin gives an indirect signal to Fedka to get rid of her. Soon after, Marya and her brother disappear in flames.

Stavrogin has overstepped all boundaries; he has orbited himself out of the social stratosphere, but now he finds himself in a complete vacuum. This citizen of the Swiss canton of Uri, as the narrator ironically refers to Stavrogin, recognizes his situation quite clearly: "There's nothing to tie me to Russia – everything here is as alien to me as anywhere else in the world" (Pt. III, Ch. 8, 690). Stavrogin further admits to Dasha:

> Your brother said to me that a man who loses his links with his native land loses at the same time his gods and his life's goals. That, like everything, could be argued about indefinitely, but the only thing that has come out of me is negation without strength and without generosity. In fact, I didn't even have negation to offer, because everything about me was always shallow and apathetic (Pt. III, Ch. 8, 691).

Hannah Arendt argues that "evil is never 'radical', that it is only extreme, and that it possesses neither depth nor any demonic dimension."[26] Dostoevsky disagrees. Yes, evil is "thought-defying," but it is too easy, perhaps also too irresponsible, to dismiss the idea of radical evil. Dostoevsky does not believe that the phrase "radical evil" should somehow magically explain – or explain away – the nature of "demonic evil." This phrase only serves as the recognition of certain drives and mechanisms that pull human beings toward destruction and nothingness. In its philosophical forms, in its preference of ethics over religion, secular humanism denies the existence of such dark drives and mechanism. Philosophical humanism wants to place the responsibility of man's actions

26 Letter to Gerhard Scholem, July 24, 1963; quoted from *The Portable Hannah Arendt*, 396.

on his shoulders and his shoulders alone, without allowing the interference of non-human factors: Not primordial sin, but human decisions and human institutions are deemed responsible for how we live. If the world is evil, man has no one to blame but himself.

While there are many noble motives behind such a philosophical attitude, it fails to recognize the depth of man's nature and his interconnection with the forces he neither controls nor understands. Poets have always been more sensitive to this aspect of human nature. Goethe, for example, does not use the phrase radical evil but recognizes the manifestation of the demonic forces within man which cannot be denied. Such forces can be subdued and neutralized, as they are in works of Goethe and his admirer Thomas Mann, or they can be set on the loose, as they are in Dostoevsky and Mann's contemporary Hermann Hesse.

For Goethe, the devil is the spirit which always denies, but this does not mean a complete bend toward destruction. When Faust questions Mephistopheles' identity, he reveals to be "Part of that force which would/Do evil evermore, and yet creates the good."[27] Dostoevsky's devils would say just the opposite – their attempts to do good turn into evil. This is why Stepan and his generation of the liberal humanists are implicated in this majestic comedy of destruction: Their stubborn confidence that there can be a world without evil is the root of the most destructive behavior of their sons.[28]

Stavrogin is another matter. In most people evil does not dominate, but threatens to gain the upper hand. Stavrogin's soul is already lost. In him we do not find even an illusion that the

---

27 Goethe, *Faust* I, 1336–37.

28 Dostoevsky is well aware that there are two conceptions of evil in the Bible. According to one, which became the historically dominant after Augustine's interpretation of it in terms of *privatio boni* (evil as the privation of good), only good is truly substantial and real, and it is personalized in God. According to the second conception, developed by the Manicheans and the Gnostics, good and evil, as well as light and darkness, creation and destruction, are in eternal conflict. For further discussion of these two conceptions and a Jungian interpretation of them, see John Sanford, *Evil: The Shadow Side of Reality*, 18–43. Dostoevsky stands much closer to the second conception.

world's malaise can be fixed. Stavrogin's soul is the waste land of meaninglessness and emptiness. Tikhon tells Stavrogin that he may be saved if he can overcome his pride, but Stavrogin has abandoned all hope. He decides to run away: from Tikhon, from his mother, from Peter, from the rest of the world. He writes a letter to Dasha inviting her to be his "nurse" (recall that Stepan finds his nurse in Sophia Ulitin). They can spend the rest of their lives in boredom, in the canton of Uri. As soon as the letter is sent, Stavrogin realizes that this kind of escape will not do, that he needs something more radical. When Dasha and Mrs. Stavrogin arrive, it is too late. In the last act of his powerful will, Stavrogin hangs himself.

Is this a concession of defeat? Hardly so. For Stavrogin, it is an act of self-perpetuation rather than self-destruction, the last act of violating the boundaries valid for everyone else. Stavrogin – and Stavrogin alone – has fully realized the secret of the "eternal Great Idea" of his pseudo-father, Stepan. The secret is hidden in the heart of an insatiable longing for immortality – if this yearning cannot be satisfied in any form of the eternal life, we must try the eternal death. After all, could anything be greater than nothingness?

A World without Meaning?

Berdyaev once wrote that "[Dostoevsky] cannot be understood – indeed, his books had better be left alone – unless the reader is prepared to be immersed in a vast strange universe of ideas."[29] Berdyaev could have also pointed out that Dostoevsky incessantly reconsiders and develops these ideas. His works can be ordered based on the sequences of ideas, and we have established one such series: *Notes from the Underground*, followed by *Crime and Punishment*, culminating in *The Possessed*. In the *Notes*, for instance, the underground man ties the fate of humanity with the preservation of freedom: If freedom is eliminated, humanity is abolished as well. In *Crime and Punishment*, Raskolnikov continues the exploration of freedom and focuses on external obstacles to his

29 Berdyaev, *op. cit.*, 12.

freedom: This concept of freedom implies freedom from such obstacles. In *The Possessed*, the idea of freedom is developed further: not one, but several central characters – Stepan, Peter, Kirillov and Stavrogin – attempt to solve the puzzle of freedom in the positive sense: If we assume that we can be free from external obstacles, for what are we free? What is the end ideal of freedom in the positive sense? Human freedom should not be restrained by the boundaries that are too narrow, but it also cannot be unbounded. Is there a way to find a constructive path between the two extremes?

To look at a related example, in these three novels we can follow Dostoevsky's preoccupation with our worst fears. The lonely underground man is afraid of others. Like Sartre, he could say: "Hell is others." We must be strong enough to protect our individual freedom and resist others. With Raskolnikov, there is a shift in orientation. Deluded by his "unfinished ideas," Raskolnikov is not afraid of others, but of himself: Is he daring enough to carry out his plan without remorse? Not so. The pangs of conscience (which Albert Schweitzer calls "the gift of the devil") turns out to be too much. In *The Possessed*, the idea is developed further. While Raskolnikov is afraid of not being strong enough, the experience of Peter and Stavrogin, the two individuals who are not bothered by conscience, shows that we should be afraid of being so strong. If we are, the hell is not the others but ourselves.

There are also developments of one idea within the same novel. In *Crime and Punishment*, Porfiry tells Raskolnikov twice how "the butterfly flies to the light," even though that will mean its death. The attractive impulse toward nothingness can be strong enough to override all other concerns. In *The Possessed*, the idea of nothingness is illuminated differently by several characters. For Stepan, we see it through his empty dreams to which nothing in reality corresponds. In Peter, nothingness is understood as the denial of existence. It culminates in an attempt to turn the world into chaos and life into death. For Stavrogin, existence itself equals nothingness. His life is empty of qualities and emotions: Life is a boring experience of an uprooted individual in a disoriented society.

These ideas cluster together, as Dostoevsky's characters do. The ideas of freedom, hope, fear, nothingness, and death crowd together around the issue of the meaning of life. Within this cluster of ideas and within the novels we have discussed so far, there is a recognizable pattern: The characters have high hopes which end up in disappointment. Heroic dreams turn into demonic nightmares. Hoping for the better, even perfect world, they cut the branch on which they stand.

Does it have to be that way? Is human life void of any positive meaning? Is the world really delivered to evil?

Let us for a moment reconsider the generational gap in *The Possessed*. The same man who abandons his legitimate son Peter tries to awaken the highest ideals in the mind of his pupil Stavrogin. Stepan stirs up "sacred longing that a superior soul, having once tasted, will never exchange for vulgar satisfaction" (Pt. I, Ch. 2, sec. i, 42). That such sacred longing never dies in Stavrogin's soul, we can see from his description of the "Landscape with Acis and Galatea" in his written confession. Stavrogin calls this painting, which he has seen many times, "The Golden Age." He sees the painting in his dream and is part of it. The description is so revealing that it deserves to be quoted at length:

> I was in a corner of the Greek archipelago – yes, and time had slipped back over three thousand years. I remember the gentle blue waves, the islands and the rocks, the luxuriant shore line, the magic panorama on the horizon, the beckoning, setting sun – it is impossible to put it into words. This was the cradle of European civilization – the thought filled my heart with love. It was a paradise on earth, where gods descended from heaven and fraternized with men. This was the corner of the earth where the first mythological stories were enacted. Ah, and the people who inhabited that land were so beautiful! They awoke innocent and went to sleep at night in innocence. There woods and glades were filled with cheerful songs; the unspent energy of their youthful vigor went into love and simple joys, and I felt all that, visualizing, as it were, all their great three-thousand-year destiny of which they had no inkling. My heart danced

with joy at these thoughts. Ah, I was so happy because my heart danced like that and because, at last, I loved! The sun flooded the islands and the sea, rejoicing at the sight of its beautiful children. Oh, a wonderful dream, a noble delusion! It was the most improbable ideal, but an ideal for which men have striven desperately throughout the ages and for which they have given their lives; an ideal for which they have sacrificed everything, for which they have longed and pined and in the name of which their prophets have been crucified and murdered; an ideal without which men wouldn't want to live and could not even die (Pt. II, Ch. 9, sec. ii, 428–29).

Tikhon is sufficiently shocked by other parts of Stavrogin's confession to comment on this dream. Let us however suppose that Stavrogin presents this portion of the confession to the other members of the counter-Trinity: Stepan and Peter. Stepan would easily recognize his own dreams in this confession; he himself led the young Stavrogin to them. As a reflection of our reality, Peter would have preferred Picasso's "Guernica" to this painting. You are misunderstanding Claude Lorrain's painting, he would reproach Stepan and Stavrogin, and call it by an inappropriate name. This is not a painting of "The Golden Age," or a picture of paradise. The painting may create an initial impression that the artist has captured the moment of eternity. Indeed, this is the idea we associate with paradise. Time stands still; nothing and no one ages. There is no pain, suffering, conflict, or privation. Everything we could possibly want is there.

Despite the initial impression, this painting is not of "The Golden Age," Peter would insist, for at least two reasons. First, do not overlook the two mountain tops in the right corner. Both seem to be the volcano craters and at least one of them – the one on the far right – appears active. In a few hours, or a few days, months, years – it does not matter when – this volcano will start its deadly cough and the idyllic archipelago will be transformed into a barren land.

There is also another reason, Peter would continue, why the painter insists on the names of Acis and Galatea when he names his work. Galatea is a sea-nymph and Acis is in love with her. Look at the painting closely and you will notice a giant figure sitting in the forest. This is a one-eyed Cyclops Polyphemus, a rival of Acis. As Ovid describes him in book XIII of *Metamorphoses*, Polyphemus's longing for the beloved Galatea has no limits:

> I burn! The fire you fight is fanned to flame;
> All Etna's furnace in my breast I bear,
> And you, my Galatea, never care!

Love may be beautiful, Peter would add, but is it not always accompanied by someone's jealousy? It is impossible that we should all be satisfied at the same time. The painter is showing a happy couple, with a little Cupid sitting in front of them. They have concealed themselves from the sight of the fierce Cyclops, but their cunning victory is only temporary. "With a wild urge to kill, his fierceness and lust for blood," Polyphemus will find his rival Acis and devour him. Instead of your wonderful dream, Stepan and Stavrogin, you will indeed have a delusion. And it is not going to be a very noble one. Galatea and Polyphemus – would that be a version of Beauty and the Beast?

What, then, should we think of the painting? That it portrays something beautiful now, but may not be such in the next moment? Or is it beautiful even though the volcano can erupt or Polyphemus kill Acis when we turn around? If we change our judgment, should we call the depicted scene ugly, because it is only a temporary delusion? Or should we say that it is neither beautiful nor ugly? Should the painting, and the rest of our reality, be evaluated in terms of quite different values?

Nietzsche famously said that, "People would rather have void for meaning, than to accept a void of meaning." If that is so, if we are prisoners of our own compulsion to discover the meaning of life and express it in terms of the highest ideal, it is quite possible we will always end up being disappointed. Is this the message Dostoevsky wants to convey in *The Possessed* and his other works?

Let us not rush to a premature conclusion. Dostoevsky certainly wants to show in *The Possessed* that something has gone terribly wrong, not just with the two generations of Russians, but with the course of the development of a broader European civilization. His protagonists begin with the highest ideal, but in their search for the absolute, instead of finding a positive absolute, they end up unearthing its negative counterpart. Instead of the victory over evil, they are desperately fixated on achieving a "final solution," even if it is a triumph of evil.

That there is much evil in the world no one of sound mind would deny. How could things go so wrong? What does Dostoevsky identify as humanity's greatest blunder?

(1) Man's search for the highest ideal?
(2) Man's identification with the "wrong" highest ideal?
(3) Man's action in pursuit of the highest ideal?

The lessons learned from our readings of *Notes from the Underground*, *Crime and Punishment*, and *The Possessed* do not justify the acceptance of (1). These works do not exclude the possibility that there is no one ultimate ideal, but point in the different direction. They point toward (2), and, as a result of that mistake, toward (3).

In the introductory section to Part I, we identified three approaches to the issues of meaning of life: the metaphysical and religious approach, the humanistic and secular approach, and the nihilistic and relativistic approach. It is no secret that Dostoevsky favors the first, although the works presented in the first part of this book did not offer much elaboration of this approach. This will be done in Part II.

Faced with the choice between the humanistic and secular approach on the one hand, and the nihilistic and relativist approach on the other, Dostoevsky prefers the latter. Although he is deeply opposed to this approach taken by itself, he finds nihilism and relativism more honest than humanism and secularism. To nihilism and relativism people come as a result of their genuine search for truth – and their inability to find it. Humanism and secularism, by contrast, appear to him as practically opportune but spiritually dishonest: They offer a compromise that makes life more convenient but which leads away from search for the highest values.

Let us document Dostoevsky's preference of nihilism over humanism. In *The Possessed*, Kirillov is a nihilist for whom Dostoevsky shows much respect. In the early drafts of the novel he views Kirillov as "a truly Russian character, a man who is forever in search of truth and who is ready to suffer and sacrifice oneself for a noble idea." Dostoevsky writes in his notes for the novel: "God bless [Kirillov] and give him the understanding of the truth because the main concern is to clarify what one is to consider the truth. This is the main aim of the novel."

That there is "truth," Dostoevsky does not doubt. To figure out what it is is the most difficult task. (Trying to defend Raphael's "Sistine Madonna" against the charges that such a painting is useless, Stepan remarks: "The truth, my friend, is always incredible; it becomes believable only when diluted with lies" [Pt. II, Ch. 1, sec. ii, 203].) If we misidentify the truth, if we identify with a false idol, we will wander astray, whether it means destroying others, ourselves, or both.

There is no character in these works who wholeheartedly defends the humanistic and secular approach to life and with whom the author strongly sympathizes. Dostoevsky finds the humanistic and secular picture of man and society oversimplified and misguided. The significance of the rational faculty in man is exaggerated, the value of utility misunderstood, and the negative impacts of our technical civilization underestimated. In *The Possessed*, Dostoevsky lets Shatov be his mouthpiece and complain about "our age of humanitarianism, industry, and railroads" (Pt. I, Ch. 1, sec. ix, 35). According to Shatov,

> In its very essence, socialism is godless – it proclaimed in its very first statement that it aims at an organization that does not presuppose God; that is, an organization based on the principles of reason and science exclusively. But reason and science have always performed, and still perform, only an auxiliary function in the life of peoples, and it will be like that till the end of time. Nations are formed and moved by some other force whose origin is unknown and unaccountable. That force is the unquenchable will to reach an end and, at the same time, the denial of that end. It is the force of an incessant and unwavering affirmation of life and a denial of death. It is the spirit of life, "river of life" as the Scriptures call it, the drying up of which is

threatened in the Apocalypse. Some philosophers claim it
is based on an aesthetic, others on an ethical principle, but
I call it simply the search for God. (Pt. II, Ch. 1, sec. vii,
236–37).

Those who believe in socialism and social engineering are
convinced in an inevitable evolution and gradual progress of
mankind, based on the power of reason and science. They overlook that whenever we face difficult obstacles, we tend to regress,
not progress. The nihilism and relativism of Dostoevsky's era
represents the regression based upon the disillusionment of the
unrealistic optimism of the Enlightenment. The more obstacles our
grand ideals encounter and the less sure we are of our progress, the
more we postulate in theory the inevitability of the advancement –
Hegel, Marx, and positivism are all variations on this same theme.
When the numerous "adjustments" of how exactly we inevitably
progress toward the complete realization of greatest happiness for
the greatest number fail to convince and correspond to reality, the
results are disastrous. In theory, we turn to relativism and nihilism;
in practice, to violence and destruction. This, in sum, is the point
of *The Possessed*.

Whatever ideals we may endorse, Dostoevsky would argue that
their ultimate test is not theoretical coherence or reasonableness
but real life. Whether or not the world is delivered to evil, it is
clear that the world is not what we would like it to be. Our continuous efforts to make it as we desire lead to our increasing
frustrations and contempt for the world. The only good that arises
from such times of deep crisis is the unconcealment and testing of
our ultimate convictions.

When frustration and contempt border on the unbearable, to
whom or to what do we turn? When disaster strikes, what is it that
carries us through? Do we have anything that supports us when
we meet great calamity? Or does that which we thought was our
support now fail us?

Dostoevsky believes that the experiment of modernity opens
a deep wound and creates an unprecedented spiritual crisis.
The "river of life" is drying up, as threatened in the Apocalypse.
The demons have been on the loose, but they are not the ones who

are insane. In their strange ways, both Peter and Stavrogin are sane. On his way to murder Shatov, Peter stops in a restaurant to devour a steak. While waiting for Kirillov to commit suicide, Peter eats his chicken dinner. Stavrogin pulls the honorable Gaganov by the nose and bites the governor's ear. Devilish behavior, but not insane. The narrator of *The Possessed* categorically asserts in the last sentence of the novel: "After the autopsy, all our medical experts rejected any possibility of insanity" (Pt. III, Ch. 8, 693). No, it is not Stavrogin (or Peter) who has gone insane. It is the rest of the world.

The experiment of relying on man's rational capacity and his freedom has failed. Turning against the tradition to build a new, better world has led to an increase in man's confusion with regard to his own identity. By trying to dissect everything, by committing himself to solving every problem and leading every thought to its logical conclusion, he has not helped himself at all in figuring out who he is. He has only encountered new and unsuspected obstacles. Reason neither defines nor fully grasps what good and evil are. Freedom does not lead to authenticity. The experiment of relying on man's capacities in order to "correct and direct nature" has been based on deluded optimism that has brought people to the threshold of self-destruction. The experiment of modernity has revealed not man's strength but his vulnerability.

In the failed experiment of modernity Dostoyevsky discerns not merely a temporary crisis but the defeat of the secular and humanistic orientation. The hidden goal of this orientation has been an individual and collective self-deification of man. Yet when man takes on himself the prerogatives of god, the demons are let loose and a tragic end is inevitable. As Shigailov says in *The Possessed*, "I started out with the idea of unrestricted freedom and I have arrived at unrestricted despotism" (Pt. II, Ch. 7, sec. ii, 384). When all norms are treated as man-made, arbitrary, and conventional, and our freedom considered as the defining feature of our humanity, there is no reason not to violate every norm and overstep every boundary. There is no reason not to pursue that freedom to its logical end. What we find at the end, however, is not authenticity, harmony, or happiness, but artificiality, degradation, and self-destruction. A flight from Christ ends with the Antichrist.

How could that be? What did go wrong?

The three works we considered – *Notes from the Underground*, *Crime and Punishment*, and *The Possessed* – are more focused on showing that, if we start from the assumptions of the humanistic and secular approach, things do go wrong and must go wrong. Nonetheless, they also give some hints as to why things go wrong and what alternative assumptions should be considered. Here are three of them, which will be developed in Part II of this book.

First, besides freedom and its exercise, which always threatens a transgression of accepted boundaries, there must be another fundamental value which will restrict the pursuit of freedom. In Chapter 2 we have indicated that freedom stands in opposition to order, and we need to consider in more detail how the two can coexist together.

Second, despite the persistence of human dreams of eschatological ends, all such ultimate and definitive ends turn out to be negative and destructive. They are such because they involve a denial of life. In contrast to such ends, life is inconclusive and indefinite. Life flows on and on without any ultimate goal. If there is to be a meaning to human life, our goals must also be open-ended rather than conclusive, flexible rather than fixed in stone.

Third, there must be some norms that are not man-made, arbitrary, and conventional. If all norms are such, it remains hard to explain why the human conscience awakens as a result of certain transgressions. There must be something not man-made, something that should never be violated, something sacred.

Part II
Recovering Life's Meaning

Introduction to Part II

Dostoevsky's realism, as considered in the first part of the book, does not offer a comforting picture of humanity. Human life is arbitrary, full of suffering and evil. The world is not created to the advantage of humanity and is resilient to rational attempts to shape it to man's satisfaction. Rational capacities to discover or create meaning in life are inadequate in a world that seems determined to thwart them. The highest ideals cannot be achieved no matter how strong-willed human beings are. Rarely do human beings even climb close to these summits. What we continue to find more often is that the pursuit of noble ideals turns into the realization of their opposites.

However, Dostoevsky's realism does not exclude the possibility of the re-enchantment of our experience of the world. Nor does it preclude the recovery of faith. Eyes open wide for the beauties of this world and hands extended in faith to others are his response to the arbitrariness in life – not the denial of its arbitrariness, not its resolution, but a human response to it. This is Dostoevsky's reaction to the increasing desacralization of the world in the modern epoch.

One of the crowning moments of this epoch is Newton's postulation of a single set of laws which govern the motion of all objects in the universe. The modern approach of "one law for all" destroys the ancient and the medieval belief in the division between the pristine and unchanging cosmos above and our grubby and chaotic Earth below. Modern science postulates a transparency and uniformity valid for the entire spatially and temporally homogeneous universe. The world may be infinite, but it is essentially the same everywhere – because it is made of the same material constituents and governed by the same forces. All the mystery of the world is exorcized.

One of the defining aspects of Dostoevsky's worldview is an uncompromising denial of this hedgehog "one law for all" approach. In all great works of art, for instance, there is a sense of a certain fundamental inscrutability. This component of inscrutability may be considered external to man – when it is attributed to God or Fate – or internal to him – when located in the human heart or soul. Dostoevsky believes that the mysterious sense of inscrutability pervades not only works of art but is present in everything – all things alive, even all things in existence. We can close our eyes to the enigmatic nature of existence or deny the mysteriousness of life, yet the inscrutable will not be eliminated. The world will continue to astound us because in it the profane and the sacred are inseparably bound together.

This, in a nutshell, is Dostoevsky's approach to the metaphysical-religious view of nature. He develops it in a way that opposes the secular-humanistic approach of modernity. While modernity attempts to demystify the world, so that we can control it and mold it to satisfy our needs, Dostoevsky believes that we have dangerously impoverished the world in our effort to master it. We sever the ties with our tradition, which we consider a source of prejudices and false beliefs, and then wonder why we find ourselves so disoriented in the world. We have mastered the forces of disintegration and destruction, but the problem is to discover – or rediscover – the creative power active in the processes of healing and growth. We have become too preoccupied with evil and with searching for whom to blame for this valley of tears. The important thing for Dostoevsky is not to lose sight of the good, not to forget about the peaks above.

We have seen that it is difficult to find a satisfactory definition of evil. This, however, is not an insurmountable obstacle. For the most part we agree on undeniable cases of evil. The situation is more complicated with the nature of the good. Here we lack not only an adequate definition but are confused even about the exemplary cases of the good. In *The Idiot* and *The Brothers Karamazov* Dostoevsky explores this complex category in terms of purity, nobility, and richness of experience. Regardless of the variations, the good is always closely related to the sacred and the holy, which for Dostoevsky are intimately interconnected with what is secular and profane, with what is here and now.

Dostoevsky takes earnestly the words from John's Gospel (8:31–32): "If you make my Word [*logos*] your home...the truth shall make you free." He is convinced that there can be no resolution to the problem of our spiritual homelessness without reviving our religious tradition. He does not treat this tradition as a dogma established once and for all, but as a living and puzzling enterprise, which finds its own form in every epoch and every culture. Just as human nature is for Dostoevsky complex and ambiguous, so is the nature of the sacred. But whatever the sacred turns out to be, its decoding requires our interpretation and – most importantly – our participation.

Against the modern postulation of the "one law for all" approach, Dostoevsky shows that every object can be perceived and treated in diverse, though not always mutually exclusive ways. Although it is possible to take objects simply as they are in themselves, as science does, we can also perceive them with respect to what they indicate, signify, or symbolize. Following Galileo's famous postulate that the Book of Nature is written in mathematical language, modernity accepts that the structure of the universe – and everything in it, including human beings – is mathematically structured. Rationality and the validity of the scientific method are based on that structure. Dostoevsky opposes this approach. The world is a book which can be read in different ways, a text that needs our illumination.[1]

---

1   Yuri Lotman distinguishes between text on the one side and code or symbol on the other; see his *Universe of the Mind: A Semiotic Theory of Culture*, 72–74. Carl Gustav Jung makes a related distinction in terms of signs and symbols; see his "Symbols and the Interpretation of Dreams," in *The Undiscovered Self*, 65. It is worth noting that for both Jung and Dostoevsky the most important symbols are cross and circle (which Jung calls "mandala").

One way of reading this text relies on the form of communication between the first person and the third person. Another is a form of (collective) auto-communication. One approach is based on discovery, the other on recovery. One assumes that the truth is yet to be found, the other that it was revealed long ago. The text as a message conveys to us "news" about someone else; it adds something interesting to our knowledge of the world. The text treated as a symbol says something about us, not about others; it does not add to our knowledge of the world but helps us discover our nature and our destiny.

The distinction between message and symbol applies to the whole spectrum of human experience. For a secular man, space and time are homogeneous. For a religious man, they are not; some parts of space and time are qualitatively different from others. A certain object is a house, but it may also be a home. An architect (e.g., Le Corbusier) may claim that the house is "a machine to live in." Although the home is always a house, it is not a machine. Nor can we ever be sure that, when building a house, it will become and remain a home.

While searching for the meaning of life, we can approach it in terms of discovery, or in terms of recovery. We can place the emphasis on reasons for living (as Ivan Karamazov does), or on the experience of life itself (as his brother Dmitri does). What the underground man perceives as the contradictory aspects of human nature the Elder Zosima takes to be proof of life's abundance. Regardless of which of these approaches we choose, each affects our perception of the world and our understanding of life's meaning.

We can clarify this with the example of suffering. There is indeed much senseless suffering in the world. This message would exclude Dostoevsky's optimism only if it were the whole and only truth about human life. Yet we know that besides suffering there are moments of joy. Dostoevsky realizes that only at the peripheral levels of human experience can we fully separate pleasure and pain, joy and suffering. The deeper we probe into ourselves, the less distinguishable these antinomical feelings are. Hedonists forget, or overlook, that all our attempts at self-knowledge and maturing demand this kind of penetration. Besides suffering which arises from want or injustice, there is also suffering arising from increased vitality and growth. Thus, instead of the focus on escape from suffering and pain (which is never fully possible anyway), Dostoevsky wants us to keep in mind just how dreadful the world would be without the human capacity for suffering, especially the suffering for others. Could we call this world "human"? Would we like to live in this kind of world?

Dostoevsky is quoted as saying: "There is only one thing I dread: not to be worthy of my suffering."[2] Following his lead, we can draw a contrast between suffering and our attitude toward suffering. The experience of Siberia was an invaluable lesson for Dostoevsky: Under the same circumstances some people behave as swine and others as saints. Human beings contain both potentialities within themselves, and which of them they actualize depends not so much on their living conditions as on their attitudes toward life. Those of Dostoevsky's characters who stubbornly attempt to escape from all suffering end up destroying either their own or someone else's humanity. Our freedom does not manifest itself only in our ability to determine what will happen to us and whether we will suffer – for suffer we must, as long as we live. Human freedom consists primarily in choosing the attitudes which we take toward what happens to us: Are we worthy of our suffering or not?

Dostoevsky does not deny that there is pointless suffering. Nevertheless, he calls our attention to the value of suffering. The very experience of suffering is the mark of the presence of value conflicts, and the existence of such conflicts is in itself something

2   Quoted from Viktor E. Frankl, *Man's Search for Meaning: An Introduction to Logotherapy*, 105. Inspired by Dostoevsky, Frankl, a Holocaust survivor, continues (105–6): "These words frequently came to my mind after I became acquainted with those martyrs whose behavior in camp, whose suffering and death, bore witness to the fact that the last inner freedom cannot be lost. It can be said that they were worthy of their sufferings; the way they bore their suffering was a genuine inner achievement. It is this spiritual freedom – which cannot be taken away – that makes life meaningful and purposeful."

valuable. With Plato, we assume that the chains which tie us to the walls of the cave are due to ignorance. Dostoevsky disagrees and argues that the chains are primarily due to our lack of sensitivity – toward ourselves, others, and the world as a whole. The presence of value conflicts allows us to become more sensitive to what value we prefer and on what ground. It is impossible to live without value conflicts and without suffering, but not all values are equally worthy of our suffering.

Part I shows that Dostoevsky realizes that the main stream of Western development has gone astray. Like the herd of the Gadarene swine, we are rushing toward the cliff of our destruction. Even if we end up avoiding the cliff, we are made to feel like exiles in this world. But exiles from where? And exiled by whom?

Where else but this same world in which we now feel so homeless. And exiled by ourselves, for there is nobody else who could alienate us from our world.

Dostoevsky's optimism consists in his faith that we can recover our lost sense of the meaning of life. Part II of this book focuses on three different yet complementary aspects of his optimism. The first deals with our ability to rediscover a sense of wonder and look at the world with fresh eyes. The second considers the fact that those who help us reestablish such ways of looking at the world are children and social outcasts. The third turns on its head our understanding of heroism: It is increasingly more difficult to find meaning in life because we are misled by our choices of heroes. Genuine heroes are not those who are superhuman – less human and more divine – but those who are more human than ourselves.

Let us briefly clarify each of these three aspects before turning to their thorough examination in Dostoevsky's two most magnificent novels, *The Idiot* and *The Brothers Karamazov*.

(1) In mind's effort after meaning, we tend to think of reality in terms of objects, things, and substances – the word "substance" literally means that which stands beneath or under the appearance of things, and what we can understand as such. That what stands firmly, and allows itself to be understood as such, gives the sense of order and stability. The mind feels at home in the world of objects, things, and substances, which it can define in terms of

signs and concepts and express through established language. From grammar's point of view, our lives, the world, and everything else in it is primarily understood in terms of nouns – I am a noun, you are a noun, even God is a noun.[3]

That is not how Dostoevsky perceives the world. Nouns are not dominant in his grammar. With Dostoevsky we experience the world as literally animated by invisible energies. His language is not rational and abstract but imaginative and vibrant, full of symbols and mimetic playfulness. Dostoevsky shows no reluctance in recognizing the fundamental ambiguity of everything that exists. Even God does not appear to us in terms of a well-defined concept but as a confusedly sensed presence. Existence – any existence – is not a noun but a verb: to be, to exist, to live. Life itself is something beyond grammar and beyond logic. It is inscrutable. Life is a flow of unpredictable reversals. The events in it are like the proverbial fire which leaves cold those who stay too far and which burns those who come too close. We are not spectators but participants in the riddle of existence. Our challenge is to find the right distance from the fire.

(2) In mind's effort after meaning, we tend to identify the normal and the norm. The voice of the majority determines what is right and what is wrong. Dostoevsky is apprehensive of that voice. He is suspicious of the ways in which modern society draws the boundaries between normal and abnormal, healthy and sick, authentic and inauthentic. His most insightful characters are always at the periphery of society, experiencing the extreme situations which lead them to intuitions inaccessible to those living securely within the confines of the mass mentality. His epileptics and insane, murderers and sinners, drunkards and outcasts, find their champions in holy fools, such as Prince Myshkin. A strange mixture of power and powerlessness, an incurable disease and supreme health, Myshkin defies the social norms. He always speaks the truth and

---

3   Étienne Gilson points out that, "The human mind feels shy before a reality of which it can form no proper concept. Such, precisely, is existence." He then emphasizes that, "existence is not a thing, but the act that causes a thing both to be and to be what it is." Quoted from Gilson, *God and Philosophy*, pages 69 and 70 respectively.

shows his compassion. In a world bent on deception and utilitarian calculation, such a gadfly must be destroyed, or sent back to the asylum. Myshkin and other outcasts will always be defeated by the majority, but the memories of an authentic existence which they evoke in us cannot be so easily extinguished.

(3) In mind's effort after meaning, we tend to conceive of perfection in terms of what is superhuman. Everything that is human is limited, fallible, imperfect. Our heroes are super-strong, super-fast, super-rich. They are larger than life, more like gods than ordinary human beings. Dostoevsky thinks that this obsession with becoming god-like is a fundamental mistake. Even in its healthier form of striving toward self-actualization of given potentials and talents, Dostoevsky is wary that this tendency may lead toward egoism and narcissism, and in extreme cases toward self-deification.

Dostoevsky's position is that life is not a commodity with which we can do whatever we like. Rather, life is a gift of a kind. If life is indeed a gift, then in an important sense it is not ours to dispose of it. We use this gift properly only when we put it in the service of something greater than our individual striving for happiness and achievements. The proper attitude toward life is that of self-transcendence, not that of self-actualization. More precisely, the only healthy form of self-actualization is that which is accomplished through self-transcendence.[4] A hero is not someone above the human norms and boundaries, but a person who unselfishly tries to make possible a healthy life for other human beings. For Dostoevsky, heroism itself is not the exception but the norm expected of every one: We should all strive to become heroes in our own lives. When we sincerely put our lives in service of something greater than our satisfactions and goals, the meaning of life comes to us of itself.

Dostoevsky's approach may close some questions but it opens others. The most pressing issues deal with Dostoevsky's understanding of the meaning of life and his optimism. His understanding of the meaning of life needs further clarification. The affirmation of life points toward the cultivation of the vital values, such as the preservation of life and freedom. Self-transcendence, however,

4   This point is also emphasized by Frankl; *op. cit.*, 175.

points toward values which are not as basic as the vital values, but which are undoubtedly higher: The life of the spirit demands the cultivation of goodness, beauty, and truth. Does heroism refer primarily to the cultivation of the stronger yet lower values or to the cultivation of the weaker yet higher values?

Furthermore, if we accept Dostoevsky's philosophy of life, what exactly can we be optimistic about? Should it be the present life in comparison to the past? Or should our optimism be directed toward the future life, rather than to the present? One way or another, our usual conception of optimism is closely related to the idea of progress, which in turn is based on a linear conception of time. We know enough about Dostoevsky to realize that he is suspicious of progress and the linear conception of time. He is skeptical even of the religious ideas of the Second Coming and the realization of the Kingdom of God on earth.

Dostoevsky focuses more on repetition than on progress. He finds a cyclical rather than linear conception of time more appropriate. Thus, he must develop the idea of optimism without relying on progress. He must develop the meaning of life without assuming an achievement of a set goal. Dostoevsky understands optimism and meaning of life in terms of religion and myth, insofar as religion and myth depend on repetition, on turning back and reuniting with our roots. As it is indispensable to transgress the existing boundaries and move forward, for our sense of orientation in life it is equally inevitable to move backward, to reestablish the boundaries and ties with the past.[5] This dynamic of transgressing and reestablishing order Dostoevsky considers to be the essence of life, so that any sense of optimism and meaning of life can be found only within the framework of this dynamism. Meaning of life and optimism cannot, then, be stable and irreversible, accomplished and controlled once and forever. They are not atoms that cannot be split further, nor irremovable Archimedean points, nor indestructible stone walls. Rather, for Dostoevsky they are part of the inscrutably and mysterious thread of life – most precious and sacred, yet also most fragile and vulnerable.

---

5   For further discussion of the cyclical conception of time, see Mircea Eliade, *The Sacred and the Profane: The Nature of Religion*, 68–113.

5
The Idiot

The Meaning of Christ's Sacrifice

Reading Faces

At the beginning of *The Idiot*, Prince Lev Nikolayevich Myshkin is on the train heading toward St Petersburg. After spending several years in a sanatorium in Switzerland, the prince returns to his native land where he has no relatives or friends. In his crowded third-class car, the prince befriends Rogozhin and Lebedev and learns of Rogozhin's passion for the beautiful Nastassya Filippovna. That very same day, the prince will find himself thrown into a whirlwind of fascinating events which will change forever the destiny of Rogozhin and Nastassya Filippovna, as well as his own life. After the murder of Nastassya Filippovna, Rogozhin will be sent to Siberia to serve his sentence, and the prince will be headed back to the Swiss sanatorium.

By using the Christ-like figure of Prince Myshkin, Dostoevsky poses some of the deepest philosophical questions concerning the meaning of life. He offers his treatment of these questions not only in an artistic form, but through unexpected devices: reading faces and playing games. Dostoevsky's unconventional approach will allow us to understand the issues concerning the meaning of life and the sacrifice of Christ in an original and profound way.

Decoding faces plays a prominent role in this novel. Prince Myshkin reads Nastassya Filippovna's face (initially from her portrait), as well as the faces of the Yepanchin ladies the first time they meet. When the middle daughter, Adelaida, asks the prince to suggest a subject for her new painting, he recommends the face of a person about to be guillotined. Yet another face which plays an important role is the face of the prince himself, before and during his epileptic attacks. The expression of this face, together with the shriek that accompanies the attack, scares away Rogozhin when he intends to kill the prince. There is one final face to account for – the face of Christ on Holbein's painting which puzzles the prince, Rogozhin, and the dying Ipolite.

The face of Nastassya Filippovna dominates the novel. Its radiant beauty at first illuminates the whole landscape. Toward the end of *The Idiot*, Nastassya's striking face is a dark cloud that spells doom for everyone associated with her. Rogozhin tells the prince that he fell in love with Nastassya instantly and could not sleep that night. Upon seeing Nastassya's portrait in General Yepanchin's office, Prince Myshkin can understand Rogozhin's sentiments. Nastassya's beauty is so incomparable that it prompts Adelaida's spontaneous remark: "One could turn the world upside down with beauty like that."[1] Whether or not this is indeed so, and whether (physical or spiritual) "beauty can save the world," as Ipolite charges the prince of saying, these are the topics of great significance to Dostoevsky. The prince toys with them but does not reach a decisive conclusion.

Unlike General Yepanchin or Ganya, the prince sees more than Nastassya's good looks on her portrait: "Her face seems cheerful, but she has suffered terribly, hasn't she? The eyes tell this, and the cheekbones that form two points under her eyes. It's a proud face, a terribly proud face; and yet, here I can't tell, is she a good person? Ah, if only she were! Everything would be all right!" (Pt. I, Ch. 3, 37).

The prince cannot but notice Nastassya's suffering and pride. His intuition tells him that where pride is, malice lingers as well. Prince

1   *The Idiot*, trans. Henry and Olga Carlisle, Pt. I, Ch. 7, page 83. All subsequent references to the quotes from this work will be given in the text, immediately after the quotation.

Myshkin hopes this is not the case, yet his presentiment is correct. Nastassya's guardian, Totsky, seduced this gorgeous girl while she was still a teenager. Her "rite of initiation" from childhood to womanhood, her passage from light to darkness, was so painful that, even with the later help of the prince, she will not be able to find her way back to light. For Nastassya, things are never again going to be all right.

The idle and playful Yepanchin sisters develop an instant liking for the naïve prince. And so they challenge him during their first meeting to tell them what he sees in their faces. He obliges and is right on target, which fascinates them even more. The prince instantly recognizes that Madam Yepanchin is a wonderful child, despite her need to appear authoritarian. The oldest sister, Alexandra, has "a lovely and very sweet face," which reminds him "of the Holbein Madonna in Dresden" (Pt. I, Ch. 6, 78). And her face also betrays a hidden sorrow: "Your heart is certainly the kindest, but you are not gay." In the middle sister, Adelaida, the prince recognizes "a happy face, the most likeable face of all three" (Pt. I, Ch. 6, 78). He praises the spontaneity of her approach to others and her quickness in understanding them. The prince does not say anything about the other side of that simple-mindedness, about the shallowness and a short span of attention with which Adelaida approaches her paintings' subjects – and her own life.

Nor does the prince say anything about the youngest sister, Aglaya. When pressed to do so, he tells her in her face what only a child – or an idiot – would dare say so directly: "You are extraordinarily beautiful, Aglaya Ivanovna. You are so pretty that one is afraid to look at you" (Pt. I, Ch. 7, 79). Of all present, Aglaya's mother is disappointed the most that he has nothing more to say. The prince defends himself in a mysterious way: "It is difficult to pass judgment on beauty; I am not ready yet. Beauty is a riddle" (Pt. I, Ch. 7, 79).

While commenting on this sentence, Eduard Thurneysen captures well Dostoevsky's sentiments when he claims that, "The beauty of woman seems to break out of all logical and ethical contexts, out of all perceptible continuity with the rest of life."[2]

---

2   Eduard Thurneysen, *Dostoevsky*, 24. See also Malcolm Jones, *Dostoyevsky: The Novel of Discord*, 102.

Since there is perhaps nothing that our soul craves as much as the sight of beauty, we find it difficult to cease talking about something so attractive. Adelaida, who is always ready for mischief, stays on the subject by asking the question the prince already answered: "She is beautiful, isn't she?" The prince steers the ship in the wrong direction: "Extremely! . . . Almost as beautiful as Nastassya Filippovna, though her face is quite different" (Pt. I, Ch. 7, 79–80).

In this one sentence Dostoevsky reveals the character of his hero. One of the reasons why the prince is so often called "an idiot" is because of his impracticality. One does not win any woman's heart by praising another, perhaps even more beautiful, woman in her presence. The prince will repeat this mistake several times. When with Aglaya he talks about Nastassya, and with Nastassya about Aglaya.

All this chit-chat about the faces of the Yepanchin ladies starts after the prince suggests to Adelaida to paint the face of a person about to be executed. The wealthy Yepanchin daughters have been spared the difficult trials of life. They do not know rites of initiation comparable to the trials of Nastassya Filippovna. The young ladies are interested in the mysteries of love, not in the mysteries of death. They do not know what to make of Myshkin's fascination with a person about to be guillotined, even though the execution the prince witnessed left a lasting impression on his soul. The important thing about this face, the prince argues, is not its unique physical characteristics. Rather, the painting would have to capture an exemplary moment. Both Myshkin and Ipolite later cite a line from Revelation which encapsulates what he is unsuccessfully trying to explain to Adelaida: This is the moment when, paradoxically, there will be no more time. Put more precisely, this is the moment when time stops, when everything freezes, at the boundary of life and death. "Did you ever feel like that when you've been frightened, in moments of terror when your reason still functions but to no avail?" (Pt. I, Ch. 5, 66). Adelaida does not answer because she does not know what to say, but the prince presses on. These are the moments when "the brain is terribly alive and active"; the person "knows everything and remembers everything" (Pt. I, Ch. 5, 67). Paint the face, the prince continues feverishly, with its blue lips kissing the cross and eyes that reveal that he "knows everything."

What that "everything" is which the executed knows and remembers in such moments before the blade falls, the prince does not say. He either guesses or, more likely, compares the experience of the executed with his epileptic attacks. Right before an attack, "in the midst of sadness, spiritual darkness, and a feeling of oppression, there were instants when it seemed his brain was on fire, and in an extraordinary surge all his vital forces would be intensified" (Pt. II, Ch. 5, 236). In such brief instants,

> His mind and heart were flooded with extraordinary light; all torment, all doubt, all anxieties were relieved at once, resolved in a kind of lofty calm, full of serene, harmonious joy and hope, full of understanding and the knowledge of the ultimate cause of things. But these moments, these flashes were only the presage of that final second (never more than a second) with which the fit itself began. That second was, of course, unbearable (Pt. II, Ch. 5, 236).

And then – like the fall of the guillotine blade – the fit begins: "The face is suddenly horribly distorted, especially the eyes." Spasms seize the entire body and not just the face. "A terrible, incredible scream, unlike anything imaginable, breaks forth; and with this cry all resemblance to a human being seems suddenly to disappear" (Pt. II, Ch. 5, 245).

Of all the fascinating things which Prince Myshkin mentions about the face of a dying person, there is one about which he is silent, although this may well be the main issue of the entire novel. Possibly Dostoevsky thinks that, at this point in the narrative, neither his readers nor the carefree Yepanchin ladies are ready for it yet. What the prince clearly believes is that death is also a rite – not of initiation but of purification. Symbolically speaking, this passage is reversed from the one of initiation. This time human beings pass from darkness to light, from the darkness of this world to the light of another.

The prince insists that the dying person be painted in such a way as if he "knows everything." All this person can know, strictly speaking, is the past, not the future. The ancients believe that we walk toward the future backwards – our faces are turned toward what has happened, and we are walking, unseeing, toward the future. Christianity reverses this pagan attitude. Through faith Christians are convinced that death is a rite of purification, a passage from darkness to light. A priest brings a cross to the dying person and he eagerly kisses it. The prince insists that this must be captured on the painting because it symbolizes the strength of faith, the ultimate victory of life over death, the triumph of spirit over nature.

The prince does not articulate this issue clearly enough to the Yepanchin girls, and it is brought closer to light only when Hans Holbein the Younger's painting, "Christ in the Tomb" is mentioned later in the novel.[3] This life-sized painting depicts the decaying body of Christ after the torturous death on the cross and before the resurrection. The image is a shockingly realistic portrayal of a man who has met a violent death. The body is swollen and is turning green around the wounds, indicating a state of corruption. The face is painted with a wide-open mouth and the eyes gazing with astonishment at some distant, perhaps inscrutable aim. Although the face of Christ is usually portrayed with the traces of extraordinary beauty, this face is positively ugly and repulsive. The viewer is spared none of the physical aspects of putrefaction.

A reproduction of this painting hangs in Rogozhin's house. When the prince visits him, Rogozhin calls his attention to the painting, curious to hear Myshkin's reaction. The prince offers a surprisingly detached response: He correctly identifies the painting, mentions that he had seen the original in Switzerland, and complements the quality of the copy. The prince understands that the painting may be shocking "to some," but it does not appear to have much effect on him.

The painting certainly bothers Rogozhin more than Myshkin. Rogozhin's late father, who was an "Old Believer" and member of the extreme sect of "Castrates," acquired a copy of this painting.

---

3   Hans Holbein the Younger was born either in 1497 or in 1498, and died of plague in 1543. His painting, the full title of which is "The Body of the Dead Christ in the Tomb," was painted either in 1521 or in 1522. John Ruskin considers Holbein to be a "most earnest and complete" artist, with incredible attention to every detail: "what he sees, he sees with his whole soul; what he paints, he paints with his whole might"; *The Art Criticism of John Ruskin*, 339.

The whole household and its family members suffer from this symbolic denial of life and emphasis on death. The house is as dark and unpleasant as a catacomb. Rogozhin's mother lives there alone, more dead than alive. Rogozhin – whose first name Parfyon means "virginal" – also does not know what do with his life. He has a volcanic passion, directed positively toward Nastassya Filippovna and negatively toward anyone who may take her away from him. But this passion presents an unbearable burden to Rogozhin. After several months of torturous struggle, his frenzy finds its release not in his love of Nastassya but in his murder of her.

Holbein's painting has an even more disturbing affect on Ipolite. In his "Essential Statement," this "progressive" young man describes the shock that the image of the dead Christ produces on him. Ipolite is dying of consumption, and the "Statement" is written as a disillusioned farewell to his friends and acquaintances before he attempts suicide. Ipolite is preoccupied with the mystery of death. He believes his death is imminent, and he both welcomes and fears it. When he sees the painting in Rogozhin's house, Ipolite is utterly captivated by it. Just as the sight of Nastassya Filippovna put Rogozhin in a state of seizure, this painting has the effect of seizure on Ipolite. It destroys any hope of life after death that this young nihilist secretly nourishes. The painting shatters any undisclosed hope that spirit may triumph over nature. The "deaf and unfeeling machine" of nature swallows up "a great and priceless Being." Ipolite wonders about those who brought the Christ's collapsed body down from the cross: "How could they believe, gazing on such a cadaver as that, that this martyr would be resurrected?" (Pt. III, Ch. 6, 427). Then an even scarier thought enters his mind: Had Christ known what would happen to Him, how would He have reacted? "And if on the eve of the crucifixion the Teacher could have seen His own image as He would be, would He then have mounted the cross and died as He did?" (Pt. III, Ch. 6, 427).

These questions belong to the very heart of Dostoevsky's novel. Ipolite has enough courage – and enough fear – to phrase them so directly. Once brought to surface, they burn like an open wound. Ipolite can be forgiven for he does not know what he is doing. The subtitle of his "Essential Statement" is *"Après moi le déluge,"* but once the Prince scratches Ipolite's egotistical and nihilistic surface he finds a scared child.

Ipolite's honest remarks about Holbein's painting help us understand why Dostoevsky is so preoccupied with faces in this novel. Together with *The Brothers Karamazov*, *The Idiot* belongs to Dostoevsky's most "Christian" novels. While in *The Karamazovs* the references to Jesus and Christianity are direct and many, Dostoevsky approaches the same issues in *The Idiot* in a more veiled way. Reading faces is not his only device, but it is the first we confront in the novel.

The word "face" indicates the surface of things, that which appears to us. In the case of human beings, facial expressions are indicative of both bodily and mental states. The face is not part-body and part-soul but both body and soul. The face is a crossroad, a meeting point of body and soul, for it belongs equally to both.

The ancient Greeks do not pay any particular attention to human faces. Their magnificent sculptures reveal that they are far more interested in the beauty of the human body. The Romans advance over the Greeks in the sense that they relate face to a mask. The Latin word *persona* means a mask which actors use; by using various masks, the same actors can play different roles in the same play. Both in their private lives and in their theaters the Romans show more awareness than the Greeks that there are many games we play with our faces: those of revealing and hiding, of seducing and deceiving.

The relevance of face and personality dramatically increases with the development of Christianity. While in Greek and Roman ontology personality is a mere addition to the independently existing being, for Christians personality is its true essence. The body secures the identity of a human being, i.e., its individuality, but neither its personality, nor its spiritual aspect. This aspect is most fully expressed through the face. The Bible abounds with unforgettable visual images, from the face of Job to the face of Christ on the cross.

While in the West the face of God and other sacred objects are represented in sculptures and paintings, in Dostoevsky's Orthodox Christianity, icons perform this role. The Russian word *ikona* derives from the Greek *eikona*, meaning "image" or "portrait." (The Russians also use the word *obraz* [= image] together with the word *ikona*.) The function of an icon is not only to represent the divine, but also to reassure us that the human face has retained the features of the divine face. As the object of devotion, an icon is put in a corner of a room and lit with a little light.[4]

An icon in general, regardless of whom it represents, portrays the intersection of God and mankind, the unknowable and the known, eternity and history. In Dostoevsky's works we often find icons which represent the Mother of God. She is the clearest symbol of the interplay between the divine and the human, the spiritual and the physical. In Dostoevsky's novels only women pray before the icon. By contemplating the image (the face) of the Mother of God, they hope to approximate its divine archetype. Sonia Marmeladova, in *Crime and Punishment*, is one such gentle, meek woman who does not attempt to "correct nature." In *The Brothers Karamazov*, Alyosha retains the image of his mother, Sophia, praying and crying before an icon. In *The Idiot*, the prince compares Alexandra Yepanchin's face to Holbein's gentle Madonna. Interestingly, we never see Alexandra or her sisters pray before the icon. It is easier to imagine Nastassya's hands folded in prayer, although Dostoevsky does not give us any such image in *The Idiot*. Of all the female characters in this novel, the quiet Vera Lebedeva – whose first name means "faith" and who is often seen with an infant sister in her hands – is portrayed as a true Russian woman most resembling the Mother of God. Like Sonia Marmeladova, Vera is the intermediary not only between the shameless behavior of her father and the innocence of children, but also between the material and the spiritual aspects of the world.

Dostoevsky's male characters display ambiguous attitudes toward the icon. In *The Possessed*, Stavrogin accidentally breaks

---

4   My discussion here relies on Sophie Olivier, "Icons in Dostoevsky's works," in *Dostoevsky and the Christian Tradition*, ed. George Pattison and Diane Oenning Thomson, 51–68, on Chapter 6 of Harriet Murav's *Holy Foolishness: Dostoevsky's Novels & the Poetics of Cultural Critique,* and on Christopher Merrill's book *Things of the Hidden God: Journey to the Holy Mountain.*

Tikhon's icon. In *The Adolescent*, Versilov smashes an icon against the stove so that it breaks into two parts. In *The Brothers Karamazov*, Fyodor breaks the icon of Alyosha's mother, to which she reacts with hysterical fits. Later in the same novel the Elder Zosima tells the story about his dying teenage brother Markel. The beginning of his spiritual transformation and his acceptance of death starts with his long-refused approval to the old nanny to light the lamp before the icon: "Light it, dearest, light it. I was a monster before not to let you light it. For that's your way of praying to God, and watching you makes me happy and in my happiness I pray for you too, which means that both of us are praying to the same God" (Bk. VI, Ch. 1, 288; translation modified).

The dying Ipolite never reaches this point. He has no roots in his native soil and religion. In the moments of crisis, Ipolite does not remember the image of God of the Russian Orthodoxy, but the Western painting devoid of any iconographical signs of divinity. Ipolite belongs to a generation educated in the Western spirit of doubt. He is afraid that death cannot be anything like what the prince imagines it to be. It is not a recovery of harmony and a passage to light, but a transition into a cold darkness of never-ending night. In the scared mind of Ipolite, the sacrifice of Christ has lost all meaning. And if His sacrifice has no meaning, how could the sacrifice of the prince, or of anyone else, have any meaning either?

Dostoevsky's *Idiot* raises more questions than it answers. Some things, however, we understand even at this stage of our discussion of this sublime novel. For Dostoevsky, face is the point of meeting of the bodily and the spiritual, or, more generally, of the two planes of existence: the profane and the sacred. This point allows us to see a marked difference between *The Idiot* and some of Dostoevsky's more negatively oriented novels. God is absent in *Notes from the Underground*, and for the most part from *The Possessed*. There are more indications of the presence of the divine in this world in *Crime and Punishment*, and this presence is even more intensely felt in *The Idiot*. God may not be directly seen and completely understood, but His presence is manifested in a variety of ways – through icons and faces, through Holbein's painting, and through Myshkin's acts of compassion. The profane and the sacred are inseparably interlaced together, and this intimate connection has significant implications for Dostoevsky's vision of the world and his understanding of the meaning of life.

The very presence of the sacred reveals that the world is not a uniform machine but pervaded by elements which are not fully homogeneous. This heterogeneity is manifested with regard to both space and time. Some space is a sanctuary, or a home, and in terms of its quality is irreducibly different from any other. Some moments are also more precious than others, and time is not just a linear tick-tock of successive, quantitatively identical units. The prince knows how rare and special some moments are. That is why he suggests that Adelaida paint the face of a person about to be executed. Recall also what he once told Rogozhin about that special moment of illumination before the epileptic seizure: "Yes, one might give one's whole life for this moment! . . . That moment by itself would certainly be worth the whole of life" (Pt. II, Ch. 5, 237).

Yet another lesson regarding the reading of faces and, more generally, of the experience of the sacred, deals with our being captivated by them. Rogozhin and Myshkin are "seized" by Nastassya's beauty; Myshkin experiences his epileptic seizures; Ipolite is captivated by the image of the dead Christ. Dostoevsky thinks it is better to be captivated by some ideal than be apathetic. Lebedev complaints about the spirit of our age in comparison to, say, the twelfth century. After admitting the backwardness and evils of the previous epochs, Lebedev issues an emphatic challenge to his audience during the surprise celebration of Myshkin's birthday:

> There must have been something stronger than the stake and fire, even stronger than a habit of twenty years. There must have been an idea stronger than all the calamities, the crop failures, torture, plague, leprosy, and all that hell which mankind could not have endured without that idea binding men together and guiding their hearts and fructifying the "water of life"! Show me anything as strong as that in our age of vice and railroads – that is, one should say in our age of vessels and railroads, but I say in our age of vices and railroads because I'm drunk but right. Show me an idea that binds men together with even half of the strength as in those days. And dare say, then, that the "water of

life" has not been weakened and polluted under this "star,"
under this network that has entangled people. And don't
try to scare me off with your prosperity, your wealth, the
rarity of famine, and the rapidity of the means of communication! There's more wealth, but there's less strength; the
binding idea doesn't exist anymore; everything has turned
soft, everything is rotten, and people are rotten (Pt. III,
Ch. 4, 397).

The crucial issues, then, are: (i) whether there is any ideal that
seizes us, (ii) what this ideal is, and (iii) how strongly it captivates us.

It is not accidental that Lebedev gives this speech during the
prince's birthday celebration. Birthdays symbolize our remembrance and celebration of events of the past. Reading faces turns
us also in the direction of the past; our faces resemble those of our
ancestors. Dostoevsky strengthens this connection of faces and the
past by making Myshkin and Nastassya express their conviction
that they have seen each other's faces somewhere before. We know
that this is physically impossible, and Nastassya herself remarks,
"I seem to have seen your eyes somewhere – but that can't be! . . .
Perhaps in a dream" (Pt. I, Ch. 9, 109). "Perhaps in a dream"
is an indication that Dostoevsky thinks that reading faces transposes us to a primeval plane of existence, that faces are related
to archetypes.[5] Reminding us of the past and of the sacred is also
the function of an icon. The very word "religion" means "to trace
back," to return to our origin, to our ultimate parents, to our home.
Like religion, reading faces takes us backward, toward the past that
still has an impact on how we are and what we strive toward. If
we are to find the meaning of human life, we have to face our

5   In *The Art of Creation*, 353, Arthur Koestler clarifies that the literal
    meaning of the word "archetype" is "implanted (*typos* = stamp) from the
    beginning." The archetypal material points to the roots of our thinking
    and our being, in contrast to the surface preoccupation of modern man,
    who lives under the illusion that, following one of his utopian visions of
    a blissful future, he can recreate or restructure the world *ex nihilo*. The
    locus classicus for the discussion of archetypes is Carl Gustav Jung, *The
    Archetypes of the Collective Unconsciousness*.

past in hope of remembering our spiritual origin and of recovering our home.

As reading faces is not a matter of abstract and calculative thinking, Dostoevsky does not expect that rediscovering life's meaning is either. Reading faces belongs to thinking not in concepts and abstractions but to thinking in pictures and images. It is not accidental that mythological stories and the Bible are full of concrete visual representations, but mythology and religion are not the only occasions when we think in pictures and images. The same kind of thinking dominates the manifestations of the unconsciousness in dream, in hallucinatory or epileptic states, in the creative works of artists and scientists, and in the play of children. Besides reading faces, playing games belongs to the core of *The Idiot* as well.

Playing Games

According to Lebedev's interpretations of the Apocalypse – and Nastassya Filippovna concurs with this reading –

> we're living in the age of the third horse, the black one, whose rider carries the scales in his hand; for everything in our century is weighted on scales and settled by agreement, and people are seeking only for their rights: "A measure of wheat for a penny and three measures of barley for a penny," yet they still want to have a free spirit, a pure heart, a sound body, and all the gifts of God. But they won't hang on to these things just by rights alone, and the pale horse will follow, and he who is named Death behind whom is Hell (Pt. II, Ch. 2, 210).

What to make of Lebedev's interpretation? Edward Wasiolek takes it seriously and claims that it "can be the epigraph to *The Idiot*."[6] Everyone in Petersburg society where the prince suddenly finds himself demands some rights, and the common denominator of these rights is money. Burdovsky and his fellow nihilists demand that his rights regarding the inheritance be satisfied; Ganya and his sister Varya believe that their family has been treated unfairly; Totsky and General Yepanchin seek the rights that

---

6   Edward Wasiolek, *Dostoevsky: The Major Fiction*, 85.

belong to them based on their social status and charitable deeds. Yes, indeed, we have arrived at the age in which all the insulted and the injured seek their rights, and "a penny" is customarily taken as the measure of these rights.

Whether all of this is indeed in the Apocalypse is ultimately irrelevant. What certainly matters for Dostoevsky is that there is a different way to approach life than through seeking one's rights, just as there is a different economy than the economy of the market. The prince himself is a messenger and a symbol of that alternative view of the good and the holy. He creates a commotion in the stale social hierarchy by his childish playfulness and his utter disregard for rights and riches. One immediate effect of his presence is to provoke others into playfulness and lead them, at least for the time being, to suspend their usual ways of behavior. Playfulness does not exclude seriousness – the prince cannot be accused of not being serious – but it allows for a new spirit which provokes imagination and brings different attitude toward life.

To illustrate this and penetrate deeper into the meaning of *The Idiot*, we will consider only three of the numerous "games" played in the course of the novel. The first is Ferdyshchenko's game at Nastassya's birthday party. This game consists of telling the worst of all the actions committed in the course of one's life. The second occurs at the conclusion of the same party, when Nastassya tempts Ganya by throwing a large bundle of rubles into the fireplace. The third game unfolds throughout the novel, the "love" game of Aglaya and Prince Myshkin, culminating in their engagement and sudden break-up.

The set for the first two games is intentionally theatrical. It is Nastassya Filippovna's twenty-fifth birthday and at her evening party the queen of beauty will announce who she is going to marry. Totsky and General Yepanchin have every reason to believe that it will be their protégé Ganya, which would suit their plans perfectly: With Nastassya Filippovna removed from his life, Totsky is free to marry Alexandra Yepanchina. The General, on his part, is hoping he can enjoy the favors of Nastassya Filippovna through Ganya. Ganya, who loves Aglaya, not Nastassya, is also present, as is the clown Ferdyshchenko and several other characters. The tense atmosphere is relaxed by the arrival of the prince, who comes uninvited. The stage is set, but Nastassya does not make her announcement – she appears to be waiting for something to happen or someone to arrive. To cheer up the guests, and also to mock them, Ferdyshchenko proposes an ingenious game, immediately supported by Nastassya Filippovna: an honest public confession of the most evil act a person has committed. While the ladies are excluded, all the gentlemen are expected to participate voluntarily.

Ferdyshchenko's proposal is not greeted with enthusiasm. From the point of view of the majority, the game is counterproductive. The stakes are high and the gain nonexistent. Unlike religious confession, in this game one is to confess without being forgiven and, quite contrary to the sacrament, publicly exposed. For the hurt pride of Nastassya Filippovna this game is just right – certain gentlemen of high reputation should be exposed for who they really are. Since the cards are in Nastassya's hands, the guests have no choice but to participate.

Dostoevsky was a great admirer of Friedrich Schiller from his youth and was certainly familiar with his famous view that nothing reveals our character as much as playing.[7] The two games played at Nastassya's birthday party are very much intended to reveal the characters of those present. After Ferdyshchenko's proposal, Ganya spontaneously reacts: "Naturally, everyone is going to lie" (Pt. I, Ch. 13, 149). Ganya says too much. He is not supposed to admit aloud, or at least not so bluntly, that the society is run on lies. Ganya cannot control himself because the lies involved around Nastassya's planned marriage hurt both his self-respect and his interests. Ferdyshchenko's reply to Ganya's "Naturally, everyone is going to lie," is equally illuminating: "Yes, and the interesting thing is just how a man will lie!" (Pt. I, Ch. 13, 149). Society is run on lies, but there is a great difference in what we lie about and how we do so.

---

7   See Friedrich Schiller, *On the Aesthetic Education of Man*, especially the famous Fifteenth Letter in which he claims that man "is wholly Man when he is playing." For further discussion, see M.I. Spariousu, *Dionysus Reborn: Play and the Aesthetic Dimension in Modern Philosophical and Scientific Discourse*, 53–66; and Frederick Beiser, *Schiller as Philosopher: A Re-Examination*, 119–68.

After the drawing of lots, Ferdyshchenko is the first to confess. He tells how he stole a small amount of money from a friend's house. One of the maids was accused and dismissed, and Ferdyshchenko himself was among those who interrogated the maid and expressed his outrage at her lack of morals. General Yepanchin is next. He had a pot stolen from him and he rushed to an old woman whom he believed had stolen it. She was sitting in her chair without saying a word to his fuming accusations, and only later did he find out why she did not move or say anything – at the time of his rage she was already dead. To relieve himself of the "sense of guilt," General Yepanchin donated a large sum of money to a charity. The next is Totsky, the seducer of the teenage Nastassya. He confesses a nasty joke he played on a friend in love. This friend told him about how his beloved greatly desired camellias for a special occasion and how lucky he has been to find a rare merchant who grows camellias. Before this special occasion Totsky meets the merchant and convinces him to sell Totsky all the camellias before his friend can buy any. After finding out that every camellia is sold, Totsky's friend is driven into delirium. He eventually recovers but is killed during his next military campaign. Many years later, poor Totsky still remembers this event with uneasiness and guilt.

At this point Nastassya interrupts the game. She is fed up with the shamelessness of her guests and their obsession with "a penny." They believe that money can buy everything – beauty, redemption, honor. Nastassya then starts her own game – the game of rebellion against the world so blatantly corrupted by money.[8] To the astonishment of all her guests, Nastassya asks the prince to determine her fate and tell whether or not she should marry Ganya. Whatever the prince says, Nastassya will accept. She only met him earlier that day, yet she has full confidence in him: "The prince is the first man I have ever met in my whole life whose sincerity and devotion I have believed in. He believed in me at first sight, and I believe in him" (Pt. I, Ch. 14, 161).

---

8   Leonid Grossman characterizes the atmosphere in *The Idiot* as worship "of the Golden Calf"; *Dostoevsky: A Biography*, 436. Malcolm Jones offers a similar interpretation; *op. cit.*, 94.

"*Ecce homo*," Nietzsche would add with a smile.

The guests are astonished that Nastassya can put her fate into the hands of the prince, whom she barely knows, but she is determined to respect anything he says. The prince is ecstatic at the chance to tell her not to marry Ganya, for this is the purpose of his attendance at the party to which he is not invited. Following his words, the feverish Nastassya announces that she will not marry Ganya. She then returns to General Yepanchin a precious necklace received earlier that day and rejects Totsky's dowry of 75,000 rubles. She will begin a new life without a penny.

The abrupt arrival of Rogozhin and his pals escalates the already heated atmosphere. Earlier that day, Rogozhin also made a bid on Nastassya's favors. He first offered 18,000 rubles, then 40,000, and finally 100,000. After a maddening day spent trying to collect this enormous amount in cash, he now throws in front of Nastassya's feet the sum wrapped in the greasy pages of *The Stock Exchange News*.

This is not the end of bidding. In an unexpected reversal of fortune, Myshkin also proposes to Nastassya and then discovers that he has inherited a large amount of money. Nastassya hesitates to accept his offer because of her stained past, but after the prince's most sincere assurances that he will always respect her, caught in the whirlwind of exasperating emotions she agrees: "Then I really am a princess! . . . I am getting married, have you heard? To the prince. He has a million and a half – he's Prince Myshkin and he's marrying me!" (Pt. I, Ch. 16, 173).

This moment is a highly significant one in Dostoevsky's opus. It captures the structure behind all the chance happenings and the unpredictability of events in his novels. As Yuri Lotman points out,

> unpredictability and even absurdity in Dostoevsky are a sign not only of scandal but also of miracle. Scandal and miracle are the poles which mark, on the one hand, final ruin and, on the other, final salvation and they are both unmotivated and abnormal. So the eschatological moment of instant and final solution to the tragic contradictions in

life is not brought into life from outside, from the domain of
ideas, but is found in life itself.[9]

In *Notes from the Underground* there are no miracles. In
The Possessed there are scandals. In *Crime and Punishment* there
are traces of miracles. Only in *The Idiot* is there a closer balance
between scandals and miracles. Nonetheless, as an illustration for
this important insight, Lotman does not have in mind *The Idiot*
but *The Gambler*. Gambling embodies both "the outrageousness of
outrageous life" and the expectation of "the eschatological miracle
as a solution to all problems." The love of gambling, as Dostoevsky
knew well, is not a matter of money but of a hunger for instant
and final salvation. This is exactly the position in which Nastassya
Filippovna finds herself – she is contemptuous of money but is
yearning for that final solution and salvation.

And then, just when everything appears settled, when it looks
that Nastassya will be walking away with the bargain of her life,
Rogozhin's shriek wakes her up from the spell. Rogozhin refuses
to admit that the game is over and demands of the prince: "Give
her up!"

In *The Gambler*, the cool Englishman Astley remarks that
"roulette is a mostly Russian game," implying the antithesis
between Western caution and utilitarianism and Russian longing for instant salvation and ruin. Alexey Ivanovich, the hero of
The Gambler, faces the same dilemma. And so does Nastassya
Filippovna.

In yet another reversal, Nastassya decides to go away with
Rogozhin because, according to her admission, she realizes that
she cannot forget her past and fears she will ruin the prince: "I'm
a shameless person myself. I was Totsky's concubine. Prince! You
ought to marry Aglaya Yepanchin and not Nastassya Filippovna,
or else – Ferdyshchenko will be pointing his finger at you!" (Pt. I,
Ch. 16, 176).

Not a very rational reason, we admit, but the shocked guests are
beginning to realize what is going on. "This is Sodom, Sodom!"
shouts the shocked General Yepanchin, but Nastassya's game is not

9   Yuri Lotman, *Universe of the Mind: A Semiotic Theory of Culture*, 167.

over yet. She realizes that Rogozhin is no prince, but also that he is the second best among the present. Like the prince, Rogozhin does not care about money but about Nastassya. His gift is for Nastassya to do with it whatever she wants. Since the money is hers, Nastassya shows her final contempt for it and the society which worships it. She declares she will throw the whole bundle of 100,000 ruble into the fireplace, and only Ganya can take it out. If he can bend so low to his deity, the money is his. If not, if he still has some dignity left, the money will disappear in the flames.

Dostoevsky is superior to any writer in describing the kind of games in which everything is pushed to the limit, in which the lives and destinies of his heroes and heroines hang on a narrow thread. The vivid images that Dostoevsky creates could not be easily duplicated. Some of them, like the one that follows, are of unmatched mastery. As the hungry flames lick the greasy wrappings, the company is captivated by the sight. They are in the "moment" of seizure which approaches the intensity of Myshkin's epileptic attack or that of the condemned's expectation of the falling blade. The low creatures Lebedev and Ferdyshchenko beg Nastassya to allow them to crawl into the fire to save the money. The others are crossing themselves. With an "insane smile on his face," Ganya faints and falls down to the floor.

His vanity, concludes Nastassya, is greater than his lust for money. Let him have the bundle, she decides. For the prince, she has a few words before running away with Rogozhin: "Good-bye, Prince, in you I've seen what a human being is for the first time in my life!" (Pt. I, Ch. 16, 182).

At the street entrance, the four troikas are already pulling away. The only thing that breaks the silence of the night is Rogozhin's hysterical, uncontrollable laughter. Inside the house, Totsky is not sure whether he is trying to console his friend General Yepanchin or himself: "Who would not sometimes be captivated by this woman to the point of losing his reason and – all the rest? . . . My God, what might have been made of a woman with such character and such beauty. But in spite of all efforts, in spite even of her education – it is all lost!" (Pt. I, Ch. 16, 183).

In *The Idiot*, Dostoevsky forces us to reflect on the nature of play and playfulness. Like Plato and Shakespeare, Dostoevsky does not think that tragedy and comedy, scandal and miracle, exclude each other. Quite the contrary, both are needed for playfulness in the highest sense. Dostoevsky engages his audience in a variety of ways. For example, he does not miss the opportunity to play with the names of his characters. The name of the prince, Lev Myshkin, brings together the allusions to two animals which we do not usually associate – lion (Lev) and mouse (Mysh; Myshka = little mouse). The name of Nastassya Filippovna is mentioned several hundred times in the novel, but her last name – Barashkova – only on rare occasions. *Barashek* is the Russian word for lamb, which in combination with her first name – Anastasia, abbreviated as Nastassya – suggests that she is marked as a victim to be resurrected by virtue of her sacrificial death. Aglaya's name means "splendor," and she is one of the "three Graces," the other two being Euphrosyne (= rapture) and Thalia (= abundance). While the mythological Euphrosyne sends forth the energy of Apollo into the world, Aglaya brings the energy back, and Thalia embraces the other two. The three Graces correspond roughly to the Christian Trinity: Euphrosyne to the Son, Aglaya to the Holy Spirit, and Thalia to the Father.

As René Girard does, it is worth pointing out that Dostoevsky does not use religious symbols to promote institutional religion; they are entirely in the function of the novel and his art.[10] Art itself is something playful that displays and reveals the nature of play and playfulness. Before we return to the further consideration of *The Idiot*, let us briefly touch upon two important features of play and playfulness: their double nature and their relatedness to abundance and gift.

When a boy builds a sand castle, he is aware that the castle is both real and unreal. It is a castle, and not an ordinary house, but it is not a castle because it is a pile of sand. The balance between the two is delicate, and children are better in maintaining it than adults. Adults are too rigidly trained in the serious logic of either/or, which kills the nature of play. There are two typical reactions to this ominous training. Either we end up being fools carried away by the game, or we become cynics who refuse to play and perhaps

10 René Girard, *Deceit, Desire and the Novel*, 312.

with time become incapable of playing. In our attempt to reconstruct Dostoevsky's understanding of the meaning of life and of
Christ's sacrifice, we need to keep both options in mind at all times.
Dostoevsky creates fiction that is not just fiction. He is a player who
plays with the most important questions of human existence.

Dostoevsky holds that we would be better people, and our age less
spiritually devastating, if we were more playful. Playfulness develops certain attitudes and contains others. Arthur Koestler's division
of human emotions into the self-asserting and the self-transcending
helps us clarify Dostoevsky's attitude. Among self-asserting emotions Koestler considers anger, fear, hatred, malice, and hostility.
Among self-transcending, he counts compassion, love, care, and
sympathy. The self-asserting emotions are focused on "here and
now," while self-transcending emotions establish a distance from
"here and now" and are more concerned with "then and there."
Self-asserting emotions are inflexible and non-participatory, while
self-transcending emotions are flexible and participatory.[11]

If we are to understand the meaning of life, we should not look
at our lives only in connection with what is worst in it, and that is
evil with everything it represents – murder, victimization, destruction, hatred, fear, or deception. We need to look at ourselves also
when we are at our best – most alive, most loving, and most playful. This is exactly what Dostoevsky tries to do in *The Idiot*, and
that is why we need to return to his narrative about the two most

---

11 See Koestler, *op. cit.*, 305: "Thus compassion, and the other varieties of
    the participatory emotions, attach themselves to the narrative told on
    the stage or in print, like faithful dogs, and follow it whatever the sur-
    prises, twists, and incongruities the narrator has in store for them. By
    contrast, hostility, malice, and contempt tend to persist in a straight
    course, impervious to the subtleties of intellect; to them a spade is a
    spade, a windmill a windmill, and a Picasso nude with three breasts an
    object to leer at. The self-transcending emotions seem to be guided by the
    maxim *tout comprendre c'est tout pardonner*; the self-asserting emotions
    are designed for assertion, not comprehension. Hence, when attention
    is suddenly displaced from one frame of reference to another, the self-
    asserting impulses, deprived of their *raison d'être*, are spilled in the
    process, whereas the participatory emotions are transferred to the new
    matrix."

splendid characters in his novel: Prince Myshkin and Aglaya, and their intriguing love-game.

Dostoevsky unfolds this love-game in three different phases. The first is the stage of the appreciation of the mutual beauty, the second is the love-game proper, which then transposes into its final stage – the marriage-game. The first phase begins during the initial meeting – the prince cannot but notice Aglaya's splendor, just as she cannot but notice that he is a prince of inner beauty. The course of events leads to their separation and thus creates an obstacle for the further development of this mutual admiration. The prince helps the cause by sending Aglaya a short but significant letter. She correctly understands the hints that the letter contains and does not show it to anyone. Aglaya hides the letter in her copy of *Don Quixote*, for she intuitively understands that the knight of La Mancha and the prince are distant spiritual cousins.

The next meeting between the two shows how strong their initial attraction had been. With time and distance it did not die. If anything, it grew stronger, at least in Aglaya's case. The meeting is playful to the highest degree. It takes place a few days after the prince returns to Petersburg and has a serious epileptic attack. He is recovering in Lebedev's summer house in Pavlovsk, a short distance from the summer residence of the Yepanchins. Upon hearing the news, Madam Yepanchin typically overreacts: "He is on the deathbed," and rushes with her daughters to see the prince, now nearly recovered. In the days before this meeting, the secret of the "Poor Knight" has somehow become familiar to Aglaya's sisters. To the annoyance of the baffled mother, who does not understand what they are giggling about, the sisters tease Aglaya and provoke her to reveal in the prince's presence more than she desires. Besides Don Quixote, Aglaya also associates Myshkin with Pushkin's poem "Poor Knight." To those present in Lebedev's house, Aglaya explains: "This poem presents a man who is capable of having an ideal and, what's more, who having set himself an ideal believes in it, and having believed in it blindly devotes his whole life to it. This does not often happen in our days" (Pt. II, Ch. 6, 260). How does Aglaya perceive him whom she admires so much? She holds that "the 'poor knight' is the same as Don Quixote, but a serious one and not comic. At first I didn't understand and I laughed, but now I love the 'poor knight', and most of all, I respect his deeds of valor" (Pt. II, Ch. 6, 261).

Aglaya does and does not understand the prince. She understands how unique he is and how his ideals are higher than those of the people who surround her. Unfortunately, Aglaya confuses two rare but distinguishable virtues, those of nobility and purity. The spirit which is directed toward the highest ideal is noble, and thus turned away from everything small and average. Nobility is associated with high-mindedness and generosity. Don Quixote is one example of a person striving for nobility, as are the medieval Knights of the Round Table.

Purity, by contrast, means something untainted by evil. This is the principal Christian virtue, and Jesus is its greatest model. Purity is the highest spiritual value which, however, is not the result of "deeds of valor," nor the result of fighting and conquering evil. Purity is an original state before all guilt, the virtue of an innocent person. As Nicolai Hartmann explains,

> One who is pure has nothing to hide; concealment, secretiveness is alien to him. He . . . lacks the shame of the guilty. He needs no covering, no mask. . . . The same goes for his directness in conduct. He lacks both the occasion and the worldly wisdom for tricks. He has no need of deception.[12]

Hartmann recognizes Prince Myshkin as an exemplar of purity, not of nobility. Aglaya does not, and this is the source of many of her disappointments. She cannot understand why he is not excited about having a duel with an officer he offended while defending Nastassya Filippovna. Aglaya is shocked even more when she learns that the prince has no idea how to load or fire a pistol.

From the whole confusion surrounding Aglaya's passionate recitation of Pushkin's poem and her account of it, the prince understands that she may well be in love with him. The surest sign

12 Nicolai Hartmann, *Ethics*, vol. II, 213; translation modified. Hartmann offers elaborate distinctions between nobility, purity, richness of experience, and goodness, as well as between justice, brotherly love, love of the remote, and personal love.

of her strong feelings is her jealousy toward Nastassya Filippovna. While citing the poem, Aglaya changes the original initials of A.M.D. ("*Ave, mater Dei*"; "Hail, the Mother of God") into A.N.B. ("*Ave, Nastassya Barashkova*"). Neither the prince nor Aglaya could at that point imagine to what extent this jealous love will contribute to his doom, so well anticipated by Pushkin's poem:

> Returning to his distant castle,
> He lived a lonely season,
> Ever sad and ever silent,
> And dies, bereft of reason (Pt. II, Ch. 7, 263).

Like romantic medieval lovers, the two spend time together playing games. Aglaya beats him badly in chess, but the prince is incontestably better in playing "Fools." Aglaya is not used to losing and displays all of the colorful feathers of her temper after the loss. She then tries to compensate for her outburst by convincing Kolya and his friend to sell her their hedgehog, which she sends immediately to the prince as a sign of her affection.

There is nothing more difficult to handle than love. Beauty is a tricky thing, but love is far tougher. We have already seen the mismatch of beauty and love in Nastassya Filippovna – instead of trusting her feelings and marrying the prince, she would rather "sacrifice" herself and suffer with Rogozhin. The issue now is whether the beautiful Aglaya is better versed in the mysteries of love.

For Aglaya, to be in love is to be possessed by the desire to possess the beloved. This, at any rate, is how she understands love and its demands. She is possessed and she wants to possess, which, she finally accepts, should be translated into marriage. As far as Aglaya is concerned, her union with the prince has to exclude Nastassya Filippovna – love does not leave any room for the third.

Dostoevsky provides plenty of illustrations that the prince does not see things in the same way, neither with respect to beauty nor to love. Recall the prince's accounts of how he liked to spend his days in Switzerland. Every afternoon he would to go to see the waterfall, a typical example of natural beauty, but also a unique kind of beauty. As Dudley Young clarifies,

> The waterfall is not only beautiful, as flowers and birdsong are beautiful, but it also embodies power and violence. The roaring water crushes upon itself with great force . . . and yet nothing changes, nothing dies: extraordinary violence is unleashed and yet contained, and contained moreover in an experience both awesome and delightful. No wonder such things tend to draw us to them hypnotically, as if all of life's wearying contradictions might be resolved by surrendering to the mystery of such changeless change, harmless harm, and terrible beauty.[13]

The prince reacts to this "terrible beauty" by sitting next to it in reflection. The "terrible beauty" of the waterfall does not excite him to leap – which is the original meaning of the word "play"[14] – but to sit in quiet appreciation of this majestic gift of nature.

The prince treats love in a similar manner. The story of Marie and the children at the beginning of the novel shows that just as his virtue – purity – is Christian, so is his love. Platonic *Eros* presupposes that there must always be a reason for erotic attraction: the beauty and attractiveness of the person or, in more sophisticated cases, her virtue. The Christian conception of love means precisely the absence of any reason for love. Christian love is moreover universal and cannot be limited to one person or object – to love one is to love none. The gift of love is – like any gift – to be passed on and spread around, not possessed for oneself. The prince does not quite understand our concept of possession, and thus has a very unconventional conception of love and marriage.

Taken by themselves, these differences between the prince and Aglaya need not lead to the scandal that occurs in the novel. The prince does have very strong feelings for Aglaya as a unique individual, and this feeling is stronger than any he may have for other persons. Moreover, Aglaya forgives him for the "scandalous" behavior during the party at the Yepanchins where the prince was to be presented to the "respectable society" as her bridegroom. It is the set of circumstances, combined with the differences in the

---

13 Dudley Young, *The Origins of the Sacred: The Ecstasies of Love and War*, 190.
14 Johan Huizinga, *Home Ludens: A Study of Play Element in Culture*, 37.

understanding of love, which leads to the scandalous outcome of the meeting between Aglaya, Nastassya, and the prince.

Aglaya's tension leads her to force the issue: No matter if it ends in scandal or miracle, once and forever she needs to clarify the relationships between the three of them. The anxiety builds because before the fateful encounter Nastassya and Aglaya exchange letters. Nastassya, who initiates the exchange, suggests that Aglaya marry the prince and find her happiness with him; Nastassya would step away and marry Rogozhin. This fits Aglaya's plans, except that she senses from the letters just how much Nastassya loves the prince. Aglaya thus forces the meeting of the three, hoping to relieve her anxiety by seeing for herself that the prince does not love Nastassya but only her.

By forcing the issue, Aglaya commits a terrible mistake. She demands proof of love, which is a cardinal sin, equivalent to asking for a proof of the immortality of the soul before we become genuine believers in God. Two later episodes show that Aglaya's behavior is not an accidental whim but a revelation of her immaturity. First she demands proof of love from Ganya by asking him to burn his finger in the candle flame. Since poor Ganya does not understand what she wants, out of spite Aglaya runs away with a Polish "count" and converts to Catholicism.

The bitter exchange between Aglaya and Nastassya displays just how fragile these two proud women are. Aglaya gets carried away and loses control over her words. Nastassya realizes what is going on and hits her right in the heart: "You wanted to find out for yourself whether he loves me more than you or not, because you are terribly jealous" (Pt. IV, Ch. 8, 595). Nastassya feels instantly that her enemy is shaken and continues her counterattack. Like a gambler possessed completely by the game, Nastassya then stakes the future of all three of them on the last card: "There he is – look!" she cries at last to Aglaya, pointing to the prince. "If he doesn't come to me at once, if he doesn't take me and doesn't give you up, take him for yourself, I give him up, I don't want him!" (Pt. IV, Ch. 8, 596).

Caught between the persons he loves more than anybody else, the prince is the one who makes the last blunder. As Nastassya and Aglaya "both stood there in expectation, staring at the prince like insane women," he "perhaps did not understand the whole force of the challenge. . . . He only saw before him the face, despairing and demented, which he had once told Aglaya had 'pierced his heart forever.'" The prince could not bear it and turned reproachfully to Aglaya: "How can you? She's – so unhappy!" (Pt. IV, Ch. 8, 596).

This is not exactly what you expect your bridegroom to say to you, and the humiliated Aglaya runs out. "The prince ran too, but at the threshold a pair of arms seized him." After asking him: "You're following her?" Nastassya drops unconscious into his arms. The prince stays with Nastassya. In the scene that represents a reversal of the pieta, the prince "at once began caressing her head again, and tenderly drawing his hands over her cheeks, soothing and comforting her like a child" (Pt. IV, Ch. 8, 597). The game was (almost) over. And all have lost.

The Meaning of Sacrifice

From the beginning of the last part of *The Idiot* (Part IV), the narrator turns against the prince. He wants to convince us to blame Myshkin for the disaster that occurs. The narrator does not tell us about the implications of this scandal, but I have already indicated some of them in connection with Ipolite's reflections on Holbein's painting of the dead Christ. The questions that Ipolite raises reduce to two. First: How can those who had seen the distorted body of Christ taken down from the cross and put in the grave still believe in Him and in the possibility of resurrection? Second: Had Jesus been able to foresee what would happen to Him, would He have considered His sacrifice worth making?

At the end of the novel, we are left with these same questions. If we sympathize with the Jesus-like character of the prince, what do we make of the events that take place? Are Ipolite's despair and the narrator's disappointment the last words on the subject?

These issues are of such crucial importance to Dostoevsky that he makes Yevgeny Pavlovitch discuss them with the prince himself. Yevgeny Pavlovitch is a wealthy and socially well-respected suitor of Aglaya. Despite that, there is no personal animosity between him and the prince. Yevgeny Pavlovitch even displays signs of sympathy for Myshkin, both before and after the scandalous event. Nevertheless, as the narrator's representative of practical wisdom and common sense, Yevgeny Pavlovitch takes Aglaya's side.

The dialogue between the prince and Yevgeny Pavlovitch is yet another masterpiece of Dostoevsky's art. While the prince is understandably emotional and confused, Yevgeny Pavlovitch is articulate and intelligent. He seems to understand everything, yet in his lucid reconstruction of what has happened it becomes increasingly clear that he misses or distorts virtually every important point. Yevgeny Pavlovitch is a character-type later developed in the person of the prosecutor at Dmitri's trial in *The Brothers Karamazov*.

The prince tells Yevgeny Pavlovitch that he is going to marry Nastassya Filippovna, not to make her happy, but "I'm simply marrying her – that's all." But that marriage changes nothing, "it doesn't matter." He is marrying Nastassya, yet he cannot bear to face her eyes: "'I am afraid of her face,' he added in extraordinary terror." So, concludes Yevgeny Pavlovitch, you are marrying Nastassya even though you do not love her. Prince Myshkin shocks him one more time:

"Oh, no, I love her with all my soul! For she's – a child. She's a child now, a complete child. Oh, you know nothing!"

"And at the same time you assured Aglaya Ivanovna that you loved her?"

"Oh, yes, yes."

"How is that? Do you want to love both of them?"

"Oh, yes, yes!"

"For heaven's sake, Prince, what are you saying? Come to your senses!"

"Without Aglaya I – I absolutely must see her! I – I shall soon die in my sleep. Oh, if only Aglaya knew, if she knew everything – I mean absolutely everything. For in this matter you have to know everything – that's what is most important! Why can we never learn *everything* about another person, when we have to, when that other person is at fault. But I don't know what I'm saying, I'm all mixed up. You've shocked me terribly" (Pt. IV, Ch. 9, 608).

Yevgeny Pavlovitch concludes that the prince is not in his right mind. While this may be part of the truth, it is not the whole of it. To come an inch closer to the truth, and also nearer to answering Ipolite's questions, let us separate two issues intermingled in

The Idiot. The first deals with whether what happens at the end of the novel had to happen, considering the prince's character. The second and more important issue deals with the meaning of the scandal that occurred, and ultimately, with the meaning of the prince's sacrifice. As Christ ends up in the tomb on Holbein's painting, Myshkin "dies in his sleep" and ends up in the asylum, in the tomb of his own deranged mind. What should we make of this?

The first issue is easier to resolve: A disaster had to occur. As much as Dostoevsky resisted this conclusion and played with other options, there is no other consistent way to conclude the novel. The prince's role in this scandal is anticipated several times during the course of the narrative. The most obvious and the best-developed episode is the one when Prince Myshkin disappoints the Yepanchins and their class on the one hand, and Burdovsky and the representatives of the younger, nihilistic group on the other. The Yepanchins cannot understand why the prince even associates with such lowly "bastards," much less why he is willing to take their unfounded demands seriously. The nihilists cannot grasp why this nice person who shows his contempt toward the higher classes and their greed by throwing his money around has anything to do with those "parasites" who live on the blood and sweat of the poor. Standing alone between the two groups, the prince is scrutinized by both parties with the greatest attention. To the disappointment of the both, he behaves according to his kind, gentle, child-like nature, willing to assume responsibility for everyone's fault. By smiling innocently and answering seriously the most shameless questions and demands, the prince annoys everyone present. The two groups ignore for once their irreconcilable differences and turn their indignation on the only one among them who is pure. To all their reproaches he replies with gentleness, for what they quarrel about is irrelevant. What really matters, they do not even try to understand.[15]

For further clarification of Prince Myshkin's character, recall one of the funniest and most telling encounters in the novel, which

15   My presentation in this paragraph relies on Hermann Hesse's interpretation of *The Idiot*; see Hesse, "Thoughts on *The Idiot* by Dostoevsky," in *My Belief: Essays on Life and Art*, 88–89.

occurs during the first meeting of the prince and the Yepanchin ladies. Madam Yepanchin asks the prince about his initial impression of Switzerland, and he gives her more than she bargains for. "My first impression was very strong," began the prince in a solemn manner, explaining that he had a hard time adjusting to how foreign everything was:

> This foreignness was killing me. I completely recovered from this depression, as I recall, one night after I had reached Switzerland and was in Basel, when I was awakened by the braying of a donkey in the marketplace. The donkey made a great impression on me and for some reason pleased me intensely, and at the same time everything seemed to clear up in my head (Pt. I, Ch. 5, 57).

We can easily imagine the shocked face of Madam Yepanchin and the hearty laughter of her daughters after this reply. Of all the remarkable things in Switzerland, a donkey made the strongest impression on the prince! While speaking of Basel, he could have mentioned Holbein's painting of Christ, where it is exhibited and which the prince later told Rogozhin he saw there. Already during this first meeting, we see that the reactions of others do not distract Prince Myshkin from his course. Like a stubborn mule, he continues:

> From that time on I developed a great fondness for donkeys; it's even a kind of special affection. I began to ask questions about them, because I had never really seen them before, and I was immediately convinced that it is the most useful of animals, hardworking, strong, patient, cheap, and long-suffering (Pt. I, Ch. 5, 57).

Even Madam Yepanchin could not resist the temptation to identify the prince with a donkey after this. While for her the donkey is a symbol of stupidity, an image of a donkey "pleased the prince immensely" and "cleared up his head." It could also be that the prince had in mind an image of Jesus on the back of a donkey on his final trip to Jerusalem, or the famous words of St. Paul (1 Cor. 1:20): "Hath not God made foolish the wisdom of this world?"

For Dostoevsky, Prince Myshkin is a "holy fool," one of those "fools for Christ" who possess the "wisdom of the fool."[16] The idea behind this archetype is that, in the purity of their hearts, the untutored and simpleminded can penetrate profounder truths than those who have accumulated academic learning or conventional wisdom. According to this tradition, whenever human intelligence questions itself and acknowledges that the heart has its reasons that reason does not know, a kind of wisdom is attributed to the fool.

The tradition of the holy fool involves such major figures of Western civilization as Jesus and Socrates, though it has always survived only in the undercurrents of the mainstream culture. Writers as celebrated as Sophocles, Aristophanes, Thomas More, Erasmus, Rabelais, Cervantes, Shakespeare, and Tolstoy create some of their best characters within this tradition, and yet the idea of the holy fool has always remained something of an aberration. Philosophers of the Enlightenment are especially hostile to the tradition that reveres holy fools. They find it impossible to reconcile reason and nature – notwithstanding our sophisticated rational schemes, nature is always recalcitrant. While human intelligence is guided by the principle of sufficient reason – the principle that holds that for every occurrence there must be sufficient reason for its happening – nature does not reveal any reason for some of its occurrences. In *Crime and Punishment*, Raskolnikov wants to correct this irrational nature, and in *The Idiot* Ipolite compares nature to a dumb, irrational beast.

If it is impossible to reconcile reason and nature, why condemn nature? There are thinkers before Dostoevsky – Pierre Bayle, Blaise Pascal, Alexander Pope, and later Albert Schweitzer – who wonder about this and conclude that we cannot rationally comprehend the order of the universe. They think it foolish and arrogant even to try. For the philosophers, such as Hegel, who nevertheless insist

---

16 The preparatory notes for *The Idiot* indicate that Dostoevsky struggled mightily with the right conception of Myshkin, until he decided that he must be a holy fool. Here is a typical entry: "*Enigmas*. Who is he? A terrible scoundrel or a mysterious ideal? . . . He is a *Prince* . . . Prince *Yurodivyi* [holy fool]. (he is with children.)"; quoted from *The Notebooks for The Idiot*, 14.

that everything real must be rational, or that sooner or later we will figure out the hidden laws of nature, Erasmus coined the phrase "foolosophers." Nicolas of Cusa made a related contribution of his own by coining a beautiful phrase: *docta ignorantia* – "learned ignorance."

Dostoevsky belongs among those thinkers who refuse to glorify reason. His assault begins with the underground man who claims that reason is the twentieth part of who we are. Dostoevsky does not hold rationality to be the governing faculty within our soul, nor does he think that it should be. When we treat rationality as a quasi-deity, we end up worshiping false idols.

If we dethrone rationality, the problem is whom or what to trust as authority, a source of values, and a guide to our decisions and actions. Like Bayle, Pascal, Pope, and Schweitzer, Dostoevsky believes that we need to turn to faith. If there is a solution to the mystery of the meaning of human life, faith should be our authority and our guide.

Dostoevsky has a unique understanding of faith. In *Crime and Punishment* his comprehension of faith seems to remain mostly within the confines of the Orthodox Christianity. In *The Idiot*, his understanding is more advanced and also more idiosyncratic. Since it is questionable whether Dostoevsky ever completely develops his conception of faith, I will try to reconstruct it with utmost caution.

Traditional Christian views often display remarkably little interest in nature and this world. When St. Paul talks about God making foolish the wisdom of this world, he believes that this world is not our destination but only our temporary station; to rely on it and its wisdom is foolish. This is not how Dostoevsky understands "fools for Christ," nor how he treats nature. Dostoevsky does not share in the contempt for nature which is often found in the Western Christianity and, no less frequently, in secular doctrines of modernity. Despite Raskolnikov and Ipolite, Dostoevsky thinks that nature is not a dumb mechanism which needs to be corrected, nor an irrational beast which needs to be tamed.

This does not mean that Dostoevsky glorifies nature. Despite the interpretations of some Russian scholars, the mystical return to "Mother Nature" is not the ultimate credo of Dostoevsky's faith in *The Idiot*. Although nature does play a more prominent role in *The*

Brothers Karamazov, in *The Idiot* Dostoevsky insists that nature
has its limitations and that they must be recognized. For instance,
nature does not distinguish between Nastassya Filippovna and the
fly that buzzes over her dead body. Nor does nature tell us why
Ipolite has to die, while some scoundrels, such as Lebedev, live full
lives. The natural processes continue, and it does not make any
difference as to who lives and who dies. Life continuously devours
life, just as it continuously creates new life.

Had this been the whole story, Raskolnikov and Ipolite may have
been right. But, in his foolish wisdom, Prince Myshkin understands
some things – more intuitively than rationally – which the others do
not. Nature does not discern a buzzing fly from Nastassya's beauty,
but nature has made Nastassya astonishingly beautiful. Why is
someone born so beautiful? Why Nastassya rather than someone
else? There are no answers to these questions. Yet even without
such answers, the beauty remains. And beauty is truly a gift of
nature, a miracle of nature that can be neither rationally explained
nor rationally recreated.

Love belongs to the mystery of a different order. Just as beauty
is a gift of nature, love is a gift of spirit. They both have something
inscrutable, but their inscrutability comes from different sources.
And if beauty poses many challenges, love outmatches it in this
regard.

Dostoevsky thinks of a ladder of beauty and love in terms of the
steps we have to climb before we can reach faith and hope. Earlier
we have seen how many characters in *The Idiot* cannot appreciate
beauty. They do not understand that beauty is a gift, something
which cannot be controlled or manipulated, but which must be
appreciated and shared. They think of Nastassya's beauty – and to
a lesser extent of Aglaya's as well – as a commodity, something they
can possess or buy with "a penny."

Those who think of beauty as a commodity are stuck in the trap
of their own egos, forced to observe the world from their "frog perspective," the same perspective from which Holbein makes us view
the body of Christ in the tomb. Those who think of beauty as a
commodity cannot climb the next step of the ladder, the one of
love, and will never reach faith and hope. Nastassya and Aglaya
know that beauty must be appreciated for what it is, but they both

fail in the mysteries of love. Their failure is not that of nature but the failure of spirit. Just as Totsky and General Yepanchin think that they can manipulate beauty, Nastassya and Aglaya think they can do the same thing with love. Yet love cannot be controlled, and in an attempt to do so, they spoil it. They both end up lacking faith, which leads them to disbelief, fear, even madness.[17]

The prince is the one character in *The Idiot* who is capable of love and who has faith. Myshkin is different from others because he does not see them in relation to his desires. This makes him stand above the usual daily concerns and see things from a higher perspective. And his perspective affects not only his behavior and his judgments of others, but also the behavior and the judgments of those who associate with him. The prince's disinterestedness, his purity and sincerity invite others to put off all disguise before him.

Pure and good-natured, Prince Myshkin obviously does not understand some things that occur around him. Despite these faults, he knows exactly who Lebedev is and how he tries to manipulate the prince. He understands what the crowd behind "Pavlishchev's son" wants. He senses that it is Rogozhin's blood-thirsty eyes that are following him. He has no illusions about Nastassya Filippovna and the madness that overcomes her. The prince cannot be accused of expecting to find the final paradise on earth, or of being oblivious to other people's faults. Nor does Myshkin like people because he is under the illusion that they are better than they really are. What separates him from the rest of the characters is unique: The prince accepts even the worst in others and likes them in spite of it. He does not judge others. He has faith in them.

---

17 According to Stefan Zweig, "the most amazing of all Dostoeffsky's achievements is his analysis of the love sentiment. For hundreds of years, ever since the days of classical antiquity, literature has taken the relation of man to woman and woman to man as its central theme and as the fountainhead of existence. Yet Dostoeffsky has pushed his researches in this domain into deeper channels and on to higher peaks; indeed he has won to an ultimate knowledge of the topic, and that is perhaps the greatest of his deeds. Love is for other imaginative writers the aim of life, the goal towards which the story as a work of art is directed; for Dostoeffsky, however, love is no more than a stage on life's highway. . . . Dostoeffsky's heaven is at a far greater altitude"; *Three Masters: Balzac, Dickens, Dostoeffsky*, 211.

This is something that Yevgeny Pavlovitch and other persons of conventional wisdom find so hard to understand. The prince hopes that Aglaya's love may help her understand where he stands. Love can, indeed, overcome many obstacles, but is Aglaya's love deep enough and pure enough to pass this trial? The fact that in her hurt pride Aglaya does not even consider giving Myshkin a chance to explain himself suggests otherwise. Yevgeny Pavlovitch tries to defend Aglaya: "No, Prince, she won't understand! Aglaya Ivanovna loved you like a woman, like a human being, not like – a disembodied spirit. Do you know, my poor Prince? Most likely, you never loved either one of them" (Pt. IV, Ch. 9, 609).

Yevgeny Pavlovitch is again both right and wrong. The prince does not love either one of them in the sense in which Yevgeny Pavlovitch understands love. Prince Myshkin loves like a disembodied spirit because love is a gift of spirit, not of body or of nature. The manifestations of that spiritual love in the body and in nature are only of secondary importance. Such manifestations are important only when the spiritual purity of that love is secured. Put differently, whenever the choice is between passion and compassion, the prince will choose compassion because the humanity in a person is of a higher value than her individuality. He tries to awaken compassion in the hearts of those around him, whether Nastassya or Aglaya. Yevegeny Pavlovich may rightly argue that the prince fails to evoke compassion in any one of them. The prince would nonetheless insist that compassion – as the opening of one's heart for the suffering of other human beings – is the way toward faith and hope.

Suppose, then, that we accept as Dostoevsky's "ladder" something along the following lines:

$$\text{beauty} \rightarrow \text{love} \rightarrow \text{faith} \rightarrow \text{hope}$$

How would this line of thought help us answer the questions raised by Ipolite?

This ladder can aid us with the second question: Had Jesus known what would happen to Him, would He make this sacrifice again? The answer is: Yes, because His sacrifice is a gift of spirit. It is an act of love.

In the *Symposium*, Plato's outlines his "ladder of beauty" – to climb up to the vision of the Beauty itself, or the Idea of Beauty, demands an uncommon sacrifice and devotion.[18] Dostoevsky differs from Plato: Our sacrifice is not needed for the appreciation of beauty but for the cultivation of love. The measure of the meaning of someone's sacrifice is not an external success; it cannot be measured in hedonistic, utilitarian, or pragmatic terms. What happens after the sacrifice is utterly irrelevant for any meaning of sacrifice performed for love, in the same way that it is irrelevant what happens to a gift given to someone out of love. The sacrifice of Jesus, and by analogy the sacrifice of Prince Myshkin, is a gift of love, an act of grace.

The sacrifice of Jesus and His suffering on the cross do not belong to the cause-effect chain of natural events. Nor should we treat them as the means-ends relation of the calculative morality. The sacrifice of Jesus and His suffering on the cross belong to a different order of "logic," the logic of spirituality, the logic of part and whole. They signify an act of solidarity between various parts of the same whole. While the notion of right is negative – because it means someone's right against someone else's right, the notion of sacrifice is positive – it is sacrifice for someone. Sacrifice means our participation in a larger whole, a willing and loving participation in the game of life, regardless of the final outcome. One of the central problems of the modern era, Dostoevsky maintains, is that – unlike the people of by-gone epochs – we do not have any ideal that seizes us. Without such an ideal, it is hardly possible to escape the dominance of what Koestler calls "self-assertive tendencies": I want to be a center of the universe, if necessary at the expense of others. In that frame of mind, I cannot but be weary of sacrifice and death.

Without sacrifice and faith, there can hardly be genuine dialogue with others. Without them we cannot establish that kind of relatedness to the other on which a developed personality can be grounded. Sacrifice implies self-transcending tendency, a positive ideal of a higher order not based on self-oriented calculus of pleasure and displeasure. By sacrificing myself for someone else,

---

18   Plato, *Symposium*, 209c–211c.

I show my reverence for this person. I am rendering the other sacred, in the original Latin meaning of the word *sacer*: "set apart," "untouched," "taboo," and, therefore, "sacred."

The prince shows us how this self-transcending attitude of reverence opens up for us the mystery of everything that exists and the value-depth of that existence. This reality discloses itself on a different level and reveals the layers that the self-asserting mind cannot perceive. Prince Myshkin's reverent attitude and the penetrating eye lead to a sense of trust: He trusts others and they trust him. This is how Dostoevsky wants us to understand "incarnation," which literally means: "to cause flesh to grow," or, symbolically, "the word becoming flesh" – an ideal becoming reality. Prince Myshkin recognizes that sacrifices are worthy, that life is given back to those who are willing to sacrifice it for others.

Thus, Prince Myshkin is not bothered by Holbein's painting of the dead Christ. He has no fear of death, nor is he scared of "dumb, unfeeling nature." In those rare moments of supreme insight before his epileptic attacks – the moments when time stops, the moments worth an entire life – he is able to empathize with everything and recognize the interconnectedness of all life. All life is sacred and everything can be accepted. "Yes" can be said to anything that belongs to the mysterious dance of life.

Prince Myshkin also participates in the dance of life through everything he does, and this is where he loses Yevgeny Pavlovitch. He says "Yes" to Aglaya, and "Yes" to Nastassya, and the prince sees no contradiction. He says "Yes" to Lebedev and to Burdovsky, to Ganya and to Ipolite, to Keller and to General Ivolgin. He says "Yes" even to Rogozhin, who tries to kill him. The prince is "out of this world."

The prince's purity is powerless, yet by no means harmless. The likes of Yevgeny Pavlovitch will either put the prince back into an asylum or execute him publicly, as a warning to anyone else who may come up with similar, "other-worldly" ideas. Every society establishes firm boundaries between right and wrong, good and evil, acceptable and unacceptable. Prince Myshkin defies these boundaries. He is a game-spoiler, a "spoil-sport," who could be far more dangerous for our social games than any cheat. As Johan Huizinga clarifies in his book *Homo Ludens*,

By withdrawing from the game [a spoil-sport] reveals the relativity and fragility of the play-world in which he had temporarily shut himself with others. He robs play of its *illusion* – a pregnant word which means literally "in-play" (from *inlusio*, *illudere* or *inludere*). Therefore he must be cast out, for he threatens the existence of the play-community.[19]

Prince Myshkin is as much of a game-spoiler as was Jesus, and this spirit of game-spoiling also pervades Holbein's painting of Christ. Dostoevsky knew of this painting from his childhood, from the time he read Karamazin's *Letters of a Russian Traveler*. Karamazin reports his interest in the "paintings by the celebrated Holbein who was born in Basel and was a friend of Erasmus." Having first been impressed by Holbein's majestic painting of "Madonna" in Dresden, which he considered "the supreme embodiment of quiet and secret sorrow," Dostoevsky travels to Basel to see Holbein's painting of the dead Christ. His expectations are not disappointed. In an entry to her *Diary*, written shortly after the event, Dostoevsky's wife describes how her husband "was completely carried away by it, and in his desire to look at it closer got on to a chair, so that I was in a terrible state lest he should have to pay a fine, like one is always liable to here." She changes the story in her published (and unfortunately much edited) *Reminiscences*. Her later account is that Dostoevsky was so excited about the painting that, after standing in front of it for fifteen or twenty minutes, she pulled him away in fear that his epileptic seizure might begin. Dostoevsky was indeed experiencing seizure, but it was of a different kind.[20]

Hans Holbein the Younger lived at the crossroads of Christianity and Humanism, but his painting of the dead Christ is as little the product of an atheistic mind as Erasmus's *Praise of Folly* is. His uncompromising realism – Holbein used as his model the corpse of a man found dead in Rhein – was an abiding element in late

19 Johan Huizinga, *op. cit.*, 11. Girard similarly argues in *Violence and the Sacred* that the idea of sacred violence can function only as long as there is complete unanimity of all the participants.

20 My presentation in this passage is based on Joseph Frank, *Dostoevsky: The Miraculous Years, 1865–1871*, 220–22.

medieval meditations on Christ's Passion. Such paintings, like Erasmus's book, were intended to be as dramatic as possible so that the audience's imagination would be greatly intensified in contemplating the Passion and Christ's sacrifice. As John Rowlands explains,

> It was this heightened sense of drama for revealing the events that was taken up later by St. Ignatius and used to such effects by his followers. [Holbein's] painting aptly demonstrates the need to understand it in terms of its milieu and the purpose for which it was originally intended. . . . Far from conveying despair, its message is intended as one of belief, that from the decay of the tomb Christ rose again in glory on the third day.[21]

Myshkin is not bothered by this painting, but Rogozhin and Ipolite are. What may disturb a viewer of the painting are two things. Most obviously, the open mouth and eyes of Christ are in violation of the burial ritual. The ritual itself, however, is more pagan than Christian, and it reveals the fear of the demonic. Nevertheless, since the thirteenth century, Christian Europe has closed the eyes of the deceased, "out of fear of the evil eye." Similarly, the mouth is closed, "lest this evil spirit seizes the living and drags them down with him into death." The second disturbing aspect of the painting, more symbolic than literal, is the lack of opening of any kind. Everything about the painting is coffin-like, including its size. The fact that there is no opening, no gate, no bridge, symbolizes that there is no passage from one mode of existence to another. The sacred is entrapped by the profane. The divinity of Christ is double-bounded by the profane: Not only does the coffin ensnare him, but the body itself is symbolically a tomb. Holbein's friend Erasmus liked to quote the famous line from Plato's *Gorgias*: "Who knows whether living is not dying and dying living? And perhaps we are actually dead, for I once heard one of our wise man say that we are now dead and our body is a tomb."[22]

---

21   John Rowlands, *Holbein*, 52–53.
22   Plato, *Gorgias*, 492d–493a.

Rogozhin shows Holbein's painting to Myshkin and asks him whether he believes in God. Myshkin tells him a few stories, the last of which involves a mother of a baby who smiles for the first time. That peasant woman told the prince: "There is joy for a mother in her child's first smile, just as God rejoices when from heaven He sees a sinner praying to Him with his whole heart" (Pt. III, Ch. 4, 231). In this sentence of a simple, illiterate woman, Myshkin tries to explain to Rogozhin, "the whole essence of Christianity is expressed – I mean the whole conception of God as our own Father and of God's joy in man, like a father's in his own child." Since Rogozhin probably continues to stare at Myshkin with a dazzling look, the prince tries again: "The essence of religious feeling doesn't depend on reasoning, and it has nothing do to with wrongdoing or crime or with atheism. There is something else there and there always will be, and atheists will always pass over it and will never be talking about *that*" (Pt. III, Ch. 4, 231).

About what? About that joy of the mother looking at the child's smile, about the joy of the Father looking at the sinner praying to Him with his whole heart.

Everyone has difficulty understanding *"that,"* because of the notorious absence of the moral categories from Myshkin's account. The trapped and decaying body of Christ does not bother him, and he even claims that the essence of religion does not have anything to do "with wrongdoing or crime." The prince never reproaches anyone for wrongdoing, nor does he think that sinners should be threatened with punishment from God: "God rejoices when . . . He sees a sinner praying to Him with his whole heart." Myshkin's own purity is not the same as goodness,[23] and our reconstruction of Dostoevsky's ladder (beauty → love → faith → hope) does not mention any moral category either.

---

23 As Hartmann explains, "The meaning of goodness is entirely positive, that of purity – as the word itself implies – is negative as regards the intended content; it means untainted by evil. Here the pursuit of values, even of the higher ones, is confronted by the non-pursuit of disvalues, especially of those that are lower and elemental. He is pure whom no desire leads astray, no temptation allures. His ethos consists of an inner tendency turned away from disvalues altogether and as such"; *op. cit.*, 211.

Should we then understand Dostoevsky's positive worldview in entirely non-ethical terms, or should we assume that his outlook is ethical in an unusual sense?

Dostoevsky wavers between the two options. He thinks, for instance, that although Myshkin's purity is not identical with goodness, it is not opposed to it either. Had Dostoevsky been a philosopher, he may have developed a moral philosophy quite different from both utilitarianism and Kantianism. Unlike the former, Dostoevsky is not preoccupied with the instrumental and teleological aspect of human activities, which focus on the end result of our actions. What is practically useless and aimless does not turn Dostoevsky away. Nonetheless, the argument may go that he is far more interested in the inter-subjective aspect of human lives, in the dialogical relationship between two or more persons: Instead of justice he is preoccupied with mercy; instead of human rights he considers caring and compassion the exemplary human attitudes.

The focus on caring and compassion would also explain how Dostoevsky differs from Kantianism, although this approach would be closer to him than any utilitarian ethics. Kant emphasizes not the consequences of our actions but their motives and our good will. Instead of the enlightened egoism of utilitarianism, Kant insists on the ethics of principles (formulated as the famous "categorical imperative") which treats every person as an end and never as a means only. Dostoevsky nonetheless rejects Kant's rigid ethics of principles: Caring and compassion do not presuppose any moral principles, no moral law, and no a-priori deduced sense of duty, expressed in the form of a categorical imperative. If Dostoevsky were to write a moral philosophy, it would be the ethics of sympathy, not the ethics of principles.[24]

There are also good reasons to believe that Dostoevsky wants to separate ethics and religion. Myshkin's purity is not something that can be earned, as all moral achievements must be earned, but

---

24 An ethical theory of such a kind has never been fully developed. Two noteworthy attempts involve: Max Scheler, *The Nature of Sympathy*, and Tzvetan Todorov, *Facing the Extreme: Moral Life in the Concentration Camps*.

is a gift which in its ultimate nature is incomprehensible. While not opposed to goodness, purity borders on holiness. The tie of purity to the religious realm is even more obvious when purity is lost. Morally speaking, once purity is lost, it can never be restored. Hartmann rightly argues that religion tries to accomplish what is ethically impossible:

> For ages past religious thought has met this need [of restora-
> tion of innocence], just at the point where the value of
> purity as such is drawn into the centre of moral conscious-
> ness. The ancient concept of "purification" (*catharsis*) as
> the superstitious "wiping away of guilt" is here joined with
> the thought of forgiveness and salvation through the suffer-
> ing and sacrifice of the divinity intervening for man. Purity
> returns as a gift of grace. The condition which man must
> fulfill is simple belief. The mystery of the new birth resolves
> the antinomy of the values.[25]

Although Hartmann's line of thought does not directly refer to Prince Myshkin (he mentions Alyosha Karamazov as an exem-plar of purity), we can easily recognize Dostoevsky's concern in the quoted passage. Since we will discuss Alyosha in the following chapters, let us here focus on Myshkin's account of the essence of religion. Rogozhin is touched by the prince's account, how-ever he happens to understand it. He wants to exchange with the prince the crosses they wear around their necks, which is equiva-lent to sharing blood and becoming spiritual brothers. And to his new-found brother Rogozhin is willing to present a gift of what is the dearest to him in the whole world – Nastassya Filippovna: "Well, take her, then, since it's fated to be! She's yours" (Pt. II, Ch. 4, 233). Yet, whatever string the prince touches in Rogozhin, its vibration does not last very long. A miracle turns into a scan-dal when, later that same day, Rogozhin tries to murder the prince.

    Ipolite is even more scared by Holbein's painting than Rogozhin. His disease and the inevitability of death place Ipolite in a similar

---

25 Hartmann, *op. cit.*, 221. See also Jaroslav Pelikan, *Fools for Christ: Essays on the True, the Good, and the Beautiful*, 83–84.

position to that of the prince – he does not belong to society, he is an outcast, a spoil-sport. Unlike the prince, he does not accept his role, or the fate intended for him. More precisely, he does not accept it all of the time. For this reason, Ipolite goes back and forth, between the desire to belong and the disgust that he might be just like the mediocre others. This unsettled status puts him in a good position to express what others do not dare, or do not understand in the first place. Ipolite is the dying man, who, unlike the dying man the prince tells about, does not realize that life is a gift bestowed on him. He does not marvel, as the man about to be guillotined does: Why is it that people do not live their lives to the fullest? He does not wonder, as Jesus does when looking from the cross: How is it that they do not see what they are doing?

Yet Ipolite is dying. His fear of death is childish, but it does not make it any less authentic or primordial. Primitive man must have often wondered: What if the sun does not rise tomorrow? He must have had persistent fears of darkness, the bareness of the land, and the death from which there is no sequel. The fears of a modern, non-believing man are the same fears; they are simply expressed and manifested differently.

A modern day Ipolite would doubt the meaning of beauty, of play, of love, of life, of death, and of sacrifice. He would want a reassurance, a proof that we are not helpless in the face of contingency. But are such proofs needed?

In an attempt to explain the nature of play, Johan Huizinga uses a wonderful German expression: "*zwecklos aber doch sinnvoll*." The translator renders it as "pointless but significant."[26] This is a correct translation, but it does not do a full justice to the phrase. The English "but" is too weak, too abbreviated for the intentional double negation phrase "*aber doch*," which is translated more accurately as "yet nonetheless." The first word, *zwecklos*, is rendered better as "purposeless," as it is always done in the translations of Kant, who uses this word in his discussion of the playfulness of art and the questions of teleology. The last word of the German phrase, *sinnvoll*, literally means "full of meaning," thus "meaningful."

26 Huizinga, *op. cit.*, 19.

The phrase "purposeless yet nonetheless meaningful" captures what Dostoevsky wants to say about beauty, play, sacrifice, life, and death in *The Idiot*. They are strange things. But, then, the whole issue about the meaning of life is peculiar as well. Does not the phrase "meaning of life" sound like a contradiction in terms? We understand that word "meaning" refers to something ordered, determined, and purposive, while the word "life" refers to the opposite characteristics of flow, indeterminacy, and chance. What to do about this incompatibility? We cannot understand life differently than it is, but are we equally stuck with our established understanding of the meaning of "meaning"? Do we not have to look for a different meaning of "meaning" because there is apparently some meaning in all of the transformations and tribulations of life? Any good dictionary will tell us that "meaning" is "something in the mind." But is that really so? Why must "meaning" be understood in terms of conscious purpose, aim, or intent? The meaning of "meaning" is actually weaker: to signify, to express, to indicate. It is our modern distortion to take for granted that these characteristics do require "meaning" to be in the mind. Nevertheless, "meaning" can be found in our interactive relation with the things or events perceived to signify, or express, or indicate something. Furthermore, "meaning" need not be understood in any strictly intellectual way. "Meaning" need not be something that is grasped rationally, but can also be – and often is – merely something that is felt or intuited.[27]

To illustrate this, think again about beauty. What is the meaning of beauty? Beauty is its own meaning. What is the meaning of play? Why, play itself! Not the individual players. Not the outcome of the game but play itself. Think about poetry. As Arthur Koestler states: "The effect of the rhythm of a poem . . . is not due to our perceiving pattern in something outside us, but to our becoming patterned ourselves."[28] This rhythmic periodic cycle is a fundamental characteristic of any play or game, and the foundation of life's meaning as well. Rhythm means measure and this measure – unless it is too

---

27 For further discussion, see Stewart R. Sutherland, *Atheism and the Rejection of God*, 38–39.

28 Koestler, *op. cit.*, 311.

rigidly mechanical and repetitive, as is the case with machines – reminds us of the pulsations of life. The measure does not have to be perceived consciously, as it does not have to be quantifiable. We subconsciously and intuitively recognize this measure in face readings and in games played.

Beauty, dance, poem, life – there is rhythm in them all; there is something meaningful in them even without any explicit purpose and without any rational apprehension of what their meaning is.

Ipolite's fear, intensified after looking at the dead body of Christ locked in that tomb, is that he will never rise again. The prince looks at the painting and believes: "Christ has died, Christ has risen, Christ will come again."

Christ's is the sacrifice whose blood conquers darkness. The holy blood will purify the "water of life," the polluted blood of the world. Life will continue. The sun will rise tomorrow.

But what kind of life will it be? What kind of day will it be?

What the prince realizes, and what Rogozhin and Ipolite do not, is that nature is not to blame for whatever kind of life and whatever kind of day it turns out to be tomorrow. Regardless of the gifts it bestows on us, or fails to do, it is not nature that obscures man's life and his chances of salvation. It is human beings and our attitudes toward what nature (and God) presents to us. For Dostoevsky, a miracle and a scandal are the two aspects of the same event. Yet how can that be?

Of the two questions that Ipolite poses, the one about those who witness the burial of Christ is far more difficult to answer. How can anyone who has seen His tortured, distorted body still have faith in resurrection? How can anyone who has witnessed the scandal still believe in the miracle?

Beauty is cast into the world, and we are not capable of appreciating it. A gift is cast into the world, and we are not capable of appreciating this gift. Prince Myshkin is a holy fool, and this fool is a gift. What is such a man doing in this world?

The purpose of his gift is not to initiate a crisis in this world, nor to resolve an already existing one. As Dostoevsky sees it, the purpose of his holy fool is to intensify the crisis so that we feel it more intensely, so that it becomes unbearable for us. How can we look at the prince without being shamed into righteousness?

A gift, any gift, enriches us. Yet it also puzzles us. In our age of "the third horse, the black one, whose rider carries the scales in his hand" (Pt. II, Ch. 2, 210), we understand the meaning of penny, but the meaning of gift escapes us.

Dostoevsky sometimes offers answers but more often leaves us with questions. *The Idiot* poses one of the most difficult riddles: Given a gift, what will we do with it?

6
The Brothers Karamazov (I)

The Gift of Life

The Framework of Discussion

In *The Idiot*, Dostoevsky wrestles with the idea of a "beautiful man." He is aware of the immensity of the challenge, for entirely good and pure characters are few in literature. In the biblical story of Cain and Abel, for instance, Cain is far more interesting as a literary character than Abel because of his guilt; he has both an exterior and an interior life. Cain lives – to carry on his mark and become a founder of the first city, thus indirectly the founder of culture. Abel perishes – he has no line, no dialogue. He is a victim, and victims are usually silent. His victimization creates an impression of the transparency of his character; we suspect we know all there is to know about him. With Cain, we do not. His deeds and struggles are fascinating. He holds our attention.[1]

---

1 This distinction between Cain and Abel as literary types has been made following Mary Douglas; see Bill Moyers (ed.), *Genesis: A Living Conversation*, 82–83. See also Dudley Young, *Origins of the Sacred: The Ecstasies of Love and War*, 347–54; and René Girard, *I See Satan Fall Like Lightning*, 82–86.

Dostoevsky realizes that it is possible to pay more attention to Abel; it is also possible to portray a beautiful man. As the inspirations for Prince Myshkin, in his correspondence he mentions Don Quixote, Dickens's Pickwick, and Hugo's Jean Valjean. Nevertheless, as *The Idiot* unfolds, it is clear that he has in mind the story of Jesus of Nazareth. The Christian exemplar gives voice to the victims and also offers a positive message in which Dostoevsky is especially interested. More than any other, the example of Jesus suggests to Dostoevsky that it is not only possible but indispensable to wonder about the inner drama of a beautiful person: What is it like to give with a pure heart and without reservation? What is it like to live your life as a gift to others?

Prince Myshkin is Dostoevsky's first major attempt to portray a beautiful man as the central character. Alyosha Karamazov is the second.[2] Alyosha is the proclaimed hero of *The Brothers Karamazov*, although in the preface Dostoevsky warns us that Alyosha will come to full bloom only in the sequel-novel. Despite the unfinished nature of Alyosha's life trial, his character represents significant improvement over the hero of *The Idiot*. Recall the principal weakness of Prince Myshkin: He is too disembodied, too detached from life. Dostoevsky conceives Alyosha as more instinctual, more "earthly" than the prince. The presence of the "Karamazov blood" makes Alyosha less Jesus-like, but it allows him to be more realistic and believable. The demands of realism will also specify more clearly the parameters of Dostoevsky's project: If Alyosha is to become a beautiful man, it will come not by renouncing the bodily aspect of his nature but by finding a way to integrate it with the spiritual realm.[3]

---

2   Leonid Grossman argues that Dostoevsky's very first hero, Makar Devushkin (from *Poor Folk*), was his "first 'beautiful man,' his earliest 'poor knight'"; *Dostoevsky: A Biography*, 54. While there is some justification for this view, Makar does not represent any ambitious attempt to develop this character to the greatest human height.

3   George Steiner advances a similar estimate of Alyosha (in comparison with Prince Myshkin); see *Tolstoy or Dostoevsky: An Essay in the Old Criticism*, 171 and 293. I can nonetheless agree with Nicholas Berdyaev that "Zosima and Alyosha, in whom [Dostoevsky] gave voice to his positive theories, cannot be numbered among his best-drawn characters; Ivan

That Prince Myshkin is utterly alone, one of a kind in a hostile world, without a physical or spiritual brother, is another distinction between the two heroes. Dostoevsky hints at this solitude in the novel's title, *The Idiot*, which indicates how the rest of the world perceives the Prince. In more ways than one, Alyosha is not alone. He is only one of the brothers, and the title of the novel does not refer to him alone. Dostoevsky's last novel is about brothers and brotherhood, about "the Karamazovs." To be a Karamazov means, above other things, to have an insatiable thirst for life, to love life with all of its sorrows and trials. Dostoevsky himself felt such a craving:

> In spite of everything I have lost, I love life ardently, I love life for life's sake, and seriously, I am still planning to *begin* my life. I will be fifty soon, yet I cannot make out whether I am ending my life or only beginning it. This is a principal attribute of my character and, perhaps, of my work.[4]

Nowhere in Dostoevsky's work is this love of life manifest more fully than in *The Brothers Karamazov*. This novel can be characterized as a hymn of life, a celebration of life in all its aspects. This portrayal of life is so complex, covering such a vast span ranging from pure instinctuality and vitality to pure spirituality and holiness, that we need some help, a framework within which we can situate this work. Together with *The Idiot*, this novel offers Dostoevsky's positive philosophy of life, his own understanding of the metaphysical and religious approach to life. In the consideration of *The Idiot* we followed the ladder:

$$\text{beauty} \rightarrow \text{love} \rightarrow \text{faith} \rightarrow \text{hope.}$$

This pattern will be further examined in this and the following chapters, especially with regard to faith and hope. Besides these general points, we need to recognize that the tacit assumptions of

---

Karamazov is infinitely more strong and convincing, and his very darkness is pierced by a shaft of strong light"; *Dostoevsky*, 205.

4   Quoted from Grossman, *op. cit.*, 49. Stefan Zweig comments on Dostoevsky's affirmation of life, as well as on a need for all of us to learn how to appreciate life; see his *Three Masters: Balzac – Dickens – Dostoeffsky*, 235–37.

the entire Karamazov drama are the following: 1. the unfinished nature of humanity; 2. the idea of life as a gift; 3. the corresponding need of the protagonists to figure out what to do with the gift of their lives. This need is not considered in isolation from their relationship with others, and it takes two dimensions: vertical and horizontal. The vertical dimension deals with the relationship with other generations, the most symptomatic of which in *The Brothers Karamazov* is the relation of fathers and sons. The horizontal dimension concerns our sense of brotherhood with others. In this novel, the task is presented in terms of becoming brothers, not only in the biological but in the spiritual sense.

To illuminate these points and come to a closer understanding of our subject, I will use two devices: one visual, one conceptual. Auguste Rodin's statue, "The Hand of God," will help us clarify Dostoevsky's view of the incompleteness of human nature, as well as his assurance that human life is a gift of God. Dostoevsky introduces these ideas in the context of the quarrels between Fyodor Karamazov and his oldest son, Dmitri. They fight over Grushenka, whose love both attempt to buy, and over several thousand rubles of inheritance. A conceptual distinction between an "exchange economy" and an "economy of gifts" will aid us in describing their quarrels. This distinction will lead us to one of the central issues posed by *The Brothers Karamazov*: What to do with the gift of life?

Rodin's "The Hand of God" gives fine visual expression to the theological and anthropological conception which underlies Dostoevsky's work. In Rodin's statue (also called "The Hand of Creation") a hand shapes the figures of the first man and the first woman out of a mass of clay. The figures are not completely formed and there is plenty of clay to play with; all is still entangled together. Nevertheless, we recognize Adam and Eve. The work of creation has not been completed by the Divine Hand, nor will it be finished by it. The Hand is opening up to let the primal couple establish its identity and finish the work of creation on its own. Impressed by Rodin's statue, Rainer Maria Rilke describes "The Hand of God" as the hand which "opens in the air as though to let something go, as one gives freedom to a bird."[5]

5   Quoted from Athena Tasha Spear, *Rodin Sculpture*, 79.

Dostoevsky would have appreciated this image. The symbolism of the Hand of Creation is rich enough to refer not only to God, but also to our biological and spiritual (perhaps even political) father-figures as well – an important preoccupation both in Dostoevsky's private life and in his work.[6] Dostoevsky would also appreciate that Rodin's statue does not give us a definitive image of God. Instead, it shows us God's work. The statue emphasizes the intimate relationship between the divine and the human. God does not withdraw from the world after finishing His Creation, for the Creation has not been finished. Nor is God's intention to complete it alone. Human beings participate in this process as well.

The novel pushes each of the three Karamazov brothers to his personal limit and forces them to change. We can follow the nature of their transformations in terms of their relationship to the creating Hand. Alyosha, the youngest of the brothers, is unwilling to leave the loving protection of the Hand. Ivan, four years older than Alyosha, wants to depart from the Hand once and forever. He dreams of being independent and of correcting the serious flaws of creation. Four year older than Ivan, Dmitri has long ago left the protective shelter and is yet another lost soul in the world. Dmitri is transformed by his newfound love for Grushenka, on the night he is accused of his father's murder. Alyosha embodies a balance between the disorderly passion of his biological father (Fyodor) and the devotion of his spiritual father (Zosima). Ivan represents a plunging of the intellectual into the incontrollable caldron of impulses and urges. Dmitri illustrates how vital impulses and irrational urges find their way to spirituality.

If *The Brothers Karamazov* is a celebration of life, it also is a guidebook of the proper and improper ways of life. Dostoevsky's aim in composing this guidebook is to expose two main misconceptions: that life is akin to our property, and that life is a promise

6   Freud was the first to call attention to the existential and artistic relevance of this subject, centered on the murder of Dostoevsky's father, when Dostoevsky was seventeen years old. Malcolm Jones offers a more balanced discussion of parricide for Dostoevsky's work. See Jones, *Dostoyevsky: The Novel of Discord*, 171–72. For a criticism of Freud's patriarchally oriented outlook, see Erich Neumann, *The Creative Man*, 241–45.

given to us. His understanding of life as a gift is opposed to both misconceptions. Dostoevsky is firmly convinced that life is not something one *has* but something one *is*. Life is not a possession or property, with which one can do whatever one wants. As one cannot possess a home, even though one owns the house, similarly one cannot possess life, even though he or she "owns" a body. Dostoevsky believes that what I am is not mine. What I am is a gift.[7]

Yet another widespread misconception consists in approaching life as a promise that is given to us. When we realize that no fulfillment of the alleged promise is forthcoming, we start wondering if we are not deceived. We question life and its meaning. Such doubts, Dostoevsky maintains, are misdirected. They are due to our erroneous expectations. After all, what could be promised to us? Happiness? Salvation? And promised by whom? Unless the primordial image imprinted on the human clay is treated as a promise, there is no promise to consider. There are potentials and expectations, talents and shortcomings. What we do with them is another matter.

If life is a gift, what can and should we do with it?

Generally speaking, there are quite diverse ways of giving or receiving gifts, and many things we can do with them. We can use them or misuse them. We can appreciate them or find them burdensome. There are gifts which are welcomed, and also those which leave a sense of obligation. Some gifts are genuine signs of appreciation, while others are used to manipulate or humiliate. There are gifts that create bonds and overcome separation, and there are gifts that establish or maintain hierarchies.

---

7   Dostoevsky first expressed this idea that life is a gift in his letter to the older brother Michael, immediately after the mock execution, in December of 1849: "Life is a gift, life is happiness, every minute can be an eternity of happiness." Joseph Frank finds this insight so important for the proper interpretation of Dostoevsky that he mentions it in each of his five volumes on Dostoevsky. In his *Dostoevsky: The Mantle of the Prophet, 1871–1881*, he comments (208): "This ecstatic feeling for life as an incomparable gift – one at which we never cease to marvel and to wonder – remained with him to the very end of his days, and he would soon incorporate it into the rhapsodic celebration by Father Zosima of the wonders of God's world."

As there is an economy of the market, Dostoevsky insists that there is also an "economy of gifts." The crucial point is that some aspects of life must remain outside the circle of exchange values. These aspects cannot be assigned a market price. While in *The Idiot* the relationship of these two economies is never explicitly clarified, Dostoevsky is far more decisive in *The Brothers Karamazov*. He does not argue that these two economies must exclude each other. In fact, both are necessary for life, although their fundamental principles are quite different. If we agree that every commodity has value, we should say that a gift does not; it has its worth, but not a value that can be expressed in terms of the market's currency. Although no price can be ascribed to human life, it has unique worth as a gift. This worth is manifested in the quality of life, in its richness and meaningfulness.[8]

The demarcation between the exchange economy and the gift economy is important for our proper understanding of *The Brothers Karamazov*. The preference for one kind of economy over the other affects the entire way of life. It affects what one does with the gift of life. A spirit of commerce, even when most successful, is not an agent of positive bonding. The spirit of commerce is the spirit of separation into "mine" and "yours." In the exchange economy, interest is understood as self-interest. In a world in which we treat virtually everything as property or possession, there can only be a society of strangers, of people who are spiritually homeless. Dostoevsky goes even further in his criticism of a society that worships self-interest and property. The meaning of sin, he holds, is "falling away" and "splitting apart." A man who sins separates himself from his fellow human beings and from God. As the only adequate antidote to disgrace is an act of grace, Dostoevsky insists that the only remedy to sin is atonement – reconciliation

8   The distinction between the two economies is based on the remarks of Lewis Hyde; see his book, *The Gift: Imagination and the Erotic Life of Property*, especially 25–73. Erich Fromm argues that the differences between the two economies reflect the two modes of existence: one focused on acquisition and hoarding, the other on the will to give and to sacrifice for others; see *To Have or to Be*, especially pages 69–129. Stewart R. Sutherland makes similar points in terms of Wittgenstein's phrase "forms of life"; see his *Atheism and the Rejection of God*, 85–98, 141–43.

and reunification with those from whom the sinner has fallen. Such reunification needs an economy of gifts, a spirit of giving and forgiving.

There are several further features which the art of giving gifts shares with the art of having faith. Both gift-giving and faith are disinterested: They are based on trust and appreciation, not on calculation or measuring. Religion establishes a circle of the gift economy which also includes God. This circle is enlarged beyond any particular society and even beyond the realm of nature.

The contours of Dostoevsky's positive worldview are now becoming more visible. The spirit of the religiously interpreted gift economy fosters union, cohesion, and brotherhood. Compassion is based on an awareness of the interdependence of all human beings, and indeed of all living beings. A gift exchange economy should lead to fertility, growth, and rebirth. To those who give (of) themselves, a new life will come. This is the meaning of the words from the Gospel of John which Dostoevsky, a lover of mysteries and paradoxes, uses as the epigraph to *The Brothers Karamazov*:

> Verily, verily, I say unto you,
> Except a corn of wheat fall into the ground and die,
> It abideth alone;
> But if it die, it bringeth forth much fruit (John 12:24).

As the title of Dostoevsky's novel suggests, the task is to create a sense of brotherhood. The question, then, is: How to use the gift of life to create a sense of brotherhood? The biological factor is neither decisive nor necessary. Dostoevsky indicates this by complicating the biological ties between the brothers to the maximum: They neither have the same mother, nor grow up with their father. Dmitri is born from Fyodor's first marriage, Ivan and Alyosha from the second. Then there is also Smerdyakov – most likely the illegitimate son of Fyodor.

The beginning of this "chronicle of the death foretold," as Gabriel Garcia Márquez would call it, finds the brothers living in the same town for the first time in their lives. They are there for a variety of reasons, but it is hard to avoid the impression that their real task is to get to know each other and become "brothers."

Would we ever find the brothers together in the sublime harmony and calm in which we find the three angels seated on Andrei Rublyov's masterful icon "The Holy Trinity"? Rublyov's icon depicts the well-known story from the Old Testament about the three heavenly beings who bring to Abraham and Sarah the announcement that they will get a long awaited son. The angels are seated at the table, upon which, according to the biblical account, lies the feast the couple presented them. Dostoevsky was familiar with Rublyov's icon. In contrast to Rublyov's mood of the majestic calm and divine harmony, *The Brothers Karamazov* presents the opposite picture.[9] Fyodor does not in any way resemble the ancient Abraham. He is not going to be tested with the murder of his son Isaac. Rather, the sons are tempted to kill the father. Unlike the Old Testament story, in Dostoevsky's novel there is a notorious absence of the mothers and wives; Fyodor neither has Sarah nor is he pious and hospitable toward the angels, his sons. Perhaps even more importantly, the three brothers do not travel their journeys together. In the entire novel, all three brothers come together only three times.

The first time the three brothers gather together is in the cell of the Elder Zosima. The disaster that occurs there leads to deeper divisions between Fyodor and Dmitri and between Fyodor and Ivan.

The second gathering for a "family portrait" occurs shortly after the first meeting. The jealous Dmitri, suspecting that Grushenka is visiting the old man, slams into his father's house at the moment when Ivan and Alyosha are offering opposing answers to Fyodor's inquiries regarding the existence of God, the immortality of the soul, and the existence of the devil. Fyodor almost has the chance to check for himself whether heaven and hell exist, for Dmitri beats

---

9   We have already noticed this contrast in the works for which Dostoevsky himself depicts one painting as an integral part of his novel (e.g., Raphael's "Sistine Madonna" in *Crime and Punishment* and Claude Lorraine's "Acis and Galatea" in *The Possessed*). The only painting mentioned in *The Brothers Karamazov* (once and in a passing association with Smerdyakov) is "The Contemplator," by I.N. Kramsky (1837–1887). This painting was first exhibited in 1878.

him badly enough to kill him. Alyosha and Ivan prevent Dmitri from committing the parricide.

The third and final meeting of the brothers takes place a few months later, at Dimitri's murder trial. By this point much has changed in their lives. Dmitri and Alyosha have grown more intimate. Dmitri will soon be on his way to serve his sentence in Siberia. Will he have the same desire to embrace his brothers upon his return, many years later? Will the three ever be able to sit together in the blissful harmony of the brotherhood, as the angels on Rublyov's idyllic icon do?

Perhaps Dostoevsky intended to answer these questions in his next novel. Nonetheless, some of his thoughts on brotherhood are clear in *The Brothers Karamazov*. If becoming a human being is not simply something given to us, but is a task on which we need to work our entire lives, becoming and being a brother is no less a complex and enduring task. Each of the brothers responds to the question of what to do with the gift of life in his unique way. Dmitri uses his gift by wavering between wasting it and appreciating a fuller sense of personal accountability. Ivan falters between his Karamazovian love of life and the regrets that he was ever born. Unable to resolve his indecisions and trapped in the awareness of his moral responsibility for the murder of Fyodor, Ivan sinks into the darkness of a mental disorder. Alyosha, whose story is supposed to come to its climax in Dostoevsky's next novel, oscillates less than the other two brothers. Yet even he cannot avoid a few difficult ordeals on his way to fuller growth and more secure faith.

Since Dostoevsky designates Alyosha as a beautiful man and the principal hero of the novel, we will begin our interpretation of *The Brothers Karamazov* with his appreciation of the gift of life. From there we will move to examine Dmitri's thorny (external and internal) trials. We will conclude with an account of Ivan's regret that he was ever born.

Alyosha – The Gift Appreciated

Alyosha Karamazov is Dostoevsky's quintessential hero. More than any other character, he expresses Dostoevsky's positive philosophy of life. Alyosha summarizes this philosophy to his skeptical brother

Ivan: "I think that everyone should love life before everything else in the world. . . . Love it before logic . . . and only then will [you] understand its meaning" (Bk. V, Ch. 3, 231).

Before we fully appreciate Alyosha's words and Dostoevsky's message, we need to take a closer look at the youngest of the brothers. The first things we learn about him are his indifference to money and dedication to a spiritual way of living. Alyosha is not interested in any learned discussion of progress, as the youngsters of his generation are. He has a strong sense of divine authority present in the world and surrenders reverently to this higher Will. He does not judge anyone and is not interested in power-games. Alyosha has a deep indebtedness for the gift of his life. Abraham Heschel aptly describes this attitude as "an awareness of *owing gratitude*, of being *called upon* at certain moments to reciprocate, to answer, to live in a way which is compatible with the grandeur and mystery of living."[10]

The introductory chapter of this book outlines Dostoevsky's metaphysical-religious framework in terms of a unique combination of realism and optimism. Alyosha is the author's most complete illustration of this combination. The narrator of *The Brothers Karamazov* emphasizes Alyosha's realism, repeating several times that he is "more of a realist than the rest of us" (Bk. I, Ch. 5, 25). In the early drafts of the novel Dostoevsky calls Alyosha an "idiot" and a "prince." To distance Alyosha from the sickly prince Myshkin, he calls to our attention Alyosha's health – the health of a red-cheeked and well-built twenty-year old. This health is both physical and mental. Unlike the frail prince Myshkin, there is no shortage of physical strength and vitality in Alyosha. His mental health is no less remarkable. In him it is not miracles that generate faith, but faith that generates miracles.

The previous chapter gives us a better grip on the second important aspect of Dostoevsky's positive philosophy, his optimism, by means of the following formula: beauty → love → faith → hope. Alyosha's character clarifies further the meaning and significance of this line of thought. Alyosha's physical beauty is not particularly emphasized, but neither is it hidden. The ugly and cheap cassock

10   Abraham Heschel, *Who is Man?*, 111.

which Alyosha wears as the monastery novice cannot hide his physical attractiveness. Grushenka notices this even though Alyosha
frequently passes her with his face turned away. Father Zosima
does not conceal how much he likes Alyosha's "beautiful face,"
which he confesses reminds him of his brother Markel, who died
as a teenager.

Alyosha's spiritual beauty is manifest in his relations to others
and in the manner in which they receive him. Like Prince Myshkin,
Alyosha also loves everyone and his chastity warms everyone's
heart. Although Alyosha seems to have a special gift for inspiring
universal trust and love, even his father Fyodor is sometimes surprised by how good-natured, honest, and forgiving Alyosha is. Can
he really be the father of this angelic boy? What puzzles Fyodor
most is the depth and sincerity of Alyosha's faith. Fyodor is an old
cynic, skeptic, and atheist. From where, then, does Alyosha receive
his faith?

Initially, Alyosha receives it from his mother. Although he lost
his mother in his fourth year, Alyosha remembers her face and her
caresses all his life "as if she were standing alive before me." The
narrator emphasizes the relevance of such memories and gives a
particularly impressive image of one of them:

> He remembered a quiet summer evening, an open window,
> the slanting rays of the setting sun (these slanting rays he
> remembered most of all), an icon in the corner of the room,
> a lighted oil-lamp in front of it, and before the icon, on her
> knees, his mother, sobbing as if in hysterics, with shrieks
> and cries, seizing him in her arms, hugging him so tightly
> that it hurt, and pleading for him to the Mother of God, hold-
> ing him out from her embrace with both arms towards the
> icon, as if under the protection of the Mother of God . . . and
> suddenly a nurse rushes in and snatches him from her in
> fear (Bk. I, Ch. 4, 18–19).

Alyosha retains forever the image of his mother's frenzied but beautiful face. Her name was Sofya Ivanovna, and her first name links
her with Sofya Andreyevna (the mother of the main character in
The Raw Youth) and with the "little mother" Sofya Semyonovna
(Sonia, from *Crime and Punishment*).

In the overall structure of *The Brothers Karamazov*, Alyosha's vivid memory of his mother is crucial for two reasons: (i) the notorious absence of mothers from this novel, and (ii) the role memory plays in Alyosha's choice of what to do with the gift of his life.

There is a notable absence of mothers in *The Brothers Karamazov*. Dmitri's mother dies very young, as is the case with Ivan and Alyosha's mother. Smerdyakov's mother dies at childbirth. The most prominent mother-role in the novel is Madame Khokhlakov, but she does not in any way resemble the archetypal, all-loving and protective Mother. This young widow is on the constant verge of hysterics; her faith is shallow and she desperately desires miracles to reaffirm her faith. Ilysha's mother, Arina Petrovna, is sick and mentally deranged. Kolya Krasotkin's mother and Zosima's mother add little to the work. The world described in *The Brothers Karamazov* is a patriarchal one. Although mothers are really the ones who bestow the gift of life, their role in the novel is reduced to a shadowy presence – in Alyosha's case, to an everlasting memory of an all-forgiving and unconditionally loving being.[11]

That Alyosha retains such strong memories of his mother and of his early childhood is of great importance for Dostoevsky's comprehension of reality. Although four years older than Alyosha, Ivan has no memory of their mother. Ivan tries to repress the past. Dmitri also retains no memory of his mother. He has her violent passions and her inheritance, the exact amount of which is the source of constant hostility between him and his father.

Fyodor is astonished by Alyosha's return to their town: He has come to see his mother's grave. While the boys were little, Fyodor frequently forgot that he had children. Initially, his faithful servant Grigory took care of them before they were dispatched to distant relatives. It is not surprising that Fyodor, who is always focused on the pleasures of the moment, has no recollection of where the grave is. The simple-minded but deeply religious Grigory, who was very

---

11   For further discussion of this important topic, see Liza Knapp, "Mothers and Sons in *The Brothers Karamazov*: Our Ladies of Skotoprigonevsk," in *Dostoevsky: New Perspectives*, ed. Robert L. Jackson, 31–52.

fond of Alyosha's martyr-mother, takes him to the grave. Shortly after, Alyosha enters the monastery as a novice to the famous Elder and healer Zosima, who also emphasizes remembrance as a foundation of faith.

Mircea Eliade argues that by virtue of an eternal return to the sources of the sacred, human existence appears to be saved from nothingness and death. "Their whole religious life is a com- memoration, a remembering. . . . The true sin is forgetting."[12] Eliade talks about religion in general, especially the early, pre- Christian religions, but his point applies to Dostoevsky's Orthodoxy as well. This emphasis on memory is especially important in the context of Dostoevsky's insistence on freedom as the crucial component of humanity. As we have seen in our discussion of the underground man, the elimination of freedom amounts to nothing less than the elimination of humanity. Memory and remembering, as the metaphysical components of religion, amount to repetition and imitation. We are given our lives as a gift, and our lives come to us imprinted with primordial images. Of these images, two are most important: the image of our Mother and of our Father. In Russian Orthodoxy, a primordial image (*obraz*) is preserved and represented as an icon. When the gifts of life are bestowed upon us, our task is to "give an image" to our life. We have to find a model or an exemplar to follow. Alyosha retains with gratitude the image of his mother praying to the Mother of God, and this image prompts him to enter the monastery. There Alyosha finds Father Zosima and regains the image of the Father. In the notes for *The Brothers Karamazov*, Dostoevsky envisions Zosima instructing Alyosha: "Preserve the image [*obraz*] of Christ and if you can, depict [*izobrazi*] it in yourself."[13]

---

12 Mircea Eliade, *The Sacred and the Profane: The Nature of Religion*, 101. For further discussion, see Robert Belknap, "Memory in *The Brothers Karamazov*," in *Dostoevsky: New Perspectives*, ed. Robert L. Jackson, 227–42.

13 Quoted from Murav, *Holy Foolishness: Dostoevsky's Novels & the Poetics of Cultural Critique*, 149. In the same context (150), she quotes Gregory of Nyssa (4th century): "Every person is a painter of his own life."

How does Dostoevsky reconcile his demand for freedom and his conviction that we should imitate the divine images imprinted in us? Do freedom and imitation not exclude each other?

Dostoevsky believes that the contradiction, created by the Enlightenment's exaggerated insistence on the alleged autonomy of man, is an illusion. Our freedom does not consist in creating a new model or an exemplar for ourselves. Our true choice is whether or not to remain faithful to God and further develop the archetypal images already imprinted in us.[14] Zosima does; Fyodor does not. Alyosha does; Ivan does not. Because of their strong bias against tradition and religion, advocates of the Enlightenment argue that what we do with the gift of life is up to us – that our lives are the acts of self-creation. Dostoevsky claims that this unjustifiably ambitious attitude is the source of delusion, one of the main causes of our spiritual impoverishment and homelessness. Those who neglect or destroy the archetypal images must create the new ones. And in the process they resort to self-deceptions and lies. Fyodor, who has no respect for religion and no recollection of the past, identifies himself as "the father of a lie" (Bk. II, Ch. 2, 44). He has lived with lies all his life, but his approaching death worries him. As the Russian proverb says, "without truth it may be easier to live, but it is hard to die."

We first meet Alyosha at the time when both his physical father and his spiritual father are at the threshold of death. Indeed, they die on two consecutive nights. Zosima, who dedicates his life to faith and truth, finds an easy and peaceful death, while Fyodor, who lives the life of debauchery and lies, is violently murdered by one of his sons. Symbolically speaking, the fact that his fathers die means that it is time for Alyosha to begin a life on his own. To quote Eliade again,

> For every human existence is formed by a series of ordeals,
> by repeated experience of "death" and "resurrection."
> And this is why, in a religious perspective, existence is

---

14 A secular reading of the relevance of memory and faithfulness is also possible; see, for instance, Georg Simmel's essay "Faithfulness and Gratitude," 379–95.

established by initiation; it could almost be said that, in so far as human existence is fulfilled, it is itself an initiation.[15]

Life is a series of ordeals and trials. This simple statement reveals perhaps the most important difference between Prince Myshkin's purity and Alyosha's faith. Unlike purity, which a person either possesses or does not, faith is attained by striving; unlike purity, faith is the result of moral ripeness. We do not see Myshkin grow in the course of *The Idiot*; he is a "holy fool" from the beginning to the end. As much as Alyosha may resemble Myshkin, he is not a "holy fool." He is a Karamazov. Despite Alyosha's initial childish simplicity, he grows up and undergoes difficult ordeals and trials of which Myshkin is spared.

Alyosha's first major rite of "death" and "resurrection" occurs after the death of Father Zosima. This death leads to a scandal that deeply challenges Alyosha's young faith. Dostoevsky uses the opportunity of the Elder's death to show that faith can be abused and misunderstood. The frivolous expectation that a miracle must occur after the monk's death leads to a scandal that causes Alyosha to lose his sense of perspective. The bodily remnants of the venerable man create an increasingly unpleasant odor of corruption. The stench is used by the old enemies of Zosima as a sure sign – "a proof" – of how un-holy the man was. The commotion among the believers whose faith depends on proofs and miracles is so contagious that even Alyosha's heart is not spared of ugly suspicions. In the scene that reminds us of Ipolite's bewilderment in front of Holbein's painting of the dead Christ, Alyosha is afraid that the "dumb, unfeeling beast of nature" may, after all, have the last word: "Where was Providence and its finger? Why did it hide its finger 'at the most necessary moment' (Alyosha thought), as if wanting to submit itself to the blind, mute, merciless laws of nature?" (Bk. VII, Ch. 2, 340).

We may be surprised by Alyosha's reactions. Recall that he is present when Father Zosima explains to Madame Khokhlakov that faith cannot be proved:

15 Eliade, *op. cit.*, 209. For further discussion of this immensely important topic for Dostoevsky, see Erich Neumann, *The Origins and History of Consciousness*, especially 131–91 and 261–312.

"One cannot prove anything here, but it is possible to be convinced."

"How? By what?"

"By the experience of active love. Try to love your neighbors actively and tirelessly. The more you succeed in loving, the more you'll be convinced of the existence of God and the immortality of your soul. And if you reach complete selflessness in the love of your neighbor, then undoubtedly you will believe, and no doubt will even be able to enter your soul" (Bk. II, Ch. 4, 56).

How is it, then, that such doubt manages to enter Alyosha's soul after the death of Father Zosima? Dostoevsky's point is that it is one thing to hear someone talk about active love and faith, and quite another to pursue such love and establish such faith based on one's own personal experience. This is the task that awaits Alyosha, for his love and faith are not yet grounded in his own ordeals and trails.

After the scandalous occurrences related to the earthly remains of Father Zosima, the visibly shaken Alyosha leaves the monastery. He does not have any particular aim or destination in mind, but his Mephistopheles, Rakitin, is waiting for him. As the devil presents three temptations to Christ in the desert, Rakitin takes Alyosha to Grushenka for his version of the three temptations: to eat, to drink, and to lust. Alyosha obediently and absentmindedly follows Rakitin to Grushenka's "garden."

Grushenka – "a red-cheeked, full-bodied Russian beauty, a woman of bold and determined character, proud and insolent, knowing the value of money, acquisitive, tight-fisted, and cautious, who by hook or crook had already succeeded, so they said, in knocking together a little fortune of her own" (Bk. VII, Ch. 3, 344) – is delighted to receive Alyosha. This woman, whose charms have brought Fyodor and Dmitri into murderous rivalry, has promised a considerable sum of money to Rakitin if he brings Alyosha to her, so that she can "eat him up."

Rakitin wants the usually fasting Alyosha to "gobble sausage." A bottle of champagne – Dmitri's gift to Grushenka – is opened to make the inexperienced novice drunk, and Grushenka shamelessly jumps into Alyosha's lap. Rakitin is ready to celebrate his victory: He "took a glass, drank it in one gulp, and poured himself another" (Bk. VII, Ch. 3, 351), but his celebration is premature. Upon hearing about the death of Father Zosima and realizing the reason for grief on Alyosha's face, Grushenka springs from his knees and crosses herself.

These gestures are of outstanding significance for Dostoevsky. They reveal his deepest conviction in the element of virtually innate chastity of the ordinary (Russian) people. Ivan and his Grand Inquisitor believe that we are essentially selfish and self-preoccupied creatures. Dostoevsky does not deny that we are selfish and self-preoccupied, but he also believes in the fundamental good in people, which can be evoked at times of crises and by genuine acts of goodness. Father Zosima has the gift of recognizing the best in people and helping them retrieve it, and so does Alyosha – as his later speech to the twelve boys after Ilyusha's funeral testifies. As soon as Grushenka jumps from his lap, Alyosha wakes up from his perilous slumber:

> "Rakitin," he suddenly said loudly and firmly, "don't taunt me with having rebelled against my God. I don't want to hold any anger against you, and therefore you be kinder, too. I've lost such a treasure as you never had, and you cannot judge me now. You'd do better to look here, at her: did you see how she spared me? I came here looking for a wicked soul – I was drawn to that, because I was low and wicked myself, but I found a true sister, I found a treasure – a loving soul . . . She spared me just now . . . I'm speaking of you, Agrafena Alexandrovna. You restored my soul just now" (Bk. VII, Ch. 3, 351).

In a critical moment of his life Alyosha is helped not by one of his brothers, but by a fallen woman, "a sister," as he calls her. Alyosha needs the help of another human being and is not able to resolve his crisis on his own. We come to the truth of ourselves only in the presence of others and in a dialogue with them. That a friendly gesture need not amount to any great sacrifice but can be just an uncalculated and spontaneous act of good will – a simple gift – Dostoevsky further clarifies by Grushenka's narration of the folktale about an onion.

According to Grushenka's story, there was a woman who "was wicked as wicked could be" (Bk. VII, Ch. 3, 352). She never did anything nice to other people and, upon her death, the devils took her into the "lake of fire." Her guardian angel pleads her case to God that the poor woman might escape hell, but the angel cannot remember any good deeds done by the woman. Then the angel recalls that at one time this woman pulled up an onion and gave it to a beggar. God then orders the angel to take that same onion, hold it out to her in the lake and, if it is strong enough to pull her out of the lake, she will enter paradise; if the onion breaks, she must remain in hell. The angel begins to pull out the woman and almost succeeds, but the other sinners see this and begin holding on to her so as to be rescued together with her. The wicked woman kicks them all off: "It's me who's getting pulled out, not you; it's my onion, not yours" (Bk. VII, Ch. 3, 352). As soon as she says this, the stem breaks and she falls into the lake, where she burns in the fires of hell. Her guardian angel weeps over her fate, but finally must give up and leave.

Grushenka relates this story to Alyosha because she does not want to be praised beyond measure. She offered only one onion to Alyosha. Yet the meaning of that simple gift is not lost on her or on Alyosha. It is a small gift, almost nothing; but how far more difficult would human life be without small yet spontaneous gifts of kindness and goodness to other human beings?[16]

Grushenka emphasizes that she heard the tale as a child and has remembered it ever since. In this way, Dostoevsky again calls our attention to the role of memory, of what we cherish from the past and how it guides us in our behavior and choices. This point is developed in the follow-up to Alyosha's visit to Grushenka. With the help of his newfound sister (for whom Alyosha's recognition is a beginning of her own conversion), he escapes the temptations that lure him toward sin. Upon his return to the monastery, Alyosha visits the cell of Zosima where the coffin of the venerable teacher still stands and where Father Paissy is reading the Gospel over

16 For further discussion, see Gary Saul Morson, "The God of Onions: *The Brothers Karamazov* and the Mythic Prosaic," in *A New Word on The Brothers Karamazov*, ed. R. Jackson, 107–24.

the coffin. He is reading the passage from "Cana of Galilee" (John 2:1–11), a story deeply symbolic of the interplay of the divine and the human. Alyosha has loved this story from his childhood.[17] As he kneels down and begins to pray, his soul – overwhelmed with so many experiences and exhausted from a previous sleepless night – slips into a half-dream. Images of the gospel dance in front of him, and Father Zosima appears at the biblical wedding, pointing out to Alyosha the presence of Jesus and his Mother. Following the demand of his Mother, Jesus performs his first miracle by turning water into wine. As the walls of the cell become blurred in his vision, Alyosha hears the voice of his beloved teacher addressing him from the banquet:

> "I, too, my dear, I, too, have been called, called and chosen. . . . Why are you hiding here, out of sight . . . ? Come and join us. . . . Why are you marveling at me? I gave a little onion, and so I am here. And there are many here who only gave an onion, only one little onion . . . What are our deeds? And you, quiet one, you, my meek boy, today you, too, were able to give a little onion to a woman who hungered. Begin, my dear, begin, my meek one, to do your work!" (Bk. VII, Ch. 4, 361).

Alyosha wakes up and departs into the starry night, filled with joy and a renewed appreciation of life. Perhaps at the very same time when his father Fyodor is murdered, Alyosha bows down and kisses the earth, "weeping, sobbing, watering it with his tears, and he vowed ecstatically to love it, to love it unto ages of ages" (Bk. VII, Ch. 4, 362).[18]

---

17 Dostoevsky himself loved this story from his childhood. Irina Kirillova argues that the number of marks in Dostoevsky own copy of the Bible displays a clear preference for the Gospel of St John and its companion text the First Epistle of John, even over the Sermon on the Mount. See Kirillova, "Dostoevsky's Markings in the Gospel according to St John," in *Dostoevsky and the Christian Tradition*, edited by George Pattison and Diane Oenning Thompson, 41–50, esp. 42.

18 For further discussion, see Christopher Merrill, *Things of the Hidden God: Journey to the Holy Mountain*, 95; and Arthur Koestler, *The Act of Creation*, 271–84.

Alyosha has left behind his first passage of initiation. His soul is filled with faith and gratitude. He is ready to leave the monastery and begin his "work."

Father Zosima once quotes the Epistle to the Hebrews (10:31), which warns: "It is a fearful thing to fall into the hands of the living God" (Bk. VI, Ch. 2 [d], 309). This warning was issued to his "mysterious visitor" who is responsible for a murder. The same warning will later apply to Ivan and Smerdyakov. The venerable priest could also have cited the next verse (11:1), which gives the most succinct explanation of faith in the Bible: "And what is faith? Faith gives substance to our hopes and makes us certain of realities we do not see."

This explanation has three elements, each of which is important for Dostoevsky. Faith grounds our hopes, so that they are not imaginary or unrealistic. Faith gives confidence and supports the attitude of trust: We come to trust what we do not see and cannot see with our physical eyes. Finally faith involves a leap from the visible to the invisible, from the tangible to the intangible.

Faith can be subjective ("faith in . . . ," an attitude and disposition of trust), or objective ("faith that . . . ," which relates to a specific content). The common element of both is an orientation toward what is best in other human beings (and in the world as a whole). As Nicolai Hartmann explains, this orientation "manifests itself as a capacity to detect what is good and genuine in another's disposition amidst the less worthy tendencies and to seize upon the good, even to draw it out and develop it by the influence of one's trust."[19]

Father Zosima's command to Alyosha to leave the monastery and begin his "work" corresponds to what Hartmann describes as faith. The venerable priest does not challenge Alyosha to become a martyr. Nor does he expect Alyosha to perform a heroic deed the world has never seen. On the contrary, he must do what many have already done. Alyosha must help those in need, his brothers and sisters, by seizing upon the good in them and encouraging them to develop what is best in them. Alyosha's time has come, his faith is strong, and he is prepared for his "work."

---

19 Nicolai Hartmann, *Ethics*, vol. 2, 296.

He is ready to sit down with his brothers in a joyful harmony, as the three angels sit on Andrei Rublyov's icon. Are his brothers ready to join him?

Dmitri – The Gift Used

In the story of Cana of Galilee, Jesus turns water into wine. The meaning of this miracle is that nature can be transformed into something which is the result of a union with spirit. Alyosha's embrace of the earth has a similar message: Even the wild, passionate, uncontrollable Karamazov nature can be ennobled. It is ennobled not in the way in which Freud envisions we treat the eruptive *id* – by taming and containing it through the *superego* – but through miraculous, almost mystical experience of love and grace. Dostoevsky insists that even the unruly Karamazov blood can be spiritualized.

A skeptic may not be convinced so quickly. Alyosha is an easy case, but what about "a true Karamazov"? Can Dmitri or Fyodor, with their enormous vitality and much stronger ties to the earthly passions find their way to faith?

Dostoevsky concedes that it is too late for Fyodor, but he does not give up on Dmitri. Fyodor's name derives from the Greek name Theodore and means "gift of God." It is hard to resist the impression that this gift is misused and wasted, not only in Fyodor, but also in Dmitri who – at least initially – seems to follow his father's footsteps. With his unruly behavior and unbridled passion, mostly channeled through sexual energy and drunken orgies, Dmitri resembles his father more than he resembles any brother. Their vitality and sensualism are so alike that they desire and fight over the same woman and come to hate each other.

Even before their struggle over Grushenka, father and son are involved in the wrong economy, the economy of the market. They fight over the inheritance of Dmitri's mother. Due to his ignorance and arrogance, Dmitri imagines that its value is far greater than it actually is. As was typical of a Russian officer of the nineteenth century, Dmitri lives a reckless life far beyond his means and expects that the money from the inheritance will constantly flow to him. Fyodor is far more experienced in the matters of money – he actually manages to amass a small fortune. He pays Dmitri little by little, keeping a careful record of the amounts, so that later he can legally manipulate his careless son and avoid further obligation.

As the novel unfolds, we come to realize how different Dmitri is from his father. Dmitri constantly needs money because of his wild and irresponsible life-style, but unlike his father he does not value money inherently. For his father money is both means and end, but for Dmitri it is always and only a means. Just as Alyosha is willing to give his savings to anyone in need, Dmitri does not appreciate money and throws it around with the greatest of ease. As Perkhotin reproaches his friend, "money is like trash or water to you" (Bk. VIII, Ch. 5, 401).

Dmitri's playful pursuit of the joys of life, which swings him mercilessly from one hazardous adventure to another, is colored by his appreciation of poetry.[20] All Karamazovs are blessed with rhetorical gifts. Although Fyodor often lies, when he does not, he (like Alyosha) tells the truth directly and in no uncertain terms. Ivan is a brilliant rhetorician who does not tell the truth simply and directly but through various fictional accounts, the most famous of which is "The Legend of the Grand Inquisitor." For his part, Dmitri is an incurable Schillerian romantic who expresses himself better in verse than in prose. In a magnificent chapter, "The Confession of an Ardent Heart in Verse," Dmitri opens his soul for his youngest brother. He does so not only by confessing to Alyosha but also by citing Schiller, including his "Ode to Joy."[21] Citing Schiller displays Dmitri's joy of life and also the realization of his proper place in

---

20 The following statements, which Zweig makes of Dostoevsky, apply well to Dmitri: "He does not want to conquer life but to feel it. Nor does he choose to be the master of his fate; rather does he prefer to remain a loyal servitor. It was only thus, by electing to be God's thrall, the most abject of his slaves, that he could attain to so profound a knowledge of all things human"; op. cit., 141. Hartmann thinks that this attitude is an insufficiently appreciated value of a special kind, which he calls "richness of experience"; see op. cit., 205–10.

21 Is it probable that a poorly educated Dmitri is able to cite Schiller by heart, or even that he is familiar with Schiller in the first place? Dostoevsky would definitely say that this is quite possible. In A Writer's Diary (June 1876, vol. 1, 507), Dostoevsky argues that Schiller "was absorbed into the Russian soul; he left his mark on it and all but gave his name to a period in the history of our development."

nature. To Alyosha, he compares himself to an insect with a sensual lust, but Alyosha can sense that Dmitri is capable of noble impulse as well. He is a man able to refocus his life around some uplifting ideal, instead of merely wasting his gift on sensual pleasures and unseemly quarrels with his father. Like Alyosha, Dmitri is attracted toward that which is great and superior, but will he ever redirect his pursuit of sensual pleasure toward the sublime?

Remarkably, while citing the "Ode to Joy," Dmitri skips over the central verses that talk of the universal brotherhood ("*Alle Menschen werden Brüder*") "in the soul of God's creation," inspired by "life's mysterious fermentation." Despite "all that custom has divided," says Schiller, the "Divine magic power" will reunite all human beings into one brotherhood. This intentional omission is due to Dmitri's self-preoccupation – he cannot yet think about how all human beings will become brothers. In the course of the novel Dmitri becomes far more aware of deeper issues, and his character transforms itself before our eyes.

Although Dmitri has a long journey in front of him, at the moment when he sings Schiller's "Ode to Joy," he is more than an imitation of Fyodor Karamazov.[22] While Fyodor declares that "there has never been an ugly woman" (Bk. III, Ch. 8, 136) and chases any skirt, Dmitri has developed a refined appreciation for female beauty. Since this distinction places Dmitri on the path of beauty → love → faith → hope, let us explain how he understands beauty in the language of Schiller (and Kant, whose ideas Schiller develops).

Schiller argues that our choices and behavior are based either on irrational inclinations (emotions) or on reason. Acting according to inclinations gives us a sense of freedom in the sense of self-determination – I choose to do what I want to do. The focus of interest is on me and my desires. Following Kant, Schiller argues

22 Dmitri's name comes from the Greek *Demeter*, which literally means "Mother Earth" and which refers to the goddess in whose honor the Eleusian mysteries were celebrated. It is thus fully appropriate that Dmitri cites Schiller's "Eleusian Festival." On the name symbolism in *The Brothers Karamazov*, see Victor Terras, *A Karamazov Companion*, 117–18, and Ralph Matlaw, "Myth and Symbolism in *The Brothers Karamazov*," 109–10.

that there is a more dignified way of choosing and acting than focusing on the self. This type occurs when we choose and act following the precepts of reason. Reason allows for freedom in a deeper and more authentic sense because it makes possible genuine moral autonomy. In the case of rational and autonomous freedom, the focus shifts from "I" toward an intelligible and supersensible realm, toward how things "ought to be." Schiller further develops these distinctions to mark a difference between the realm of beautiful and the realm of sublime. Beauty attaches itself too closely to the sensible world, by focusing on our inclinations and on what is present. The experience of sublimity, by contrast, requires lifting our eyes (and expectations), toward what is not visible, toward an ideal.[23]

While Dostoevsky agrees with some of Schiller's finer distinctions (e.g., the focus on an "I" versus the focus on the supersensible, the difference between beautiful and sublime), much of that theory he finds abstract and inadequate. Dmitri penetrates the mysteries of beauty in a way that indicates quite different insights:

> Beauty is a fearful and terrible thing! Fearful because it's indefinable, and it cannot be defined, because here God gave us only riddles. Here the shores converge, here all contradictions live together. I'm a very uneducated man, brother, but I've thought about it a lot. So terribly many mysteries! Too many riddles oppress man on earth. Solve them if you can without getting your feet wet. Beauty! Besides, I can't bear it that some man, even with a lofty heart and the highest mind, should start from the ideal of the Madonna and end with the ideal of Sodom. It's even more fearful when someone who already has the ideal of Sodom in his soul does not deny the ideal of Madonna either, and his heart burns with it, verily, verily burns, as in his young, blameless years. No, man is broad, even too broad, I would narrow him down. Devil knows even what to make of him, that's the thing! What's shame for the mind is

---

23 For further discussion of Schiller's theory of beautiful and sublime, see Frederick Beiser, *Schiller as Philosopher: A Re-Examination*, especially 47–76, 213–62. For a criticism of Schiller and Kant's aesthetic approach, see Nicolai Hartmann, *Ästhetik*, Ch. 32.

beauty all over for the heart. Can there be beauty in Sodom?
Believe me, for the vast majority of people, that's just where
beauty lies – did you know that secret? The terrible thing is
that beauty is not only fearful but also mysterious. Here the
devil is struggling with God, and the battlefield is the human
heart (Bk. III, Ch. 3, 108).

Two of Dmitri's points stand in the striking contrast to Schiller: the
complexity of our experience of beauty, and the emphasis on irrationality (and riddles), which either eliminates the role of reason
or relegates it to the background. We must not overlook the complex, virtually contradictory nature of our experience of beauty –
the Madonna and Sodom are inseparately linked. By bringing them
together, Dostoevsky turns not only against Schiller but against
some of his own speculations regarding the nature and role of
beauty. In this passage he transcends the naïve hope voiced in
The Idiot that perhaps beauty can save the world. Beauty cannot
save the world, but its appreciation can serve as a path to the more
hidden mysteries and perplexities of human nature. As in Plato's
Symposium, the appreciation of physical beauty is the first step
on a ladder toward higher insights and further growth. Such appreciation leads not only to pleasure but also to pain. Pleasure and
pain are separable only in the most peripheral layers of our experience; the further we probe ourselves, the less distinguishable they
become. The playful and illogical Dmitri sees them as inseparably
connected.

Dmitri does not mention reason or sublimity in the quoted
passage, but he indirectly refers to both. Dostoevsky agrees with
Schiller that our experience of the sublime points toward the supersensible or, as he would say, toward the divine. But even the divine
is, for Dostoevsky, complex and ambiguous. Divine reason might
be as puzzled by the world as is its human counterpart. The divine
and the sublime do not lead toward any neatly delineated moral
category of freedom. (As I argue in Chapter 2, freedom is for
Dostoevsky primarily a metaphysical, not a moral category.) Dmitri
is seized by female beauty, especially by Grushenka's "infernal
curves," but this intoxication does not lead him to become a better person. Rather, it throws him into a love-fever which brings

him to the threshold of parricide. Due to unusual and "lucky" circumstances, Dmitri's infatuation with Grushenka leads to his rediscovery of love and faith.

The decisive step in Dmitri's maturation occurs when he learns that Grushenka has run away from both him and his father. She hopes to be reunited with her lover who seduced her five years ago and for whom she has been waiting. After dealing with feelings of betrayal and deception, Dmitri comes to understand Grushenka's avoidance of both Karamazovs. In the pain of the moment, he realizes how much he really loves her and he makes a resolution that will completely change his life. Despite his burning desire for Grushenka, he will "remove himself out of the way" and bless her newfound happiness. Precisely out of his love for Grushenka, he will restrain his own feeling and sacrifice himself for her happiness. In the night of their reunion, Dmitri will join Grushenka and her lover to let them know that he will not be an obstacle to them. And with the first rays of light announcing a new day, with the first appearance of "golden-haired Phoebus," he will commit suicide (Bk. VIII, Ch. 5, 402).

Here, again, Dostoevsky illustrates this transformation with his epigraph: "Except a corn of wheat fall into the ground and die, it abideth alone: but if it die, it bringeth forth much fruit." Dmitri, with his Karamazovian love of life, is willing to sacrifice himself for the woman he loves. His gift to Grushenka "bringeth forth much fruit." As with other gifts, love is not lost when given away. Grushenka realizes that her Polish seducer is not the one she has dreamed about for five years. He is a pitiful, disgusting, greedy individual who is more interested in her money than in her love. In contrast to him stands Dmitri, who in the generosity of his heart is willing to give up everything he has for the happiness of his "queen of beauty." In a sudden change of heart, Grushenka realizes that Dmitri is the man with whom she wants to spend her life.

While Dmitri is on his second spree with Grushenka, someone kills Fyodor Karamazov. The police commissioner and the public prosecutor are quickly alerted and they arrive in Mokroye a few hours after the murder, arrest Dmitri, accuse him of parricide, and begin a preliminary investigation.

According to Anna Grigorievna, during his work on *The Brothers Karamazov* Dostoevsky frequently turned to the Book of Job. Book Nine, which describes the preliminary investigation of Dmitri, resembles structurally Job's encounter with his friends. The fact that Job is suffering, and suffering mightily, proves for the friends that God is punishing him. They are assured of his guilt and want to figure out what sins he has committed. While Job persistently denies any accusation, his friends try to secure Job's confession, so that – after being properly punished – he can reconcile with God. Job continues to deny any guilt and, in the torturous process, comes to learn more about himself, his friends, and his God than he has ever known before.

Dmitri similarly claims: "I've found out more in this one cursed night than I'd have learned in twenty years of living" (Bk. IX, Ch. 6, 486). We have already seen that Dmitri has learned of Grushenka's love and devotion for him. The accusation against him only strengthens Dmitri's and Grushenka's resolve to spend the rest of their lives together. Dmitri also finds out that his former acquaintances and the present interrogators are no friends of his. They have different values from his and live according to different economies of life. Dmitri believes that, since they know each other, since they played cards and gossiped about women together, the investigation will proceed in the spirit of mutual trust between them. He is bitterly disappointed. The investigation is based not on the spirit of camaraderie but on the formalities of detached and cold legal procedures.

Western civilization has always regarded truth as one of its highest and most important values. In ancient and medieval times truth has often been understood as a secret revealed to a few. These few are persons in a state of *mania*, like the Delphic priestess in the temple of Apollo, or those who have purified themselves to become worthy of true insight, like Augustine. Modernity radically breaks with this tradition. Descartes and his successors tie the concept of truth to publicly available evidence, demonstration, and proof. They shift the attention from the truth itself to a reliable criterion of truth. Dostoevsky's insight is that human beings can miss the truth in spite of the best available evidence. We see the most notable occurrences of this insight in connection with Dmitri's preliminary interrogation and his trial.

The investigators are interested in evidence and facts which Dmitri views as irrelevant for the discovery of the truth. They want to know everything about the money he brought with him to Mokroye, as if the money could have killed his father. They want to know all of his motives, but Dmitri does most things impulsively, without being conscious of any particular motive. They want proofs, while Dmitri is concerned about feelings – especially feelings of shame, which burn in his soul like open wounds ever since he borrowed Katerina Ivanovna's three thousand rubles. That money was a dishonor for him, and led him to lie and feel like a thief. Dmitri tries to explain to the interrogators the difference between a scoundrel and a thief, but they laugh at him and humiliate him by asking him to undress so they can check his clothes. This, to Dmitri, is the ultimate disgrace: for them to see his dirty socks and underwear, for him to stand naked in front of these hard-hearted strangers. Dmitri feels that the investigators treat him not as a human being but as an object to be examined, just as the pestle with which he hit Grigory will be examined as a piece of material evidence in the court of law.

Abraham Heschel claims that religion depends upon what human beings do with their ultimate embarrassment. An individual (like Dmitri) experiencing such embarrassment stands at the crossroads at which he can – through wisdom or grace – find his or her way toward a new life, toward a spiritual rebirth. The exhausted Dmitri, humiliated and disgraced, finds himself at such crossroads. As the "friends" finish the transcript of the preliminary investigation, Dmitri's eyes close with fatigue. In the darkest hour of his life, he lies down on a large chest covered with a rag, and falls asleep.

Arthur Koestler calls dreams "underground games," and Dmitri's dream certainly falls into this category.[24] He has "a strange sort of dream, somehow entirely out of place and out of time" (Bk. IX, Ch. 8, 507). He dreams of being driven through a steppe, in a place

24 Koestler, op. cit., 178.

where he served as an officer long ago. While the big flakes of snow are falling down on a cold November day, half of the nearby village is burning. A long line of destitute village women stand along the road, hungry and cold. At the very end of their line, there is a mother holding a baby in her hands. The baby cries desperately, as the mother's "breast must be all dried up, not a drop of milk in them. And the baby is crying, crying, reaching out its bare little arms, its little fists somehow all blue from the cold" (Bk. IX, Ch. 8, 507).

Dmitri cannot understand why the baby is crying and repeats this question to his driver. To all reasonable answers that "the wee one" is hungry and cold, that their house is burned out, that they need bread, Dmitri fixates himself on the same impossible to answer "why" questions:

> "No, no," Mitya still seems not to understand, "tell me: why are these burnt-out mothers standing here, why are the people poor, why is the wee one poor, why is the steppe bare, why don't they embrace and kiss, why don't they sing joyful songs, why are they blackened with such black misery, why they don't feed the wee one?"
>
> And he feels within himself that, though his questions have no reason or sense, he still certainly wants to ask in just that way, and he should ask in just that way. And he also feels a tenderness such as he has never known before surging up in his heart, he wants to weep, he wants to do something for them all, so that the wee one will no longer cry, so that the blackened, dried-up mother of the wee one will not cry either, so that there will be no more tears in anyone from that moment on, and it must be done at once, at once, without delay and despite everything, with all his Karamazov unrestraint.
>
> "And I am with you, too, I won't leave you now, I will go with you for the rest of my life," the dear, deeply felt words of Grushenka came from somewhere near him. And his whole heart blazed up and turned towards some sort of light, and he wanted to live and live, to go on and on along the same path, towards the new, beckoning light, and to hurry, hurry, right now, at once! (Bk. IX, Ch. 8, 507–8).

Dmitri is ready to surrender to this light. His heart is awakening from his own personal drama, which preoccupied him to the point of madness. Now that his father is dead and Grushenka has accepted his gift, he is beginning to realize that his previous life was a horrible delusion, a nightmare from which he must wake up. At the point of his dream when the cries of "the wee one" become unbearable and Dmitri is ready to redirect his entire life toward helping others, the prosecutor wakes him up to check the transcript. Another surprise awaits Dmitri:

> It suddenly struck him that there was a pillow under his head, which, however, had not been there when he had sunk down powerlessly on the chest.
>
> "Who put that pillow under my head? What good person did it?" he exclaimed with a sort of rapturous gratitude, in a sort of tear-filled voice, as though God knows what kindness had been shown him. The good man remained unidentified even later – perhaps one of the witnesses, or even Nikolai Parfenovich's clerk, had arranged that a pillow be put under his head, out of compassion – but his whole soul was as if shaken with tears. He went up to the table and declared that he would sign whatever they wanted.
>
> "I had a good dream, gentlemen," he said somehow strangely, with a sort of new face, as if lit up with joy (Bk. IX, Ch. 8, 508).

The narrator of *The Brothers Karamazov* tells us from the first page, and reminds us later as well, that he is writing a "chronicle" of this unfortunate family, and that the central focus of this chronicle is the murder of the old Karamazov. The word "chronicle" literally means "to be plunged into time." Chronicles are based on a "historical approach" and a linear conception of time, with their indispensable beginnings and ends. But we know that Dostoevsky is more interested in the cyclical conception of time, according to which the most important events, the only ones worth recording and remembering, are those which repeat themselves. In the mythological cycle of life – death – resurrection (renewal), a person enters into a closed space and emerges from it renewed. Something of this kind of cycle is clearly taking place in Dmitri's spiritual transformation. Dostoevsky describes Dmitri's rite of initiation, his definitive turn toward faith, toward the Hand of Creation. Although his transformation is more complex and consequential, it parallels the one which Alyosha undergoes that same night. The pillow that somebody puts under his head, which touches Dmitri so much, is analogous to Grushenka's onion – it is a small, simple gift which nonetheless makes a powerful impression on the one who receives it, especially when that person seems abandoned by his former allies. Like Alyosha's, Dmitri's passage toward light takes the form of a dream in which a message coming from the source of his being penetrates his conscious surface.

Dmitri has always believed that the source of life is irrational. Now he comes into a more direct contact with this source which transforms his soul. Dmitri is willing to sign any transcript. His true, inner trial is over. The trial that awaits him in court is a formality to which he will not pay too much attention. The prosecutor and the police commissioner do not hide that, from their point of view, Dmitri has transgressed some "sacred" boundaries and will have to be punished for it. Even if there is no direct evidence that Dmitri killed his father, his contemptuous treatment of money makes him a "spoil-sport" who threatens the existence of the community fixated on the value of money. As such, he must be cast out. Katerina Ivanovna will present Dmitri's letter to the court which will provide "undeniable" evidence that Dmitri is the murderer. The letter of the law will be followed, sending him to penal servitude in Siberia.

None of this disturbs Dmitri's newfound faith. During the night he plunges to the depths and there, in his darkest hour, he finds his way to God. Immediately after the pillow episode, Dmitri turns to his interrogators with kind words: "Well, gentlemen, I don't blame you, I'm ready . . . I understand that you have no other choice" (Bk. IX, Ch. 9, 509). Like Job's friends, they do not understand his spiritual transformation.

Suffering, Dmitri now comes to understand, is neither punishment nor coercion. Suffering offers the possibility of purification of the conscience. Purification does not mean establishing moral or religious quality. Rather, it means the awakening of the ability to discriminate genuine from base qualities, a gradual sharpening of the vision on the central goods and values and on an authentic source of the meaning of life. Suffering enables Dmitri to see his previous blindness and notice values which were hidden before. In suffering for the sake of love, a person awakens to a deeper moral and religious order. In *Notes from the Underground* the main character poses his tormenting question: "Which is better: cheap happiness or exalted suffering?" (Pt. II, sec. x, 376). He is inclined to choose cheap happiness, as would Dmitri at the beginning of *The Brothers Karamazov*. After the fateful night in Mokroye, after being struck by "the thunder," Dmitri reverses his judgment. Those like the underground man overlook that besides the suffering which arises from want or need there is also suffering which evolves from the increase of vitality, from spiritual growth and faith.

At the end of his farewell speech, in the spirit of his rediscovered faith and sense of brotherhood, Dmitri offers his hand to the prosecutor. Dmitri accepts his responsibility and is ready to atone for his sins, but the prosecutor murmurs that "the investigation is not over yet" and refuses to shake hands with him. Dmitri forgives him. He knows that there will be others, Alyosha among them, who will not be ashamed to take his hand and who will always sit with him at the same table. Alyosha will always be his brother, no matter how low he may sink.

And Ivan? Will Ivan join his brothers? "Ivan is a grave," says Dmitri (Bk. III, Ch. 4, 110). "Ivan is a riddle," thinks Alyosha (Bk. V, Ch. 3, 229). Later, Dmitri corrects himself: "Ivan is a sphinx" (Bk. XI, Ch. 4, 592).

Ivan – The Gift Regretted

Little is known about the life of Andrei Rublyov, who painted Russia's most sublime icon – "The Holy Trinity." He lived in a difficult era of his country's history (1360–1430), the period of continuous Tartar invasions, when Russia was politically divided and when the role of the Church was not well secured and defined. Rublyov was a monk in The Trinity – St. Sergius monastery where a strong emphasis was placed on fraternity, spiritual self-improvement, and love of God. In this era of general turmoil, the monks most sincerely believed that Christ was born and died to make peace between God and man. These convictions are manifest on Rublyov's icon.

In his unique approach to the biblical story of the three wanderers who visit Abraham and Sarah and receive their hospitality, Rublyov simplifies to the maximum the structure of his icon. Abraham and Sarah are not (directly) represented, and the only trace of the feast is a cup on the table (resembling the Eucharistic cup on the altar) with a lamb-head in it. The focus is on the three angels and their mutual relationship. The angels are quiet, gentle, almost sorrowful; the mood permeating the icon is meditative and intimate. The slightly tilted figures suggest humility and love for each other. All the angels are equally important, and, seated around the table, they form a circle. "The Trinity" epitomizes the ideal of brotherhood, love, and quiet sanctity. Rublyov's icon is a majestic portrayal not of one beautiful person, but of three.

Dostoevsky must have admired the simplicity and sublimity of Rublyov's icon.[25] Nonetheless, his own approach to the task of portraying a beautiful man and the ideal of brotherhood is opposite to Rublyov's. The relationship between the three Karamazov brothers is complex and their journeys thorny. The circle between the brothers is constantly shifting, never complete, and continually threatening to dissolve beyond repair.[26] Even the boundaries of the circle are not clear: Is Smerdyakov in or out? An even greater obstacle for the closure of the circle is Ivan. Despite the disparities between Alyosha and Dmitri, and they are considerable, both find their way to faith and both believe in purification through suffering and service to others. Alyosha clearly appreciates life from the beginning, and what he has to learn – what his Elder demands of him – is how to use his gift, not in the secluded world of the monastery but in "real" life. Alyosha inclines toward the economy of gifts, and he has to learn about the exchange economy as well. Dmitri has a different, more convoluted path to travel.

25 According to Malcolm Jones, Dostoevsky's parents made with their children an "annual pilgrimage to the St Sergius Trinity Monastery, about 60 miles outside Moscow. These major family events continued until Dostoevsky was ten"; *Dostoevsky and the Dynamic of Religious Experience*, 1.

26 Girard reinserts Clyde Kluckhohn's thesis that the most common of all mythological conflicts is the struggle between brothers, which generally ends in fratricide; *Violence and the Sacred*, 61.

While Alyosha comes to the boundaries of the permissible without crossing them, Dmitri is no stranger to transgressing such limits. His Karamazovian passion for life leads him to use, misuse, and abuse his gift of life, without worrying much about the consequences of his actions for himself or those affected by them. From being a playful Bacchus who lives only for the pleasures of the moment, Dmitri finds his way to a different shore, where compassion and responsibility are the dominant values. He learns when not to mix the two economies. The lesson of his ordeals is that a sinner can find a way to repent, and Dmitri learns this the hard way.

Ivan has a different story. The narrator gives us compelling reasons for the presence of Dmitri and Alyosha in their father's town, but we never quite grasp what Ivan is doing there. At the age of twenty-four Ivan is a highly cultivated man of progressive convictions. Good looking and meticulously dressed, superbly intelligent and well educated, with grace and ease Ivan finds his way into higher social circles, where the economy of the market sets the norms. Without difficulty we imagine Ivan engaged in a sophisticated discussion in the literary circles of Moscow, attending a performance in a luxurious Parisian theater, or wandering pensively through the ancient ruins of Rome. But what is he doing in the town of Skotoprigonievsk (meaning "beast coral," or "beast pen")? Not interested in the grave of his mother, as Alyosha is, or in his father's money, which preoccupies Dmitri, Ivan remains a riddle to the narrator. During his stay he hardly establishes any genuine contact with his brothers or his father.

Our first good look under Ivan's polished surface occurs during the family gathering which takes place at the monastery. It is Ivan's idea to have the venerable priest give council to his father and his brother regarding their dispute. Despite his fragile health, Father Zosima receives them. Through his cryptic remarks, penetrating insights, and unexpected symbolic gestures, he helps us understand Ivan's character and future.

In a few words, the Elder points out the two extreme poles between which Ivan oscillates. While they are discussing Ivan's recently published article, it becomes clear that the middle brother defends the following radical view: *If there is no God and subsequently no immortality of the soul, there can be no such thing as virtue and everything is permissible* (Bk. II, Ch. 6, 69–70).

Thanks to Dostoevsky, we are so familiar with this conditional that it is easy to overlook how brilliantly it summarizes some of the central dilemmas of the modern secular civilization.[27] Since the same conditional resurfaces in the "Legend of the Grand Inquisitor," we will discuss its merits in the next chapter. Here we focus primarily not on the tenability of Ivan's philosophical arguments but on his personality. As Edward Wasiolek remarks, Ivan's revolt is rooted in something deeper than his reason. It is based on his Karamazov belly, on his sensibilities, and his personal revulsion toward the troublesome historical reality.[28]

Father Zosima does not hide his admiration for Ivan's intelligence. What worries him is that Ivan's emotions seem to be detached from his intellect. In this regard, Ivan is unlike any other Karamazov and more like a European intellectual – like Schiller or, perhaps even better, Kant.[29] As a result of the detachment of his intellectual and emotional aspects, Ivan is troubled by the terrible "if" of his conditional – we can never know whether there is a God and immortality of the soul. The law of nature does not prompt people to love each other. Ivan holds that they love their neighbors (when they do) only as a result of their unverifiable belief in personal immortality. Although European liberals and socialists often assume that their vision of brotherhood is equivalent to those defended by Christians, this assumption is wrong.[30] In fact, argues Ivan, provided that this shared belief is indeed possible, liberals

---

27 This conditional does not represent only the view of a fictional character (Ivan). See Dostoevsky's letter to Osmidov of February 1878. See also James P. Scanlan, *Dostoevsky the Thinker*, 19–40.

28 Edward Wasiolek, *Dostoevsky: The Major Fiction*, 161.

29 In his *Dostoevskii i Kant*, Jakov Emmanuilovich Golosovker argues that it is not accidental that Ivan Karamazov and Immanuel Kant have the same initials; the reason for this is that in *The Brothers Karamazov* Dostoevsky wanted to confront and resolve Kantian antinomies of pure reason, especially the last one, concerning the existence and nature of God.

30 In *Dostoevsky: The Stir of Liberation, 1860–1865*, Frank elaborates on Dostoevsky's convictions that that brotherhood is the very antithesis of

and socialists have to defend their vision of brotherhood on very different terms from believers because they cannot take for granted the existence of God and immortality of the soul. As Ivan's later discussion with Alyosha clarifies, liberals and socialists must rely on law and justice, not on repentance and forgiveness; on exact retribution, not on gifts of grace. Alyosha and Dmitri are led to the table by the economy of gifts; Ivan, by the economy of the market. This is why Ivan has a hard time sitting at the same table with Dmitri and Alyosha. If the ideal of brotherhood is possible, Ivan's understanding of it will be quite different than, and even incompatible with, that of his brothers.

Recognizing Ivan's indecisiveness, and knowing the power of the Karamazov passion, Father Zosima encourages Ivan to confront himself and figure out what he believes, before it is too late: If he does not believe in any higher authority, how can Ivan avoid the conclusion that everything is permissible? Perhaps even more importantly, if Ivan really believes that everything is permissible, how is he going to live with the consequences of his actions? How will he confront his own conscience?

Dostoevsky expresses Ivan's later guilt in terms of the "moral responsibility" for the murder of his father. Yet here, as in *Crime and Punishment* and several other novels, Dostoevsky is not so much interested in the act of crime *per se*, but in what leads to it, and in what happen afterwards. Why, then, does Ivan, who seems so much better off than his brothers at the beginning of *The Brothers Karamazov*, plummet so low?

The narrator gradually realizes that, despite initial impression to the contrary, Ivan most resembles Fyodor Karamazov. When Dmitri says that "Ivan is a grave" (Bk. III, Ch. 4, 110), he may mean that Ivan closes his own feelings within and also that it is not easy to penetrate his secret. Alyosha's exclamation that "Ivan is a riddle" (Bk. V, Ch. 3, 229) confirms that there is a secret inside Ivan that bothers him. Toward the end of the novel, Dmitri comes even closer

---

the European character, that brotherhood demands a much higher development of personality than has been obtained in the West, and that the ideal of brotherhood cannot be obtained either by reason, or by social contract, or by pursuing self-interest; see pages 243–45.

to understanding his younger brother when he says that "Ivan is a sphinx" (Bk. XI, Ch. 4, 592). Why a sphinx?

In the Petersburg of Dostoevsky's time, there were a number of statues of Egyptian sphinxes (figures having the body of a lion and the head of a man, ram, or hawk), but he probably had in mind the Sphinx of Greek mythology.[31] If this is indeed so, Dostoevsky is talking about a monster that perched on a rock near Thebes and asked a riddle of every passerby, strangling all who could not answer. When Oedipus finally solves the riddle, the Sphinx kills herself.

Why would Ivan resemble this Sphinx and what would be his riddle? What would be his forbidden knowledge which, when revealed, would lead to his doom?

To answer these questions, let us see where Ivan stands with regard to Dostoevsky's ladder of beauty → love → faith → hope.

Strangely enough, Ivan does not display any particular appreciation of beauty throughout the entire novel. Yes, he is attracted to the extraordinarily beautiful Katerina Ivanovna, but we never get the slightest intimation that this is so because of her beauty. The narrator leads us to suspect that the attraction has more to do with the hidden rivalry (a first trace of Ivan's forbidden knowledge?) between the brothers than with Katerina Ivanovna's beauty (Katerina is Dmitri's fiancée, whom he abandons because of his passion for Grushenka). And while many others – regardless of what they think of her moral qualities – also notice Grushenka's exceptional beauty, Ivan will have none of it. While the narrator compares Grushenka with the celebrated Venus of Milo, for Ivan this woman is at best just a "creature," and at worst a "beast" (Bk. III, Ch. 10, 148–49).

Ivan may not appreciate beauty, but is he not capable of loving? Ivan says he is in love with Katerina Ivanovna, and Madam Khokhlakov claims several times that Ivan and Katerina love each other. Fyodor Karamazov, who may be a shrewder observer than either Ivan or Madame Khokhlakov, has a different opinion: "But Ivan loves nobody, Ivan is not one of us" (Bk. IV, Ch. 2, 175).

31 Strictly speaking, the Greek mythology inherited the story of the Sphinx from Egypt; see J.J. Bachofen, *Myth, Religion, and Mother Right*, 180.

We have already seen in the previous chapter, in connection with Nastassya and Aglaya, that love is a complicated affair. It gets no simpler in *The Brothers Karamazov*. Dmitri, for instance, both loves and hates Katerina Ivanovna, although he has far more straightforward feelings toward Grushenka. Ivan notices that Katerina Ivanovna's inability to choose between Dmitri and himself has nothing to do with which of them she loves: Katerina Ivanovna does not love either. If she loves at all, she is in love with herself and her misery. Hers is that imaginary love, as Father Zosima calls it, which yearns for a quickly achieved heroic act seen by everyone.

One of the persistent features of Ivan's superb intelligence is that, like Oedipus, he understands others – their problems, motives, emotions, or values – much better than he understands himself. What Ivan does not recognize is that he and Katerina Ivanovna are mirror images of each other. They torture each other and secretly enjoy the torment. If Katerina Ivanovna is not capable of loving others, the same holds for Ivan; he is attracted to Katerina Ivanovna, but not for the reasons of beauty or love.

Ivan's struggles with love are by no means limited to his relationship with Katerina Ivanovna. The feud between Fyodor and Dmitri gives several occasions to see Ivan's abhorrence of both. The dialogues which most reveal his hatred are those between Ivan and Alyosha, occurring at the end of the second family gathering, when Dmitri bursts into his father's house, suspecting that Grushenka is there. With a spontaneous "God forbid!" Alyosha voices his fears regarding what might have happened if they did not pull Dmitri away and convince him to leave the house. Ivan's reaction is quite different: "Why 'forbid'? . . . Viper will eat up viper, and it would serve them both right!" (Bk. III, Ch. 9, 141). A few minutes later, the conversation which Alyosha initiates with Ivan becomes even more revealing:

> "Brother, let me ask you one more thing: can it be that any man has the right to decide about the rest of mankind, who is worthy to live and who is more unworthy?"
>
> "But why bring worth into it? The question is most often decided in the hearts of men not at all on the basis of worth,

but for quite different reasons, much more natural ones. As for rights, tell me, who has no right to wish?"

"But surely not for another's death?"

"May be even for another's death. Why lie to yourself when everyone lives like that, and perhaps even cannot live any other way? What are you getting at – what I said about 'two vipers eating each other up'? In that case, let me ask you: do you consider me capable, like Dmitri, of shedding Aesop's blood, well, of killing him?" (Bk. III, Ch. 9, 143).

Ivan's forbidden knowledge surfaces here in a way that surprises him as well as Alyosha. But he is able to pull back just in time, before making Alyosha too suspicious. When Alyosha reassures him that such a thought has never entered his mind, Ivan abruptly departs with the final words: "Don't condemn me, and don't look at me as a villain" (Bk. III, Ch. 9, 143).

"Don't condemn me," Ivan says, although – and precisely because – he constantly condemns others. As the novel progresses, Ivan's negative attitude becomes stronger even toward his closest relatives. Yet Alyosha does not condemn him. He feels compassion for Ivan and, following Father Zosima, reiterates that hell is "the suffering of being no longer able to love" (Bk. VI, Ch. 3 [i], 322).

Father Zosima says that Ivan does not know what he really believes. Ivan tells Alyosha that he does not rebel against God but against His creation. Both Alyosha and the Elder suspect that Ivan does not believe in God. Without faith Ivan must accept the second part of his own conditional: Everything is permissible.

Ivan semi-consciously instills his forbidden knowledge in the mind of his half-brother Smerdyakov, who serves as the "lackey" of Fyodor Karamazov. This "broth maker" and "Balaam's ass" (Bk. III, Ch. 8, 132), as Fyodor vulgarly calls him, is roughly of the same age as Ivan. Since Smerdyakov's homeless and retarded mother dies in childbirth in Fyodor's garden, Fyodor's servant Grigory and his wife adopt him as their own. Smerdyakov, who regularly suffers from severe epileptic attacks, has always been a sickly child. The pious Grigory tries to instill into the sick boy at least the basic Christian values, but no such knowledge seems to stick to Smerdyakov's mind. Fyodor sends him later to Moscow to culinary course, and cooking turns out to be the only thing at which he excels. Despite continuously abusing him, Fyodor Karamazov grows increasingly dependent on Smerdyakov's presence in the house. Since Fyodor is convinced that Smerdyakov will not steal his money, he turns the unfortunate young man into his confidant. This is how this strange relationship works in the house until Ivan moves in with his father.

From the first days of Ivan's unexpected appearance, Fyodor notices a change in his lackey. Smerdyakov has found his idol in Ivan and greedily absorbs everything that he says. Ivan's presence and his ideas trigger something in Smerdyakov. With Ivan around, Smerdyakov's life – and the life of all the members of the Karamazov family – takes a different course. The allegedly stupid lackey Smerdyakov understands Ivan's forbidden knowledge and solves his hidden riddle.

Like Ivan, Smerdyakov repeats Cain's question: Am I my brother's keeper? (Bk. V, Ch. 2, 226, 231). Dmitri does not realize to what extent Ivan hates him and their father; Alyosha may be too trusting to see it; Fyodor only suspects it; Smerdyakov comprehends it fully. He understands Ivan's contempt because he himself is full of hatred. Ivan fuels Smerdyakov's revulsion – these two have far more in common than anyone would initially expect. Smerdyakov realizes Ivan's hope that the "vipers will eat each other up" – if Dmitri kills Fyodor, this will be Dmitri's end as well. What does Ivan gain from this affair? As Smerdyakov – who becomes more lucid than Ivan as the narrative advances – clarifies to him, Ivan would end up inheriting at least forty thousand rubles, a nice sum with which to start a comfortable and independent life, even if he does not end up collecting Katerina Ivanovna's weighty dowry.

Things, however, do not develop as Ivan anticipates. The Hand of God, Dmitri claims, saves him from killing his father, as the same Hand stops Abraham from slaying his first-born Isaac. (Notice the reversal of roles of fathers and sons. For Dostoevsky, this reversal illustrates the difference between ancient and modern times.) Ivan will have to rely on Katerina Ivanovna's testimony in the court to get rid of Dmitri (although at that time the older brother is already transformed and the external trial will not significantly damage his soul). To have it all in style, before the trial Katerina Ivanovna and Ivan pay an expensive lawyer to defend

Dmitri, bring a doctor from Moscow, and even think about sacrificing thirty thousand rubles for Dmitri's escape on his way to Siberia. It is hard to know whether Katerina Ivanovna comprehends to what extent Ivan uses her because the whole scenario fits so nicely into her ideal of martyrdom: She believes she will sacrifice her own life for Dmitri. In her pretentious attitude Dostoevsky portrays a gesture of a person obsessed with herself, although she is planning her own sacrifice. During the trial, inspired by her imaginary role of a martyr, Katerina Ivanovna first testifies on behalf of the accused. After Ivan's testimony, she suddenly changes her mind and presents to the court Dmitri's letter which, as Ivan explained to her a few days earlier, presents "mathematical" proof of Dmitri's guilt (Bk. XII, Ch. 5, 688). One wonders why she has this letter with her in the court if she had previously decided to sacrifice her life for the "unfortunate man."

Since Dmitri did not kill Fyodor, someone else pollutes his hands. Convinced to follow Ivan's "instructions," Smerdyakov plays the role to perfection. Because of the unusually strong attacks of epilepsy on the day of the murder, suspecting the sick man is unreasonable. Not only is Smerdyakov seriously ill, but it is hard to detect his motive for murder.

Everything appears fine, and yet it is not so. The Hand of God is still active. Smerdyakov and Ivan cannot sleep well at night. Something rebels from the depth of their beings, something which both had convinced themselves did not exist. In the times of Sophocles' tragedies, at the time of deep crises an inquiry would be made to the priestess of Apollo's temple in Delphi about what disturbs the gods and what can be done to appease them. In modern times, when heaven and hell are thought to be extinguished, the revelatory hallucinations are not made by the dancing priestess but emerge directly from the dark corners of the human soul. In Ivan's case, a seemingly all-knowing devil visits him. Ivan tries to reassure himself that his "friend" with a tail is not real, that he is only his past mocking him and reminding him of what he wants to forget. No matter how he treats his visitor – whether he speaks to him honestly or throws his teacup at him – Ivan now must confront the dark depth of the human psyche at which he used to laugh.

Ivan's internal crisis escalates rapidly, threatening to break all
boundaries of normalcy, when he suddenly gets another chance.
The night before the trial Ivan visits Smerdyakov once more, and
his double, in disbelief at Ivan's denial, tells him in no uncertain
terms that the two of them, not Dmitri, are responsible for the murder of Fyodor Karamazov. As Alyosha hits bottom after the death
of Father Zosima, and Dmitri after he almost kills Grigory, Ivan
descends into the underworld of despair the night before Dmitri's
trial. Upon hearing Smerdyakov's confession, which, with the rest
of his forbidden knowledge Ivan previously refused to acknowledge,
he leaves Smerdyakov determined to change his life and accept full
responsibility for his father's death. The first chance to show his
new resolve occurs when he rescues a drunken peasant from an
immanent death in the falling snow, the same man whom he pushed
to the ground on his way to Smerdyakov.

Alyosha and Dmitri resolve their crises by rediscovering faith and
finding spiritual rebirth. Can Ivan do the same?

Like Raskolnikov, who promises to turn himself in and confess his crime, Ivan realizes that he must immediately go to the
prosecutor and tell him who the actual murderer is. Once more in
his life, Ivan hesitates. Unfortunately for the lonely Ivan, there is
no brother or sister to help him. The loving Sonia is not there to
reproach him with her caring look and compel him to do as he
should. Grushenka is not there to offer him an onion. Nor is anyone there to put a pillow under his aching head. Ivan only has his
devil. Not trusting himself or anyone else, Ivan does not act immediately. He decides to reveal Fyodor's murderer the following day,
during the trial.

Recall Heschel: "Religion depends upon what man does with his
ultimate embarrassment."[32] He could have added that our humanity also depends on our embarrassment. This is fully congruent with
his line of thought:

> Embarrassment is a response to the discovery that in living
> we either replenish or frustrate a wondrous expectation.
> It involves an awareness of the grandeur of existence that

32 Heschel, *op. cit.*, 112.

might be wasted, of a waiting ignored, of unique moments missed. It is a protection against the outburst of the inner evils, against arrogance, *hybris*, self-deification. The end of embarrassment would be the end of humanity.[33]

Alyosha and Dmitri are quite capable of shame and embarrassment. Ivan's inner evils – his arrogance, hubris, and self-deification – are already so strong that he does not feel enough embarrassment. He has always been convinced that the opposite of the human is the animal and has hated this animal side in his father, in his older brother, and in himself as well. Against Ivan's reasoning, it turns out that the opposite of the human – the true antidote to our humanity – is not the animal but the demonic. It is the devil, whatever or whoever he happens to be, that leads Ivan into the abyss of self-destruction, into the darkness of madness. The next day, during the trial, the raving Ivan presents the missing three thousand rubles and accuses Smerdyakov and himself:

> "I got it from Smerdyakov, the murderer, yesterday. I visited him before he hanged himself. It was he who killed the father, not my brother. He killed him, and killed him on my instructions. . . . Who doesn't wish for his father's death? . . . "
>
> "Are you in your right mind?" inadvertently escaped from the judge.
>
> "The thing is that I am precisely in my right mind . . . my vile mind, the same as you, and all these . . . m-mugs!" he suddenly turned to the public. "A murdered father, and they pretend to be frightened," he growled with fierce contempt. "They pull faces to each other. Liars! Everyone wants his father's death. Viper devours viper. . . . If there were no parricide, they'd all get angry and go home in a foul temper. . . . Circuses! 'Bread and circuses!' And me, I'm a good one! Is there some water? Give me a drink, for Christ's sake!" he suddenly clutched his head (Bk. XII, Ch. 5, 686).

---

33 *Ibid.*, 113. For philosophical analysis of the related values (modesty, humility, aloofness, and pride), see Hartmann, *Ethics*, vol. 2, 298–303.

These revelations concerning parricide, which attracted Freud to Dostoevsky's novel, show that Ivan has lost his mind. This did not happen at the trial, but the night before. As Arthur Koestler explains, "The Night Journey is the antipode of Promethean striving. One endeavors to steal the bright fire from the gods; the other is a sliding back towards the pulsating darkness, one and undivided, of which we were part before our separate egos were formed."[34]

At the beginning of the novel, the well-educated, progressive Ivan aspires to steal the bright fire from the gods. At its conclusion, he ends up in the dark dungeon of his soul. During the fatal night journey of Ivan the sphinx, his carefully guarded forbidden knowledge escapes control and his riddle is apparently revealed. And when the riddle is solved, the sphinx must destroy itself.

What is this terrible riddle?

You will be as disappointed as Dmitri's interrogators were when they finally heard the secret of which he is so ashamed. But the fact that the riddle does not seem much to others does not say anything about its relevance for those whose riddle it is.

When Alyosha tells Ivan that Smerdyakov had committed suicide earlier that evening, the bewildered Ivan confesses to Alyosha: "He [the devil] got up and left. You came and he left. He called me a coward, Alyosha! *Le mot de l'énigme* is that I'm a coward! It's not for such eagles to soar above the earth! He added that, he added that! And Smerdyakov said the same thing" (Bk. XI, Ch. 10, 654).

Raskolnikov thought of himself as a Napoleon, Ivan as an eagle. A true eagle must be carnivorous enough to shed the blood of others, but Ivan cannot do it himself. He can only think, he can only conceive of a "grandiose" deed, but not execute it. He can proudly proclaim how, if there is no God, everything is permissible. Ivan even convinces himself of that. Yet he is scared to act according to his own nihilistic principle. He needs Smerdyakov and Katerina Ivanovna; he even needs Rakitin. When he needs them the most, however, they are not there to help him.

What does it mean that Ivan lacks courage and cannot soar like an eagle? It means the following. While during their Night Journeys

---

34 Koestler, *op. cit.*, 360.

Alyosha and Dmitri find faith, Ivan's descent into the darkness only reveals what Dostoevsky marks as "devil" and what Lewis Hyde calls "bad faith." As Hyde understands it,

> Gift exchange is connected to faith because both are disinterested. Faith does not look out. No one by himself controls the cycle of gifts he participates in; each, instead, surrenders to the spirit of the gift in order for it to move. Therefore, the person who gives is a person willing to abandon control. If this were not so, if the donor calculated his return, the gift would be pulled out of the whole and into the personal ego, where it loses its power. We say that a man gives faithfully when he participates disinterestedly in a circulation he does not control but which nonetheless supports his life.
>
> Bad faith is the opposite. It is the confidence that there is corruption, not just that the covenants of men may be severed, but that all things may be decomposed and broken into fragments (the old sense of "corruption"). Out of bad faith comes a longing for control, for the law and the police. Bad faith suspects that the gift will not come back, that things won't work out, that there is a scarcity so great in the world that it will devour whatever gifts appear. In bad faith the circle is broken.[35]

Alyosha is humbled by the gift of life and never wants to break the circle. Dmitri, except in the moments when he forgets himself and loses perspective on his life, also has a profound sense of humility, the appreciation of something far greater than his individual life. Dmitri is no stranger to the feelings of shame and embarrassment; to Alyosha, he willingly confesses that he is a lowly insect. Ivan is different from his brothers. He does not trust anyone, including God. He does not want gifts, nor will he be satisfied with grace. Ivan

35 Hyde, *op. cit.*, 128. Hartmann does not have a special term for "bad faith" but remarks: "Faith can transform a man, towards good or evil, according to what he believes. This is its secret, its power to remove mountains. Distrust is impotence. Trust imposes an obligation. The ethos of fidelity increases with faith"; *op. cit.*, 295.

wants law and justice, which belong to the exchange economy and not to the economy of gifts. Dostoevsky is convinced that the pursuit of money and justice, of treating money and justice as if they hold a quasi-religious nature, leads to scandal, not to a miracle. The exchange economy leads to our treatment of life as something individual and embodied, something that dies when the individual dies. The economy of gifts, by contrast, presumes that life, this most perplexing gift of God, is the unbroken tread, that the spirit of life survives the destruction of its vessels.[36]

Ivan thinks that he is an eagle, that he is so much above everybody else. Ivan the eagle cannot sit with his brothers at the same table: Neither are they his equal, nor does he recognize their God. While Alyosha and Dmitri's faith leads them to treat others in terms of compassion and brotherly love, Ivan demands justice and law. Nicolai Hartmann remarks that "justice may be unloving, brotherly love quite unjust,"[37] but Dostoevsky's claim is stronger. Ivan's pursuit of justice is based on something radically different from brotherly love and the economy of gifts: His bad faith is accompanied by hatred and contempt, and this bad faith spreads from Ivan to Smerdyakov, Rakitin, and Katerina Ivanovna.

During the fateful night before the trial, Alyosha folds his hands in prayer for Dmitri and Ivan. Alyosha is beginning to understand Ivan's illness: "The torments of a proud decision, a deep conscience!" Alyosha hopes that everything may still turn out to the best: " 'God will win! . . . [Ivan] will either rise into the light of truth, or . . . perish in hatred, taking revenge on himself and everyone for having served something he does not believe in,' Alyosha added bitterly, and again prayed for Ivan" (Bk. XI, Ch. 10, 655).

On Ivan's behalf we may ask: What does it mean that "God will win"? Will the Hand of God, the almighty Hand of the Creator, again take Ivan's clay and reshape it into a new form of life? Will Ivan be brought to faith, so that he can sit with his brothers at the same table? Or is all of this just a part of Alyosha's naïve and unrealizable

36 Hyde explains this difference in terms of the Greek distinction between *bio* and *zoë*; *op. cit.*, 33–34, 154.
37 Hartmann, *op. cit.*, 271.

hope? Is not Ivan already lost, just as his father was lost and just as Smerdyakov was lost?

Instead of believing in Ivan's recovery, it is more reasonable to expect that Alyosha must further mature, that he is not yet a beautiful man. Will he ever become one?

Art has the capacity to bring contraries into accord. At the time of turmoil and desperation, Rublyov used his art to paint the icon of the Holy Trinity, to paint an all-encompassing symbol of unity and trust of one individual in another. His icon presents a captivating example of inverse perspective, where lines seem to converge on a point in front of the icon, in order to draw the viewer into a different space and different order. Rublyov uses this inner perspective to symbolize the fact that "the action taking place before our eyes is outside the laws of earthly existence."[38]

Ivan lacks the courage to accept this unearthly, non-Euclidean order. He refuses to believe in the possibility of harmony between man and God, or even between man and man, when everything before his eyes speaks of discord and injustice. Dostoevsky wants to show in *The Brothers Karamazov* that Ivan's hesitation and doubt are not only untenable but even lead to the abyss of self-destruction. In this Dostoevsky fully succeeds, for there are many ways in which Ivan fails. Ivan does not understand the way of gifts: He gives priority to economy, politics, rationality, and law, rather than to beauty, love, faith, and hope. Ivan does not find the meaning of life and ends up alone in the prison of his own mind. Ivan is crushed and defeated.

Whatever we think of Ivan's character and his fate, however, his rebellion is not without point. If freedom to choose God means anything, then freedom to reject Him must also be meaningful. This is the path of Ivan's argumentation. Not the Holy Trinity, but the Grand Inquisitor is Ivan's hope for a better future, for a brotherhood of men. Ivan's Grand Inquisitor premises his own version of the brotherhood on the most unpleasant question for a believer: How can we be guilty of not being our brothers' keepers when God Himself allows the meaningless suffering of the innocent and is not the keeper of His own children?

38 Leonid Ouspensky and Vladimir Lossky, *The Meaning of Icons*, 42.

7

The Brothers Karamazov (II)

Meaningless Suffering

Ivan's Riddle

"What creature, with only one voice, has sometimes two feet, sometimes three, sometimes four, and is the weakest when it has the most?"

This is the riddle with which the Sphinx, settled on a mountain near the ancient city of Thebes, confronted every traveler. "If you can answer," the Sphinx would add, "I will let you go." No one could, and the terrible creature – half-beast and half-woman – devoured man after man until the city was in a state of siege. The seven great gates, the Theban's pride, remained closed, and famine threatened the lives of all the citizens.

This is how matters stood when Oedipus came to the stricken country. He was a homeless wanderer who left Corinth and went into self-exile because a Delphic oracle declared that he was fated to kill his father. The destitute Oedipus, who was running away from his fate and to whom life meant little, was determined to seek out the Sphinx and either solve her riddle or be destroyed by her. Upon hearing the question, Oedipus offered the correct answer: "Man – man is that creature. He crawls on all fours as an infant, stands firmly on his two feet in his youth and adulthood, and helps himself with a staff in old age."

According to the ancient legend, the mortified Sphinx then leaped from the mountain and dashed herself to pieces in the valley below. The Thebans were saved, and in gratitude made Oedipus their new King. And he married Jocasta, the queen. Their happy and long marriage seemed to prove that, for the first time, the prophecy of Apollo had been wrong.

It is certainly noteworthy that Sophocles, who devotes three tragedies to the fate of Oedipus and his children (*Oedipus the King*, *Oedipus at Colonus*, and *Antigone*), mentions the riddle of the Sphinx only briefly. It appears that the solution of this riddle is only a preamble to a far more difficult and relevant riddle: What is man? Sophocles' tragedies are the explorations of this wonder – human life. The framework of the explorations is man's unsettled status between the two realms: the beastly (symbolized by the Sphinx and her riddle) and the divine (symbolized by Apollo and his prophecy).

Sophocles' tragedies deal with souls that suffer greatly. Oedipus is one such soul, and he brings immense agony upon himself not only by his deeds, but also by his honest and uncompromising quest for self-knowledge. He is a man of great courage and intelligence, but Apollo knows far more than human beings. No one can escape his prophecies. Years after Oedipus defeats the Sphinx and establishes himself on the Theban throne, an unexpected challenge emerges: A plague threatens to destroy the entire city. The messengers of Apollo make it clear that the condition for the city's liberation from its new curse is the discovery and punishment of the person who killed Laius, the previous King of Thebes. Oedipus presses hard to find the murderer, but the intuitive Jocasta – his mother, his wife, and the mother of his children – senses a forthcoming tragedy and begs him: "O Oedipus, God help you! God keep you from the knowledge of who you are!"[1] In his noble aspiration to avoid the

---

1   Bernard Knox points out that, while the first part of Oedipus's name – *Oidi* – means "swell," "it is also *Oida*, 'I know', and this word is often, too often, in Oedipus's mouth. His knowledge is what makes him *tyrannos*, confident and decisive; knowledge has made man what he is, master of the

prophetic murder of his father, Oedipus commits more crimes than predicted by the oracle. At the moment they realize their guilt, Jocasta commits suicide while Oedipus blinds himself, continuing to suffer his tragic fate.

Almost twenty-five centuries separate the lives of Sophocles and Dostoevsky, but the riddle: "What is man?" has lost none of its significance. In 1839, Dostoevsky was a seventeen-year-old cadet in the Petersburg military academy of engineers. He had recently been informed of the death of his father, who was likely murdered by his own serfs. There is only one document preserved from that time which reveals the state of mind and the future plans of the young Dostoevsky, a letter to his beloved brother Michael (of August 16, 1839). After lamenting at the death of their father (their mother died two years before), Dostoevsky understands that from now on he is on his own and reveals to his brother his future plans. The aim of his life, he writes, will be to study "the meaning of life and man. . . . Man is a riddle. This riddle must be solved, and if you spend all your life at it, don't say you have wasted your time; I occupy myself with this enigma because I wish to be a man."

It is no coincidence, as Joseph Frank points out, that these words appear in the letter commenting on the murder of his father:

> For no event could have driven home to him more intimately and starkly the enigma of man and human life – the enigma of the sudden irruption of irrational, uncontrollable, and destructive forces both within the world and in the human psyche; the enigma of the incalculable moral consequences even of such venial self-indulgence as his own demands on his father. It was this enigma which, indeed, he was to spend the rest of his life trying to solve; and no one can accuse him, while doing so, of having wasted his time.[2]

---

world. *Oida*, 'I know' – it runs through the play with the same mocking persistence as *pous*, 'foot', and sometimes reaches an extreme of macabre punning emphasis"; Knox, "Sophocles' Oedipus," in *Sophocles' Oedipus Rex*, ed. Harold Bloom, 9.

2   Joseph Frank, *Dostoevsky: The Seeds of Revolt, 1821–1849*, 91.

Dostoevsky certainly dedicated his life to the resolution of this riddle, which Sophocles called the most mysterious of all wonders. There are good reasons, however, why – despite humanity's most ingenious efforts and deepest concerns – few definitive insights have emerged in the last twenty-five centuries of man's pursuit of self-knowledge. Scientific and philosophical disciplines of various kinds have been formed and advanced, yet they do not seem able to penetrate to the core of man's nature, for "too many riddles oppress man on earth" (Bk. III, Ch. 3, 108). Dmitri Karamazov explains why this is so in his own unlearned and intuitive way: "Man is broad, even too broad, I would narrow him down" (Bk. III, Ch. 3, 108).

What makes man so broad? Dmitri replies that contradictory impulses in man's heart and mind inexplicably coexist and swing man from one extreme to another. No less perplexing are man's conflicting desires regarding freedom: his yearning to be free, coupled with his fear of the burden imposed by that very same freedom. Dmitri speaks about the paradoxical nature of beauty, but he could have said the same thing about man's position between the animal and the divine impulses that flood the human soul.

These concerns trouble Ivan far more than Dmitri. The oldest brother rides on the crest of the wave; he uses up the gift of his life to its maximum, and only occasionally does he thrust himself into such questioning. In his efforts to narrow man down, Ivan the thinker is thrown into a "furnace of doubt" and for him these considerations are, literally, a matter of life and death. Alyosha compares Ivan to a riddle, Dmitri compares him to the Sphinx, but it would be more accurate to match Ivan up with Oedipus. In Sophocles' tragedy, Oedipus separates himself from other human beings, and the chorus has to remind him often that, by solving the riddle of Sphinx, he has not become a god but only "the first among equals." In *The Brothers Karamazov*, the members of the family are concerned with how different Ivan is: "But Ivan loves nobody, Ivan is not one of us," claims his father Fyodor (Bk. IV, Ch. 2, 175).

Both Oedipus and Ivan seem "marked" and preordained for the fate of extraordinary suffering. For both of them, intelligence is the decisive distinguishing mark. And not only are they exceptionally intelligent, but they have probing and persistent intelligence, guided by a self-tormenting passion for truth. For both Oedipus and Ivan, the extreme boundaries which confine our humanity are its divine height and its beastly abyss, and the dilemma is: either/or. As Ivan puts it, if God does not exist and there is no immortality (which will make us god-like), then there is no virtue and everything is permissible (which reduces us to the level of beasts). Like Oedipus, Ivan is also "driven" and cannot stop in the middle of the road, even if the consequent pursuit of self-knowledge leads to his doom. In the further course of the novel, this is, indeed, what happens. Oedipus blinds himself, and Ivan plunges into the blindness of a mental disorder. Both thereby symbolically abandon the very thing – their intelligence – that distinguishes them from their peers and counterparts.

I would like to leave Oedipus behind for the moment and focus on Ivan's fall into his furnace of doubt. It is clear to Ivan that human life is "too broad," that it is a riddle; he narrows the focus of his questioning to one of life's most perplexing aspects: meaningless suffering – especially the meaningless suffering of children. Ivan's struggles with this riddle are revealed in the three consecutive chapters of Book V of *The Brothers Karamazov*: "The Brothers Get Acquainted," "Rebellion," and "The Grand Inquisitor." We begin by considering the first two, which present the riddle of meaningless suffering. The next section of this chapter will ponder Ivan's Grand Inquisitor poem to see what kind of answer it offers to Ivan's riddle. The third section will reflect on Father Zosima's thoughts on suffering and the meaning of life. At the end, we will compare the views of the Grand Inquisitor and Father Zosima and draw some conclusions about the novel as a whole.

"The Brothers Get Acquainted" sets the stage for the novel's deepest philosophical dialogue. Ivan waits in an inn, hoping to meet Dmitri there. Alyosha passes by, and Ivan invites his younger brother to join him. Ivan probably wants to inform Dmitri what he now immediately relates to Alyosha, namely that he has resolved to leave town the next day, to depart from his father and his brothers, to forget about Katerina Ivanovna. Ivan decides to turn his life around and never to return to this wretched place. Where will he go? Ivan's answer foreshadows the things to come:

> I want to go to Europe, Alyosha, I'll go straight from here. Of course I know that I will only be going to a graveyard, but to the most, the most precious graveyard, that's the thing! The precious dead lie there, each stone over them speaks of such ardent past life, of such passionate faith in their deeds, their truth, their struggle, and their science, that I – this I know beforehand – will fall to the ground and kiss these stones and weep over them – being wholeheartedly convinced, at the same time, that it has all long been a graveyard and nothing more. And I will not weep from despair, but simply because I will be happy in my shed tears (Bk. V, Ch. 3, 230).

Alyosha comes to town to find the grave of his mother, while Ivan leaves town to find the graveyard of Western civilization. The Elder Zosima pushes Alyosha away from the monastery, so he can help his living family members, but Ivan runs from the living to be with the dead and weep over their tombs.

Alyosha's reaction to Ivan's words is no less intriguing than his brother's announcement. He is glad to hear how Ivan "loves life," but tells him that this is only one-half of his task. After Ivan's wondering what the second half is, Alyosha mysteriously answers: "Bringing back to life those dead of yours, who may have never died." And as if he had just pronounced the most trifling sentence, Alyosha continues: "Now give me some tea. I'm glad we're talking, Ivan" (Bk. V, Ch. 3, 231; translation modified).

How strange! "Bringing back to life those dead of yours, who may have never died." But, then, this whole section is puzzling, as Ivan's attempts to open the discussion of the "accursed questions" are so incoherent that they seem to be arguments from the emotional Dmitri rather than the intelligent Ivan. Ivan maintains that he loves life and wants to live, but only until he is thirty. Furthermore, Ivan postulates how the world is Euclidean. God must be a good geometer, which implies that eternal harmony must occur in the world sooner or later. He then turns his argument around to declare how he does not accept this promised harmony which will retroactively justify all human suffering. Ivan accepts God, but not His creation. His indecision extends further from the physical and the metaphysical to the psychological plane as well: Ivan promises to explain everything about the eternal problems to his curious brother, but then suddenly confesses: "My dear little brother, it's not that I want to corrupt you and push you off your foundation; perhaps I want to be healed by you" (Bk. V, Ch. 3, 236). Of what wound or disease Alyosha should heal him, we are left to speculate.

With this "enlightening" introduction the brothers prepare the ground for a firework of the most challenging forebodings and confessions. Ivan begins by confessing what has occurred to many of us, but which very few would acknowledge to others: "I never could understand how it's possible to love one's neighbors. In my opinion, it is precisely one's neighbors that one cannot possibly love" (Bk. V, Ch. 4, 236).

Ivan's admission should not be taken as a sign of perversion or inhumanity. Rather, it reveals the sincerity and depth of his struggle and alerts us that we are about to penetrate some hidden corners of his soul. Similar words can be found in Dorothy Day (a great admirer of Dostoevsky's work), whose love of humanity no one would challenge:

> But how to love? That is the question. All men are brothers, yes, but how to love your brother or sister when they are sunk in ugliness, foulness, and degradation, so that all the senses are affronted? How to love when the adversary shows a face to you of implacable hatred, or just cold loathing?[3]

This is precisely what Ivan feels for his father. Should Ivan pretend to love him? No, he simply cannot do that, and he is not even going to try. Ivan's problem with loving his father, his brothers, and his neighbors goes even deeper. Those who claim to love their brothers, he maintains, do it with the strain of a lie, or out of love enforced by duty, or out of self-imposed penance: "Christ's love for people is

---

3   *Dorothy Day: Selected Writings*, ed. Robert Ellsberg, 174.

in its kind a miracle impossible on earth. True, he was God. But we are not gods" (Bk. V, Ch. 4, 237).

There is a discrepancy, Ivan explains to Alyosha, between what is expected from us in life and how we really want to live. As philosophers put it, there is an incongruity between what ought to be and what is. We are expected to love our neighbors, but we do not; at most, Ivan maintains, we can respect them. We do not like to acknowledge other people's suffering because of our ignorance as to how to help them. We do not know how to help those in need precisely when they need our help the most.

Not only do people not love each other, continues Ivan, they are cruel, and their cruelty is far worse than anything displayed by animals. There is a beast in every man and never is that beastliness more obvious than in the torture of defenseless children.

Having prepared the ground for his frontal assault, Ivan then poses his fundamental question: Why are children suffering?

Alyosha does not reply, for Ivan has more to say. Religion, continues Ivan, tells us that children are punished for the sins of their parents, but this is incomprehensible. It is impossible that the innocent ones – "the wee ones," as Dmitri gently calls them – should suffer for the past guilt of adults. The past should not hold such a grip on the present. Ivan then presents a whole catalogue of stories dealing with the suffering of children. (Dostoevsky vouches to his editor and publisher Liubimov that all the cases that Ivan mentions are true and reported in the recent press.)[4] Their torment can neither be justified nor understood. Could it be that they are suffering in order to gain future knowledge of good and evil? The whole world of such knowledge is not worth the tears of one little child![5]

Alyosha's agreement with the last point encourages the already inflamed Ivan to expose his intimate thoughts further: Why is this

4   See Dostoevsky's letter to N.A. Liubimov, May 10, 1879.
5   Peter Vardy takes this admission to be the crowing victory of Ivan's line of reasoning; *The Puzzle of Evil*, 72–83. For further discussion, see also Stewart R. Sutherland, *Atheism and the Rejection of God*; and Roger L. Cox, *Between Heaven and Earth: Shakespeare, Dostoevsky and the Meaning of Christian Tragedy*.

nonsensical world needed and created? Before his brother can answer, Ivan declares: "The world stands on absurdities, and without them perhaps nothing at all would happen. . . . I don't understand anything . . . and I no longer want to understand anything. I want to stick to the fact" (Bk. V, Ch. 4, 243).

Ivan's claims are significant because they reveal not only the boundary of intellectual comprehension, but also the limit of his patience. His "Euclidean mind," which here is not a branch of geometry but a scientifically oriented approach to the materialistically conceived reality, tells him that there is suffering, and there is no one to blame for it. There is no one to blame because what we consider to be human consciousness is, as Rakitin explains Claude Bernard's theory to Dmitri, just a movement of neurons. Neurons have no emotions, no guilt, no conscience. In Ivan's words: "Oh, with my pathetic, earthly, Euclidean mind, I know only that there is suffering, that none are to blame, that all things follow simply and directly one from another, that everything flows and finds its level – but that is all just Euclidean gibberish, of course I know that, and of course I cannot consent to live by it!" (Bk. V, Ch. 4, 244).

In the world of the "Euclidean gibberish," there is neither virtue nor vice, "wee" children do not suffer, nor does life hold any meaning. This is the chaotic world resembling the one in which the beastly Sphinx reigns, not the world of the orderly god Apollo. This is the world in which everything is permissible, the world of Fyodor Karamazov. Ivan boasts that the world in which everything is permissible is inevitable if there is no God, yet he shivers at the thought that he may be living in such a world. Who (besides Fyodor) would consent to live in it when the suffering of children is a fact? And if it is a fact, it needs to be interpreted and comprehended. Ivan's trouble concerns how we could possibly understand it.

Ivan could have examined more carefully what is fact and what is not (is the claim that the world is Euclidean a fact?), but that would take him away from the main points of his line of thought. Ivan's riddle is truly focused on the following. Human life is supposed to have meaning and purpose; the world is supposed to be or become a harmonious whole. What we experience – particularly the suffering of children – makes it difficult to see how human life can be meaningful and how the world can be harmonious. Ivan has problems with all aspects of the human story: (i) with its finale; (ii) with the means used to accomplish this desired ending; and (iii) also with the position of man in this story.

With regard to the ending of the human history, Ivan believes there is absolutely no certainty about the blissful completion of the human drama, neither on the individual nor on the universal level. Despite high hopes promoted by all religions, despite all socialist utopias, nothing is guaranteed or knowable about our ending. We are not sure what the final design is, nor if any exists in the first place. For all we can say, the whole world and our lives in it may amount to nothing more than the meaningless movement of Bernard's neurons, or mere "Euclidean gibberish."

The situation is even worse with respect to the means for accomplishing that alleged harmony. These means are obvious to us and we cannot approve of them. They involve suffering and include the torment of children. If that is the price needed for world harmony, Ivan cannot accept it. Although this is exactly how our civilization has been built, even Alyosha readily agrees with Ivan that the happiness of future generations cannot rest on the unjustified blood of tortured victims or on the tears of children.

Further troubling Ivan is the insignificant position of man in the cosmos, both in the religious scheme of things and in Bernard's scientific movement of neurons. We have intelligence, creativity, technology, economy, jurisprudence, and yet – who are we? Does man's existence really matter in this world? If the world is designed by the all-powerful and all-knowing Creator, is not the role that he assigns to man insulting? Would not man be a more precise geometer and a more imaginative architect than God? Would not man organize the world more justly, for instance according to the model of the market economy, where the price of everything is clear and where every deed is adequately rewarded or punished?[6]

6   Susan Neiman points out that there is a significant group of modern thinkers – Bayle, Voltaire, Hume, de Sade, Schopenhauer – who are unified in "condemning the Architect," but for whom it is life, rather than

Frustrated and disappointed, Ivan abandons all calls for mercy and forgiveness and rejects any attempt at theodicy. The endless examples of pointless suffering of children indicate that the Father in Heaven behaves like the God from the Prologue to the Book of Job – it seems that, for no reason other than His own entertainment, God agrees to a bet with the Accuser (Satan). This bet allows the Accuser to test the sincerity of Job's faith by torturing him and destroying his family and reputation. Does not God already know whether or not Job's faith is sincere? But this is not the end of Ivan's complaints. For a God who ignores the cries of guiltless children and tarnishes the sincerity of Job's faith, for a Father who allows his children's lives to be used as someone's toys, for that God Ivan can have no respect. He is convinced that he has the right to refuse his participation in this cruel game of life. With Promethean enthusiasm, together with Raskolnikov and Peter Verkhovenski, Ivan takes "his own measures." He wants man to design a more just world for human beings. Not God, but man should be the measure of all things! Unlike Raskolnikov and Verkhovenski, however, Ivan is not going to act himself. He has created a poem, "The Legend of the Grand Inquisitor," which will explain to Alyosha what a just architect of the world structure should do.

Before we plunge into the complexities of "The Legend," let us review once more the central points of Ivan's position. With his Euclidean mind, Ivan would like the enigma of meaningless suffering to be as clearly defined as the riddle of the Sphinx. It would be convenient to have one and only one correct answer to this enigma, but Ivan's riddle resembles the amorphous riddle about the nature of man. To reduce its ambiguities, we can branch out the question: Why is there meaningless suffering? into three sub-questions: Where does meaningless suffering come from? What can be done about it? Can meaningless suffering be eliminated?

Ivan makes the most progress with regard to the first question. He does not shift the responsibility for meaningless suffering to the distant past and the Christian idea of original sin, nor does he allow

---

God's failed creation, that "needs to be justified and defended"; see her book *Evil in Modern Thought: An Alternative History of Philosophy*, Chapter 2, 113–202.

the present suffering to be justified by some eschatological future harmony. Ivan believes that the ends cannot justify the means, and that, consequently, the responsibility for present actions must also reside in present time. He affirms that people can be cruel and that they can behave worse than beasts. Although the responsibility for meaningless suffering falls thus on the shoulders of humanity, Ivan maintains that God has a significant share of responsibility for this sad state of affairs as well. Just what that responsibility amounts to, the Grand Inquisitor will further articulate.

With regard to the second question – what can or should be done about meaningless suffering? – Ivan is not very clear. He wavers in his attitudes, but the conviction he carries over to "The Legend" is that something – and something radical – must be done. In Ivan's eyes, the presence of such suffering reveals that we live in a polluted and chaotic world in which human life appears meaningless. Not to do anything means to condone pointless misery, and that makes us the accomplice in the suffering of the world.

With regard to the third question – can meaningless suffering be eliminated from the world? – Ivan's answers in the affirmative. He also affirms that it is the task of the Creator to create a world in which human beings – and especially children – are not exposed to such cruel and unjustifiable tortures. This tragic plight is for Ivan a strong indication, if not a definitive proof, that God has failed in His mission, and that the Promethean man, proud and independent, imaginative and intelligent, has to recreate the world. Yet this proposal leads to further questions: to recreate creation in the image of what? If God has failed and man is a cruel beast, in what image is man going to recreate the world?

The Grand Inquisitor's Thesis

There is a lot that is not immediately clear about the riddle of the Sphinx. We are never told why Oedipus is capable of answering the riddle while so many others fail. Nor do we know why the Sphinx has to destroy herself upon hearing the correct answer. Perhaps most striking of all is the riddle's relative insignificance compared to the punishment for the inability to solve it and the reward for its solution.

One way to understand the Sphinx's riddle, as well as Ivan's riddle of meaningless suffering, is by distinguishing between a question and a problem. Abraham Heschel says that "to ask a question is an act of the intellect; to face a problem is a situation involving the whole person. A question is the result of thirst for knowledge; a problem reflects a state of perplexity, or even distress."[7] The riddle of the Sphinx is a question, and the riddle of man a problem. How, then, does Ivan's riddle of meaningless suffering fit into this distinction? Is it a "mere" question, or a problem? Heschel may help us here:

> A question is due to knowing too little, to a desire to know more; a problem is often due to knowing too much. . . . The impulse to reflect about the humanity of man comes from the conscience as well as from intellectual curiosity. It is motivated by anxiety, and not simply by a desire to add to the sum of information about a member of the class of mammals.[8]

Ivan's riddle is the result of his existential anxiety, due to "knowing too much." Too much about what? Almost certainly about man and the nature of humanity. Heschel clarifies his point: "The animality of man we can grasp with a fair degree of clarity. The perplexity begins when we attempt to make clear what is meant by the *humanity* of man." Accepting the humanity of man, however, leads to other crossroads: the beastly or the divine, the rational or the irrational, the visible or the invisible, the trivial or the profane, the real or the ideal. Have we made any significant progress in understanding these crossroads since the time of Oedipus?

The ancient story of Oedipus is well known in our age because of Freud's theory regarding the "Oedipus complex." In *The Interpretation of Dreams*, his first major breakthrough in the field of psychoanalysis, Freud argues that "the incest fantasy" lies at the root of that monumental drama, the Oedipus legend.[9] Freud calls attention not to the contrasts between the beastly and the

7   Abraham J. Heschel, *Who is Man?*, 1.
8   *Ibid.*, 2.
9   Freud, *The Interpretation of Dreams*, 256–65; see also pages 397–99.

divine, but rather to the one between the female (the Sphinx and Jocasta) and the male (Apollo, Laius, and Oedipus). This contrast, argues Freud, is primarily sexual, which is most clearly expressed through the name "Oedipus." It means "the swollen footed," an age-old sexual symbol.[10] Oedipus's incestual desire toward his mother prompts him to eliminate the rival, his father. And the realization of what he has done leads to the catastrophes Sophocles describes in his tragedy. Oedipus's desire is still alive in us, holds Freud, for the fundamental human conflicts are identical, regardless of time and place.[11]

Despite the wide acceptance of the Oedipus complex, there are also wide-ranging criticisms of Freud's theory. Among the most severe is that by René Girard. In *Violence and the Sacred*, Girard argues that Freud misunderstands the nature of desire. Following philosophers of the Enlightenment, Freud believes that (i) desire is anchored in an object, and that (ii) we freely select our object of desire. Girard insists that Freud errs on both accounts, for our desire is not located either in the subject who desires or in the object desired, but in the third element – the model we imitate. This model can be a real or imaginary person and his or her desire becomes ours:

> The "father" projects into the future the first tentative movements of his son and sees that they lead straight to the mother or the throne. The incest wish, the parricide wish, do not belong to the child but spring from the mind of the adult, the model. In the Oedipus myth it is the oracle that puts such ideas into Laius' head, long before Oedipus himself was capable of entertaining any ideas at all. . . . The

10 "The foot," writes Freud, "is an age-old sexual symbol which occurs even in mythology"; *Three Essays on the Theory of Sexuality*, 155. Freud ignores J.J. Bachofen's magisterial work "Mother Right" (published in 1861), which offers a more detailed and quite different account; see Bachofen, "Mother Right," in *Myth, Religion, and Mother Right*, 180.

11 Freud, *The Interpretation of Dreams*, 262. Freud bases his interpretation on the following lines from Sophocles' tragedy: "For many a man hath seen himself in dreams/his mother's mate, but he who gives no heed/to such like matters bears the easier fate."

son is always the last to learn that what he desires is incest and patricide, and it is the hypocritical adults who undertake to enlighten him in this matter.[12]

In *The Brothers Karamazov* the behavior of God (or, more precisely, a lack of God's involvement in human affairs) and of Fyodor Karamazov provoke Ivan's rebellion. The Freudian jealousy motive does not exist in Ivan. He is not a monster who schemes to kill his father because of a sexual desire for his mother, but an outraged son whose sin consists in not doing enough to prevent Smerdyakov from murdering Fyodor.[13]

Ivan himself may not feel any Freudian incestual desire, but he would also criticize Girard's rejection of the autonomy of desire. It is not that I am imitating anyone, Ivan may say, but rather that the repulsive reality in which children are tortured leads me to desire a different, more just, and more rationally ordered world. The Legend of the Grand Inquisitor, Ivan maintains, is as much my own creation as *Oedipus the King* is Sophocles' creation. Let us, then, examine the content of Ivan's "poem."

The story takes place in sixteenth century Spain, on the blazing streets of Seville. The fires of the inquisition have just burned dozens of heretics, "*ad majorem gloriam Dei*" (Bk. V. Ch. 5, 248–49). Jesus suddenly makes His appearance, and "the insulted and the injured" recognize Him instantly. A blind man asks him to restore his vision, a despondent mother to resurrect her dead child. The miracles which Jesus performs do not escape the watchful eye of the Grand Inquisitor, a ninety-year-old cardinal in charge of the city's religious purity. He arrests Jesus and throws Him in jail. The obedient and scared crowd does not protest the incarceration of their Savior. Later that night, the proud cardinal visits the

---

12   Girard, *Violence and the Sacred*, 175. It is God, not man, Girard maintains, who comes up with the idea that man is God's potential rival.

13   For the English translation of his book on Dostoevsky (*Resurrection from the Underground: Feodor Dostoevsky*), Girard added a "Postface" to explain how his theory of mimetic desire applies to Dostoevsky (see pages 143–65). For Girard's interpretation of *The Brothers Karamazov*, however, more important are Chapters X–XI (229–89) of his book, *Deceit, Desire and the Novel*.

captive. The eyes of Jesus look straight into the eyes of the Grand Inquisitor, but the prisoner does not say a word. The cardinal does the talking, and he has much to say.

The Grand Inquisitor's speech, in which he expresses his outrage at Christ's unwanted appearance, has the following structure. First, he wants to show that the world cannot be built the way Jesus tried to build it the first time He walked the earth. Second, someone has to correct the creation that had gone astray. Third, this task is the Church's (working together with secular power), and the Grand Inquisitor is one of its servants.

To show what is wrong with the direction in which Jesus set the world, the Grand Inquisitor points to the problem of freedom. Jesus overestimated the need for freedom, and His mistake has led to all sorts of calamities. What people need, insists the cardinal, is not freedom, but happiness. Freedom and happiness are incompatible, according to the Grand Inquisitor, but the illusion of freedom and genuine happiness are not.

And how does the Grand Inquisitor plan to straighten the crooked timber of creation? How will he make people happy? His most basic principle, the one Jesus disdainfully neglected, is to give people bread. You must feed people, give them shelter, and satisfy their biological needs. This is the first and the most important step, but by no means the only one, for – as Jesus also insisted – human beings have legitimate needs which are not biological. It is, for instance, indispensable to find someone to "take over the freedom of men" and "appease their conscience" (Bk. V. Ch. 5, 254). Human beings long to bow down and worship; they need an object of devotion. While Jesus insisted on giving people freedom, He did not realize that for the vast majority of people freedom is a burden.

When the narrator first introduces Alyosha, he describes him as a realist because in him "faith is not born from miracles, but miracles from faith" (Bk. I. Ch. 5, 26). The Grand Inquisitor reverses this attitude. The "facts" lead Ivan and his Inquisitor to lose faith. (Ivan assumes that the same will happen with other intelligent human beings.) If faith can be restored at all, and it must be restored in order to have a happy mankind, it can be preserved only by miracles. As the Grand Inquisitor explains, besides someone to worship, people need miracles; besides bread, they need circuses. In fact, claims the old man, they do not seek God as much as they seek miracles. Christ demands an unconditional faith that does not depend on miracles, but for the majority of people this is impossible. Their faith is based on miracles, and those who reject miracles also reject God.

When people are given bread and circuses, when they have someone to make decisions for them, it is easy to organize a happy ant-hill and create a sense of universal brotherhood. The vast majority of people will live like children, like "happy babes" (Bk. V. Ch. 5, 259). For their happy ant-hill to become reality, the Church needs to usurp political power as well. A handful of rulers will take that power on themselves. Out of their love for humanity, they will sacrifice their happiness for the well being of the whole. Because Jesus rejected the three temptations in the desert, the Church cannot bring peace and happiness to the vast majority of people. Only with "him" – Jesus's adversary – can the Church "correct your deed" and properly organize "the unfinished, trial creatures created in mockery" (Bk. V, Ch. 5, 261).

The Grand Inquisitor hopes that the captive will respond somehow to his speech, even violently. After a prolonged silence, Jesus approaches him and "gently kisses him on his bloodless, ninety-year-old lips" (Bk. V, Ch. 5, 262). The kiss burns in the old man's heart and, as unexpectedly as the kiss comes, the Grand Inquisitor opens the door of the cell and orders his prisoner: "Go and do not come again . . . do not come at all . . . never, never!" (Bk. V, Ch. 5, 262).

How different is this reaction from Father Zosima's bow in front of Dmitri! How different is Zosima's compassion for the great suffering Dmitri will endure (if he murders his father) from the cold, merciless judgment of the old cardinal who treats Jesus as a criminal. Alyosha, who was present when the venerable Elder made his mysterious bow, may now be shocked less by the content of Ivan's poem than by the anguish that lurks in his brother's heart. For his brother – just as for his father – it all comes to the same thing: Since we are not like gods, we may behave like beasts. Thus, "everything is permitted." Ivan will not renounce this principle, but he is not sure whether or not Alyosha will renounce him.

Like Jesus, Alyosha does not say a word but gently kisses him on the lips. "Literary theft" (Bk. V, Ch. 5, 263), Ivan charges, with a sense of relief. With regained confidence, Ivan sends the puzzled Alyosha back to the monastery, intending to go abroad tomorrow to the sacred graveyard of Western civilization. The brothers think their separation is forever, but, as in the Oedipus myth, fate will surprise them.

Berdyaev considers the Legend of the Grand Inquisitor "the high point of [Dostoevsky's] work and the crown of his dialectic."[14] Dostoevsky himself believes that Ivan "puts forth the theme, which *in my opinion* is irrefutable: the senselessness of children's suffering, and deduces from this the absurdity of all historical reality."[15] Many commentators unquestioningly accept his opinion. Camus readily recognizes the revolutionary novelty of Ivan's rebellion: "With Ivan, however, the tone changes. God, in His turn, is put on trial. If evil is essential to divine creation, then creation is unacceptable. Ivan will no longer have resource to this mysterious God, but to a higher principle – namely justice. He replaces the reign of grace by the reign of justice."[16]

In the Book of Job, man is on trial and God is his judge. The roles are now reversed. Ivan rejects the essential interdependence of suffering and truth, on which the Christian vision of the world is built. If the torment of children completes the sum of suffering necessary for the acquisition of truth, Ivan maintains that truth is not worth such a price. It is not that truth does not exist, but that it is unacceptable. Truth is not acceptable if it is unjust. Against God and His flawed creation, Ivan demands justice. If this justice is to serve as a universal principle, it must bind man and God equally. If the principle of universal justice demands that the Creator be separated and detached from His creation so that man can correct

14 Nicholas Berdyaev, *Dostoyevsky*, 188. See also Konstantin Mochulsky, *Dostoevsky: His Life and Work*, 617.

15 Letter to N.A. Liubimov, May 10, 1879.

16 Albert Camus, *The Rebel: An Essay on Man in Revolt*, 55–56. For further discussion of Camus' interpretation of (Ivan's) rebellion, see Jean Kellogg, *Dark Prophets of Hope: Dostoevsky, Sartre, Camus, Faulkner*, 89–122; and Susan Neiman, *op. cit.*, 291–300.

its injustices, so be it: *Fiat iustitia, ruat cealum* (Let justice prevail, even if the heavens collapse).

Following Dostoevsky, Camus affirms that the logic of the argument unfolds flawlessly. After the authority of the Master of the world has been contested, He must be overthrown. Man will occupy God's place; man will become "the measure of all things." But what does this rejection of God's authority mean? It means, claims Nietzsche, that God is dead. Camus adds that we recognize that everything is permitted and that we refuse any law other than man's own.

Even if this rebellion does not turn us back to the reign of the beastly Sphinx, it leads to numerous difficulties. One problem with this position is the variety of human laws which arise, not all of which are reconcilable: Why accept one human law over another? Indeed, why accept any law whatsoever? If every law is arbitrary, all values relative, and everything permissible, then the centuries of crime and genocide are prepared in that very cataclysmic moment. In *The Brothers Karamazov*, this acceptance means not the ultimate victory of the Grand Inquisitor but the murder of Fyodor, the suicide of Smerdyakov, the penal servitude of Dmitri, and the madness of Ivan. In the decades that follow, the proclamation that everything is permissible will lead to the Sphinx-like terror of fascism and communism. In the centuries forthcoming, it may bring about a subtle but no less devastating social engineering of the entire human race. Despite his unmitigated admiration for Ivan, Camus is not enthused about the Grand Inquisitor's prospects of the "Brave New World."

A conspicuously different reaction to the Legend comes from D.H. Lawrence:

> If there is any question: who is the Grand Inquisitor? – then surely we must say it is Ivan himself. And Ivan is the thinking mind of the human being in rebellion, thinking the whole thing out to the bitter end. As such he is, of course, identical with the Russian revolutionary of the thinking type. He is also, of course, Dostoevsky himself, in his thoughtful, as apart from his passional and inspirational sense. Dostoevsky half hated Ivan. Yet, after all, Ivan

is the greatest of the three brothers, pivotal. The passionate Dmitry and the inspired Alyosha are, at last, only offsets to Ivan.[17]

I would agree with everything Lawrence says except his claim that Ivan is "the greatest of the three brothers." What makes Ivan, and with him also the Grand Inquisitor, so great? Lawrence replies that the Grand Inquisitor presents the "final and unanswerable criticism of Christ." It is unanswerable because it is "borne out by the long experience of humanity. . . . It is reality versus illusion, and the illusion was Jesus', while time itself resorts with reality."[18] This assessment implies that Dostoevsky himself ultimately rejects Christ, which stands against his innumerable declarations to the contrary. In the same letter in which Dostoevsky affirms that the opinions of the Grand Inquisitor's are Ivan's own, he announces that, if he writes it as he intends, Book VI will convince everyone "that Christianity is the only refuge of the Russian land from all its evil."[19] Lawrence is aware of this and nevertheless insists on his view:

> And we cannot doubt that the Inquisitor speaks Dostoevsky's own final opinion about Jesus. The opinion is, baldly, this: Jesus, you are inadequate. Men must correct you. And Jesus in the end gives the kiss of acquiescence to the Inquisitor, as Alyosha does to Ivan. The two inspired ones recognize the inadequacy of their inspiration: the thoughtful one has to accept the responsibility of a complete adjustment.[20]

This opinion is bald. It is not, however, Dostoevsky's. Why is Jesus inadequate? Lawrence answers that "Christianity is too difficult for

---

17 D.H. Lawrence, "The Grand Inquisitor," in *The Brothers Karamazov and the Critics*, ed. Edward Wasiolek, 79. Dostoevsky confirms that the opinions of the Grand Inquisitor are Ivan's own in the latter to Liubimov, June 11, 1879.

18 Lawrence, *op. cit.*, 79.

19 Letter to Liubimov, June 11, 1879.

20 Lawrence, *op. cit.*, 79.

men, the vast mass of men." He adds: "Christianity, then, is the ideal, but it is impossible."[21]

Is Christianity difficult as an ideal, or is it impossible? There is nothing wrong with an ideal being difficult – what is easy to achieve should hardly serve as an ideal. But, if an ideal is impossible, then it cannot be imposed on anyone. Since Christianity has served as an inspiration to millions of people for the last two millennia, it is strange to call it "impossible." We may argue whether it is the most appropriate ideal, whether it is not worse than other choices, but this is quite different from calling it impossible.

Let us look at the ideal and its alternative more carefully. The Grand Inquisitor insists that freedom and happiness cannot go together. Is the problem that if people are free to share bread with others, there is no guarantee that they will? Those who possess much may lack a desire to share with those who have nothing. As Lawrence puts it, that is the long experience of humanity. To make everybody happy, freedom must be replaced by organization and compulsion – it is necessary to organize life in such a way that all people receive an equal share.

One problem with compulsion (and similarly with despotism, neo-colonialism, and consumerism) is that people must be deceived about the nature of the system. The Grand Inquisitor does not hide that, although he works with the lies of the devil, he pretends to work in the name of Jesus. As he also puts it, miracles must be used, for people need to believe in their rulers.

Jesus might have answered that the Grand Inquisitor turns things upside down: In the proper order of things, faith leads to miracles. Miracles do not lead to faith. He could have objected to the Grand Inquisitor's accusation that he, Jesus, denied all miracles and mysteries. In fact, this is not the case. Lawrence repeats the Grand Inquisitor's mistake, without seeing that he contradicts himself: "The bread, the earthly bread, while it is being reaped and grown, it is life. But once it is harvested and stored, it becomes a commodity, it becomes riches. And then it becomes a danger."[22] Jesus admits that the growth of wheat, and of any living thing for that matter, is a

21 *Ibid.*, 80.
22 *Ibid.*, 84.

miracle. He not only objects to it becoming a commodity, but also refuses to restore stones to bread – for this is what earthly bread becomes when the rich hoard it and bread becomes an inert possession. Had Lawrence known that in the notebooks for *The Brothers Karamazov* Dostoevsky wrote: "The Grand Inquisitor – God like a merchant," he would have understood the meaning of the Legend more properly.[23]

The fault of the Creator, according to Ivan and his Grand Inquisitor, is that He does not behave like a merchant. Instead, He follows the economy of gifts: He bestows too much here, too little over there. A good merchant divides the world's goods more evenly and justly. He would not turn his back to the sword of Caesar but would use it for the overall good of humanity. Although the Grand Inquisitor charges Jesus with failing all three temptations, it is really the third temptation that is the cornerstone of their disagreement. Jesus accepts miracles and mystery but He does not compromise freedom and exchange it for deception, compulsion, and the use of force.[24]

Lawrence also makes an analogous mistake with regard to the human need for an object of devotion. In his words, "It is not man's weakness that he needs someone to bow down to. It is his nature, and his strength, for it puts him into touch with far, far greater life than if he stood alone. All life bows down to the sun. But the sun is very far away from the common men."[25]

Indeed, it is not man's weakness that he needs someone to worship. Ivan himself is an illustration of a man who refuses to bow down in front of anything or anyone. On the psychological level, this leads him to value his independence above everything else. On the intellectual level, this seduces him to believe that Euclidean

---

23   *The Notebook for the Brothers Karamazov*, 75. Here I follow the translation of George Steiner, *Tolstoy or Dostoevsky: An Essay in the Old Criticism*, 333. Steiner offers an interesting commentary of this fragment (333–36), which he – surprisingly and not fully convincingly – uses to argue for his thesis that the Legend of the Grand Inquisitor is directed against Tolstoy. See also Joseph Frank, *Dostoevsky: The Mantle of the Prophet, 1871–1881*, 434–35.

24   Wasiolek points this out in his book *Dostoevsky: The Major Fiction*, 167.

25   Lawrence, *op. cit.*, 84.

reason is sufficient to master life. On the metaphysical level, this leads him to deny that he has been created in the image of God. Ivan wants to establish himself in opposition to God. He wants to become a Man-god.[26]

According to Erich Fromm, having an object of devotion is one aspect of an overall "map of reality."[27] There is no culture and no epoch in which human beings do not need a general frame of reference, and an object of devotion is usually the focal point of this map. A map itself does not tell us what to do and where to go. As Girard suggests – and the Grand Inquisitor concurs – the guidelines usually come from imitating our object of devotion. The problem is to find an appropriate object of devotion, someone who helps us find our way at the numerous crossroads of life. The Grand Inquisitor accuses Jesus of not establishing sufficient guidelines and leaving human beings in the unbearable situation of having to choose on their own.

This accusation is at least partially incorrect. Jesus establishes a number of demanding guidelines, including the most fundamental ones: Love thy neighbors and love thy enemies. It is true, however, that the Christian ethic does not cover the entire ground of life with specific prescriptions. This is the case because the Hand of God does not complete creation. This is the case because Christianity is not an ideology but a religion based on freedom. The Grand Inquisitor is right to notice that the more an ideology pretends to give answers to all questions, the more psychologically attractive it becomes for many people. The more attractive, however, does not mean the more true or appropriate. As Fromm remarks, the objects of man's devotion vary: He can be devoted to an idol which requires him to kill his parents or to an ideal which requires him to respect them. Human beings can be devoted to the growth of life or to its destruction. They can be devoted to the goal of amassing a fortune and acquiring power, or to that of becoming loving and creative.[28]

---

26 In making these distinctions, I follow Victor Terras, *A Karamazov Companion: Commentary on the Genesis, Language, and Style of Dostoevsky's Novel*, 51.

27 See Erich Fromm, *The Anatomy of Human Destructiveness*, 259.

28 *Ibid.*, 261.

The Grand Inquisitor might agree with Fromm and emphasize that, insofar as he intends to bring people happiness, there is no reason to object to his reshaping of creation. And yet, insofar as the Grand Inquisitor's ideology is based on deception, there will never be a guarantee that, for the sake of the grand goal, his ideology will not slip into destruction and death. Once such radical social engineering begins, who can possibly guarantee that it will always work for the benefit and happiness of humankind? Even more fundamentally, who can know in what that benefit and happiness really consist?

The fundamental premise of the Grand Revision of the world is that people want happiness, not freedom. Freedom is too demanding, while happiness is pacifying. But is it true that all people want happiness? And at what price?

Ivan's Legend belongs to what Karl Mannheim calls "the utopian mentality," or, more specifically, "the liberal-humanitarian idea."[29] In its characteristic form, the liberal-humanistic utopia attempts to establish a "correct" rational conception to be set off against evil reality. Based on the idea of human progress, such a utopia is problematic from its beginning (a point Mannheim traces back to Herder's *Letters for the Advancement of Humanity* [1792]): "There is no definite statement of wherein the ideal consists: at one time it is 'reason and justice' which appears as the goal; at another it is the 'well being of man' that he regards as worth striving for."[30] The Grand Inquisitor's utopia suffers from the same indeterminacy and abstractness – if it is created to remedy the problem of meaningless suffering, then it must at least offer a viable alternative to the world in which such suffering regularly takes place.

Curiously, meaningless suffering is not explicitly mentioned in the Legend. Ivan is well aware that the development of modern civilization has not led to more happiness. If anything, it leads to greater, not less suffering. Humanity has invented many diverse ways to cope with the increasing suffering. Suffering can be denied, escaped, or dulled to the point of apathy. It

---

29 Karl Mannheim, *Ideology and Utopia: An Introduction to the Sociology of Knowledge*, 219–29.

30 *Ibid.*, 222.

can be justified as punishment, passively accepted, or heroically contested. Some objectify suffering as the very ground of human existence, while others achieve personal redemption through suffering with the merciful love of God.

Ivan rejects any traditional theodicy because the ends cannot justify means. No harmony, and presumably no happiness, can be allowed if it requires the death of one child. Should not Ivan apply the same standards to the methods of the Grand Inquisitor? If suffering and torture (which Ivan condemns) are unacceptable as means, why should deception and loss of freedom (which the Grand Inquisitor condones) be acceptable as means? Does not the Grand Inquisitor introduce through the back door what Ivan throws out through the front, namely the principle that some goals justify all means?

Ivan rejects the insignificant position of man in the cosmos, as it is created and ordered by the incomprehensible Hand of God. Christ's pursuit of freedom is too demanding. Only a few can live up to His standards. For the vast majority they are unapproachable. For love of mankind, creation must be decisively completed and rigid order must be imposed. For love of mankind, freedom must be sacrificed and despondence masked as genuine freedom. How would this new world order enhance the position of man in the grand building of the universe? The "happy babes" would be controlled by the Grand Inquisitor and his associates so that they would be unaware of their slavery. The elite would again be in charge. A few chosen ones would pull the strings and sacrifice themselves for humanity.

What kind of love is this, we must ask. If Ivan cannot love his father and brothers, how can the Grand Inquisitor love those repulsive, weak, beastly creatures called men? Why should anyone love such creatures and sacrifice oneself for their happiness? If Ivan and the Grand Inquisitor are right in their vision of who human beings are and what their nature is, instead of loving such worthless creatures, why not destroy them? Why not transform the so-called civilized world into the perpetual peace of a graveyard? Would that not lead to even more happiness for the chosen ones? Those brave, gifted, and smart could have the entire world for themselves.

There are those who interpret the Legend as the irrefutable criticism of the traditional religious approach, with its persistent but unsuccessful theodicy. Lawrence sees in the Legend "the final and unanswerable criticism of Christ."[31] If this is indeed Dostoevsky's intention, than he fails in presenting it. But why believe that this is his intent? In the very same letter to Liubimov in which he announces that Ivan's logic is flawless, Dostoevsky suggests an opposite meaning for the Legend: "All of socialism originated and began with the negation of the meaning of historical reality and ended in a program of destruction and anarchy."[32] This quotation sheds an entirely different light on Dostoevsky's declaration concerning Ivan's reasoning. If Ivan's logic is indeed flawless, it is the flawlessness of a *reductio ad absurdum* argument: What is taken as an initial premise is developed to its absurdity and because of that must be rejected. Dostoevsky aims to convince even the most ardent socialist that no "happy" arrangement of the human race can resolve the fundamental perplexities of life. We can reassure philosophers and pacify moralists, says Shestov ironically, but what can we do with life? How can we force life to reshape Raskolnikovs and Karamazovs? For life has neither the sense of guilt nor conscience; it is equally indifferent toward human tragedy as it is toward human comedy.[33]

Similarly, Berdyaev reminds us of Alyosha's significant words that, contrary to Ivan's intention, the Legend is a vindication of Christ. In Berdyaev's opinion, the Grand Inquisitor "argues and persuades; he is a master of logic and he is single-mindedly set on the carrying-out of a definite plan: but the Lord's silence is stronger and more convincing."[34]

While "the Lord's silence" can indeed speak, Dostoevsky does not think that it "is stronger and more convincing" than the words of

---

31 Lawrence, *op. cit.*, 79.
32 Letter to Liubimov, May 10, 1879.
33 Shestov, *Dostoevsky, Tolstoy and Nietzsche*, section XVII, 238–39.
34 Nicholas Berdyaev, *op. cit.*, 189. On the meaning of silence, see Malcolm Jones, *Dostoevsky and the Dynamics of Religious Experience*, 139–46.

the Grand Inquisitor. If he did, he would not dedicate Book VI to Father Zosima's reply to the old cardinal. And Dostoevsky is far from certain that, even with the help of Father Zosima, he can present a stronger and more convincing view. Dostoevsky writes to his editor Liubimov: "I am hurrying to send out to you the whole of Book VI. . . . But I'm not sure that it will come off. I've been able to say only a tenth of what I've wanted to say. Still, I look on Book VI as the culminating point of my novel."[35]

The Russian Monk's Antithesis

Sophocles does not invent the story of Oedipus's tragic fate, or that of his conquest of the Sphinx. They are part of the mythological tradition in which the figures of Oedipus and the Sphinx are connected with the cult of the earth-goddesses, representative of matriarchal religion. Erich Fromm relates the myth of Oedipus to "Eteonos, the only Boeotian city which had a cult shrine of Oedipus and where the whole myth probably originated, and also has the shrine of the earth-goddess, Demeter." Fromm adds that "Sophocles has emphasized this connection between Oedipus and the chthonic goddesses in *Oedipus at Colonus*."[36]

In *Oedipus the King*, the female is present in the primitive and negative role. The Sphinx is a half-woman, half-beast, who threatens to devour the civilized world and push it back into primordial chaos. Jocasta is a participant in this civilized world and not a primitive woman-beast, but she abandons her duty as a mother: She agrees to the death of her child in order to save her husband. By solving the riddle of the Sphinx, Oedipus initially overcomes this world of the primitive mother; yet through his incest with Jocasta (and the recognition of himself as father-murderer), he is again defeated by the negative side of the mother archetype (symbolized by the act of blinding). Sophocles emphasizes the positive aspect

---

35 Letter to Liubimov, August 7, 1879.
36 Erich Fromm, *The Forgotten Language: An Introduction to the Understanding of Dreams, Fairy Tales and Myths*, 211. A similar connection is also made by Bachofen, *op. cit.*, 179–83, and by Erich Neumann, *The Origin and History of Consciousness*, 162–67.

of the feminine in the later two dramas, especially in *Antigone*. Antigone's insistence on the law of burial for both of her brothers, against the specific prohibition of the new ruler, Creon, symbolizes the return of the body to Mother Earth and is rooted in the very principles of matriarchal religion. As Fromm points out, when Antigone proclaims that "'Tis not my nature to join in hating but in loving," she "stands for the solidarity of man and the principle of the all-embracing motherly love."[37]

Fromm criticizes Freud for his tendency to see in myth, as well as in dream, only the expression of irrational, antisocial impulses, rather than the wisdom of the past ages expressed in the language of symbols.[38] Contrary to Freud, Fromm insists that the central theme of the Oedipus myth is not sexual desire but attitude toward authority. The marriage of Oedipus and Jocasta is only a secondary element in the story primarily concerned with the rebellion of son against father in the patriarchal society. Fromm is not the only one who believes that Sophocles' trilogy carries residues of the ancient battle between the patriarchal and matriarchal systems of society. In the older, matriarchal world the emphasis is on blood-ties, ties to the soil, and the passive acceptance of all natural phenomena. The one sacred tie – the tie of unconditional love – is that of mother and child. Consequently, in the matriarchal world matricide is the ultimate and unforgivable sin.

The patriarchal point of view does not promise any unconditional love or faith. It is characterized by respect for man-made laws, predominance of rational thought, and man's calculated effort to manipulate the world of nature. The son's love and respect for the father are his paramount duty in the patriarchal world, while parricide is here the ultimate and unforgivable crime.[39]

37 Fromm, *op. cit.*, 224. See also Neumann, *op. cit.*, 171.
38 Fromm, *op. cit.*, 196. For a different criticism of Freud's approach, see Neumann, *op. cit.*, 162–68, and *passim*.
39 To quote Fromm again, "The patriarchal principle is that the ties between man and wife, between ruler and ruled, take precedence over ties of blood. It is the principle of order and authority, of obedience and hierarchy"; *op. cit.*, 222. Neumann makes similar claims; *op. cit.*, 172–73.

The Brothers Karamazov is a novel about the struggles within a patriarchal world: The sons rebel against the compromised authority of their father. Fyodor Karamazov is a symbol of an irresponsible parent. Alyosha blushes because of him, Dmitri wants to smash his face, Ivan despises him, Smerdyakov kills him. Ivan rebels against the Divine Father as well – He has also compromised His authority by allowing meaningless suffering of the innocent. The pollution of innocent blood reveals the arbitrariness – even chaos – of a poorly created and managed world. This chaos, in turn, eradicates any meaning from the world and turns human beings from privileged children to disoriented and homeless wanderers.

Ivan does not challenge patriarchal values and hierarchies as such. He does not deny the authority of a father figure in general. His rebellion is directed against the specific father figures whom, like Fyodor and the Father in Heaven, he believes to be immoral or incompetent. Instead of them, Ivan turns to his father figure – the imaginary Grand Inquisitor. He can fix the unjust and chaotic world and recreate a hospitable environment for the suffering humanity.

Father Zosima contests the one-sidedness of the patriarchal world and intimates an alternative to it. While Dmitri's name points toward the goddess earth (Demeter), and while Alyosha is inspired by the memories of his mother to embark on his spiritual journey, Father Zosima promotes feminine, motherly values to the highest rank.[40] Dostoevsky offers various hints to help us understand the

---

40   Father Zosima is not the only one who thinks this way. As George Gibian maintains: "To Vladimir Solovyov, S.N. Bulgakov, Alexander Blok, and many others, the concept of Sophia supplemented that of the divine trinity. It has been variously defined as 'cosmic love' or love for 'the divine ground of the created world'; through contemplation of Sophia one can merge all that is visible, admire its beauty, and penetrate to its essence. Vivid response to all that lives is a joining with the creator in creating and preserving the world; Sophia is a blissful meeting of god and nature, the creator and creature. In Orthodox thought Sophia has come close to being regarded as something similar to the fourth divine person." Quoted from "Traditional Symbolism in *Crime and Punishment*," in *Crime and Punishment: The Coulson Translation; Backgrounds and Sources; Essays in Criticism*, ed. George Gibian, 590.

Elder's attempt to redirect us toward values different from Ivan's. After the presentation of the Legend of the Grand Inquisitor, when the cardinal sends Jesus out of this world, Ivan sends Alyosha to the dying "Pater Seraphicus" (Bk. V, Ch. 5, 264).[41] Although Alyosha cannot understand all the implications of this phrase, Ivan's words reveal more than he intends. He is almost certainly aware that a "Seraphic Father" is an epithet for St. Francis of Assisi, and thus not inappropriate to the teachings of the Elder, which resemble the wisdom of St. Francis venerating the Mother Earth. The well-educated Ivan knows that Goethe uses Pater Seraphicus as a character in his *Faust* – Ivan is more familiar with foreign tradition than his own. Like Ipolite in *The Idiot*, who is moved by Holbein's painting of a dead Christ but does not react to the Orthodox icon in his room, Ivan cherishes a Western-style utopia and fails to appreciate Father Zosima as a monk who represents the Orthodox ties with the Mother Earth and Mother Nature.

Goethe himself at first presents the female-maternal element as something foreign and frightening, only to make a full circle toward the end of his greatest work. He ends his *Faust* (part II), with a celebration of the positive aspect of the feminine-mother archetype: "*Das Ewig-weibliche zieth uns hinan*" (The Eternal-Feminine draws us on high). Like Goethe, Father Zosima will evoke the positive side of the mother archetype. In the moments of crisis, he will throw himself on his knees before the icon and weep "to the most holy Mother of God" (Bk. VI, Ch. 2 [d], 310).

When Russians speak of "the most holy Mother of God," one of their first associations is to the Vladimir Icon of the Virgin and her Child. This twelfth-century icon, a gift from Constantinople to Kiev, which eventually moved to Vladimir (hence the name) and later to Moscow, is believed to be so miraculous that the

---

41 As Victor Terras points out (*op. cit.*, 239, note 331), "Pater Seraphicus" is an explicit echo from Act V of the second part of Goethe's *Faust* (lines 11918–25). "Pater Seraphicus" is traditionally an epithet ascribed to St. Francis of Assisi (1182–1226). In Goethe's poem, Pater Seraphicus leads a chorus of blessed boys (= unbaptized children who die immediately after being born and thus are without sin) to an awareness of God's presence and eternal love.

medieval legends attribute its painting to the Evangelist Luke.[42] The Russians emphasize that the Mother of God – *Theotokos* (Greek), *Bogoroditsa* (Russian) – is not just a virgin but a mother. Unlike Western Christianity, this distinctive stress on mother- hood is at the core of the Orthodox faith. This icon emphasizes motherhood by depicting the Madonna pressing her face against her child's. The fuller symbolic significance of this icon becomes clearer after we consider Book VI in which Dostoevsky coun- ters the Legend of the Grand Inquisitor with his narrative about Zosima's life.

Ivan associates Father Zosima with a Western saint, while Dostoevsky uses several Russian models for the Elder. Perhaps the most significant of them is Saint Sergius of Radonezh (1314–1392). He became the patron saint of Moscow and the founder of a monastery where Andrei Rublyov later lived as a monk and painted "The Holy Trinity." During one of the brutal Mongol invasions, Father Sergius withdrew into the forests and there founded a small community of the faithful, which eventually established itself as a center of spiritual teaching and the greatest monastery in the land. Father Sergius became known as a "*starets*" (Elder), by which Russians understand "a man of profound spiritual wisdom, guided by direct inspiration of the spirit. His special gift of 'charisma' enables him to see in a practical way the will of God in relation to each person who consults him."[43]

Book VI of *The Brothers Karamazov*, entitled "The Russian Monk," is significantly different from the rest of the narrative. It is also often judged to be the weakest part of the novel. Here is one typical criticism, coming from the pen of Edward Wasiolek, a dedicated Dostoevsky scholar: "The writing is pallid, abstract, and lacking the drama; the ideas of Father Zosima read like a list of aphorism and risk provoking the indifference that banality leaves

---

42 My description of this icon relies mostly on Henri Nouwen, *Behold the Beauty of the Lord: Praying with Icons*, 31–42.

43 Suzanne Massie, *Land of the Firebird: The Beauty of the Old Russia*, 42. See also Frank, *op. cit.*, 621–22. In *Theology of the Icon*, 55, Leonid Ouspensky argues that "the distinctive trait of the New Testament is the direct connection between the word and the image" (*obraz*).

in its train. . . . Book VI seems remote from human experience, passion, and [is] curiously verbal and abstract. It reads like a sermon."[44]

Book VI reads like a sermon because it is intended as a sermon. More precisely, it is a combination of sermon and icon, which is known in Russia as *zhitie*, "a life of a saint." To his editor and publisher Liubimov, Dostoevsky writes that "the blasphemy" of Book V will be "triumphantly overturned in the next issue [Book VI], on which I am now working with fear, trembling, and devotion."[45] Ivan presents his "blasphemy" in the form of a typical Western utopia. "The blasphemy" will not be overturned by confronting it point-by-point and argument-by-argument, but rather by presenting an alternative vision of reality, a different "form of life." Dostoevsky's choice of how to structure and present this alternative is certainly atypical for literature in general and for the novel in particular. It is, however, fully in accordance with his own emphasis on images of ideas (more precisely, on image-ideas), and also in concurrence with the content of the message he wants to convey. Dostoevsky counters Ivan's purely theoretical construction with an exemplary word and life-story (*zhitie*) of "a beautiful man."

Dostoevsky's choice is also in accord with his religious tradition. As Henri Nouwen explains, "Gazing is probably the best word to touch the core of Eastern spirituality. Whereas St. Benedict, who has set the tone for the spirituality of the West, calls us first of all to listen, the Byzantine fathers focus on gazing." The objects of gazing are primarily icons, which "are created for the sole purpose of offering access, through the gates of the visible, to the mystery of the invisible."[46] Nouwen rightly stresses the connection of the visible with the invisible, which is the essential element of faith.

---

44   Edward Wasiolek, ed. *The Notebooks for The Brothers Karamazov*, 89–90. Sergei Hackel offers a similar critical assessment of Book VI; "The Religious Dimension: Vision or Evasion? Zosima's Discourse in *The Brothers Karamazov*," in *Fyodor Dostoevsky*, ed. Harold Bloom, 212.

45   Letter to Liubimov, May 10, 1879. For a valuable discussion of how Dostoevsky approached the work on the life of Father Zosima, see Frank, *op. cit.*, 451–58, 621–35.

46   Nouwen, *op. cit.*, 13–14. It may be worth noting that Orthodox believers pray gazing at the icon and not with their eyes closed.

Ivan insists on facts, on the visible, but the facts are insufficient on their own. Facts need a glue to hold them together and present a meaningful story. The insistence on facts alone leaves the world disenchanted and its observers disoriented. Icons allow us this connection of the visible with the invisible, a transition from fragmented facts to a spirited narrative. Nouwen's next passage comes even closer to explaining what Dostoevsky attempts to do in Book VI and why our first reactions to it are so restrained:

> Icons are not easy to "see." They do not immediately speak to our senses. They do not excite, fascinate, stir our emotions, or stimulate our imagination. At first, they even seem somewhat rigid, lifeless, schematic and dull. . . . It is only gradually, after a patient, prayerful presence that they start speaking to us. And as they speak, they speak more to our inner than to our outer senses. They speak to the heart that searches for God.[47]

It is hardly possible that Dostoevsky himself would better describe the medium he intends for Book VI. Despite the obvious differences in the form of presentation – a point to which we will return – let us begin by mentioning some significant structural similarities between Books V and VI. In Book V Ivan first presents a number of examples, focusing on the inexcusable suffering of children before he launches his Legend of the Grand Inquisitor. In Book VI, Father Zosima first narrates a few stories, drawn from his own life, before "some talks and homilies" are introduced. There are numerous claims in Books V and VI presented in a strict thesis-antithesis structure: Ivan takes human beings to be weak and cruel by nature; Father Zosima holds that people are inherently good. Ivan interprets "In the beginning was the Word" as "In the beginning was Suffering"; the Elder takes it to mean "In the beginning was Love." Ivan thinks that the world must be restructured; Father Zosima believes that the inherent order should be respected. Ivan suggests that man-made order and justice are the solution to the

---

47   *Ibid.*, 14. See also Christopher Merrill, *Things of the Hidden God: Journey to the Holy Mountain*, especially pages 109 and 196–98.

riddle of meaningless suffering; Father Zosima champions freedom and forgiveness.

Father Zosima's "talks and homilies" eventually make clear that his disagreement with Ivan does not concern facts, on which Ivan insists, but our attitudes toward them. Like Ivan, the Elder sees much that is not acceptable in this world. He talks about "freedom" which men praise, yet which really amounts to nothing but "slavery" and "suicide" (Bk. VI, Ch. 3 [e], 314). Father Zosima does not overlook the artificially generated desires, habits, and fancies of the modern world. He is quick to contrast the ancient monastic life of obedience, fasting, and prayer to the contemporary slavery to desires and the mindless hording of goods. No brotherhood and no solidarity can emerge from such an "order" of things. The Elder is also aware of the factories which employ ten-year-old children and terms this practice the "torture of children" (Bk. VI, Ch. 3 [f], 315). Nevertheless, the Elder radically differs from Ivan and his Grand Inquisitor on what can be done about such a sorrowful state of affairs.

The heart of their disagreement lies in choosing between the path of power or the path of love. Will we renounce love for the sake of power? Or will we seek redemption through a love that renounces self-seeking? Ivan and his Grand Inquisitor choose power, because they have no faith in people, because of their bad faith. In this view Ivan follows a tradition in political philosophy that starts with Hobbes, according to which every man is a wolf to every other. To prevent this (alleged) perpetual war, a social contract is required. Hobbes sets his reorganization of the primitive humanity into a civilized state on four "insights" about the nature of man: his selfishness, fear of death, power of reason, and awe inspired by authority.[48] All four are accepted by the Grand Inquisitor.

Father Zosima holds the opposite conception of humanity. People are not inherently selfish, nor do they fear death. Reason is useful, but to a limited degree, and authority has to come from the

---

48 This is pointed out by Lewis Hyde, *The Gift: Imagination and the Erotic Life of Property*, 90. Hyde also ascribes to Hobbes a "double deceit" on which most modern societies are operating: "first, that passion will undo social life and, second, that coercion will preserve it" (92).

people, not from an authoritarian ruler. For the Elder, a sustainable and healthy community does not emerge when a part of our nature is inhibited and restrained, but rather when a part of the self is given away as a gift, in willing service to others. Instead of looking for servants, we should strive to be them. True equality is not achieved by legal enforcement but exists only though the spiritual dignity respected in ourselves and others. True brotherhood is not possible without gifts of love. Those who attempt to build a community based on power and force "will end by drenching the earth with blood, for blood calls to blood, and he who draws the sword will perish by the sword" (Bk. VI, Ch. 3 [f], 318). Such a community would not be paradise but hell.

An authentic community must be based on gifts of love, and it must not excommunicate sinners, criminals, or suicides: "Brothers, do not be afraid of men's sin, love man also in his sin, for this likeness of God's love is the height of love on earth. Love all of God's creation, both the whole of it and every grain of sand" (Bk. VI, Ch. 3 [g], 318–19). Father Zosima suggests this transformation of society can be accomplished by orienting ourselves toward Mother Earth. He teaches: "Fall down on the earth and kiss it and water it with your tears, and the earth will bring forth fruit from your tears" (Bk. VI, Ch. 3 [h], 321).[49]

This theme of kissing the earth and watering it with one's tears is frequent in Dostoevsky. Kissing itself has a special meaning for Father Zosima, for his words echo Jesus's silent response to the Grand Inquisitor. D.H. Lawrence sees the silence of Jesus and his kiss of the old Inquisitor as a sign of acquiescence. George Steiner disagrees. The silence and the kiss are "a parable of the artist's humility and one of the truest insights given us into the necessary defeats of language."[50]

The archaic meaning of a kiss is that it represents an exchange of souls, a mystery rarely matched by any other human gesture. Lewis Hyde's words on the meaning of mystery apply

---

49   For further discussion, see Jaroslav Pelikan, *Imago Dei: The Byzantine Apologia for Icons*, 134–51. See also Orlando Figes, *Natasha's Dance: A Cultural History of Russia*, 321.

50   Steiner, *op. cit.*, 292.

both to the mystery of the kiss and to the mystery of artistic creation:

> The root of our English word "mystery" is a Greek verb, *muein*, which means to close the mouth. Dictionaries tend to explain the connection by pointing out that the initiates to ancient mysteries were sworn to silence, but the root may also indicate, it seems to me, that what the initiate learns as a mystery *cannot* be talked about. It can be shown, it can be witnessed or revealed, it cannot be explained.[51]

Steiner offers a radical criticism of Lawrence, but there is a less radical yet fully acceptable interpretation of Dostoevsky's text. A kiss need not be a sign of acquiescence, but a sign of acceptance, regardless of this person's deeds (and words). Alyosha kisses Ivan while Ivan wonders whether Alyosha will renounce him, after Ivan has renounced God. Alyosha's kiss is meant to reassure him: You are my brother and I love you for who you are, not for what you do or say. I do not judge you. I forgive you despite your blasphemy. You have my unconditional love.

With its intense immediacy, the kiss speaks louder than words. Ivan has shown that words can lie, and Alyosha wants to deliver a message that will not be misunderstood. Jesus's kiss of the Grand Inquisitor could be interpreted similarly, but Father Zosima adds a new dimension to the meaning of the kiss:

> And if, having received your kiss, he goes away unmoved and laughing at you, do not be tempted by that either: it means that his time has not yet come, but it will come in due course; and if it does not come, no matter: if not he, then another will know, and suffer, and judge, and accuse himself, and the truth will be made full. Believe it, believe it without doubt, for in this lies all hope and all the faith of the saints (Bk. VI, Ch. 3 [h], 321).

Yet another dimension of Jesus's kiss shows how, despite his disagreement with the Grand Inquisitor, Christ refuses to exercise pressure on the cardinal. Christ must be loved and honored for

---

51 Hyde, *op. cit.*, 280.

Himself, as faith can only be accepted for its virtues. An atheist has to find his or her way (back) to faith on his or her own, as in the following example, in which a non-believer feels attracted to the "marvelous power" of the icon:

> I once stood at a shrine and gazed at a wonder-working icon of the Mother of God, thinking of the childlike faith of the people praying before it; some women and infirm old men knelt, crossing themselves and bowing down to the earth. With ardent hope I gazed at the holy features, and little by little the secret of their marvelous power began to grow clear to me. Yes, this was not just a painted board – for centuries it had absorbed these passions and these hopes, the prayers of the afflicted and unhappy; it was filled with the energy of all these prayers. It had become a living organism, a meeting place between the Lord and men. Thinking of this, I looked once more at the old men, at the women and the children prostrate in the dust, and at the holy icon – and then I too saw the animated features of the Mother of God, and I saw how she looked with love and mercy at these simple folk, and I sank on my knees and meekly prayed to her.[52]

Father Zosima's homilies emphasize faith as an attitude of unconditional love and dedication, associated with the Mother of God. He also stresses the connectedness of human beings with Mother Earth and Mother Nature, and for him these three figures are one. We are not isolated and alone in this world full of pointless suffering, Father Zosima tells us, for we always belong to the Mother of God. As she is represented on Russia's most venerated icon, "The Vladimir Mother of God," her face and the gestures of her hands reveal her profound patience and unquestioning forgiveness. Her sorrowful eyes, which look past the Child to the outside world, seem to communicate her apprehension of the sufferings which await Him – indeed, which await all of her children. She knows what it means to be poor, oppressed, and a refugee. She knows what it means to stand under the cross and be the bearer of the thoughts and feelings that

52   Quoted from Figes, *op. cit.*, 299.

cannot be shared with anyone. What the Mother of God conveys she cannot speak with words but can express with a kiss or a loving gesture. The patience, love, and forgiveness of the Mother of God are strong and unwavering. Father Zosima's homilies seem to be telling us to learn these virtues from the Mother of God and become like her.

How, then, does the Elder resolve Ivan's riddle of meaningless suffering? How does he answer the three sub-problems into which we divided the riddle: Where does meaningless suffering come from? What to do about it? Can meaningless suffering be eliminated from this world?

Unfortunately, Father Zosima is more elusive than we would like him to be. It is not clear, for instance, whether he admits that there is meaningless suffering in the first place. The Elder declares that life is a paradise, although we are usually not able to see it. And yet, he recognizes the injustice of ten-year-old children working like slaves in factories. The Elder also criticizes the isolation of modern man and his addiction to artificially created needs and habits. How, then, can he call this world a paradise?

Father Zosima does not see the death of his brother Markel as meaningless, just as Alyosha does not consider the death of his little friend Ilysha as meaningless. What would Father Zosima say, however, about the death of the woman killed by his mysterious visitor? Or, had he not experienced a conversion the night before the duel and proceeded to kill an innocent man, what would he say about that murder and the suffering it would cause for that man's wife?

The Elder does not see the contrast between life and death in the exclusive categories of our logical reasoning. Having faith in the Mother of God and Mother Nature, he sees life and death in terms of recurring cycles. As the sowing, growth, and gathering of the crops is one process which continually revives itself in nature, so are human birth, death, and rebirth part of the same cycle. Experiencing both joy and suffering is part and parcel of these processes and cannot be considered in isolation from each other.

Father Zosima's answer to the second part of the riddle is also elusive. He puzzles us because, once more, his views can be interpreted differently. Father Zosima encourages his disciples to "work

tirelessly" (Bk. VI, Ch. 3 [h], 321), although he does not separate
suffering and action in the way we usually do. Just as he does not
see any strict separation between the divine and the human, the
Creator and the creation, the Elder does not experience suffering
(normally associated with passivity) and action as opposite from
each other. Hermann Hesse explains this view better than Father
Zosima:

> Action and suffering, which together make up our lives, are
> a whole; they are one. A child suffers its begetting, it suf-
> fers its birth, its weaning; it suffers here and it suffers there
> until in the end it suffers death. But all the good in a man,
> for which he is praised or loved, is merely good suffering,
> the right kind, the living kind of suffering, a suffering to
> the full. The ability to suffer well is more than half of life –
> indeed, it is all life. Birth is suffering, growth is suffering,
> the seed suffers the earth, the root suffers the rain, the bud
> suffers its flowering. In the same way, my friends, man suf-
> fers destiny. Destiny is earth, it is rain and growth. Destiny
> hurts.[53]

Although Father Zosima often sounds this way, there are other
passages in his homilies which are not quite consistent with this
Nietzschean *amor fati*. For instance, there are the particular passages where Father Zosima indicates that the Russian people, being
closer to Mother Earth and Mother Nature than their Western
counterparts, have a historical mission to accomplish. Unlike the
Grand Inquisitor, who expects that the chosen elite can rearrange
the creation from the top toward the bottom, Father Zosima sees
the restructuring of the world from the bottom toward the top. The
Russian peasants have to be the catalyst of change that will bring
an awakening of Europe, which has for centuries been sinking into
decadence.

There are several problems already pointed out with Father
Zosima's insistence on the historical mission of the Russian peasants. He wavers between accepting the world, for it is a paradise,
and changing it for the better. The second problematic point is to

53 Hermann Hesse, "Zarathustra's Return," in *If the War Goes On*, 98–99.

expect that peasants, Russian or any other, can carry out a radical change in our attitude toward the world. Even if this position has a trace of plausibility in it, what separates the Russian peasants from the rest of the world? As Sergei Hackel points out, Dostoevsky is here carried away by his nationalistic feelings which go against the universal spirit of Christianity: "What seemed to begin as an assertion of the age-old tradition of Orthodoxy is unobtrusively transformed into an expression of nineteenth century Russian nationalism, if not messianism. No longer is the Church the guardian of the truth . . . but the members of a particular nation."[54]

How, then, should we judge Dostoevsky's attempt to overturn "the blasphemy" of Book V? If that is Dostoevsky's sincere intention and he does not change his mind about his goal during the process of writing Book VI, he fails. What interests us about this failure and what leads us to suspect that Dostoevsky shifts strategies is the structure of the argument. Father Zosima's mistakes are structurally the same as those of the Grand Inquisitor. We have already seen that both visions are untenable, for in each approach we find an extreme one-sidedness which undermines its credibility. The Grand Inquisitor insists that what people want is happiness; Father Zosima insists that they want love. Yes, people want love. But love is not all human beings need, just as happiness is not all we need. The problem is that people do not want one value, but a variety of them.

The more we read Books V and VI of *The Brothers Karamazov*, the more apparent the similarities between The Grand Inquisitor and Father Zosima become.[55] In the Grand Inquisitor's scheme, innocent suffering seems to disappear; with Father Zosima,

---

54   Hackel, *op. cit.*, 228.
55   According to Joyce Carol Oates, Father Zosima and the Grand Inquisitor "are the same person, viewed by different temperaments. Zosima is the mystic, and his mysticism has the psychological power of ridding the peasant (most of humanity) of his burden of freedom; the Grand Inquisitor is the mystic-turned-political figure, the organizer and savior of mankind. Both Zosima and the Grand Inquisitor are altruistic, ruled by love of man; "Tragic and Comic Visions in *The Brothers Karamazov*," in *The Edge of Impossibility: Tragic Forms in Literature*, 104.

meaningless suffering becomes almost indistinguishable from meaningful suffering and also from joy and every other experience of life. With the Grand Inquisitor, we are not responsible for anybody and anything; with Father Zosima, we are responsible for everybody and everything. They both miss something and lose too much in such sweeping generalizations. With the Grand Inquisitor, human personality dissolves into an ant-hill; with Father Zosima, it dissolves into an ocean involving the entire divine creation.

Must it be that way? Must the human personality dissolve? Can we not retain our contradictions and paradoxes? Do not the Mother of God and her Son accomplish this?

Meaningless Suffering and the Meaning of Life

When the seventeen-year-old Dostoevsky writes to his brother that the aim of his life is to study "the meaning of life and man," he cannot but underestimate how difficult his task is going to be. Man is a riddle, and at the very heart of that riddle the young Dostoevsky properly places the puzzle of "the meaning of life and man." As Dostoevsky matures, the problem of pointless suffering and the issue of the meaning of life merge together: How can human life be meaningful when meaningless suffering exists in the world?

Many of Dostoevsky's characters feel the pressure of this riddle, though none as powerfully as Ivan. Gifted with an unquenchable Karamazov thirst for life, and also with a superb, perpetually probing intellect, Ivan cannot accept the unbearable thought that the manifestation of the Karamazov vitality cannot be sublimated into any higher meaning of life. He cannot accept that, at the end, when all illusions are dispersed, what remains is the unrestrained pursuit of sensual pleasure, as exhibited by the remorseless life of his father. In attempting to divert the human condition from the principle that everything is permissible, Ivan intends to establish boundaries which will protect man from the unpredictable flow of life's contingencies. When this noble, Faustian hope turns out to be utopian, Ivan is devastated. The more he insists that there must be some definite, provable higher meaning to life, the more he chokes in the quicksand of his bewildering ideas. Ivan's pursuit of truth then turns into a rebellion against it. Instead of the biblical promise that "the truth shall make you free," Ivan, like Oedipus, comes to a different conclusion: The truth shall make you mad. Ivan feels betrayed and turns against the God who seduces him and the rest of humanity on the path of tragedy. He comes to believe that human life is too fragile. One blow of fate, one cruel game from the uncaring God, and human life is destroyed. The best chance to survive with this immoral God is in the bliss of ignorance. The most realistic hope for the achievement of happiness is by nurturing an illusion of an all-powerful, knowing, and benevolent God. If the sorrowful lot of humanity can still be rearranged, this is how it should be done: People ought to be turned into "happy babes," the slaves of their own blissful ignorance and self-imposed deceptions. For Ivan, who knows too much, a different, more tragic fate is destined. He endlessly wavers between two positions, both of which he recognizes as untenable: having false ideals or having none.

Dostoevsky must have felt the same anguish many times when it appeared to him that Ivan's tragic truth is the ultimate solution to the riddle of man. Most commentators believe that Dostoevsky must have experienced Ivan's crucible of doubt in order to create the Legend of the Grand Inquisitor. Yet, we know that the Grand Merchant is not the final word of Dostoevsky's art and life. Dostoevsky had high hopes for his book on the Elder Zosima, which is supposed to overturn the blasphemy of the Grand Inquisitor. He does not succeed in this particular task. Father Zosima does not offer a convincing resolution to the riddle of meaningless suffering. Still, the venerable Elder dies in the middle of the novel and there are several hundred pages left to finish the job started in Book VI. The pages on the Elder Zosima do not provide a convincing solution to the riddle of meaningless suffering, but they set a foundation for a solution of a different, more important riddle – the riddle of the meaning of life. To see what this foundation is, we will take another look at Book VI and its messages in connection with the remaining part of the novel.

Human beings cannot survive very long without attaching some meaning to their lives and the world as a whole. In our eagerness to figure out what that meaning is, we often accept unjustified and false assumptions. The history of mankind provides a long list of such assumptions. Four of them are the most frequent and consequential.

(i)   We think of the world in analogy with the human mind. We assume that the world itself must be governed by reason (*logos*) and its purposeful consciousness. From the position of its cognitive and moral authority, this world-reason must set purposes for the future and must choose rational means for their accomplishment.

(ii) The meaning of the world and human life is inseparably linked to such purposes. For this reason, meaning can only reside in the initial determination of purposes, in the initial planning of the world, and no subsequent meaning can enter into the world.

(iii) The meaning of the world and human life can only reside in the whole, and not in its parts. Meaning cannot appear only in one part of the world and then expand toward a larger whole.

(iv) The meaning of life needs to be considered and expressed in moral terms. The most frequent values mentioned in this context are justice and happiness. How can an unjust world have meaning? How can an unhappy life be meaningful?[56]

Instead of convincing us that life is meaningless, or that we should return our tickets, Ivan helps us see such assumptions regarding the meaning of life as untenable. His reasoning starts with the last assumption and moves toward the first. Ivan's crucible of doubt leads him to two realizations. One is his devastating insight of the criminal and deprived tendencies which reside in every human soul. The second is his realization that injustice is inherent in the structure of human life and can hardly be extricated from it.[57] The first of these two insights leads Ivan to rebellion, the second to madness. He concludes that the presence of numerous moral shortcomings in the world reveals just how inherently

---

56 My presentation of these four assumptions relies on Nicolai Hartmann's *Ästhetik*, Ch. 35, 406–12, and *Ethics*, vol. II, 318–39.

57 These two points are made by Eliseo Vivas: "Two Dimensions of Reality in *The Brothers Karamazov*," in *The Brothers Karamazov and the Critics*, ed. Edward Wasiolek, 67.

flawed the whole structure of creation is. Moreover, if the world is indeed guided by the world-reason, then the existence of unjust and senseless suffering shows that such an authoritative reason is counter-productive. There can be no purpose which justifies such unacceptable means. The logic of means and ends, together with the vision of a rational, morally responsible ruler of the world, collapses in the face of meaningless suffering. Such suffering is a violation of justice, of any rational and moral purpose which is supposed to be inherent in the world from the moment of its creation. More broadly speaking, meaningless suffering is the violation of the borders of what is permissible and impermissible. Such borders must be established by law in order to prevent the return to the primordial chaos and maintain equilibrium indispensable for a meaningful life. Following the traditional logical principle of the excluded middle, Ivan reasons that the only alternative to order is chaos. If the Father in Heaven is not capable of establishing an order which enables a meaningful existence, Ivan rejects His creation, and declares this chaotic world unbearable. The alternatives become either the chaos of reality, or the order of a man-made structure.

Given the outlined four assumptions, Dostoevsky is right to maintain that Ivan's conclusions seem as inevitable as they are disturbing. Moreover, this verdict is not only his own, but a culmination point of an entire tradition of European thinking. Ivan's ruling, and the verdict of this tradition, is directed against the divine Creator: God has either neglected or betrayed us, and man must reject any moral authority that may come from such a negligent or irresponsible Father. Man assumes that authority and, following his own autonomous intellect and will, establishes a new beginning and a new purpose in life. If necessary, new meaning will be established over the dead body of the failed Father. Man, not God, is the measure of all things. This credo determines the further fate of humanity. For is man capable of carrying the difficult loads that he so carelessly puts on his shoulders? Is he really up to this task?

Ivan's desperation reaches a critical point when, despite the Legend of the Grand Inquisitor, he realizes that human beings are most likely unable to restructure the world in such a way as to eliminate injustice and pointless suffering.

Unfortunately for Ivan, he does not see that his pessimistic line of reasoning is not the only way of thinking. As Job learns that the human conception of justice is not God's conceptions of justice, and the human conception of chaos and order is not God's conception of chaos and order, we need to question the tacit assumptions which structure our thinking about the meaning of life. This is exactly what Father Zosima does, and both Alyosha and Dmitri provide viable examples of an alternative approach.

Father Zosima does not try to show that the suffering of children is in any way justified. He does not cite any future harmony as a justification of such suffering. The logic of means and ends belongs to the framework of an exchange economy, while the Elder approaches the world in terms of the economy of gifts.

From children's suffering Ivan concludes that the universe is arbitrary and chaotic – thus fundamentally flawed. Father Zosima believes that the limited facts on which Ivan relies in his reasoning are not sufficient grounds for such a general conclusion. The Elder refrains from defending God or from saying that God should be blamed for this suffering. Philosophically speaking, Father Zosima does not attempt to offer any theodicy. He does not even make any determinative statement with regard to the nature of God, which we automatically take for granted: The Elder does not say anything about God's benevolence, omniscience, and omnipotence.

Nor does Father Zosima offer any theological explanation of the concept of sin. He does not say much about sin at all, yet from what he says it appears that he does not understand sin as a moral category but rather as a religious one: not as a violation of any moral prohibition, but rather as a feeling of profanes and unworthiness. This rendering of sin is closer to our understanding of chaos than of pollution, as is usually the case. Ivan ties the spilling of the blood of innocent children with pollution, and only indirectly to chaos, but Zosima sees it differently. Chaos does not necessarily mean the absence of order in the outside world, but the lack of order in ourselves. This internal chaos can result from our inability to see any unifying element which would bind various aspects of the world together. Having a profound trust in the invisible divine order, the Elder is concerned precisely with this human chaos, with our inability to feel the significance of what we say and do. This rendering of chaos is congruent with his conception of hell, by which Father Zosima understands not as a place of literal torture, but as "the suffering of being no longer able to love" (Bk. VI, Ch. 3 [i], 322).[58]

Father Zosima's message is that we should approach the issue of the meaning of life differently from Ivan. Contrary to the four firmly entrenched assumptions cited earlier, meaning does not depend on the purposes set in advance. The venerable priest suspects that God does not necessarily make the world meaningful – certainly not in the sense of the fully regulated exchange economy. If, like Rodin's "Hand of the Creator," God does not finish creation, meaning does not have to come from a firmly established rational and moral authority, operating within a well-defined system of purposes. There can be meaning without any definitive authority, without prohibitions and without a flawless system of judicial norms. There may be many things which are individually meaningful, although their meaningfulness is not derived from any general purpose or principle. Sincere gestures, such as Father Zosima's bow in front of Dmitri, or Alyosha's kiss of Ivan, contain their meaning in and of themselves. The meaning of such gestures does not derive from any external source. We experience them as meaningful, regardless of what happens in the rest of the world, or in other experiences of our individual lives.

We are beginning to grasp Dostoevsky's conception of the meaning of life. His central idea is that, even if the world as a whole does not have meaning – and we can never know whether or not this is the case – this would not prevent our human lives and experiences from being meaningful. What matters is that the world is not absurd, chaotic, or counter-purposive. Even if the world is not just, this does not make it absurd. The initial sculpting of the primordial clay out of which the world is made is in God's Hand. We are then given the gift of life, and the gift of the world, as well as freedom to shape it into something beautiful or something distorted. This freedom is based on a partial indeterminacy – Ivan would

---

58 For further discussion, see Dudley Young, *The Origins of the Sacred: The Ecstasies of Love and War*, 235. See also Pelikan, *op. cit.*, 72–74, and Fromm, *You Shall Be As Gods*, 125–40.

say "arbitrariness" – of the world. Yet Ivan confuses arbitrariness for chaos. It is true that this arbitrariness gives ample space for a display of the demonic in man, but it also creates the room for the angelic element in him. As V.V. Zenkovsky sums it up, "The impulses of freedom comprise a dialectic of evil, but also a dialectic of good."[59]

Ivan is afraid of arbitrariness and freedom, and the Grand Inquisitor eliminates freedom in his utopian society of "happy babes." Father Zosima has a different insight: While freedom may not be necessary for our acceptance of conventional morality, it is indispensable for faith. Faith is precisely our response to the arbitrariness of life – not a denial of arbitrariness, but a humble response to it. Faith is the manifestation of our trust in the invisible – even if incomplete – order of the universe. The insights of religion are based not only on the testimony of the things seen, but also on the things unseen. For Dostoevsky, this implies that, by way of faith, freedom is also necessary for any genuine meaning of life.

Whether or not something is meaningful depends on the qualities and values associated with it. Interestingly enough, and despite his strong religious orientation, Dostoevsky is not primarily preoccupied with ethical values. To display his positive philosophy of life, he wants to portray "a beautiful man." This is not just a phrase covering the moral grounds, as we have seen in the previous two chapters when we considered Dostoevsky's ladder: beauty → love → faith → hope. The confrontation with beauty, rather than the confrontation with good and evil, provides the first test of the meaningfulness of life. We appreciate beauty regardless of its use, regardless of any purpose which may or may not be attached to its creation, existence, or recognition. Beauty strikes us as meaningful, independently of the four previously cited assumptions attached to possibility of the meaning in life. In fact, beauty can make such an impression on us that we feel that even a temporary experience of exceptional beauty – natural or artistic – makes life worth living. In the words of Rémi Brague: "The simple fact that we are sensitive

---

59   V.V. Zenkovsky, "Dostoevsky's Religious and Philosophical Views," in *Dostoevsky: A Collection of Critical Essays*, ed. René Wellek, 136.

to beauty shows that, without having a permanent dwelling in the world, we are not purely strangers in it; we are guests."[60] Although the appreciation of beauty by itself does not provide a permanent dwelling in the world, in combination with our appreciation of love and with faith, we can recreate such a dwelling.

Another important point worth emphasizing is the following. Beauty is something that must be immediately and intuitively experienced in order to be known. Insofar as we talk about the conceptual grasp of beauty, the concepts in questions are not abstract and general, but concrete and intuitive – "aesthetic" – concepts. In contrast to such aesthetic concepts are what Northrop calls "postulation" concepts, which constitute a theoretical com-ponent of our knowledge of the world. Although both kinds of concepts are equally indispensable, the one being the complement of the other, in Western civilization we overvalue the concepts by postulation and assign a much lower value to intuitive concepts. In Northrop's words:

> What has happened throughout our history is that the West became so fascinated with this theoretic component and with the quest for a more and more adequate theory of its nature, that it (the West) has tended to turn the equally primary, real, and basic aesthetic component into a mere appearance and a mere handmaid, whose sole value is the conveying of the theoretic component.[61]

What also strikes us about beauty is that it is a gift. Possessing and controlling beauty are contradictions in terms. Any attempt in this direction perverts beauty into something contrary to its nature. Beauty cannot be an object or a commodity. This spe-cial nature of beauty – that it is experienced as a gift – affects our general attitude toward life. The experience of beauty spreads through our lives and enlightens the dullness of ordinary experi-ences, half-measures, compromises, and suffering. The experience

---

60 Brague, *The Wisdom of the World: The Human Experience of the Universe in Western Thought*, 224.
61 F.S.C. Northrop, *The Meeting of East and West: An Inquiry Concerning World Understanding*, 305.

of beauty does not accomplish a tangible, material change, but creates room for a spiritual reorientation of ordinary life. As an addition to the routine of human life, the experience of beauty brings a treasure, the value of which can never be assigned any price on the market.

While moral values, indispensable as they are, bind us with commands, obligations and permissions, Dostoevsky believes that they do not sufficiently "elevate" human beings. They ground us to the soil and make us "heavy," while the experience of beauty makes us "light." The appreciation of beauty fills us with new spirit. The gift of beauty recharges our vital and spiritual energy and stimulates in us a desire to participate in life, not only by receiving but also by sharing and giving. Thus, for Dostoevsky, the appreciation of beauty leads to love, and through the sharing and giving of love, it leads to faith, to trust in life and the whole of the creation. This trust in both the visible and the invisible aspects of the world is possible even though the path of life includes meaningless suffering and even though we cannot know the world's ultimate destination or purposes. These aesthetic and spiritual values do not impose anything on us, nor do they demand anything except our responsiveness to the world. When we are responsive, our participation in the world is the experience of pure joy, or, as Father Zosima, calls it, "paradise on earth." Such experiences bring us a gift and make us feel that our lives are a gift which we must appreciate and use. The highest value of life is the "spending" of life.

This experience of the joy of being alive is for Dostoevsky the crucial connection between beauty and faith (via love), between the aesthetic and the spiritual values. This is exactly the point at which Ivan becomes lost and bewildered. He starts from the widely accepted position that the Holy is related to the True (by means of the intellect) and to the Good (by means of the will). Resolved to discover the True and the Good, Ivan cannot understand the "irrationality" of the world, nor can he appreciate a world in which justice is so manifestly violated by the senseless suffering of children. Such a world appears to him as both unjust and incorrigible, and Ivan, who does not recognize any rational or ethical rules in this cruel game of life, decides to return his ticket.

Jaroslav Pelikan recognizes Dostoevsky's shift from the usual association of the spiritual (Holy) with the cognitive (Truth) and the ethical (Good):

> In delineating the distinctiveness of the Holy as a reality far transcending the morally Good, Dostoevsky succeeded in stating a profoundly Christian judgment. It may be easier to identify the Holy and the Good, it may be more practical, it may even be more rational and normal to do so. But the Christian faith does not pretend to be easy or rational or normal. It claims only to be an account of how the Holy has addressed himself to men decisively in Jesus Christ. This was the insight that Dostoevsky was determined to carry out, even if it should cost him his sanity. In the twilight zone of his insanity he rediscovered some of the most profound implications of the Christian gospel. As a fool for Christ, he directs those implications at us, too, calling us into that fellowship with God in Christ which reaches beyond all morality and all ethics, the fellowship he knew in the madness of the Holy.[62]

Whether or not Dostoevsky was a "fool for Christ" is open for debate. He was certainly hoping to be one. Of more significance is Pelikan's claim regarding Dostoevsky's effort to show "how the Holy has addressed itself to men decisively in Jesus Christ." According to Book VI, this point is not correct. When we think again about Father Zosima's "talks and homilies," the most striking thing about them is the disappearance of Christ. The Grand Inquisitor denies Christ and makes a pact with the devil. In his emphasis on Mother Earth, Father Zosima mysteriously sidesteps discussion of the divine Creator and of the Son of God. Perhaps this can be justified by the context: The Inquisitor's insistence on justice is countered by the Elder's love for the entire creation. Regardless of their respective merits, both visions assume that human beings are equal and try to convince us of the best way to realize that equality. In the Grand Inquisitor's version, every person has

62 Pelikan, *op. cit.*, 83–84.

equal rights in the eyes of justice: Every person is innocent until proven guilty. Alternatively, the Elder sees that the Mother of God loves each of her children equally. She needs no ethical precepts or moral laws, no utilitarian calculus or categorical imperative, to approach every child with unconditional motherly patience and forgiveness.

What is glaringly missing from Books V and VI of *The Brothers Karamazov* – although not for the rest of the novel – is the recognition that human beings are both equal and not equal. The emphasis on equality has overshadowed any striving toward the worthiest, the purest, and the noblest. The majestic icon of The Virgin of Vladimir completes this picture and corrects its one-sided emphasis of equality. Besides the caring and loving Mother of God herself, there is no person more unique than her Son. Just as being a mother and a virgin are no longer mutually exclusive, a similar paradoxical duality of the worldly and the divine is present in the person of the Son. He is a child who – as his face on the icon reveals – is not a child. Despite the body of a child, he is a mature and wise man dressed in adult clothes. His luminous face and golden tunic indicate that this person is truly the Word of God, full of majesty and splendor.

Contemplating the Child of the Virgin on this twelfth-century icon is, as Henri Nouwen points out in the words that resemble Father Zosima's homilies, like discovering a light that has always been there but could not been seen because of our blindness. The light that shines on the face of the child comes both from without and from within: "The light illuminates and gives warmth. There is no sudden, intrusive flash, but the gradual appearance of a tender and radiant intimacy."[63] This tender embrace of the mother and the child contains no forbidden secret of the Freudian Oedipus complex. This embrace reconciles the differences of the male and the female, of the ruler and the ruled, of the divine and the human. As Nouwen puts it, "It is the portrayal of the mysterious interchange between God and humanity made

63 Nouwen, *op. cit.*, 38–39.

possible by the Incarnation of the Word."[64] One of Father Zosima's central messages to his followers deals with the appreciation of this interchange:

> When you are alone, pray. Love to throw yourself down on the earth and kiss it. Kiss the earth and love it, tirelessly, insatiably, love all men, love all things, seek this rapture and ecstasy. Water the earth with the tears of your joy, and love those tears. Do not be ashamed of this ecstasy, treasure it, for it is a gift from God, a great gift, and it is not given to many, but to those who are chosen (Bk. VI, Ch. 3 [h], 322).

Dostoevsky does not conceptually articulate this joyful ecstasy, although it shines through his entire novel. We can help him by developing what Nietzsche introduces in his *Thus Spoke Zarathustra* as "*schenkende Tugend*," variously translated as "radiant virtue," or "bestowing virtue," or (most literally) "gift-giving virtue."[65] "Tell me," Zarathustra addresses his disciples, "how did gold come to have the highest value? Because it is uncommon and useless and shining and mellow in luster; it always bestows itself." This radiant, bestowing virtue is very different from material values and goods, for we cannot possess it. The one who bestows a spiritual gift does not become poorer but stands as the recipient of a gift. In addition to that, such a person enhances the spiritual insights of those who accept his gift. In motherly love for our neighbors, there is dispensing because of the other's need and our awareness of that need. The task of loving our neighbors is their well being. Radiant virtue dispenses values worthless for immediate practical needs. It invites the opening of our eyes to the riches hidden everywhere. It encourages our participation in the fullness of the real. Deviating from Nietzsche, Dostoevsky insists that (as the Elder expresses it), "Your work is for the whole, your

---

64 *Ibid.*, 40.
65 Nietzsche introduces this virtue in the last section of Part I of *Thus Spoke Zarathustra*. In my presentation of it, I will rely more on Hartmann's analysis of it in chapter XXXI of the second volume of his *Ethics*, rather than on Nietzsche, who turns it toward his idea of *Übermensch*. For a valuable criticism of Nietzsche's philosophy of life, see Albert Schweitzer, *The Philosophy of Civilization*, 243–48, and Pelikan, *Fools for Christ*, 118–44.

deed is for the future. Never seek a reward, for great is your reward on earth without that: your spiritual joy, which only the righteous obtain" (Bk. VI, Ch. 3 [h], 322).

Our spiritual joy is our reward, and this reward is unlike what we usually understand by "reward." The serviceable, useful, utilitarian values do for us nothing more than what is needed. Radiant virtue does the opposite. In its presence our hearts and souls are filled. No one goes away from the person with radiant virtue except laden with gifts, says Nicolai Hartmann, yet no one can say what he or she has received. "One only feels that in such men the meaning of life is somehow perceptibly fulfilled, the meaning which one else-where seeks in vain. And one feels that in mere communion with [them] something of this meaning is carried over into one's own personality."[66]

Radiant virtue is rare: "A single individual can be the giver of meaning for a whole world, in so far as it participates in him. A life in which only one such exists becomes full of significance for everybody."[67] Christians believe that this person is Jesus Christ, Hartmann thinks of Socrates as another appropriate example, and Dostoevsky would like us to count Father Zosima among those who radiate this virtue into the world. Regardless of who that person is, what matters the most is the impact that such a person has on others. To quote Hartmann again,

> [T]o the imparter of spiritual goods it is not the just, the truthful, the loving or the faithful man who is the worthi-est, but he who receives with an open heart, the unspoilt spirit which is still capable of unlearning everything. That is why the man of radiant virtue loves those who are ethically imperfect, unripe, unspent and still flexible, with the love peculiar to one who has mellowed, is blessed and is filled with gratitude. He is the eternal *erastes* [lover] of youth.[68]

66 Hartmann, *Ethics*, vol. II, 336. In *The Human Condition*, 153–54, Hannah Arendt offers even sharper criticism of all attempts to base life-meaning on utility.

67 Hartmann, *op. cit.*, 339.

68 *Ibid.*, 338.

Hartmann is again thinking of Socrates surrounded with Athenian boys, but in this context we can substitute Zosima and Alyosha. We cannot all be persons of radiant virtue, for this indeed is something rare. Nonetheless, we can all cultivate the spirit of openness and maintain the willingness to unlearn what we have mistakenly conceived. We should wish for nothing more than humility and openness, the pure heart and the wakeful mind which will allow us to endure happiness and disappointment, victory and defeat, love as well as suffering.

We now come to see what Dostoevsky suspects all along. Life derives its meaning from useless virtues and values, such as the esthetic and the spiritual. It is our willing participation in the world through which the experience of such meaning-bestowing worth is possible and which makes life meaningful.

Ivan, like Oedipus, expects a different lesson. By virtue of his intellect, Oedipus manages to solve the riddle of the Sphinx. Symbolically speaking, he overcomes the beastly part of his human nature. Oedipus's status becomes more elevated when he becomes the king. The chorus warns him that he is the first among humans but not equal to the gods, but Oedipus does not appreciate this warning. Has he not only defeated the world below but also the world above?

In the same century in which Sophocles lived, the sophist Protagoras declared: "Man, not gods, is the measure of all things." Oedipus takes this "oracle" to his heart: Man is the center of the universe, for his intelligence overcomes all obstacles. He is the master of his destiny and a self-made ruler who can attain prosperity and happiness on his own. One of Oedipus's favorite words is "measure" in its numerous variations: measuring, number, calculation. These are the most important inventions that have allowed man to overcome his savage nature and establish his own dominance. In Aeschylus's drama *Prometheus*, this mythical civilizer of human life counts numbers (and not just fire) among his foremost gifts to human beings: "And number, too, I invented outstanding among clever devices."[69] "Measure" and "number" belong to the very core of

69   Quoted from Knox's article, "Sophocles' Oedipus," 8.

the exchange economy, and Oedipus's life – indeed, any human life – is full of equations. Of those equations some are more consequential than others. Oedipus confidently measures himself against gods and the result is not favorable. Man is not the measure of all things. Oedipus must learn that the riddle of the Sphinx is just a preamble. The tricky riddle is: What is man? If man is different from beasts yet not equal to gods, what or who is he? In *Oedipus the King*, Sophocles' intelligent and persistent hero fails to resolve this second, far more important riddle.

It is astonishing how similar to Oedipus's journey Ivan's path is. He does not want to identify humanity with the beastly passions of his father, for human beings are not meant to live according to the words: "Everything is permissible." Hubris seduces Oedipus to believe that he is smarter than Apollo, and Ivan similarly believes he can outsmart the imperfect architect of the world and recreate creation. The result of this effort only shows how little Ivan understands the nature of humanity. There is something profoundly misleading, dangerous, even tragic, in our attempts to solve the riddle of human nature by an exclusive reliance upon the intellect.

To help Oedipus and Ivan, Dostoevsky could have restructured the riddle of the Sphinx: Yes, man can walk on four legs (as a child), or on three (as an old man), or on two (as an adult). But which stage of his life is the most representative of his humanity?

The answer to this riddle is: all of them. The benefit of posing the riddle in this way is to help us see what Oedipus and Ivan have difficulty grasping: Our nature is not one, singular, well defined, or finished. We have various and contradictory impulses, which sometimes make us look like beasts, at others moments like gods. One, as much as the other, is representative of our nature riddled with paradoxes. Yet however baffling the nature of humanity may be, it is different from either the beastly or the divine nature – it is human. That is what Ivan overlooks when he ties the meaning of life too closely with the riddle of meaningless suffering. Ivan never asks: Why is there beauty in the world? Why is there love and faith? Why is it that people give gifts to each other? When we take these other aspects of our lives into account, we notice that meaningless suffering does not exclusively determine the meaning of human life. Moreover, Ivan associates meaningless suffering too closely with the beastly aspect of our nature, when in fact the worst suffering is produced by human pride.[70] "You shall be like gods," the devil whispers in man's ear and seduces him to pretend to be what and who he is not. Ivan, who poses the riddle of meaningless suffering, does not progress with the puzzle of the meaning of human life. He never appreciates Alyosha's instruction to "love life more than its meaning" (Bk. V, Ch. 3, 231).

Ivan approaches the issues of life's meaning with the four previously mentioned untenable assumptions. Despite these assumptions, to be meaningful, the world does not have to consist of an all-rational order, nor should its meaningfulness be manifested in ethical categories. Furthermore, the meaning of life is not contained in some pre-determined purposes, imparted in the world as a whole at the moment of its creation. Creation itself is not complete but an ongoing process. After the initial shaping by the Divine Hand, the meaning of life is bestowed from inside, through the confrontation with conflicting values and through struggles with different sides of our nature. Finding that meaning is not a discovery of something new, but a continuous recovery of what has been and what we have neglected or forgotten. This is why we become puzzled by the riddle of meaning most strongly when we lose something or someone of value. The experience of loss sharpens our appreciation for what was there for a long time and what – because of its continuous presence – we tended to take for granted.

In Dostoevsky's last novel, all three brothers experience loss, when pain and suffering sharpen their vision and focus their attention on the central spiritual goods of life and its meaning. For Ivan, such a moment occurs after Smerdyakov's suicide: He finally discerns to what extent he had desired his father's death, and to what extent he had been Smerdyakov's accomplice in the shameful affair. When he realizes what he has done, Ivan collapses under the weight of his own guilt. He does not lack the resolve to confront the riddle of the meaning of life, nor does he lack intelligence or courage.

70 As Joyce Carol Oates puts it, "To kill with one's brain is evil, but to kill with one's passion is excusable"; *op. cit.* 95.

What he lacks is the appreciation of beauty, love of life, and faith in the invisible.

For Alyosha, the transforming moment occurs after the death of the Elder, when he almost betrays his beloved teacher. Shaken by Grushenka's onion, Alyosha's faith is reconfirmed and is nourished not by an external source (such as Father Zosima), but from within his own being and through his own connectedness with Mother Earth. Alyosha then kneels down and kisses the earth. From that moment, even the death of those he dearly loves will not prevent him from loving and affirming life.

For Dmitri, the awakening occurs after the murder of his own father. Again, Grushenka is instrumental in this transformation, this time by tying her fate to the destiny of the unjustly accused man. Within a few hours, Dmitri swings from almost killing his own father and Grigory, to experiencing his first genuine feeling of love for Grushenka and the deepest sense of compassion for the "wee one." When Dmitri wakes up from his nightmarish dream and finds a pillow under his head, his gratitude for life becomes virtually endless, regardless of the suffering which he will have to experience for the next twenty years. He realizes that life is full of joy, despite meaningless suffering. Dmitri intuitively grasps what Alyosha puts in words: "I think that everyone should love life before everything else in the world" (Bk. V, Ch. 3, 231).

There is one last riddle to encounter: Is there a genuine hero in *The Brothers Karamazov*?

Ivan is the novel's tragic hero. Alyosha is the nominal one. If there is a real, positive hero in this novel, it must be Dmitri. Whether or not that happens against Dostoevsky's intentions, Dmitri is more alive and more human than either of the other two brothers. Dmitri is beastly. He is also divine. He is a living contradiction. With his noble heart and uncontrollable passions Dmitri sins, but he also genuinely repents his sins. What makes him heroic is that at the moment of his greatest fall, Dmitri accepts his responsibility and lovingly extends his hands even to those who punish him.

When we think of Ivan and his tragic fate, our eyes turn downward. With Alyosha, they are lifted up again. With Dmitri, things are different. His eyes look straight into the world, into this great and incomprehensible mystery of life. Dmitri may never find out the meaning of his life; he may never answer the riddle that life throws at him. Yet in his pursuit of all values, positive and negative, Dmitri does not search for the meaning of life but the experience of being alive. He does not ask what the meaning of life is but senses that it is he who is being asked. Dmitri recognizes that he is questioned by life, and that he must answer with his own life. His answer consists in reverence and awe for life – he serves this life without any demands for rights, or pretensions of greatness. Dmitri is the incarnation of the affirmation of life, even in the face of evil. If there is a hero in *The Brothers Karamazov*, Dmitri is it.

8

The Unwritten Novel

A Prodigal Son Returns

Dostoevsky's Ideas for a New Novel

The Brothers Karamazov is an elaboration of the biblical words: "Verily, verily, I say unto you, except a corn of wheat fall into the ground and die, it abideth alone: but if it die, it bringeth forth much fruit" (John 12:24). Dostoevsky tries to convince us that death – of a nine-year-old Ilyusha, of Father Zosima and Fyodor Karamazov, or any other death – need not be the last word. A loss is not just a loss, for it brings closer those who remain. A newfound spirit ties Ilyusha's friends together, so that the conclusion of the novel is also a new beginning. Alyosha does not turn his grief over the death of an innocent child into anger toward God, as his brother Ivan does, but has to show the confused friends of Ilyusha that life can have a meaning even in tragedy. To these twelve boys, Alyosha's message is: Cherish the memory of your friend and this loss will make you more sensitive toward each other and toward all human beings. Despite such blows as the death of a dear friend, the boys should not be afraid of life; when they do good and rightful things, life is also good and worth living. Faith in life and dedication to noble deeds are stronger than death.

Kolya, the most intelligent among the boys, suspects that more than faith in life and noble deeds are needed to overcome the loss incurred by death; perhaps only a new birth – rebirth or resurrection – can conquer death. Trustingly, Kolya asks Alyosha whether it can "really be true, as religion says, that we shall all rise from the dead, and come to life, and see one another again, and everyone, and Ilyushechka?" Alyosha – "half laughing, half in ecstasy" – replies: "Certainly we shall rise, certainly we shall see and gladly, joyfully tell one another all that has been" (Epilogue, Ch. 3, 776).

How will the lives of the boys unfold? Will they meet again, as Alyosha promises them, or are these just the words of consolation we customarily exchange in such situations? What will become of Alyosha? We do not have definitive answers.

Physically and mentally exhausted after the completion of *The Brothers Karamazov*, Dostoevsky planned to write a sequel-novel after a two-year break. Since he did not leave developed sketches for this new novel, any attempt to reconstruct what his final work would be like must rely on the testimony of his contemporaries, particularly his wife. Yet all that Anna Grigorievna tells us in her *Reminiscences* about the planned novel is that "almost all former characters would reappear after an interval of twenty years, almost in our own day, after accomplishing and experiencing much in their lives."[1]

In the "Author's Preface" for *The Brothers Karamazov*, Dostoevsky mentions two times that the second part of the narrative will resume after thirteen years, not twenty. It is, of course, possible that he later changes his mind. Leonid Grossman quotes Dostoevsky's wife (from a source he does not identify) as saying that, "Twenty years were to have elapsed since the last pages of the first volume. The action had moved into the 1880s. Alyosha was no longer a youth, but a mature man, who had already gone through a complicated emotional drama with Liza Khokhlakova. Dmitri was on his way back from penal servitude."[2]

Nina Hoffmann, an Austrian biographer of Dostoevsky, provides additional and more intriguing details. Her book on Dostoevsky

---

1   Anna Dostoevsky, *Reminiscences*, 340.
2   Leonid Grossman, *Dostoevsky: A Biography*, 586.

(published in 1899) is based partly on personal interviews with Anna Grigorievna, and she quotes Dostoevsky's wife as giving the following account of the plot for the future novel:

> It was the author's plan for Alyosha, by Father Zosima's last testament, to go out in the world, to take upon himself its suffering and its guilt. He marries Liza and then leaves her for the beautiful sinner Grushenka, who arouses the "Karamazov sensuality" in him. After a stormy period of moral straying, doubt, and negation Alyosha, left without his own children, returns to the monastery once more. There he surrounds himself with children and dedicates the rest of his life to them, loves them truly, teaches and guides them.[3]

A significantly different account of the plot comes from A.S. Suvorin, who visited Dostoevsky a few times during the last year of the writer's life. According to Suvorin's testimony, Dostoevsky was planning to "take [Alyosha] through the monastery and make him a revolutionary. He would commit a political crime. He would be executed. He was to search for the truth and in those searchings would naturally have become a revolutionary." Joseph Frank quotes Suvorin as saying that Alyosha would become "a type of Russian Socialist," and also reports that Alyosha would "become an anarchist. And my pure Alyosha will kill the Tsar."[4]

James Rice argues that this line of thought should be taken as Dostoevsky's definitive idea for his last novel.[5] Rice rightly points out that during the last few years of Dostoevsky's life there were several (unsuccessful) attempts to assassinate the Tsar – until the assassins succeeded a month after Dostoevsky died. This topic was certainly of great interest to Dostoevsky who often ties the themes of his novels to current events. Yet we also know that Dostoevsky frequently changes his mind about the course of his novels and

3   N. Hoffmann, *Th. M. Dostojewski. Eine biographische Studie*, 427.
4   Joseph Frank, *Dostoevsky: The Mantle of the Prophet, 1871–1881*, 727.
5   James L. Rice, "Dostoevsky's Endgame: The Projected Sequel to *The Brothers Karamazov*," *Russian History/Histoire Russe*, 33:2006, 45–62.

ends up relegating the events that initiate his desire to write a novel into the background (e.g., *The Possessed*).[6]

Besides these two lines of thought with regard to the content of Dostoevsky's never-written novel, there is one more. After Dostoevsky's famous "Pushkin speech," on June 8, 1880, while he is still working on the concluding books of *The Brothers Karamazov* and half a year before he dies, he is reported as saying this to several people: "I will write a new novel, 'The Children' (*Deti*), and then I will die."[7] Alexei M. Slavitsky, a writer of books on children, with whom Dostoevsky discussed various issues related to the lives of children, confirms this. He testifies that Dostoevsky was planning a novel, "The Children," in which the main characters were to be the children of the previous novel.[8] Slavitsky had helped Dostoevsky visit schools and corrective institutions and recommended to him what pedagogical works to read, even before he began writing *The Brothers Karamazov*. Dostoevsky inquired with Slavitsky whether it is possible for a child to lie between the rails under the train, as Kolya Krasotkin does in his novel. They also discussed the idea of founding a brotherhood of children, an idea Dostoevsky toyed with already in *The Idiot* (Bk. I, Ch. 6).

As Alyosha is able to turn around the boys who are initially fighting against Ilyusha, Prince Myshkin manages to bring the village children to help and love the prosecuted girl, Marie. The prince experiences far less success with uniting adults in St. Petersburg, and his "work" only contributes to an already existing moral and spiritual disorientation. Alyosha is similarly successful with children, but not with adults – he does not manage to prevent the

---

6   As Geir Kjetsaa points out, "It was possible at this time that he had the idea of writing a sequel to *The Brothers Karamazov* in which Alyosha would appear as a revolutionary and be executed for a political crime. Suvorin's account of this plan is, however, far from being authenticated. Recent studies of his diary have set a question mark over the word 'executed', and indeed such a denouncement would have been quite uncharacteristic of Dostoevsky"; *Fyodor Dostoevsky: A Writer's Life*, 355.

7   Quoted in *The Dostoevsky Archive*, ed. Peter Sekirin, 252.

8   Quoted in Sekirin, *ibid.*, and in Anna Dostoevsky, *op. cit.*, 410n1. See also Dostoevsky's letter to V.V. Mikhaylov, March 16, 1878; and Frank, *op. cit.*, 390.

murder of his father Fyodor, the madness of his brother Ivan, or the penal servitude of his brother Dmitri. Will Alyosha be more successful when he himself matures? Furthermore, can a brotherhood of children serve as a model for a brotherhood of adults? Can there be any brotherhood of adults if they abandon Christ? These are the issues that Dostoevsky wanted to write about in his last, never-written novel.

The reminiscences of Dostoevsky's contemporaries with regard to what that novel would look like are not consistent, but they point toward a few recognizable directions. The novel would indeed be about the twelve boys, and it would show them as they matured in twenty years. As Dostoevsky promises in the "Author's Preface" for *The Brothers Karamazov*, Alyosha will take the central stage in the new novel. He will develop before our eyes by becoming a "great sinner." Whether this would involve leaving his wedded wife Liza Khokhlakova for Dmitri's wife Grushenka, or an attempt to assassinate the Tsar, or both, Alyosha's trials will be greater than those of Dmitri and Ivan. Dostoevsky says of Raskolnikov at the end of *Crime and Punishment* that "he did not know that the new life would not be given him for nothing, that he would have to pay dearly for it, that it would cost him great striving, great suffering" (Epilogue, 430). Nothing less awaits Alyosha. From the beginning of *The Brothers Karamazov*, Alyosha's defining characteristic is that he is consecrated. This devotion and striving toward the highest values will push him to transgress many accepted boundaries. But what will happen after Alyosha's transgression?

If Alyosha is to assassinate the Tsar literally and not merely symbolically, he will almost certainly be executed, and that would be the end of the story. This course of events would follow the pattern of "crime and punishment," which Marcel Proust claims to be the defining characteristic of all of Dostoevsky's novels.[9] Yet, as we have already seen, even in the novel the title of which is translated as *Crime and Punishment*, Dostoevsky is interested in giving Raskolnikov a second chance – for repentance and rebirth. It is, then, more likely that – no matter what boundaries he ends up

9   Marcel Proust, "Dostoievski," *On Art and Literature*, 381.

transgressing – Alyosha will also get an opportunity for repentance and rebirth. He will lose his innocence and will become a prodigal son (*bludny syn*) in a distant land, but will be given a chance to return. Alyosha will have a chance to become a hero – not of a revolutionary type, but of a new kind more consistent with Dostoevsky's overall worldview, which he failed to fully develop.

Exactly what kind of a hero? A clue may be found in the last day of Dostoevsky's life. Joseph Frank gives us an admirable account of it. Aware that his hours are numbered, Dostoevsky asks his family – his wife Anna Grigorievna, daughter Lyubov, and son Fedya – to gather around him.

> He requested that his copy of the New Testament be given to his son Fedya and that the parable of the Prodigal Son be read to the children. Lyubov later recalled him telling them that, if they should ever commit a crime (*prestuplenie*, which has a wider meaning than a merely legal offense) to trust God as their Father, plead with Him for forgiveness, and be certain that He would rejoice in their repentance, just as the father had done on the return of the Prodigal Son. It was this parable of transgression, repentance, and forgiveness that he wished to leave as a last heritage to his children, and it may well be seen as his own ultimate understanding of the meaning of his life and the message of his work.[10]

Frank is right in reconstructing what final message Dostoevsky intended for his children and his readers. Dostoevsky always loved the biblical tale of the prodigal son. Frank does not stress enough, however, that it is precisely this legend of the prodigal son, rather than the usually favored parables of Prometheus or Faust, that Dostoevsky takes to be the most revealing of human nature, of our destiny and our hopes. Although the tale of the prodigal son was well known, Dostoevsky believes that it has not been properly understood nor taken seriously by modern intellectuals. This conviction may explain a remarkable fact that the only time this

10 Frank, *op. cit.*, 748.

story is mentioned in *The Brothers Karamazov*, Ivan not only misrepresents its first element – transgression – but also omits the last member of the sequence: transgression, repentance, and forgiveness.

In the section entitled "Rebellion," Ivan presents to Alyosha the story of Richard, who has been recently executed in Geneva. As an illegitimate child, at the age of six Richard is given to some mountain shepherds to work for them. They send him out to tend the flock, and Richard grows up like a wild beast. "Like the prodigal son in the Gospel," Ivan narrates, "he wanted terribly to eat at least the mash given to the pigs being fattened for market, but he was not given even that and was beaten when he stole from the pigs, and thus he spent his whole childhood and his youth, until he grew up and, having gathered strength, went out to steal for himself" (Bk. IV, Ch. 4, 239–40). After robbing a man and killing him, Richard is caught and condemned to death.

Before the execution, some philanthropic ladies and members of various Christian brotherhoods teach Richard to read and write, expound the Gospel to him, and urge him to repent. Richard does, and all of Geneva is stirred to tears: "You are our brother, grace has descended upon you!" (Bk. IV, Ch. 4, 240). Richard himself could hardly control his emotions. On the day of the execution, Richard weeps and keeps repeating: "This is the best day of my life, I am going to the Lord!" (Bk. IV, Ch. 4, 240). The whole city of Geneva gathers at the plaza in front of the cathedral to see Richard escorted to the scaffold on the cart of shame. "And so," Ivan concludes, "covered with the kisses of his brothers, brother Richard is dragged up onto the scaffold, laid down on the guillotine, and his head is whacked off in brotherly fashion, forasmuch as grace has descended upon him, too" (Bk. IV, Ch. 4, 240).

The word "prodigal" derives from the Latin prefix *pro-*, which means "for," "forth," and "forward," and the Latin *ago*, which means "to act," "to drive," "to move," or "to do." "Prodigal" thus means "to move forth," "to move forward." More generally, "prodigal" is related to moving beyond the present boundaries; it is related to transgressions (of which Dostoevsky spoke to his children), and also to pilgrimage and progress, or pilgrimage in search of progress.

Ivan's story of Richard reveals his lack of understanding of the biblical tale: Richard is a victim of the unfortunate circumstances; he is no pilgrim, nor does he transgress the existing boundaries in any search of progress. A more appropriate example of the prodigal son would be Raskolnikov, who rebels against the existing boundaries in order to test the limits of his humanity. A pilgrim is someone who travels far away from home, who wonders through the fields and over the countryside to distant lands, often to the Holy Land. When Raskolnikov confesses his crime at the crossroads and bows to kiss the earth, one witness says that he may be a pilgrim on his way to Jerusalem (Pt. IV, Ch. 8, 413).

Strictly speaking, nothing in the word "prodigal" indicates the process of return, although this is how we usually understand the phrase "prodigal son." Richard finds his way back from the wilderness, and that is what, in Ivan's eyes, makes him a prodigal son. He is reintegrated into a Christian society, only to be executed by his "brothers."

I do not believe that Ivan's story of Richard indicates what the end of Alyosha's life would look like, for the crucial elements of forgiveness and reconciliation are missing from Ivan's narrative. For a more likely continuation of Alyosha's life it may be better to turn to the Gospel's version of the prodigal son. It is a tale of a wealthy father with two sons. The younger asks the father to give him his share of the estate, and when the broken-hearted father divides the property between them, the younger son gathers everything he has and takes off for a distant country. There he soon squanders all his money on a life of debauchery. To survive, he hires himself out with one of the local farmers who employs him to feed his pigs. Penniless and hungry, he wants to fill himself with the mash the pigs are eating, but no one would let him have the pig food. Hitting the bottom of his desperation and dying of hunger, the son remembers how his father's servants have all the food they want. He decides to return home and repent: "Father, I have sinned against heaven and before you; I no longer deserve to be called your son. Treat me as one of your hired men."[11]

---

11 All quoted passages from the biblical parable of the prodigal son come from Luke, 15:11–32.

Seeing his lost son return, the father is overtaken by pity. He embraces the son and kisses him. The repenting son expresses his shame, and the father orders his servants to wash and cloth the son. "Bring the calf we have been fattening, and kill it," orders the joyful father, "we will celebrate by having a feast, because this son of mine was dead and has come back to life; he was lost and is found."

The elder son is then working in the field, and on his way home he hears music and dancing. One of the servants tells him the reason for the celebration, and the angry son refuses to enter into his father's house. The father comes out and urges him to join them, but the elder son declines: "All these years I have slaved for you and never once disobeyed any orders of yours, yet you never offered me so much as a kid for me to celebrate with my friends. But, for this son of yours, when he comes back after swallowing up your property – he and his loose women – you kill the calf we had been fattening."

The father lovingly responds to his angry child: "My son, you are with me always, and all I have is yours. But it was only right we should celebrate and rejoice, because your brother here was dead and has come to life; he was lost and is found."

If this story of the prodigal son is to provide the model for Dostoevsky's novel, we get a better idea of how he intends to structure it. Dostoevsky does not accidentally mention to his children in the last moments of his life that they may transgress the existing boundaries. With the psychological shrewdness he possessed, he could have told them that, in order to grow into mature human beings, they must transgress many boundaries. Willingly or not, we all have to leave the parental garden protecting us. Life is a trial on which we are severely tested, so severely that it is impossible not to transgress some boundaries of the permissible. But just as death is not the last word, neither is transgression. Our humanity is tested through temptations which lure us over the borders of the permissible, but a far more difficult challenge is to find our way back to community with other human beings and with God.

Dostoevsky believes that repentance is both more difficult and more important than transgression, just as showing mercy is more difficult and more important than the insistence on justice. Not righteousness but repenting and forgiving are the true ordeals of our humanity. Saying: "Father, I do not deserve to be your son," are among the most difficult words to pronounce. Yet if we are capable of genuine repentance, we may also hope for forgiveness; we may hope to be granted a homecoming and a second chance.

Leaving Home and Returning Home

I do not know whether Dostoevsky ever saw Rembrandt's painting "The Return of the Prodigal Son"; he could have. Catherine the Great acquired it in 1766 for the Hermitage Museum in St. Petersburg. The painting is still there – imposing and majestic, so human and yet so otherworldly. Being an avid visitor of art collections, Dostoevsky was familiar with several other works of Rembrandt. In this particular painting, "The Return of the Prodigal Son," he would have recognized some of the themes and insights that also inspire his last works.

Rembrandt has left countless drawings and paintings which deal with the biblical parables. "The Return of the Prodigal Son," painted shortly before his death, is his last and most monumental religious painting. Rembrandt is then sixty-two-years old and feels that his death is approaching. The painting is a reflection on his life, which, like Dostoevsky's own, was often far from easy or pleasant. Three of Rembrandt's children die in infancy, and the only son that lives (Titus), dies eleven months before his father. Rembrandt also has to bury his wedded wife Saskia and two other women with whom he lives after the death of his wife. It is also very likely that Titus's death occurs while Rembrandt is working on this painting, which he never manages to complete.

The Russian phrase for "prodigal son" – *bludny syn* – literally means "sinful son."[12] Just as Dostoevsky himself must have often felt like a sinner, so did Rembrandt. His earlier well-known painting, "Self-Portrait with Saskia," (on which he with one hand embraces Saskia who sits on his lap, and cheers with a glass

---

12 This is how Dostoevsky uses this phrase in *The House of the Dead* (Part I, Ch. 1, 37–38), when he describes the parricide which inspired the central theme of *The Brothers Karamazov*.

of wine with another) is also a portrayal of the prodigal son.[13] Especially in the early stages of his marriage to Saskia, who is from a wealthy family, Rembrandt does not shy away from any pleasure of the flesh. He lives in a grand style, spending money carelessly. When Saskia dies (one year after giving birth to Titus), Rembrandt finds himself in serious debt and is forced to declare bankruptcy. The rest of his life brings more losses and disappointments, but also insights into the most important values in human life. Rembrandt never again squandered his money on a life of debauchery.

When Ivan narrates the story of Richard, he ties it to the biblical parable of the prodigal son for superficial reasons. Richard wants to eat the pig mash; he is the lowest of the low. This is just an external correlation with the biblical narrative. Henri Nouwen points toward a more essential aspect of the story: "I am a prodigal son every time I search for unconditional love where it cannot be found."[14] For Nouwen, the parable of the prodigal son is not about our youthful flight and squandering of money but about the highest human strivings. It is about the strivings which get misdirected and lead to failure and waste, unless followed by repentance and forgiveness. The prodigal son leaves his father's home on his own, not out of a sheer whim, but because of one of our deepest psychological needs – to search for our own place under the sun. The separation from the father's home is as necessary as it is painful. When the prodigal demands his part of the inheritance while his father is still alive, he betrays a common desire that Ivan expresses in court: "Who doesn't wish for his father death . . . ?" (Bk. XII, Ch. 5, 686). The point of such desire is not a literal but a symbolic parricide: My father is the obstacle in my way; I must break away from him, from his home, and from his values. I must go to a distant country, where I am not my father's son and where people will not have the

---

13 This painting (c. 1635) is alternatively called "Self-portrait with Saskia" and "The Prodigal Son with a Whore." Dostoevsky saw this painting in Dresden's *Gemälde Galerie*, where he also saw, for example, Raphael's "Sistine Madonna" and Claude's "Acis and Galatea."

14 Henri Nouwen, *The Return of the Prodigal Son: A Story of Homecoming*, 43.

same expectations of me that my father does. I must go to a place where people will judge me for who *I* am.

The prodigal's desire for the father's symbolic death and his separation from father's home are not necessarily sinful; the prodigal's journey is a human journey, the striving for the establishment of our own personality. This journey goes on from the time of Adam and Eve, Cain and Abel, and it will continue as long as human beings search for the realization of their potential.[15] This is not the story of Richard, but this is what Alyosha is supposed to go through in the new novel.

Leaving the father's home is not easy, but being on our own is even more difficult. At first, being alone may feel like liberation. Gradually it dawns upon us that there is something different going on, especially if we strive for the noblest and the purest. The imperfections of the world and the deficiencies of our own nature hit us hard, and disillusionment becomes the prevailing mood. The seeker of the truth and the pursuer of the highest meaning of life, such as Alyosha, will hit a wall, the same wall of which the underground man warns us and of which Ivan bitterly complains. What to do next? What to do when life does not appear meaningful any more? When he finds himself in front of the darkest abyss, Alyosha must find a way to turn around. Dostoevsky knows that this is the most difficult thing to do.

Why expect that Alyosha will be able to do something that Ivan cannot? Because Alyosha's primary attitude toward life is consecration. This attitude manifests itself through a strong belief in the natural and supernatural order; it involves a trust in life to unfold as it should and a trust in the Father-God. Ivan's attitude is that of a rebel, of someone who refuses that faith in the world and its ruler. The only serious alternatives to Alyosha's trust are the wish to rearrange the world by means of reason on the one hand, or the desperation in the face of impotence on the other. Ivan swings from the former to the latter: After he realizes that reason is not an adequate means for the understanding of life, and even less for

15 Martin Buber claims that to "decide for the 'good' . . . means to set out in the direction of the divine"; *Good and Evil*, 87. In *Between Man and Man*, 78, he defines 'good' as the movement in the direction of home.

mastering the world, Ivan abandons his Grand Inquisitor's ambition and intends to "return his ticket."

In the major part of the unwritten novel Alyosha, Kolya, and the other boys will probably try to improve and master the world. If not the other boys, at least Alyosha will come to realize that this is not possible, that our continuous efforts to conquer the world only increase our *hubris* and push us in a wrong direction. When he hits bottom, the childhood memories will help Alyosha turn around and humble himself. He will give up his striving for power and his belief in progress. Like the prodigal son in Luke (15:11–32), the sinner Alyosha will remember his Father Zosima and go back home, to the monastery. He will return and repent.

Prince Myshkin refers to Jesus's words that "joy shall be in heaven over one sinner that repenteth more than over ninety-and-nine just persons, which need no repentance" (Pt. II, Ch. 4, 231), yet Dostoevsky never fully explains how he understands the process and the result of repentance. We can, however, rely on the work of Max Scheler for help. Unlike the majority of modern philosophers (such as Spinoza, Kant, or Nietzsche) who in repentance see merely a negative and even pointless act, Scheler argues that repentance is a form of self-healing. He claims that it is the only way of regaining the soul's lost power; repentance is the only force that can overcome the paralyzing sense of guilt and the self-crippling attitude of pride.

The essential element in Scheler's account, which he believes escapes the attention of other philosophers and leads to their negative attitude, is that a deed is not the actual object of repentance; the person repenting is. Thus, by repentance we should understand primarily the repentance of one's being, and only indirectly of this person's conduct. The result of repentance is not a correction of the past injustice, but a change of heart and a transformation of the person's outlook.[16] Repentance thus turns us back to confront the past, while it works for the future, for the liberation from the past

16 "[Repentance] cannot drive out of the world the external natural reality of the deed and its causal consequences, nor the evil character which the deed acquires *ipso facto*. All that stays in the world. But it can totally kill and extinguish the *reactive* effect of the deed within the human soul, and

and the renewal of the entire personality. Scheler even goes as far as to proclaim: "Not utopianism but repentance is the most revolutionary force in the moral world."[17]

The father in the biblical parable and on Rembrandt's painting has no desire to punish his repentant son. He has already been punished excessively by his (inner and outer) waywardness. Instead, the father forgives his son. Alyosha will also be forgiven. Since (together with repentance) forgiveness plays such an important role in Dostoevsky's opus, we should reflect on some of its fundamental characteristics.

Christianity insists on the supreme role of forgiveness, both in our relationship to God and in our dealings with each other. Our actions are irreversible and their consequences can never be fully predicted. We cannot foresee the outcomes of our actions because of our limited knowledge, and – as Hannah Arendt points out – also because actions have no end: "The process of a single deed can quite literally endure throughout time until mankind itself has come to an end."[18] The chain of happenings that one's action initiates "is never consummated unequivocally in one single deed or event, and its very meaning never discloses itself to the actor but only to the backward glance of the historian who himself does not act."[19] The power to forgive, like the capacity to repent, can release us and make us free: "Without being forgiven, released from the consequences of what we have done, our capacity to act would, as it were, be confined to one single deed from which we could never recover; we would remain the victims of its consequences forever."[20]

---

with it the root of an eternity of renewed guilt and evil"; Max Scheler, "Repentance and Rebirth," in *Person and Self-Value*, 113.

17 *Ibid.*

18 Hannah Arendt, *The Human Condition*, 233.

19 *Ibid.* For a similar view, see Scheler, *op. cit.*, 95–96.

20 Arendt, *op. cit.*, 237. On pages 239–40, Arendt quotes the famous words from Luke, 17:3–4: "And if he trespass against thee seven times a day, and seven times in a day turn again to thee, saying, I repent, thou shalt forgive him," and insists that the Greek word *hamaranein* be translated not as "sin," as it is usually done, but as "trespassing": "*Hamartanein*, finally,

The first fundamental similarity between repentance and forgiveness is that the deed is not the actual object of repentance and forgiveness; the person who is capable of committing such a deed is. Arendt also points out the second similarity between repentance and forgiveness – the relevance of love:

> Forgiving and the relationship it establishes is always an eminently personal (though not necessarily individual or private) affair in which *what* was done is forgiven for the sake of *who* did it. This, too, was clearly recognized by Jesus . . . and it is the reason for the current conviction that only love has the power to forgive. For love, although it is one of the rarest occurrences in human lives, indeed possesses an unequaled power of self-revelation and an unequaled clarity of vision for the disclosure of *who*, precisely because it is unconcerned to the point of total unworldliness with *what* the loved person may be, with his qualities and shortcomings no less than with his achievements, failings, and transgressions. Love, by reason of its passion, destroys the in-between which relates us to and separates us from others.[21]

Repentance and forgiveness are for Dostoevsky a foundation of his reply to the challenge so powerfully presented by Ivan, a foundation of hope. Repentance and forgiveness lead to a transformation of the person's attitudes and to a renewal of the personality; they lead to a rebirth. Yet Dostoevsky does not clarify in any detail how we should understand the outcome of this renewal. At this point we can rely on Carl Gustav Jung, who specifies five different understandings of the concept of rebirth:

(1) Metempsychosis, or transmigration of souls. According to this view, mostly known from Hinduism and Buddhism, one's life is prolonged in time by passing through different bodily existences. More specifically, it is a life-sequence interrupted

---

is indeed very well rendered by 'trespassing' in so far as it means rather 'to miss', 'to fail and go astray', than 'to sin'."

21 *Ibid.*, 241–42.

by different reincarnations. This view does not imply the continuity of one and the same personality.

(2) Reincarnation, or rebirth in a human body. The human personality is treated as continuous and, at least in principle, accessible to memory. This memory of previous life-cycles can, under special circumstances, be partially or fully retrieved. Plato's theory of recollection is one illustration of this view.

(3) Resurrection, or a re-establishment of human existence after death. This concept, crucial for Christianity, usually assumes that rebirth is the process no longer to be understood in the crude material sense, since death leads to rising up to the state of incorruptibility.

(4) *Renovatio*, or rebirth within the span of individual life. From one point of view, frequent in pagan religions – and still mixed together with the Russian Orthodoxy in Dostoevsky's time – rebirth is a renewal of the same person (without his or her essential nature being changed), but subjected to mystical healing, strengthening, or improvement. From another point of view, favored by Christianity, renovation means the total rebirth of the individual, with a change in his or her essential nature. Well-known examples are the transfiguration and ascension of Christ, and the bodily assumption of the Mother of God into Heaven.

(5) Indirect rebirth, or participation in the process of transformation. One has to witness, or take part in some rite of transformation, such as the Christian Mass, where there is a transformation of substances. Through presence at the rite, the individual participates in the gift of divine grace.[22]

Dostoevsky's pronouncements on rebirth and resurrection combine the third, the fourth, and the fifth meanings. In the minimal sense, rebirth is a significant redirection of consciousness. In the maximal sense, it means what Alyosha promises to Kolya: rising

22 Carl G. Jung, "Concerning Rebirth," in *The Archetypes and the Collective Unconscious*, 113–15. See also Mircea Eliade, *The Sacred and the Profane*, 68–159.

from the dead.[23] Usually, rebirth and resurrection suggest for Dostoevsky something in between these two, less definable and more ambiguous than either of the extremes. In this case rebirth and resurrection mean becoming like children: Children need to learn how to become adults, and, as the Bible teaches, adults have to become children again (*cf.* Matthew 18:3). Symbolically speaking, first we need to leave home, then find our way back. We must build our individuality and personality, then humble ourselves, abandon our proud attempts to control our lives and the world, and accept that we are ultimately defenseless against life (and death). We must give up our wish to play the role of God; instead, like children, we need to regain our trust in life and the Father who creates it.[24]

Regaining the Sense of Belonging

With which character on Rembrandt's painting do we identify?

Our first reaction is to identify with the prodigal son. He seems to be in the focus of attention, and the painting is called after him. We would all accept being that lost son, provided we could find our way home and be embraced by the forgiving father.

When we continue to think about the painting and how difficult it is to gather enough courage to be humbled, return, and ask for forgiveness, we must also realize how intricate the role of the father is. His beloved son wished him dead and rejected him. Now he is back, poor and humiliated. Should not the son be taught a lesson, so that he never repeats such a mistake again?

If this thought crosses the father's mind, we hear and see nothing of it in the biblical parable or on Rembrandt's painting. Instead what we hear and see is an ocean of forgiveness and love, embracing the fallen and repentant son. The contrast in the appearance between the two figures cannot be more striking: the age, the social

---

23   In his correspondence, Dostoevsky makes it clear that he believes "in real, literal, personal resurrection and in fact that it will take place on earth"; for the source of this letter and its discussion, see James P. Scanlan, *Dostoevsky the Thinker*, 24–56.

24   Among his numerous commentators, no one has described Dostoevsky's call to become children better than Eduard Thurneysen; see his *Dostoevsky*, 81.

position, the bodily posture, the clothing . . . With his clothes torn and head shaven, the son has indeed the appearance of a swine-herd. Humiliated to the core of his being, his head – and his prideful ego – ebbs into the father's hug.

The longer we look at the painting, the more we realize that the father may be the true hero of the parable. His parental love and forgiveness – manifested through the embracing hands gently laid on the son's back and the glow radiating from his face with kindness and serenity – are the painting's true focus. The father's eyes appear closed, or perhaps blinded by old age, but his heart is open and welcomes the fallen son. He was lost and is now found. He was dead and is alive again. What else could possibly matter?

What does matter is not to alienate the elder son. Rembrandt brings him inside the father's house (the biblical parable offers a different scenario), but the elder son is so distanced from the main characters that he appears to be related to them no more than the onlookers who happened to be there. As there is a striking contrast between the father and the prodigal son, there is also a distinct gap between the father and the elder son. Their dress is almost identical, but the body language could not be more dissim-ilar. In contrast to the father who is bending his old body and stiff arms to touch his younger son, the elder son is standing as erect and distant as possible. His hands are not eager to embrace anyone.

At the end of his preliminary examination and after his dream of the wee one, Dmitri offers to shake hands with the prosecutor, but he refuses. The elder son in Rembrandt's painting would do the same. With the long staff standing parallel to the father's extended arms, the elder son has the body position of a prosecutor, or maybe of an executioner ready to raise and swing down his weapon. He, the righteous one, feels betrayed. Why does this so-called brother of mine come back? And why is my father celebrating his return?

Ivan understands the resentment of the eldest son. Indeed, what is there to celebrate about the return of the prodigal son? He was lost and now is found. Does his return promise anything? Does it guarantee that he will not be lost again?

Dostoevsky would probably reply that, although it carries no guaranties, the return of the prodigal son is, indeed, the most appro-priate reason for celebration. With his repentance and the father's forgiveness, he is given another chance. The rebirth of the prodigal son marks a new stage in his life. His rebirth is not a return to immaturity; it is not a reversal of all the growth of character to which the intervening suffering has contributed. Through his suffering, he has gained an innocence of a different order, that of a mature person.

The return of the prodigal son does not imply, however, that he is already physically and spiritually at home. Beyond a call to return, there are two more calls awaiting him. One of them deals with gratitude, for life consists not just of receiving but of giving as well. The call to gratitude is a trying one. Together with the consciousness of the prodigal son that he needs to return a gift to his parents, there is also awareness that no gift that the son can offer will be fully equivalent to what he has received from his parents.[25]

If gratitude to our parents involves the realization that we can never entirely return the gift we have received from them, what, then, can we do? Dostoevsky believes that beyond the calls to the prodigal son to return and be grateful there is one more call – to become a father. This call is not only the most difficult one, but it is also the most puzzling. As there are no mothers in *The Brothers Karamazov*, there is no mother on Rembrandt's canvas either. But as Nouwen points out, the more we look at Rembrandt's painting, the better we recognize another point of importance. Just as the prodigal son also symbolizes all prodigal daughters, the father is not just a father but a mother, too; he is a universal parent. In addition to that, he is not just a human father but a Heavenly Father as well.[26] How should we understand this Father, His nature and His complex relationship to human beings?

25 Nouwen argues that the proper understanding of gratitude is that "all life is a pure gift," and opposes gratitude and resentment: "Along with trust there must be gratitude – the opposite of resentment. Resentment and gratitude cannot coexist, since resentment blocks the perception and experience of life as a gift"; *op. cit.*, 85. For further discussion, see George Simmel, "Faithfulness and Gratitude," in *The Sociology of Georg Simmel*, 379–95.

26 This point is made by Nouwen; *op. cit.*, 99. According to Stefan Zweig, *Three Masters: Balzac, Dickens, Dostoeffsky*, 186, "The deeper we penetrate into Rembrandt's pictures or into Dostoeffsky's books, the easier it becomes to solve the riddle of earthly and of spiritual forms, the answer to which is: universal humanity."

Étienne Gilson directs our attention to one of the most fundamental differences in the traditional conception of the Christian God, the shift from the medieval to the modern understanding: "Whereas the God of Saint Thomas was an infinite ocean of existence, the God of Descartes is an infinitely powerful fountain of existence."[27] For Aquinas, the essence of the Christian God is not to create (although He may and does create), but simply to be. For Descartes, God is the first cause: the omnipotent, omniscient, and most benevolent Being which brings everything else into existence.

Dostoevsky's pronouncements about the Divine Being are not unified. They are closer to Aquinas than to Descartes, but they are far more ambivalent than those of Aquinas. Dostoevsky does not attempt to produce any proof of God's existence, because for him religion is intuitive and not abstract: Faith which requires proofs (or miracles) is no real faith. "Much on earth is concealed from us," Father Zosima speaks in Dostoevsky's name, "but in place of it we have been granted a secret, mysterious sense of our living bond with the other world, with the higher heavenly world" (Bk. VI, Ch. 3 [g], 320). There is something inherently ambiguous, almost paradoxical in the very nature of the Divine Being. Dostoevsky agrees with another medieval philosopher and theologian, Nicolas of Cusa, who thinks of God in terms of the *coincidentia oppositorum*. Dostoevsky would have also appreciated Alfred North Whitehead's proclamation that, "God is the ultimate limitation, and His existence is the ultimate irrationality."[28]

This "irrationality" of the father – of his existence and his behavior – is what annoys the elder son. The same "irrationality" drives Ivan to despair: How can any humanitarian progress be accomplished with a God who is the *coincidentia oppositorum*? Progress can consist only in the parting of the opposites, only by separating wheat from chaff, good from evil. Thus our forgiveness and love of the sinner do not contribute anything to the pursuit of justice. They instead abort any attempt to establish adequate retribution.

27 Étienne Gilson, *God and Philosophy*, 87.
28 Alfred North Whitehead, *Science and the Modern World*, 249. For further discussion of Dostoevsky's understanding of God, see Malcolm Jones, *Dostoevsky and the Dynamic of Religious Experience*.

Dostoevsky approaches religion through mythology, rather than by way of theology (as Aquinas does) or cosmology (as Descartes does). For Dostoevsky, God is not separate from His creation but is incarnated in the world. While reading his novels, we sense a tangible, if hardly definable, presence of the sacred and holy in the world. Without speaking of Dostoevsky, Gilson expresses the thought which captures well the Russian author's point of view: "God spontaneously offers Himself to most of us, more as a confusedly felt presence than as an answer to any problem, when we find ourselves confronted with the vastness of the ocean, the still purity of mountains, or the mysterious life of the midsummer starry sky."[29]

Such a God, who lacks any discernable essence and who is the God of existence, the God of the mysterious flow of life, is too alien and perplexing for modern man. This God is paradoxical and no less puzzling than the riddle of man. Ivan does not know what to make of this ambiguous God and His unjust world. Albert Camus, who characterizes Ivan's rebellion against God's creation as the predicament of modern man, argues that there seem to be only a few possible options in the face of this agonizing absurdity. One is to escape from reality, for instance by losing oneself in debauchery, as Fyodor Karamazov does. The other is to escape from reality by committing suicide, as Smerdyakov does. The third option is to refuse to escape and bear our absurd fate. Ivan chooses this path, which, if it does not drive him to madness, comes down to Sisyphus and his proverbial rock.[30]

That Camus does not explore all possible options is clear, for instance, even from a cursory look at the works of his contemporary, Franz Kafka. In his novels (e.g., *The Trial* and *The Castle*), Kafka typically presents a hero who feels excluded from the world and who does not know how to find a reentry into it. He is spiritually homeless, a prodigal son without a world to which he can return and belong.[31]

---

29 Gilson, *op. cit.*, 116.
30 See Albert Camus, *The Myth of Sisyphus*, 1–48.
31 For a good discussion of Kafka along these lines, see Günther Anders, *Franz Kafka*.

Camus and Kafka, together with Sartre and Faulkner, may lead the list of the early twentieth-century writers who believe that the Freudian discontent with our civilization is the prevailing human condition. Together with Freud, they may feel that not only do we not have home in this world, but also that our continuous quest to find one is pointless and embarrassing.[32]

What would Dostoevsky say to this prevailing sense of homelessness and disorientation of modern man? Although he often feels Ivan's anguish, Dostoevsky wants Alyosha to have the last word. He intends for him a fate that Camus and Kafka do not discuss. The first thing that Dostoevsky would point out against the absurd and lonely heroes, such as Camus's Meursault and Kafka's Joseph K., is that faith and hope are not matters of fact but matters of attitude. They are not about what the world is like, but about how we relate to it. Furthermore, faith and hope are not just individual but pre-eminently communal attitudes. Due to their faith, believers are never as alone as Meursault and Joseph K. Dostoevsky would agree with Nicolai Hartmann's insistence that,

> Solidarity of faith is more fundamental than any other kind, it is the basis of all commonalty. Community, whether national or intimately private, is always community of faith. The distrustful man is not adapted to it; he excludes himself. Distrust breaks all bonds. Lack of faith in a cause, like lack of faith in a man, means separation. Faith is capacity for co-operation. Upon it rests the tremendous extension of the individual's sphere of power by his uniting with many; it is like solid earth under his feet at every step in life.[33]

Learning first from his mother and later from Father Zosima, the trusting Alyosha has accepted a God who is not separate from man and from the Mother Earth. Father Zosima does not have to invent a religious view but rather rediscover through his own prodigal

32 See Sigmund Freud, *Civilization and Its Discontent*, 9.
33 Nicolai Hartmann, *Ethics*, vol. II, 294. Dostoevsky would also agree with Hartmann that faith is "a creative power": "Faith can transform a man, towards good or evil, according to what he believes. This is its secret, its power to remove mountains. Distrust is impotence"; *ibid.*, 295.

wandering what his dying brother told him while he was still a child. Alyosha is in an analogous position. After his unsuccessful search for a perfect God, or a perfect worldly ruler (the Tsar), Alyosha can recover the memories of his childhood and the teaching of his Elder. The wayward son will come to realize that it is not God who hides from man but man who runs away from God. God does not abandon man but man abandons God. Like the father of the prodigal son, God is always here, waiting for his children to return home when they are ready to do so. Alyosha will return to the monastery – that would be his home and his sanctuary. According to the testimony of Anna Grigorievna, Alyosha will dedicate his subsequent life to children. Symbolically speaking, this means that Alyosha will become a father. He will find his way from being a prodigal son to becoming a father. This, I believe, is how Dostoevsky envisions the ending of his last, never-written novel.

Does this conclusion mean a happy end for Dostoevsky's hero? A completion of the torturous story of becoming a human being? Well, yes and no.

The parable of the prodigal son is a story of homecoming. If Alyosha finds a way to return home and repent, he will thereby accomplish something that Ivan would not think possible. If Alyosha can in addition become a father to whom his future wayward sons can return, he will reestablish our trust in life and God. He will make the search for the meaning of life not embarrassing but obsolete. The forgiving father, so characteristically missing from Ivan's interpretation of the parable of the prodigal son, is a symbol of the person who affirms life, even in the face of the greatest evil. Dostoevsky is convinced that, if the repentant prodigal son does not fully assuage our doubts as to whether life has meaning, when our eyes meet the father, our search for meaning comes to a rest.

The problem is that someone like Ivan may still not be satisfied. The gains of the prodigal son are minimal. The noble hopes of humanity are geared toward something greater than that. Before we consider what they may be, let us recall that the idea of hope contains two elements: expectation and confidence. To hope is to have an expectation that something positive will happen in the future. To hope is, moreover, to have confidence that the expected outcome will come true. To connect this discussion with the previous consideration of the original meaning of the word "prodigal," we can say that an expectation of a future outcome can have two forms: a movement upward and a movement forward. For believers, the upward impulse is the expectation of a greater proximity to, or union with, God. The secularly colored impulse forward is associated with an expectation of further advancement of the entire human race. These two movements can be combined, but they can also exist separately.

Dostoevsky is keenly aware of the possibility that our expectations may be unrealistic and unfounded. He knows that they may subsequently lead to a loss of confidence and disappointments. Indeed, the two greatest dangers for humanity are to have ideals that are too high, or to have no ideals at all.

The confidence that Dostoevsky's positive characters display is based on the ladder of "beauty → love → faith → hope": The appreciation of beauty and love will lead to a build-up of appreciation of and trust in something greater than the human ego, which in turn will inspire confidence in a positive outcome. Exactly what positive outcome?

Dostoevsky is very cautious about defining this outcome, and for several reasons. One of them is that, whether or not Alyosha becomes a repentant prodigal son and a forgiving father, there will always be plenty of lost children in the world. There will also be no lesser number of resentful brothers. Rembrandt called his painting "The Return of the Prodigal Son," but he could have equally justifiably entitled it "The Welcome by the Forgiving Father," or "The Resentment of the Elder Son."

Besides the already considered sociological and psychological, there are also religious and metaphysical reasons why the parable of the prodigal son does not offer a melodramatic happy ending. The expectations of a definitive end dominate our religious and metaphysical views. Eschatology, or "the doctrine of the last things," is often used as a comprehensive term for religious ideas about the afterlife. Our religious hopes for the future are connected both with the world as a whole and with the salvation of the individual soul after death. In the metaphysical context, we treat eschatology as an attempt to explain the ultimate destiny of human history, whether such a goal is "utopian" or "realistic." In the secular version of eschatology, we understand history – collective and individual – as goal-oriented and thereby meaningful. Such eschatological expectations are manifest in the use of the linear plot-development and linear time.[34]

Dostoevsky's disappointed characters come to realize that the historical reality will always remain incomplete. Instead of the expected progress of humanity, all that takes place is an endless change. There is only an apparently random stream of events, without goal or purpose. If there is no goal or purpose to the history of the world, reasons Ivan, there can also be no responsibility: Everything is permissible.

Father Zosima agrees with Ivan that the expectations of "the end of history" are illusory. Yet the Elder draws a different conclusion than Ivan. Hope, Father Zosima can say in Dostoevsky's name, is not a historical category. Instead of the inevitable or continuous progress of humanity, in the seemingly endless stream of changes we can recognize some patterns of development. The key pattern, as the parable of the prodigal son indicates, is that of departure and return, of transgression of established boundaries and a re-establishment of new boundaries. Put differently, hope is not related to an accomplishment of a definitive historical goal, but to the process of self-regeneration, to the cycle of life, death, and rebirth. What we need to trust is not the world's historical or religious development, but life and its power of regeneration.

If the ending of Dostoevsky's last, never-written novel is not to be a happy or melodramatic one, the main reason is that he does not believe in endings. Instead of beginnings and endings, there is a flow of life, the mystery of affirming existence, especially in the face of evil. Yet, not all would be evil in the last novel, as not all is evil in life.

Without closing his eyes to evil that exists in the world, Dostoevsky encourages us to approach the world with trust. He challenges us to put our trust in life, in ourselves, in people, in

34 For further discussion, see Yuri Lotman, *Universe of the Mind: A Semiotic Theory of Culture*, 158–59.

nature, and ultimately in God. His ladder of "beauty → love → faith → hope" does not promise or guarantee anything, but invites an appreciation of various aspects of life. Beauty is practically useless, as are love, faith and hope. They can protect us from no enemy determined to harm us. They leave us as defenseless as little children. And yet, like radiant virtue, they give a positive meaning to life. Beauty, love, faith, and hope bestow meaning upon human existence, a splendor shed upon our path covered with thorns. In the world which will never be perfect, they create a sense of belonging, a sense of home.

It has now become clearer that, when Dostoevsky announces that Alyosha is – or will become – a hero, he understands heroism in his own peculiar way. According to our traditional understanding, a hero is someone who is more than human, and a victim is less than human. While victims are those whose humanity is violated, those who are treated like objects or things, heroes are larger than life – they are supermen, semi-gods. Dostoevsky reminds us that a victim is not someone who is less than human, but someone who is forced to be less human than other human beings. By analogy, a hero is not more than human, but instead someone who is more human than other human beings.

We normally think that heroes, victimizers, and victims are three separate categories. For Dostoevsky, they are intimately connected, because a prerequisite for being a hero is being a victim, or being a victimizer. Dostoevsky is so concerned with the seductive power of pride that he believes only those who are humbled enough can become heroes. Only those who have been insulted and injured, or those who come to repent their insults of others, can understand the pain of other human beings and suffer with them.

While we usually understand heroes to be those who break the new frontiers (the trans-processes), Dostoevsky conceives of heroes in terms of the re-processes. His heroes use their courage to restore what is broken. They do not deliver justice but help the wound heal. They do not enter the world with a sword or a gun but face it with helping hands and caring hearts. We conceive of heroism in terms of greatness which cannot be demanded of everybody. Dostoevsky thinks that every human being must strive to become a hero – in his or her own life. While our heroes are distinguished individuals, Dostoevsky's heroes are those human beings who have developed their spirituality. Each person has something unique and thus is an individual, but, more importantly, each person has a developed sense for the common core of humanity, as well as a commitment to its highest values. The greatness of a person does not consist in external and measurable achievements but in an internal greatness, in the inner commitment to certain values and the unique approximation to them.

While we think of heroes in terms of the categories of vitality – a hero is someone with more vitality than the rest of us – Dostoevsky understands heroes in terms of spirituality. A hero is not someone who corrects the injustices of the world, but the one who accepts human beings for who they are – lovingly and with appreciation for their weaknesses and strengths, for their humanity. Spirituality is the key word for Dostoevsky's philosophy of life, for his approach to the riddles and paradoxes of life. Spirituality is the ultimate source of his optimism and affirmation of life, even in the face of evil.

Epilogue

Dostoevsky's most disturbing character is Ivan Karamazov. His struggle reflects the failure of human beings to find their place in the world and to understand the meaning of life. Ivan is devastated by the overwhelming presence of evil. What kind of world is this, Ivan despairs, in which little children are tortured? What kind of meaning can this life have, if the world – and its Creator – is so incomprehensible and unjust?

Dostoevsky's uncompromising realism demands that we take seriously the numerous examples of evil, without explaining them away as illusory. Nevertheless, Dostoevsky hopes to convey the message of optimism: Life should be affirmed even in the face of evil. Human beings can regain their sense of belonging to this world; they can recover the sense of life's meaning. When it comes to elaborating this optimistic outlook, Dostoevsky is not as explicit as when he paints the disappointed expectations of modernity. In this book, I set as my goal to reconstruct Dostoevsky's optimism. Besides articulating in what it consists, my task has been to explain what the ultimate ground of Dostoevsky's optimism is and how this optimism can be reconciled with the recognition of evil.

Ivan suggests that the problem of evil arises because the existence of innocent suffering undermines the basic trust in the world and its Creator. If we cannot trust the world, how can we feel but as exiled wanderers? Ivan's criticism is so powerful because it shows that our trust is betrayed with regard to the world's intelligibility and its justice: The world full of evil defies both our intelligence and our sense of justice.

The beginning of Dostoevsky's answer to Ivan's charges consists in the realization that the demand that the world be trustworthy does not imply it must be either intelligible or just. This trustworthiness can be understood by means of a different criterion. To uncover it, Dostoevsky takes a closer look at the problem of evil. Evil usually occurs when some established boundary is transgressed. Yet not every such transgression leads to evil (or crime). It is wrong to identify transgressions as the source of evil, and then structure our moral precepts in terms of prohibitions to violate these established boundaries. Transgressions are the results of our freedom and our vital desire to explore such boundaries and open new frontiers. They are the consequence of our natural impulse to become more than what we already are – smarter, better, larger . . . While transgressions may lead to crimes, they are also responsible for much good, in cases when the boundaries are inappropriate and unjust. Violating unfair boundaries and establishing the more appropriate ones make possible the important advances of humanity.

Besides transgressions, Dostoevsky emphasizes the presence of another vital impulse in every human being – a desire for order, stability, and security. What is broken should be mended; what is sick, healed; what is transgressed needs to be restored. In addition to the trans-processes, which lead to transgressions of established boundaries, Dostoevsky calls our attention to the re-processes, which aim at regenerating order, stability, and security. He expresses this distinction in terms of the symbolic cycles of death and rebirth – a death of the old and a birth of the new.

The cycles of trans-processes and re-processes are based neither on intelligence nor on justice. They are indifferent to our rational and moral categories. Nature does not reveal any plan or purpose. Yet the cycles of trans-processes and re-processes have a meaning without purpose. They provide the pattern which, like glue, connects together an enormous swirl of individuals and events, all of which partake in the gigantic drama we call reality. This pattern helps us make sense of the world's past, present, and future.

The sources of Dostoevsky's optimism are that (i) there are recurring cycles of trans-processes and re-processes in nature, and that

(ii) regardless of what kind of transgressions human beings commit (victimizers) or suffer (victims), they can distance themselves from evil deeds and respect their common humanity. Dostoevsky maintains that these points are crucial for our trust in the world and other human beings. The world can be trusted because of the cycles of deaths and rebirths, of trans-processes and re-processes. Human beings can be trusted because regardless of what happens to us, regardless of what kind of evil we commit or suffer, a path toward becoming more human is still open.

This striving to become more human than we already are, coupled with the appreciation of what already exists, is not simply a natural impulse. Dostoevsky treats it as the highest expression of human spirituality. A striving of this kind may begin as a natural impulse, with the appreciation of beauty. No intelligence and no morality are needed for the appreciation of what is beautiful. We are drawn to beauty naturally, without prerequisites, ulterior motives, or future expectations. Dostoevsky insists that the fact that we are sensitive to beauty is a clear indicator that there is structure and order in the world independent of human beings and their reasoning, intentions, and actions. Symbolically speaking, the fact that we are appreciative of beauty shows that, even when not having a permanent dwelling in the world, we are not strangers in it either. We cannot be masters of the world, but we can be its guests, grateful for the gift of life inexplicably granted to us. Our gratitude for the gift of life is intensified when we extend our appreciation from beauty to love, and then move on toward faith and hope. While the appreciation of beauty is our preparation for the positive reception of other "useless" values, love is the crucial turning point for the development of human spirituality. The appreciation of love teaches us that we should turn with care and sympathy even toward those human beings from whom our natural impulse would lead us away. We can learn to accept and appreciate even those who strike us as irrational and unjust.

Love always involves a leap of faith, because it places trust into something that is not tangible, or not yet. Dostoevsky understands faith in its biblical sense: "Faith gives substance to our hopes and makes us certain of realities we do not see" (Epistle to the Hebrews 11:1). Faith is not primarily a possession of dogmatic beliefs but an inner attitude of trust in the visible and the invisible aspects of reality. For Dostoevsky, this means the interconnectedness of the profane and the sacred. Nature is not a blind and pre-determined Newtonian mechanism, but a living organism permeated with various kinds of energies and forces. The sacred is not transcendent but immanent in the world and present in multiple aspects of human life. Dostoevsky does not understand the sacred – or the holy – in the intellectualistic and moralistic terms. For him, God is not the omniscient, omnipotent, and benevolent being, but is as ambivalent as human beings are. Dostoevsky's God does not resemble the Divinity praised by the pious friends of Job. His God is far closer to the unnamed voice which addresses Job from the whirlwind. This God is the principle of creativity as well as of destructivity, of death no less than of life. This God is the God of paradoxes, and only faith can come to terms with this ambiguous God and His perplexing creation.

Dostoevsky concedes that not everything in reality, perhaps not even most of it, is meaningful. Nor does he have any qualms about accepting that our intellectual capacity is not a fully adequate means for comprehending what goes on in human life. The meaning of life is for Dostoevsky a spiritual category expressed through the joy of being alive and the affirmation of the aspects of life that deserve to be appreciated. Dostoevsky's optimism is ultimately grounded in spirituality. His attitude toward life is optimistic in the sense that there is always a chance for people to become more human than they are. This optimism, minimal as it may be, is also realistic and compatible with the presence of evil in the world. Dostoevsky maintains that it is usually the experience of evil which stimulates our spiritual growth and leads us to overcome the ego-centeredness by becoming more sensitive, caring, and forgiving.

Disappointed by the unrealistic expectations of modernity, Ivan goes to the opposite extreme and denies meaning to human life. Yet if the world were indeed as absurd as Ivan tries to convince us, human beings could not have survived in it for any prolonged time. This does not mean that the world must have been created with a meaning fixed into it, but only that its various fragments must be capable of meaning being bestowed upon them. There are many human emotions, acts, and attitudes which, like gifts, can bestow meaning on the fragments of reality. Dostoevsky thinks that such bestowing comes from a variety of spiritual attitudes. No one capable of appreciating the beauty of the setting sun wonders at that moment whether the world is absurd. No one capable of feeling gratitude or love doubts for a second whether life is meaningful. No trusting person thinks of suicide. At least in the moments when we are capable of appreciating beauty and love, in the moments in which we have faith in ourselves, other human beings, nature, or God, our existence is experienced as a miracle which cannot but be affirmed, regardless of whether any plan or purpose hides behind its always shifting surface.

When reason fails to understand the riddles and paradoxes of life, faith comes to terms with them. No person of faith, no one appreciative of the gifts bestowed upon us, would demand a proof of the meaning of life. This spirit of appreciation is the glue which makes life worth living. Dostoevsky's philosophy of life and his optimism are based on this awareness of our gifts, which crystallizes in the central messages of his affirmation of life: that we give gifts to others, and, even more importantly, that we ourselves become gifts to others.

Acknowledgments

In preparing this book, I received help from several institutions.

I am grateful to the College of the Holy Cross for granting me a sabbatical leave during the 2005–2006 academic year, as well as a Faculty Fellowship Leave in the spring semester of 2007.

The earlier versions of Prelude, Chapter 2 and Chapter 5 were published as, respectively, "On the Central Motivation of Dostoevsky's Novels," *Janus Head: Journal of Interdisciplinary Studies in Literature and Philosophy*, Volume 10 (Summer/Fall 2007) No. 1, 277–92; "Notes from the Underground: Dostoevsky's Anatomy of Modernity," *The Dostoevsky Journal: An Independent Review*, 11:2010, 25–44; and "The Meaning of Christ's Sacrifice: Reflections on Dostoevsky's *Idiot*," Philotheos: International Journal for Philosophy and Theology, 7:2007, 52–79. I am grateful to the editors of both journals for their permission to reprint these articles.

I had been also helped by a number of individuals. I am most grateful to Tom Lawler, Adam Musser, and Michael Grandone for their detailed comments on one or more drafts of my manuscript; they were most patient readers and constructive critics. My gratitude is also extended to Maria Granik, Lawrence Cahoone, Nalin Ranasinghe, and Richard Matlak for their help with various parts of the manuscript.

Finally, my deepest gratitude goes to my wife, Jadranka, to whom this book is dedicated.

Bibliography

A. Works by Dostoevsky

The Adolescent, trans. Andrew MacAndrew. New York: W.W. Norton, 1981. (Also translated from Russian as *A Raw Youth*.)

The Brothers Karamazov, trans. Richard Pevear and Larissa Volokhonsky. New York: Farrar, Straus and Giroux, 2002.

"The Christmas Tree and a Wedding," trans. David Magarshack, in *The Best Short Stories of Dostoevsky*. New York: The Modern Library, 1979, 89–98.

Complete Letters, ed. and trans. David Lower and Ronald Mayer. 5 vols. Ann Arbor, Mich.: Ardis, 1987–1991.

Crime and Punishment, trans. Constance Garnett. New York: Dover, 2001.

"The Double," trans. George Bird, in *Great Short Works of Fyodor Dostoevsky*. New York: Harper & Row, 1968, 1–144.

"The Dream of a Ridiculous Man," trans. David Magarshack, in *Great Short Works of Fyodor Dostoevsky*. New York: Harper & Row, 1968, 715–38.

"The Gambler," trans. Constance Garnett, in *Great Short Works of Fyodor Dostoevsky*. New York: Harper & Row, 1968, 379–519.

"A Gentle Creature," trans. David Magarshack, in *The Best Short Stories of Dostoevsky*. New York: The Modern Library, 1979, 241–95.

The House of the Dead, trans. David McDuff. New York: Penguin, 1985.

The Idiot, trans. Henry and Olga Carlisle. New York: Signet Classics, 2002.

The Insulted and the Injured, trans. Constance Garnett. Westport, Conn.: Greenwood Press, 1975.

"The Landlady," trans. David McDuff, in *Poor Folk and Other Stories*. New York: Penguin, 1988, 131–213.

"Mr. —bov and the Question of Art," in *Dostoevsky's Occasional Writings*, ed. and trans. David Magarshack. Evanston, Ill.: Northwestern University Press, 1997.

Netochka Nezvanova, trans. Jane Kentish. New York: Penguin, 1985.

The Notebooks for The Brothers Karamazov, ed. and trans. Edward Wasiolek. Chicago: University of Chicago Press, 1971.

The Notebooks for Crime and Punishment, ed. and trans. Edward Wasiolek. Chicago: University of Chicago Press, 1967.

The Notebook for The Idiot, ed. Edward Wasiolek, trans. Katherine Strelsky. Chicago: University of Chicago Press, 1967.

The Notebooks for The Possessed, ed. Edward Wasiolek, trans. Victor Terras. Chicago: University of Chicago Press, 1968.

"Notes from the Underground," trans. David Magarshack, in *Great Short Works of Fyodor Dostoevsky*. New York: Harper & Row, 1968, 261–377.

"The Peasant Marey," trans. David Magarshack, in *The Best Short Stories of Dostoevsky*. New York: The Modern Library, 1979, 99–105.

Polnoe Sobranie Sochinenii v Tridtsati Tomakh. 33 vols. Leningrad: Izdatel'stvo Nauka, 1972–1990.

"Poor Folk," trans. David McDuff, in *Poor Folk and Other Stories*. New York: Penguin, 1988, 1–129.

The Possessed, trans. Constance Garnett. New York: The Modern Library, 1963. (Also translated from Russian as *The Devils* and *Demons*.)

Selected Letters of Fyodor Dostoevsky, eds. Joseph Frank and David I. Goldstein, trans. Andrew MacAndrew. London: Rutgers University Press, 1987.

"White Nights," trans. David Magarshack, in *Great Short Works of Fyodor Dostoevsky*. New York: Harper & Row, 1968, 145–201.

Winter Notes on Summer Impressions, trans. David Patterson. Evanston, Ill.: Northwestern University Press, 1997.

A Writer's Diary: 1873–1881, trans. Kenneth Lantz. 2 vols. Evanston, Ill.: Northwestern University Press, 1993–94.

B. Works about Dostoevsky

Bakhtin, M.M. *Problems of Dostoevsky's Poetics*, trans. Caryl Emerson. Minneapolis: University of Minnesota Press, 1984.

Beardley, Monroe C. "Dostoevsky's Metaphor of 'Underground'." *Journal of the History of Ideas*, 3:1942, 265–90.

Belknap, Robert L. *The Genesis of The Brothers Karamazov: The Aesthetics, Ideology, and Psychology of Making a Text*. Evanston, Ill.: Northwestern University Press, 1990.

——. "Memory in *The Brothers Karamazov*," in *Dostoevsky: New Perspectives*, ed. Robert L. Jackson. Englewood Cliffs, N.J.: Prentice-Hall, 1984, 227–42.

——. *The Structure of The Brothers Karamazov*. The Hague: Mouton, 1967.

Berdyaev, Nicholas. *Dostoevsky*, trans. Donald Attwater. Cleveland: The World Publishing Company, 1965.

Cascardi, Anthony J. *The Bounds of Reason: Cervantes, Dostoevsky, Flaubert.* New York: Columbia University Press, 1986.

Catteau, Jacques. *Dostoevsky and the Process of Literary Creation*, trans. Audrey Littlewood. Cambridge: Cambridge University Press, 1989.

Cicovacki, Predrag. "The Enigmatic Conclusion of Dostoevsky's *Idiot*: A Comparison of Prince Myshkin and Wagner's Parsifal," *Dostoevsky Studies* 9:2005, 106–14.

———. "Searching for the Abandoned Soul: Dostoevsky on the Suffering of Humanity," in *The Enigma of Good and Evil: The Moral Sentiment in Literature*, ed. Ann-Therese Tymieniecka. Lancaster, UK: Springer, 2005, 367–98.

———. "Trial of Man and Trial of God: Reflections on Job and Dostoevsky's Grand Inquisitor," in *Destined for Evil? The Twentieth Century Responses*, ed. Predrag Cicovacki. Rochester, N.Y.: University of Rochester Press, 2005, 249–60.

Cox, Roger L. *Between Heaven and Earth: Shakespeare, Dostoevsky and the Meaning of Christian Tragedy.* New York: Holt, Rinehart & Winston, 1969.

Dostoevsky, Anna. *The Diary of Dostoyevsky's Wife*, ed. and trans. Beatrice Stillman. New York: Macmillan, 1928.

———. *Reminiscences*, ed. and trans. Beatrice Stillman. New York: Liveright, 1975.

Efortin, René. "Responsive Form: Dostoevsky's *Notes from Underground* and the Confessional Tradition," in *Gaining Upon Certainty: Selected Literary Criticism of René Efortin*, eds. Brian Barbour and Rodney Delasanta. Providence: Providence College Press, 1995, 291–314.

Fanger, Donald. *Dostoevsky and Romantic Realism: A Study of Dostoevsky in Relation to Balzac, Dickens, and Gogol.* Cambridge, Mass.: Harvard University Press, 1965.

Frank, Joseph. *Dostoevsky: The Mantle of the Prophet, 1871–1881.* Princeton: Princeton University Press, 2002.

———. *Dostoevsky: The Miraculous Years, 1865–1871.* Princeton: Princeton University Press, 1995.

———. *Dostoevsky: The Seeds of Revolt, 1821–1849.* Princeton: Princeton University Press, 1976.

———. *Dostoevsky: The Stir of Liberation, 1860–1865.* Princeton: Princeton University Press, 1986.

———. *Dostoevsky: The Years of Ordeal, 1850–1859.* Princeton: Princeton University Press, 1983.

Freud, Sigmund. "Dostoevsky and Parricide," in *The Brothers Karamazov and the Critics*, ed. Edward Wasiolek. Belmont, Cal.: Wadsworth, 1967, 41–55.

Gibian, George. "Traditional Symbolism in *Crime and Punishment*," in *Feodor Dostoevsky, Crime and Punishment: The Coulson Translation. Backgrounds and Sources. Essays in Criticism*, ed. George Gibian. New York: W.W. Norton, 1964, 575–92.

Girard, René. *Resurrection from the Underground: Fyodor Dostoevsky*, trans. J.G. Williams. New York: The Crossroad Publishing Company, 1997.

Golosovker, Jakov Emmanuilovich. *Dostoevskii i Kant*. Moscow: Izdatel'stvo Akademii Nauk, 1963.

Grossman, Leonid. *Dostoevsky: A Biography*, trans. Mary Mackler. Indianapolis: Bobbs-Merrill, 1975.

Hackel, Sergei. "The Religious Dimension: Vision or Evasion? Zosima's Discourse in *The Brothers Karamazov*," in *Fyodor Dostoevsky*, ed. Harold Bloom. New Haven: Chelsea House, 1988, 211–35.

Hoffmann, N[ina]. *Th.M. Dostojewski. Eine biographische Studie*. Berlin: Ernst Hoffmann, 1899.

Ivanov, Vyacheslav. *Freedom and the Tragic Life: A Study in Dostoevsky*, trans. Norman Cameron. New York: The Noonday Press, 1957.

Jackson, Robert Louis. *Dialogues with Dostoevsky: The Overwhelming Questions*. Stanford: Stanford University Press, 1993.

——. *Dostoevsky's Quest for Form: A Study in his Philosophy of Art*. New Haven: Yale University Press, 1966.

Jones, John. *Dostoevsky*. Oxford: Clarendon Press, 1983.

Jones, Malcolm V. *Dostoevsky and the Dynamics of Religious Experience*. London: Anthem Press, 2005.

——. *Dostoyevsky: The Novel of Discord*. New York: Harper & Row Publishers, 1976.

Kellogg, Jean. *Dark Prophets of Hope: Dostoevsky, Sartre, Camus, Faulkner*. Chicago: Loyola University Press, 1975.

Kirillova, Irina. "Dostoevsky's Markings in the Gospel According to St. John," in *Dostoevsky and the Christian Tradition*, eds. George Pattison and Diane Oenning Thompson. Cambridge: Cambridge University Press, 2001, 41–50.

Kjetsaa, Geir. *Fyodor Dostoyevsky: A Writer's Life*, trans. Siri Hustvedt and David McDuff. New York: Fawcett Columbine, 1989.

Knapp, Liza. *The Annihilation of Inertia: Dostoevsky and Metaphysics*. Evanston, Ill.: Northwestern University Press, 1996.

——. "Mothers and Sons in *The Brothers Karamazov*: Our Ladies of Skotoprigonevsk," in *Dostoevsky: New Perspectives*, ed. Robert L. Jackson. Evanston, Ill.: Northwestern University Press, 2004, 31–52.

Kostalevsky, Marina. *Dostoevsky and Soloviev: The Art of Integral Vision*. New Haven: Yale University Press, 1997.

Kozhinov, Vadim. "The First Sentence in *Crime and Punishment*, the Word 'Crime,' and Other Matters," in *Twentieth Century Interpretations of Crime and Punishment: A Collection of Critical Essays*, ed. Robert L. Jackson. Englewood Cliffs, N.J.: Prentice-Hall, 1974, 17–25.

Lawrence, D.H. "The Grand Inquisitor," in *The Brothers Karamazov and the Critics*, ed. Edward Wasiolek. Belmont, Cal.: Wadsworth, 1967, 78–85.

Leatherbarrow, W.J. *Dostoyevsky: The Brothers Karamazov*. Cambridge: Cambridge University Press, 1992.

Lord, Robert. *Dostoevsky: Essays and Perspectives*. London: Chatto and Windus, 1970.

Lukács, Georg. "Dostoevsky," in *Dostoevsky: A Collection of Critical Essays*, ed. René Wellek. Englewood Cliffs, N.J.: Prentice-Hall, 1962, 146–58.

Matlaw, Ralph E. "Myth and Symbolism in *The Brothers Karamazov*," in *The Brothers Karamazov and the Critics*, ed. Edward Wasiolek. Belmont, Cal.: Wadsworth, 1967, 108–18.

Merejkowski, Dmitri. *Tolstoi as Man and Artist, with an Essay on Dostoevsky*. Westminster: Archibald Constable, 1902.

Miller, C.A. "Nietzsche's 'Discovery' of Dostoevsky." *Nietzsche-Studien* 2:1973, 202–57.

Miller, Robin Feuer. *The Brothers Karamazov: Worlds of the Novel*. New York: Twayne, 1992.

——. *Dostoevsky and The Idiot: Author, Narrator, and Reader*. Cambridge, Mass.: Harvard University Press, 1981.

——. *Dostoevsky's Unfinished Journey*. New Haven: Yale University Press, 2007.

Mochulsky, Konstantin. *Dostoevsky: His Life and Work*, trans. Michael A. Minihan. Princeton: Princeton University Press, 1967.

Morson, Gary Soul. "The God of Onions: *The Brothers Karamazov* and the Mythic Prosaic," in *A New Word on The Brothers Karamazov*, ed. Robert L. Jackson. Evanston, Ill.: Northwestern University Press, 2004, 107–24.

Murav, Harriet. *Holy Foolishness: Dostoevsky's Novels and the Poetics of Cultural Critique*. Stanford: Stanford University Press, 1992.

Oates, Joyce Carol. "Tragic and Comic Visions in *The Brothers Karamazov*," in *The Edge of Impossibility: Tragic Forms in Literature*. New York: The Vanguard Press, 1972, 87–113.

——. "Tragic Rites in Dostoevsky's *The Possessed*," in *Contraries: Essays*. New York: Oxford University Press, 1981, 17–50.

Ollivier, Sophie. "Icons in Dostoevsky's Works," in *Dostoevsky and the Christian Tradition*, eds. George Pattison and Diane Oenning Thomson. Cambridge: Cambridge University Press, 2001, 51–68.

Proust, Marcel. "Dostoievsky," in *On Art and Literature: 1896–1919*, trans. Sylvia Townsend Warner. New York: Carol & Graf, 1984, 381–82.

Rahv, Philip. "Dostoevsky in *Crime and Punishment*," in *Feodor Dostoevsky, Crime and Punishment: The Coulson Translation. Backgrounds and*

Sources. Essays in Criticism, ed. George Gibian. New York: W.W. Norton, 1964, 592–616.

Rice, James L. "Dostoevsky's Endgame: The Projected Sequel to *The Brothers Karamazov*," *Russian History/Histoire Russe*, 33:2006, 45–62.

Rosenthal, Richard. "Raskolnikov's Transgression and the Confusion between Destructiveness and Creativity," in *Do I Dare Disturb the Universe: A Memorial to Wilfred R. Bion*, ed. James Grotstein. Beverly Hills, Cal.: Ceasura Press, 1981, 199–235.

Rozanov, Vasily. *Dostoevsky and the Legend of the Grand Inquisitor*, trans. Spenser E. Roberts. Ithaca: Cornell University Press, 1972.

Scanlan, James P. *Dostoevsky the Thinker*. Ithaca: Cornell University Press, 2002.

Schmidl, Fritz. "Freud and Dostoevsky," *Journal of the American Psychoanalytic Association*, 13:1965, 518–32.

Sekirin, Peter. *The Dostoevsky Archive: Firsthand Accounts of the Novelist from Contemporaries' Memoirs and Rare Periodicals*. Jefferson, N.C.: McFarland, 1997.

Shestov, Lev. *Dostoevsky, Tolstoy and Nietzsche*, eds. and trans. Bernard Martin and Spencer E. Roberts. Athens: Ohio State University Press, 1969.

Shneidman, N.N. *Dostoevsky and Suicide*. New York: Mosaic Press, 1989.

Simmons, Ernest J. *Dostoevsky: The Making of a Novelist*. New York: Random House, 1962.

Slonim, Marc. *Three Loves of Dostoevsky*. New York: Chekhov Publishing House, 1953.

Steiner, George. *Tolstoy or Dostoevsky: An Essay in the Old Criticism*. New York: Alfred A. Knopf, 1971.

Sutherland, Stewart R. *Atheism and the Rejection of God: Contemporary Philosophy and "The Brothers Karamazov."* Oxford: Blackwell, 1977.

——. "Death and Fulfillment, or Would the Real Mr. Dostoyevsky Stand Up?" in *Philosophy and Literature*, ed. A. Phillips Griffiths. Cambridge: Cambridge University Press, 1984, 15–27.

Terras, Victor. *The Idiot: An Interpretation*. Boston: Twayne Publishers, 1990.

——. *A Karamazov Companion: Commentary on the Genesis, Language, and Style of Dostoevsky's Novel*. Madison: University of Wisconsin Press, 1981.

——. *Reading Dostoevsky*. Madison: University of Wisconsin Press, 1998.

Thompson, Diane Oenning. *The Brothers Karamazov and the Poetics of Memory*. Cambridge: Cambridge University Press, 1991.

Thurneysen, Eduard. *Dostoevsky*, trans. Keith R. Crim. Richmond: John Knox Press, 1964.

Vivas, Eliseo. "Two Dimensions of Reality in *The Brothers Karamazov*," in *The Brothers Karamazov and the Critics*, ed. Edward Wasiolek. Belmont, Cal.: Wadsworth, 1967, 55–72.

Wasiolek, Edward. *Dostoevsky: The Major Fiction*. Cambridge, Mass.: MIT Press, 1964.

Zander, L.A. *Dostoevsky*, trans. Natalie Duddington. London: SCM Press, 1948.

Zenkovsky, V.V. "Dostoevsky's Religious and Philosophical Views," in *Dostoevsky: A Collection of Critical Essays*, ed. René Wellek. Englewood Cliffs, N.J.: Prentice-Hall, 1962, 130–45.

Zweig, Stefan. *Three Masters: Balzac, Dickens, Dostoeffsky*, trans. Eden and Ceder Paul. New York: Viking, 1919.

C. Other Cited and Used Works

Anders, Günther. *Franz Kafka*, trans. A. Steer and A. K. Thorlby. London: Bowes & Bowes, 1960.

Arendt, Hannah. *The Human Condition*, sec. ed. Chicago: University of Chicago Press, 1995.

———. *The Portable Hannah Arendt*, ed. Peter Baehr. New York: Penguin Books, 2000.

Aristotle. *The Basic Works of Aristotle*, ed. R. McKeon. New York: Random House, 1941.

Auerbach, Erich. "Representations of Reality in Homer and the Old Testament," in *The Bible*, ed. H. Bloom. New Haven: Chelsea House Publishing, 1987, 45–58.

Bachofen, J.J. *Myth, Religion, and Mother Right: Selected Writings of J.J. Bachofen*, trans. Ralf Manheim. Princeton: Princeton University Press, 1967.

Barker, F. *The Tremulous Private Body*. New York: Methuen, 1984.

Beiser, Frederick C. *Schiller as Philosopher: A Re-Examination*. New York: Oxford University Press, 2005.

Belinsky, Vissarion G. *Selected Philosophical Writings*. Moscow: Foreign Languages, 1948.

Berlin, Isaiah. *The Crooked Timber of Humanity*. New York: Alfred A. Knopf, 1991.

———. "The Hedgehog and the Fox: An Essay on Tolstoy's View of History," in *The Proper Study of Mankind: An Anthology of Essays*. New York: Farrar, Straus and Giroux, 1998, 436–98.

———. *The Power of Ideas*. Princeton: Princeton University Press, 2000.

———. *Russian Thinkers*. London: Hogarth Press, 1978.

Brague, Rémi. *The Wisdom of the World: The Human Experience of the Universe in Western Thought*, trans. Teresa L. Fagan. Chicago: University of Chicago Press, 2003.

Buber, Martin. *Good and Evil*, trans. R.G. Smith. New York: Charles Scribner's Sons, 1952.

——. "What Is Man?" in *Between Man and Man*, trans. R.G. Smith. New York: Macmillan, 1965, 140–244.

Burrow, J.W. *The Crisis of Reason: European Thought, 1848–1914*. New Haven: Yale University Press, 2000.

Butler, Ruth. *Rodin: The Shape of Genius*. New Haven: Yale University Press, 1993.

Camus, Albert. *The Myth of Sisyphus and Other Essays*, trans. Justin O'Brien. New York: Vintage Books, 1955.

——. *The Rebel: An Essay on Man in Revolt*, trans. Anthony Bower. New York: Vintage Books, 1956.

Carlyle, Thomas. "Heroes and Hero Worship," in *The Best Known Works of Thomas Carlyle*. New York: The Book League of America, 1942, 159–309.

Cervantes, Miguel de. *Don Quixote*, trans. Samuel Putnam. New York: Random House, 1949.

Chekhov, Anton. *Great Stories by Chekhov*, ed. David H. Greene. New York: Dell Publishing, 1959.

Chernyshevsky, Nicolai G. *What Is to Be Done? Tales about New People*, trans. Ludmilla B. Turkevich. New York: Alfred A. Knopf, 1961.

Colté, Sabina. *Toward Perfect Harmony*, trans. Helen Sebba. New York: George Brazilier, 1970.

Cottingham, John. *Descartes*. Oxford: Blackwell, 1986.

Day, Dorothy. *Selected Writings*, ed. Robert Ellsberg. Maryknoll, N.Y.: Orbis Books, 1992.

Descartes, René. *Philosophical Works of Descartes*, trans. E. Haldane and G. Ross. 2 vols. New York: Dover, 1955.

Douglas, Mary. *Purity and Danger: An Analysis of the Concepts of Pollution and Taboo*. London: Routledge, 1991.

Eliade, Mircea. *Mephistopheles and the Androgyne: Studies in Religious Myth and Symbol*, trans. J.M. Cohen. New York: Sheed and Ward, 1965.

——. *The Sacred and the Profane: The Nature of Religion*, trans. Willard R. Trask. New York: Harcourt Brace Jovanovich, 1959.

Feuerbach, Ludwig. *The Essence of Christianity*, trans. George Eliot. New York: Harper, 1957.

Figes, Orlando. *Natasha's Dance: A Cultural History of Russia*. New York: Henry Holt, 2002.

Frankl, Victor E. *Man's Search for Meaning: An Introduction to Logotherapy*, trans. Ilse Lasch. New York: Washington Square Press, 1965.

Freud, Sigmund. *Civilization and Its Discontents*, trans. Joan Riviere. New York: Dover, 1994.

——. *The Interpretation of Dreams*, trans. James Strachey. 2 vols. London: Hogarth Press, 1958. (Volumes V and VI of the Standard Edition of the Complete Psychological Works.)

——. *Three Essays on the Theory of Sexuality*, trans. James Strachey. London: Hogarth Press, 1953. (Volume VII of the Standard Edition of the Complete Psychological Works.)

Fromm, Erich. *The Anatomy of Human Destructiveness*. New York: Henry Holt, 1992.

——. *The Forgotten Language: An Introduction to the Understanding of Dreams, Fairy Tales and Myths*. New York: Grove Press, 1957.

——. *To Have or to Be*. New York: Continuum, 1999.

——. *You Shall Be as Gods: A Radical Interpretation of the Old Testament and Its Tradition*. Greenwich, Conn.: Fawcett, 1966.

Gerstein, Linda. *Nikolai Strakhov: Philosopher, Man of Letters, Social Critic*. Cambridge, Mass.: Harvard University Press, 1971.

Gilson, Étienne. *God and Philosophy*, sec. ed. New Haven: Yale University Press, 2002.

Girard, René. *Deceit, Desire and the Novel*, trans. Y. Freccero. Baltimore: The Johns Hopkins University Press, 1976.

——. *I See Satan Fall Like Lightning*, trans. James G. Williams. New York: Orbis, 2001.

——. *Violence and the Sacred*, trans. Patrick Gregory. Baltimore: The Johns Hopkins University Press, 1977.

Goethe, Johann Wolfgang von. *Faust: A Tragedy*, trans. Walter Arndt. New York: W.W. Norton, 2001.

Gogol, Nikolay V. *Diary of a Madman and Other Stories*, trans. Ronald Wilks. London: Penguin, 1972.

Gronicka, André von. *The Russian Image of Goethe. Goethe in Russian Literature of the Second Half of the Nineteenth Century*. 2 vols. Philadelphia: University of Pennsylvania Press, 1985.

Hartmann, Nicolai. *Ästhetik*. Berlin: Walter de Gruyter, 1953.

——. *Ethics*, trans. S. Coit. 3 vols. New York: Macmillan, 1932.

Hegel, G.W.F. *Phenomenology of Spirit*, trans. A.V. Miller. New York: Oxford University Press, 1988.

——. *Philosophy of Right*, trans. T.M. Knox. New York: Oxford University Press, 1952.

Herzen, Alexander. "From the Other Shore," in *"From the Other Shore" and "The Russian People and Socialism,"* ed. Moura Budberg. New York: Meridian, 1963, 3–162.

Heschel, Abraham J. *Who Is Man?* Stanford: Stanford University Press, 1965.

Hesse, Hermann. *My Belief: Essays on Life and Art*, trans. Richard and Clara Winston. New York: Henry Holt, 1974.

———. "Zarathustra's Return," in *If the War Goes On*, trans. Ralph Manheim. New York: Farrar, Straus and Giroux, 1971.

Huizinga, Johan. *Home Ludens: A Study of the Play Element in Culture*. Boston: Beacon Press, 1955.

Hyde, Lewis. *The Gift: Imagination and the Erotic Life of Property*. New York: Vintage Books, 1983.

Jung, Carl Gustav. *Answer to Job*, trans. R.F.C. Hull. Princeton: Princeton University Press, 1969. (Volume 11 of the Collected Works.)

———. *Archetypes and the Collective Unconsciousness*, trans. R.F.C. Hull. Princeton: Princeton University Press, 1968. (Volume 9, Part I, of the Collected Works.)

———. *The Undiscovered Self*, with *Symbols and the Interpretation of Dreams*, trans. R.F.C. Hull. Princeton: Princeton University Press, 1990.

Kaufmann, Walter, ed., *Existentialism from Dostoevsky to Sartre*. New York: Meridian Books, 1956.

Knox, Bernard. "Sophocles' Oedipus," in *Sophocles' Oedipus Rex*, ed. Harold Bloom. New Haven: Chelsea House Publishing, 1988, 5–22.

Koestler, Arthur. *The Art of Creation*. London: Picador, 1975.

Lossky, Vladimir, and Ouspensky, Leonid. *The Meaning of Icons*. Crestwood, N.Y.: St. Vladimir's Seminary Press, 1982.

Lotman, Yuri. *Universe of the Mind: A Semiotic Theory of Culture*, trans. Ann Shukman. Bloomington: Indiana University Press, 1990.

Mann, Thomas. *Essays of Three Decades*, trans. H.T. Lowe-Porter. New York: Alfred A. Knopf, 1965.

———. *Past Masters and Other Papers*, trans. H.T. Lowe-Porter. Freeport, N.Y.: Books for Libraries Press, 1968.

Mannheim, Karl. *Ideology and Utopia: An Introduction to the Sociology of Knowledge*, trans. L. Wirth and E. Shils. San Diego: Harcourt Brace & Company, 1985.

Massie, Suzanne. *Land of the Firebird: The Beauty of Old Russia*. New York: Simon and Schuster, 1980.

Merrill, Christopher. *Things of the Hidden God: Journey to the Holy Mountain*. New York: Random House, 2005.

Moyers, Bill D., ed., *Genesis: A Living Conversation*. New York: Doubleday, 1996.

Muchnic, Helen. *Russian Writers: Notes and Essays*. New York: Random House, 1971.

Münz, Ludwig. *Rembrandt*. New York: Harry N. Abrams, 1954.

Murdoch, Iris. *The Sovereignty of Good*. London: Routledge & Paul Kegan, 1970.

Neiman, Susan. *Evil in Modern Thought: An Alternative History of Philosophy*. Princeton: Princeton University Press, 2002.

Neumann, Erich. *The Creative Man: Five Essays*, trans. E. Rolfe. Princeton: Princeton University Press, 1979.

——. *The Origins and History of Consciousness*, trans. R.F.C. Hull. Princeton: Princeton University Press, 1970.

Nicholi, Armand M., Jr. *The Question of God: C.S. Lewis and Sigmund Freud Debate God, Love, Sex, and the Meaning of Life.* New York: Free Press, 2002.

Nietzsche, Friedrich. *Thus Spoke Zarathustra*, trans. R.J. Hollingdale. London: Penguin, 1969.

Northrop, F.S.C. *The Meeting of East and West: An Inquiry Concerning World Understanding.* New York: Macmillan, 1947.

Nouwen, Henri J.M. *Behold the Beauty of the Lord: Praying with Icons.* Notre Dame: Ave Maria Press, 1987.

——. *The Return of the Prodigal Son: A Story of Homecoming.* New York: Doubleday, 1994.

Ouspensky, Leonid. *Theology of the Icon.* Crestwood, N.Y.: St. Vladimir's Seminary Press, 1978.

Ouspensky, Leonid, and Lossky, Vladimir. *The Meaning of Icons.* Crestwood, N.Y.: St. Vladimir's Seminary Press, 1982.

Ovid. *Metamorphoses*, trans. David Raeburn. New York: Penguin, 2004.

Pamuk, Orhan. *Others Colors: Essays and a Story*, trans. Maureen Freely. New York: Alfred A. Knopf, 2007.

Pelikan, Jaroslav. *Fools of Christ: Essays on the True, the Good, and the Beautiful.* Philadelphia: Fortress Press, 1955.

——. *Imago Dei: The Byzantine Apologia for Icons.* Princeton: Princeton University Press, 1990.

Plato. *Collected Dialogues*, eds. Edith Hamilton and Huntington Cairns. Princeton: Princeton University Press, 1978.

Price, Martin. *Forms of Life: Character and Moral Imagination in the Novel.* New Haven: Yale University Press, 1983.

Pushkin, Alexander S. *The Poems, Prose, and Plays of Alexander Pushkin*, ed. Avrahm Yarmolinsky. New York: The Modern Library, 1964.

——. *The Queen of Spades and Other Stories*, trans. Rosemary Edmonds. London: Penguin, 1962.

Rousseau, Jean-Jacques. *Confessions*, trans. Angela Scholar. Oxford: Oxford University Press, 2000.

Rowlands, John. *Holbein: The Paintings of Hans Holbein the Younger.* Boston: D.R. Godine, 1985.

Ruskin, John. *The Art Criticism of John Ruskin.* New York: Da Capo Press, 1964.

Sanford, John A. *Evil: The Shadow Side of Reality.* New York: The Crossroad Publishing Company, 1981.

Schama, Simon. *Rembrandt's Eyes*. New York: Alfred A. Knopf, 1999.

Scheler, Max. "The Meaning of Suffering," in *On Feeling, Knowing, and Valuing*, trans. Harold J. Bershady. Chicago: University of Chicago Press, 1992, 82–115.

——. *The Nature of Sympathy*, trans. Peter Heath. New Haven: Yale University Press, 1954.

——. "Repentance and Rebirth," in *Person and Self-Value: Three Essays*, trans. M.S. Friggs. Boston: Martinus Nijhoff Publishers, 1987, 87–124.

Schiller, Friedrich. *On the Aesthetic Education of Man*, trans. R. Snell. New York: Frederich Ungar, 1965.

Schweitzer, Albert. *The Philosophy of Civilization*, trans. C.T. Campion. Amherst, N.Y.: Prometheus Books, 1987.

Seidlin, Oscar. "Hermann Hesse: The Exorcism of the Demon," in *Hesse: A Collection of Critical Essays*, ed. Theodor Ziolkowski. Englewood Cliffs, N.J.: Prentice-Hall, 1973, 51–75.

Simmel, Georg. "Faithfulness and Gratitude," in *The Sociology of Georg Simmel*, ed. and trans. Kurt H. Wolff. Glencoe, Ill.: Free Press, 1950, 379–95.

Simmons, Ernst J. *Introduction to Russian Realism*. Bloomington: Indiana University Press, 1965.

Sophocles. *Oedipus the King, Oedipus at Colonus, Antigone*, trans. David Green. Chicago: University of Chicago Press, 1991.

Spariousu, Mihai I. *Dionysus Reborn: Play and the Aesthetic Dimension in Modern Philosophical and Scientific Discourse*. Ithaca: Cornell University Press, 1989.

Spear, Athena Tasha. *Rodin Sculpture in the Cleveland Museum of Art*. Cleveland: Cleveland Museum of Art Press, 1967.

Terras, Victor. *A History of Russian Literature*. New Haven: Yale University Press, 1991.

Todorov, Tzvetan. *Facing the Extreme: Moral Life in the Concentration Camps*, trans. Arthur Denner and Abigail Pollak. New York: Henry Holt, 1996.

Tolstoy, Lev N. *Anna Karenina*, trans. Constance Garnett. New York: Barnes & Noble Classics, 1993.

——. *The Death of Ivan Ilych and Other Stories*, trans. J.D. Duff and Aylmer Maude. New York: Penguin, 1960.

——. *War and Peace*, trans. Louise and Aylmer Maude. New York: Simon and Schuster, 1942.

Turgenev, Ivan S. *Fathers and Sons*, trans. Rosemary Edmonds. New York: Penguin, 1965.

Vardy, Peter. *The Puzzle of Evil*. London: HarperCollins, 1992.

Volkov, Solomon. *St. Petersburg: A Cultural History*, trans. Antonina W. Bouis. New York: Free Press, 2002.

Whitehead, Alfred North. *Science and the Modern World*. New York: Macmillan, 1925.

Wilson, A.N. *Tolstoy: A Biography*. New York: W.W. Norton, 1988.

Young, Dudley. *The Origins of the Sacred: The Ecstasies of Love and War*. New York: HarperPerennial, 1992.

Yovel, Yermiyahu. *Spinoza and Other Heretics*, vol. 2: *The Adventures of Immanence*. Princeton: Princeton University Press, 1989.

Index

Idea, 140, 277, 285.
Ideal, 145, 171, 195, 274, 335.
Idiot, The (Dostoevsky), 8, 10, 83, 160-
   205, 206-08, 315;
      Aglaya, 162-63, 179, 181-87, 192-
      94;
      Ippolite, 169, 186, 201-02;
      Lebedyev, 170-71;
      Myshkin, 157-58, 160-64, 175-79,
         181-90, 193, 196-99, 201-02,
         204, 207-08, 216, 221, 315;
      Nastassya, 161-62, 163, 175-79,
         185-86, 187, 192-93;
      Rogozhin, 165-66, 176, 199, 201.
Image, 172, 219, 285;
   divine, 219, 222;
   and icon, 168, 219.
Immortality, 240-42.
Inscrutability, 152, 157.

Jesus. *See* Christ
Job, and God, 8, 233, 264, 298, 342.
Jung, Carl Gustav, 326-37.
Justice, 21-23, 34, 42, 200, 271, 277,
   298, 305, 339-40;
   and love, 252, 303, 331;
   and repentance, 320-21.

Kafka, Franz, 332-33.
Kant, Immanuel, 38-39, 49, 135-36,
   200, 229, 241, 324.
Kiss, 98, 225, 270, 271, 273, 288-89,
   291, 299, 305.
Knowledge, forbidden, 245-46, 250;
   of good and evil, 261;
   self-, 49-50, 53, 70, 257, 288.
Koestler, Arthur, 180, 195, 203, 250.

Ladder of beauty, love, faith, and hope,
   192, 194-95, 199, 208, 229, 243,
   300-01, 335, 337.
Landscape with Acis and Galatea (Lorrain), 118, 125-26, 142.
Language, 157;
   and truth, 115-16.
Law, 87, 97, 129.
Lawrence, D. H., on Grand Inquisitor,
   272-75, 279, 288.
Legend of the Grand Inquisitor, 268-
   69, 271, 277, 278, 283, 286.
Life, 12, 26, 49, 60, 62, 72, 81, 91, 92,
   96, 103, 104, 105-06, 110, 117, 120,
141-42, 149, 147, 149, 157, 159,
   195, 196, 204, 208-09, 210-11, 234,
   252, 258, 275, 276, 294, 310, 312-
   13, 323, 332, 334;
      affirmation of, 5-6, 10, 12-13,
         101, 107, 146, 311, 338, 339,
         342, 343;
      arbitrariness of, 151, 300;
      and death, 75, 133, 140, 198, 203,
         236, 291, 312-13;
      gift of, 158, 202, 209, 212, 215,
         220, 239, 240, 299, 341, 343;
      love of, 10, 12-13, 208, 216, 232,
         259, 309, 310;
      meaning of, 5, 10, 13, 15-16, 18,
         23, 40, 43, 108, 133, 142, 145,
         151, 156, 159, 170-71, 180,
         203, 211, 238, 256, 262-63,
         265, 294, 295-96, 297, 298,
         299, 300-01, 307, 308-09, 310,
         311, 342, 343;
      paradoxes of, 338, 343;
      purpose of, 15-16;
      as a trial, 221, 320.
Limit. *See* Boundary
Lorrain, Claude, *Landscape with Acis
   and Galatea*, 118, 125-26, 142.
Lotman, Yuri, 115, 116, 176.
Love, 66-67, 102, 104, 124-25, 136,
   183-85, 187, 192-94, 232, 238, 244,
   260-61, 278, 281, 286, 287, 288,
   293, 305, 307, 326;
      and beauty, 183-84, 192, 195, 302,
         343;
      and faith, 192, 222, 232, 281, 308,
         341-42;
      gift of, 103, 184, 192, 195, 288;
      and justice, 252, 303, 331;
      of life, 10, 12-13, 208, 216, 232,
         259, 309, 310;
      unconditional, 281, 290, 322.

Madonna, 230-31, 284.
Man, 30, 47, 50, 56, 58, 60, 61, 71,
   87, 148, 154, 255, 256, 257;
      beautiful, 206-07, 215, 285, 300;
      definition of, 47-48;
      extraordinary, 89, 107;
      and God, 25-26, 35-37, 38, 52,
         90, 118, 122, 133, 134-35, 168,
         212, 253, 276, 297, 304-05,
         320, 334-35;

CPSIA information can be obtained at www.ICGtesting.com
Printed in the USA
LVOW05s0005050314

376089LV00010B/297/P